Dear Fellow Stargazers,

Since childhood, understanding astrology has given me both the courage and inspiration to live the life of my dreams. However, the greatest gift I have received from working with astrology has always been the incredible insights I have learned about the various signs.

How wonderful it is to have this information to draw on when it comes to understanding myself, family and everyone else around me.

I hope that by sharing my views of the signs with you (and my personal impression of what makes them tick) that it enriches your life, as much as this knowledge has enriched mine.

Much love,

Athena

New York, March 2000.

ZODIAC

Athena Starwoman

HarperCollins*Publishers*

HarperCollins*Publishers*

First published in Australia in 2000
by HarperCollins*Publishers* Pty Limited
ACN 009 913 517
A member of the HarperCollins*Publishers* (Australia) Pty Limited Group
http://www.harpercollins.com.au

HarperCollins*Publishers*
25 Ryde Road, Pymble, Sydney NSW 2073, Australia
31 View Road, Glenfield, Auckland 10, New Zealand
77–85 Fulham Palace Road, London W6 8JB, United Kingdom
Hazelton Lanes, 55 Avenue Road, Suite 2900, Toronto, Ontario M5R 3L2
and 1995 Markham Road, Scarborough, Ontario M1B 5M8 Canada
10 East 53rd Street, New York NY 10022, USA

National Library of Australia Cataloguing-in-Publication data:

Starwoman, Athena.
Zodiac: your astrology guide for the new millennium.
ISBN 0 7322 6781 1.
1. Zodiac. 2. Astrology. I. Title.
133.5

Illustrations by Stella Danalis
Cover photograph by Verko Photography USA
Printed in Australia by Griffin Press on 79gsm Bulky Paperback

5 4 3 2 1   00 01 02 03

To all those who read this book

······●(CREDITS AND THANKS

Writing a book of this size and magnitude can be an overwhelming project and it would not have been possible without the help of Toni Robino, my dear Capricorn friend and editor. Toni, without your creative assistance, chapter organisation and follow-through, this book could not have become a reality.

Also, my sincerest thank you to John F. Demartini, my Sagittarian husband, best friend and soulmate. Darling John, your love, wisdom and life-transforming seminars (like 'Breakthrough') changed my life. I hope that this book reflects some of the blessings that your teachings and insights have given to me.

Thank you also Helen Littleton (Taurus) of HarperCollins for being so excited and enthusiastic about this book from the moment I mentioned it to you. Your confidence and belief in me helped me to get this book done. Special thanks to Anne Reilly and Katie Mitchell for their talented contributions to this book.

Also to Fiona (Aries) and Georgina (Taurus) Russell, my nieces, who are both astrologers and writers, and like their mother (my sister), Planet Janet, provided me with inspiration and useful astro-advice.

Particular thanks as well to Scorpio, Shelley Rahim for helping me find the physical stamina to complete this task (thank you Shelley so much for those wonderful daily healing walks through Central Park talking about the zodiac signs).

Special thanks also to my friend and co-writer of *How to Turn your Ex-Boyfriend into a Toad*, Deborah Gray, for her Virgo contributions and friendship. As well as Jennifer Fox, Christiane Mack and Jennie Angel for their Capricorn wisdom and understanding. And Verko for his photographic artistry.

Much love to Della Rounick (a Gemini) for being such a wonderful friend and also for providing so many unique glimpses into Geminis. To Nurit Kahane Haase (Taurus) — thank you for your incredible generous heart, for being such a super hostess and also allowing me to get to know your daughter, little Ariella, who is a gorgeous example of a beautiful Libran.

And to so many others who I've met and travelled with through my spiritual journey through life. So many of you have contributed and played a role in making this book a reality and shaping its form. You all know who you are and you are always with me, and part of me!

CONTENTS

·····(ARIES

·····(TAURUS

······ (GEMINI

······ (CANCER

······(LEO

VIRGO

LIBRA

······(SCORPIO

······(SAGITTARIUS

CAPRICORN

AQUARIUS

(PISCES

THE SUN SIGNS CHART

ARIES	21 March – 20 April
TAURUS	21 April – 21 May
GEMINI	22 May – 21 June
CANCER	22 June – 23 July
LEO	24 July – 23 August
VIRGO	24 August – 23 September
LIBRA	24 September – 23 October
SCORPIO	24 October – 22 November
SAGITTARIUS	23 November – 21 December
CAPRICORN	22 December – 20 January
AQUARIUS	21 January – 19 February
PISCES	20 February – 20 March

If you were born on the first or last day of a Sun sign, in astrological terms you were born on a cusp. If that's the case, you will probably benefit from reading your own Sun sign and the Sun sign that ends or begins right before or after your date of birth. For example, if your birth date is 22 December, your Sun sign is Capricorn, but you probably have some Sagittarian traits as well.

NOTE: Because of leap years, time zone differences and other factors, the exact day and time when the Sun changes signs varies from year to year. If you are born close to the changeover dates (close to the cusp) of the signs, you would need to have your own personal horoscope drawn up in order to know exactly which sign you are. The above dates are guidelines only.

Dear Reader

All my studies of astrology and the other metaphysical subjects have led me towards one specific realisation: the most important thing in life is to be grateful for everything and anything. For whatever life presents us with — our joys, tests, trials and triumphs — all are gifts from above. We polish and refine our characters by adapting to the changing experiences of our everyday lives. We learn through our mistakes just as much (sometimes even more) as we learn through our successes and blessings.

I truly believe that gratitude is the key to mastering life in all its forms, and if there is one thing I would love to do within the pages of this book, it is to share my gratitude for life, love, others, the stars, nature and destiny with you all.

Athena Starwoman
www.starwoman.com

ARIES

[21 march — 20 april]

aries aries aries aries aries aries aries
aries aries aries aries aries aries aries
aries aries aries aries aries aries aries
aries aries aries aries aries aries aries
aries aries aries aries aries aries aries
aries aries aries aries aries aries aries
aries aries aries aries aries aries aries
aries aries aries aries aries aries aries
aries aries aries aries aries aries aries
aries aries aries aries aries aries aries
aries aries aries aries aries aries aries
aries aries aries aries aries aries aries
aries aries aries aries aries aries aries
aries aries aries aries aries aries aries
aries aries aries aries aries aries aries

element: fire

planetary ruler: mars

symbol: the ram

quality: cardinal (= activity)

colours: carmine, red, scarlet

gem: amethyst

best companions: leo and sagittarius

strongest virtues: resilience, loyalty and daring

traits to improve: impatience, over-

reactions and ability to create unnecessary dramas

deepest desire: to gain recognition and

approval from others

Aries celebrities

Russell Crowe, Celine Dion, Dennis Quaid, Marlon Brando, Ellen Barkin,

Matthew Broderick, Doris Day, Sarah Jessica Parker, Elle MacPherson,

Diana Ross, Marsha Mason, Ayrton Senna, Keri Russell, Timothy Dalton,

Matthew Modine, Joan Crawford, George Benson, Aretha Franklin,

Elton John, James Caan, Alec Baldwin, Harry Houdini, Steven Tyler,

Gary Oldman, Reese Witherspoon, Andrew Lloyd Webber, Chaka Khan,

Marcel Marceau, Kelly LeBrock, Quentin Tarantino, Steve McQueen,

Warren Beatty, Richard Chamberlain, Mariah Carey, Jennifer Capriati,

Lucy Lawless, Emma Thompson, Eric Clapton, Robert Downey Jr,

Gregory Peck, James Woods, Rosie O'Donnell, Claire Danes, Tiny Tim,

Paloma Picasso, Ashley Judd, Ewan McGregor, Eddie Murphy,

Julian Lennon, Francis Ford Coppola, Rolf Harris, Charlie Chaplin,

Leonardo da Vinci, Jackie Chan, Arthur Murray and David Cassidy.

[General outlook]

Get ready Aries! You enter the new millennium filled to the brim with your trademark enthusiasm and contagious love of life. The end of the twentieth century was a time for Rams to observe and reflect, but now new millennium energy pulls you towards what you love best — action. To make the most of the new millennium, you will be in the flow where you focus on travelling, meeting people, creating, exploring, learning and teaching.

Life will be your oyster now, and like a beacon of light, you will shine forth with an irresistible energy that attracts fascinating people and projects into your realm. New and exciting opportunities for living, working and loving arise and you are there, ready and waiting to grab them. Trust your instincts and follow your heart's messages, right through the first five years of the new millennium. If you do (and you remain true to yourself) your stars indicate that you can't lose.

Romance

Aries enter a new, more mature phase concerning love and romance. You know what you want now. Carefree and impulsive single Aries look for stability in a relationship over fleeting affairs, whilst married Aries strengthen their union by spending time together working on a mutual project. Whatever occurs in your romantic world, Aries are radiating a new millennium romantic and relationship glow. Take advantage of it and remember that love really does make the world go around.

Health

Relaxation is the key to your good health as the new millennium gets underway. It's important to limit your stress. Be sure to get frequent rest and relaxation (lack of sleep will trigger a cranky temperament, so do try to get eight hours of sleep most nights). A friend introduces you to new relaxation techniques (possibly massage, reflexology, yoga or tai chi) and you find it works wonders for you! Look after yourself healthwise, and you'll discover that everything else falls into place.

Finance

It is time for you to become a tough business negotiator, a conscientious money manager and a long-term financial planner as well. Be warned — money and financial security will soon mean a great deal more to you than it ever did in the past. Money will provide you with the freedom of choice to do the ghings you love (especially to live well, study and travel). What is more, it can also provide the sense of self-worth and independence you need to boost your confidence up to a new more resilient level.

So, while impulse might rule affairs of the heart, don't let it take charge where money matters are concerned. You have the ability to make great financial breakthroughs right through the first decade of the new millennium (especially where real estate or other investments are concerned). Be careful not to fall prey to overspending or quick money-making schemes. Water-tight investments are preferable. Money matters are good now, so think 'abundance'.

Career

The new millennium ushers in a lucrative new work and career phase for Aries, and many Rams find themselves moving quickly and delightfully up the work ladder, taking on extra responsibilities or even starting their own business. Although it might seem that employers are trying to push your limits, keep in mind that you need pressure in order to come up with your best work. Be creative. Don't follow the party line; the new millennium is your time to dare to be different in your career. Keep in mind that you need to leave your individual stamp on all that you do.

[Millennium wildcards to watch for]

Keeping focused is going to be your biggest challenge as the new millennium gets into full swing. A plethora of projects, people and places are competing for your attention. If anything is likely to bring down your new millennium potential, it's your belief in trying everything at least once, and doing everything at once. While it's good to be confident, there is also wisdom in being selective and taking things slowly. Rushing into things or volunteering for too many responsibilities could be your biggest new millennium downfall.

Understanding Aries

> *You Aries are the zodiac's rule-breakers and you rarely do anything in a traditional or ordinary way.*

If you aligned each zodiac sign with a certain type of car, then you Aries would be a turbo-charged racer! Signs such as Capricorn might resemble something solid and reliable like a Mercedes, Geminis a zip-along model like a sports car, and Taurus a four-wheel-drive truck. But you are the zodiac's interpretation of the racing car because you like to put your pedal to the metal, race ahead and stay out in front. Moreover, you usually only know one speed to travel through life, and that speed is fast. This desire to zoom down the fast track can leave you with some physical scars and tends to make you accident prone.

Although the benefits you derive from your gung-ho approach and attitude provide you with the capacity to live every day to its fullest, this fast-lane existence often comes with a high price. There will be days when you find yourself feeling like a road-wreck rusting at the side of life's roadway, rather than a turbo-charged racer. However, usually the times when you feel like this are short-lived because you do have a courageous fighting spirit and, generally, you quickly bounce back from emotional upheaval, ill-health or other difficult circumstances.

Most times, the saying 'I love trouble' — even if subconsciously — relates to you. Reckless behaviour may also come naturally to you. You love to take risks, break records, stir things up and sometimes delight in leaving others gasping at the things you say, do, or believe in.

Aries is also a quick-thinking sign. Your mental wheels (as well as your physical wheels) spin rapidly. Whether sharing statements, giving opinions or making plans, you usually are unafraid to speak your mind (even if you know your viewpoint may not be a popular one). Many times, however, you speak in haste and then have to learn to live with the consequences. Your impetuous nature spills over into other areas, too. I have noticed that when you truly want something or someone, you can be audaciously impulsive.

Small wonder that patience is not a word that generally exists in your Aries vocabulary, and when you are waiting for something to happen, even instant gratification can take too long for you.

One of the reasons you are so gung-ho at times and live life in the fast lane, stems from the fact that you're the first sign of the zodiac. You have the initial spark of cosmic expression within. This provides you with an abundance of enthusiasm, energy and curiosity. Because the life-spark energy flow in you is so potent, yours is also often an overly dramatic, wild-at-heart and fiery zodiac sign.

Being the first sign of the zodiac makes you the fearless pioneer and sometimes the vulnerable wild child, too. Many inventive and pioneering minds have been Aries-born — including wonderful astrologer Linda Goodman, whose astrological insights reached millions around the world through her writings.

Because you are one of the more fired up signs of the zodiac, you Aries are trailblazers. You love to lead, and feel best when you are free and independent. Restriction weighs heavily on you (that's one of the reasons some Aries tend to over-eat). When you are on track, you can set other people afire with your passionate way of living. When you are in the flow, your dedication and enthusiasm are unmatched, especially when you use your talents and expressions without caution or reservation.

However, the exact reverse applies when you get down at heart — or lose your good health, confidence, vision, drive or purpose. You can become incredibly negative in your thinking and focus only on problems. When you get into this downhearted state, you are somewhat like a balloon with the air going out of it. You sink into yourself!

Nobody can truly sing the blues like an out-of-sorts, down-in-the-dumps, heartbroken Aries, as Aries blues singer Billie Holiday proved. When you are down and out, it takes something or someone special to come into your life to lift you up and dust you off again. If you are sometimes a 'blue mood' type of Aries, remember that you always need something to look forward to in the future. Future dreams keep you eager and enthusiastic. Lack of recognition by others, boredom, disillusionment or disappointment quickly take away your lust for life (and Aries artist Van Gogh is a great example of this).

However, bad times usually do not deflate you for too long. You are a natural fighter and survivor and often you need to be a survivor, too, because of the predicaments you find yourself in. In all kinds of ways, those born under Aries remind me of the movie *The Terminator*, where no matter what happened to the Arnold Schwarzenegger character, he was seemingly indestructible. So many Aries I know have been through hell and high water, but somehow or other, they have an innate 'I'll be back' physical and psychological resilience that helps them survive and bounce out of many a testing situation, including severe problems with health.

Aries are not only endowed with psychological and emotional strength, you have abundant physical power, too. Your tremendous energy and vigour impress your friends . . . and sometimes exhaust them. As you already know from your own life story, all that extra energy can lead you into living the motto, 'act first, pay the price later'. You run your life wanting the excitement of the moment — and as you do this, you sometimes zoom head first into excess and complications of every kind, even when you don't mean to get into any mischief at all.

Astrologically it is easy to see why you are so headstrong — and such a warrior as well. After all, your ruling planet, Mars, is the ancient god of war, aggression and conflict and this strong influence places you in plenty of extreme predicaments. But the unusual and challenging situations that spring up without warning (when you find yourself in hot water through your own actions) provide many opportunities for you to learn about yourself, if you're willing to face them.

You love to push the envelope of life, but one of the most difficult things for a Ram to accept is that no matter how fast you run, or no matter how many hijinks you get up to, you can't run away from yourself. And you are quite a worrier as well as a warrior — you're great at beating yourself up internally, too. Nobody feels worse than an Aries who thinks they've said or done the wrong thing. You also have a capacity to concern yourself over situations or scenarios that may not ever happen anyway.

You have many soft emotional spots, too, which complicate your moods, actions and deeds. Just about all the Aries I know are animal lovers. In fact, if you ask Aries children what they would love to be when they grow up, most of them will say an animal doctor, a zoo-keeper, a wildlife photographer, an animal activist, or something that involves animals.

In childhood and in grown-up years, you are the type of person who walks past the pet shop and falls instantly in love (or rather infatuation) with the cutest doggie or kitten in the window. On impulse you will race in and buy your little pet (assuming that you are rescuing it from some kind of horrible fate) and then wonder what you are going to do with the cute pooch now that you have it!

Your ability to assume a responsibility, like buying the puppy or kitten, can be expanded onto even larger life-transforming levels. You are liable to marry in haste, buy properties without thinking about how to pay for them, and switch jobs on a whim as well.

With hindsight, it is natural that you often have cause to regret your headstrong actions. However, even when you really create a problem for yourself or others, or go through sad situations, or hold within you a sense of wrong-doing, the experiences are often the ones that are the stepping stones towards enlightenment for you. So even though you Aries often feel badly about some of the things that have occurred in your life or that you have brought to pass, these experiences can actually be blessings in disguise. They force you to take a closer look at who you are and what you want and they help you to fine-tune your range of choices in life.

Sure (like most of us) there are times you do truly go out of your way big time and mess things up. Nevertheless, by the same token it's typical for you to forget that your mess-ups — whether they take the form of aggression or impulsiveness, and even your selfishness — can create as much good as they do bad, and are part of the same package that makes you passionate, idealistic and progressive.

You don't need to criticise yourself so often about what you have or haven't said or done. I feel Aries are often trying to prove something to the world, or to themselves. When you learn to laugh at yourself, you realise that life is one drama and lesson after another for you. Then, your dilemmas will turn magically into rewarding and revealing information about you and your purpose in life.

As the first sign of the zodiac, you are what you are, a most beloved child of the universe! This makes you a natural trailblazer and encourages you to ignore the rules and learn as you go along the journey of life. No wonder that you favour forging ahead now, and dealing with the consequences later. This rebellious type of behaviour is both your strength and weakness, but it is intrinsically your gift.

In fact, you Aries are known as the zodiac's rule breakers because you hardly ever do anything in a traditional or ordinary way. You make up your own rules as you go along, and this has a price, but at least you are always your own person.

With the bold, aggressive and fearless planet Mars as your ruler, you were born to be an adventurer. That's why you have incredible stamina and a strong drive to accomplish things that most people won't even consider taking on. You have childlike zeal and enthusiasm.

You sometimes enjoy being over-the-top about your experiences, and you have a knack for making the mundane dramatic. That's why so many Aries make it as actors and entertainers (Russell Crowe, Elle MacPherson, Ellen Barkin, Emma Thompson, Alec Baldwin, David Letterman, Charlie Chaplin, Marlon Brando, Eddie Murphy, Gregory Peck, Joan Crawford, James Caan, Aretha Franklin, Mariah Carey, Alan Arkin, Rhea Perlman, Paul Reiser and Diana Ross are among many Aries in the business; and interestingly Celine Dion, Rolf Harris, Warren Beatty and Vincent Van Gogh all share the same birthday of 30th March).

Drama and enthusiasm add up to make you entertaining and animated, but they also can land you in hot water. Nearly all Aries can throw a big enough tantrum to send everyone running for cover. But these storms blow over quickly, and your 'in your face' type of honesty is usually refreshing, even if it's not totally appropriate. One of the things that I personally love most about Aries is that even though you explode like volcanoes sometimes, once you settle down, you can usually laugh about it. Plus you generally don't hold a grudge either — which is a lovely side to your character.

Another great thing about you, Aries, is that you don't say one thing and mean another. (Or, at least if you do, you can't keep up the mask or facade for long.) Your pistol mind shoots honesty out like bullets of fire at times. You're usually an 'honest Jane (or John)' type. If people ask you for your opinion, they get it — sometimes in a way that they don't enjoy.

If you put on a 'pretend' or happy face, trying to please others, most people can see right away that you are trying to keep the peace. In general, what you see with an Aries, is exactly what you get. Your actions are invariably well above-board and up-front, even if sometimes misguided. You call 'em like you see 'em, and while you don't always paint a pretty picture, you're rarely accused of dodging an issue.

You love to talk, too, and occasionally get accused of spilling a secret. An Aries can let the cat out of the bag in some of the most surprising and impulsive ways. And your sense of drama often encourages you to get your revenge or make your point in the most untimely fashion, or the most unusual manner.

It was an Aries bride (another friend of mine) who, at the beginning of her wedding reception, stood to propose a toast. With champagne in hand, she said, 'Here's to my husband and my maid of honour, who I just learned had a private celebration of their own before this ceremony'. She then delightfully, to the shock of the entire bridal party, poured the champagne on her groom's head, left the ballroom, and filed for divorce the next day. Seems like a sensational way to make your point, but that's what Aries are all about. If you're going to do something, you're going to do it in an explosive, sensational fashion. No little notes tucked under pillows by Aries; more like a billboard complete with flashing lights.

My friend recovered from her five-minute marriage and, instead of dwelling on it for long, like a true Aries she bounced back and moved on. She poured her heart and soul into her acting career. Within four years she had starred in two made-for-television movies and was auditioning for her first big role in a motion picture.

She didn't have time to think about the past because she was too busy in the moment, and planning for the future. The ability to re-focus your energy is a true and valuable gift, Aries, and it can help you to triumph under any circumstances. If something doesn't go right for you, you have the capacity to switch your world, heart, or plans around, and do something else — with someone else, if necessary.

When you are busy and racing the clock — that's when you're really in your Aries element. A bored Aries is a dangerous personality and can be quite pitiful to behold.

Also when your life is not filled to the brim with things to do or think about, your thoughts quickly turn to problems or upsets. When you're kept active, busy and productive, you're adventurous, bright and optimistic. When things are quiet, you are tired, edgy, miserable and lacklustre.

You love to be your own person, and are quickly bored with routine and repetition. You love variety, too, in your friends and in your fun. You're drawn to people who march to the beat of unorthodox drummers, and bohemian traits appeal to you. Aries Leonardo da Vinci marched to his own beat, and Aries musicians — like Mariah Carey, Aretha Franklin, Chaka Khan and Ravi Shankar — and Aries authors and poets — like Erica Jong and Maya Angelou — are blazing their own trails. Aries thrive on flamboyance, wither with mediocrity and bloom with new and exciting experiences.

One of your greatest Aries assets is your ability to see life as a magnificent experience, instead of as a test or a challenge. You seem to know intuitively that in the long run, there is no finish line, and because of this you don't stop when others would think 'enough is enough!' This inner knowing that life is a journey, with no distinct finishing line, gives you the courage to do things that other people only dream about.

Aries is a Fire sign

To your advantage, you have a fiery combination of confidence, energy and passion that make it possible and sometimes even easy for you to navigate your self-styled and self-sufficient journey through life. It's no wonder the word 'ram' means to forge ahead — sometimes with force. When you're on a mission, you let no one and nothing stand in your way. You can be a ball of fiery energy when you're inspired to some great purpose and you know what it takes, and what it's worth to live your dream. You're a hero in the eyes of many, and you light up the lives of nearly everyone you meet.

To your disadvantage, your impulsive behaviour can lead to accidents and injuries. Your forcefulness can be overwhelming and you can injure or burn yourself out before you realise it. You also have an uncanny knack for alienating people — just when you need them the most. You are extremely self-critical and the more you beat yourself up for what you think you did wrong or what you could have or should have done better, the slower you grow. You give just about everyone else a break, Aries, why don't you give yourself one for a change?

[Insights into your sign]

The bright side: One of your extraordinary strengths is your courage to dare to be different from the crowd. You experiment, test your boundaries and generally do things and try things others would never consider possible, and that is how you sometimes work your miracles. You understand that experience is your greatest teacher, and you eagerly take on one lesson after another.

The shadow: You're so focused on making the experience happen (rather than just having the experience) that you miss the meaning of it. When you feel that life isn't filled with incident (or drama), you go beyond living *in* the moment and have a

Characteristics >	Benefits >	Drawbacks >
Adventurous	Get the most out of life	Live dangerously
Aggressive	Get what you want	Scare other people away
Bright	Think quickly	Outsmart yourself
Competitive	Win your battles	Play dirty
Confident	Willing to take chances	Don't prepare
Dramatic	Get attention	Cause fusses about nothing
Energetic	High stamina	Burn out
Enterprising	Bold ideas	Take big risks
Enthusiastic	Spread hope	Go too far over the top
Fearless	Face adversity	Accident-prone
Forceful	Able to dominate	Create enemies
Idealistic	Believe in justice	Fight losing battles
Impatient	Get a lot done	Short-tempered with others
Impulsive	Exciting	Leads to trouble
Optimistic	See the rainbow	Caught up in silly infatuations
Passionate	Lust for life	Overbearing
Progressive	Open-minded	Permanently restless
Selfish	You do what you want	Unreasonable
Straightforward	Speak your mind	Offensive
Volatile	Lots of energy	Explosive personality
Vulnerable	Childlike charm	Lose your shirt

spree of living *for* the moment that can be self-sabotaging. Moreover, when you do go off on your temperamental or wild-child sprees, you create chaos that shoots out sparks in all directions.

[Looking beneath the surface of your sign]

You look like you're all cool, calm and collected when in fact you are often like an atom bomb, just waiting to explode. The sorts of things that make you explode are any criticism, direction and instruction from others, or any suggestion that you have room for improvement.

You can't take other people lightly. That's why relationships can make you or break you. If it seems that others are not on your side, or do not agree with you, you often feel they are out to get you. You are a complex person underneath. You often find it difficult to behave in the appropriate way when your more volatile side runs your life. Your confidence and enthusiasm can wash right down the drain when you're not number one or you're not getting all the praise and attention you desire. Even when the feedback is meant to be constructive and helpful, you cannot take any sort of negative feedback from others no matter how justified their words may be.

It's interesting that one of your most visible traits — your straightforward nature — is something you don't tolerate well in others. You can dish it out, but you can't always take it. When your feelings are hurt, you go straight for your opponent's throat in a very aggressive and dramatic fashion. Or, you simply crumble and have to withdraw to boost yourself up again. You also have a habit of placing the blame on others when things don't turn out well and you let other people carry the burden of fixing up the messes or misunderstandings you leave behind you. Plus, you can be extremely one-eyed and self-absorbed.

You sometimes (maybe even most times) act as if you're the centre of the universe and forget about others' needs, feelings and circumstances. You would be wise to practise the art of walking a moon or two in someone else's moccasins (at least in your mind). This will help you to see situations from other perspectives and will definitely improve your relationships in all areas of life.

[How to tune into your sign's powers]

> *Believe in yourself.*
> *Learn the value of patience.*
> *Listen to your conscience — it is unwise for you to go against it.*

The Aries woman

> The Aries woman is an idealist who values truth, fairness and justice. She's fiercely loyal and will take on any challenger to defend her family or friends or to fight for a worthy cause. And if she loves you, she will die for you if necessary — such is her devotion.

Ms Aries is warmhearted, alluring and generous and she's selfish, demanding and unpredictable. Naturally independent, she needs to have a life of her own, not just to orbit around her man. She has a distinctive range of personalities. She is the girl-next-door type (like Aries Doris Day), the Amazon warrior woman type (rather like Aries Lucy Lawless — who portrays Xena the warrior goddess on television) and everything in between as well!

One thing she normally is not, however, is timid. Armed with an attitude, dry sarcasm and quick wit, the assertive and outspoken Aries can be one of the stronger females in the zodiac. No wonder, as she is, after all, the only woman of the zodiac who is ruled by the masculine planet of war, Mars. This Mars connection tends to make Ms Aries a combative, fiery and forceful gal. She is also capable of great feats of strength, resilience and endurance.

Wrap all this Mars energy up in a unique and sometimes quite dazzling feminine guise and you have the equivalent of heaven and hell adorned in high heels. Some of you may remember gorgeous Aries Kelly LeBrock in the movie *The Woman in Red*, where she was a vision of feminine sensuality. The women you see in red, looking gorgeous at a bar, party or on television — well, they're likely to be Aries (think of knockout Aries Elle MacPherson, too!).

Aries women are no pushovers when it comes to matching wits and strength with their male counterparts. If you're waiting for a green light, it is the Aries woman who pushes her foot to the floor and takes off one second before the light turns green — sometimes with the screeching of tyres and the smell of burning rubber.

Whether she is walking, driving or making love, Ms Aries usually likes to lead the field. Even though she is not necessarily the most delicate, feminine type of woman of the zodiac, she is definitely the femme fatale of all the signs. She may have big hands, big feet or even unusual (but still most attractive) shaped features, like Aries Ellen Barkin.

While she may not quite be a picture of geometric symmetry, proportion and order, whatever physical characteristics she possesses, she can put a great head-turning look together. She often has a remarkable body shape and figure (again think of super-model, Aries Elle MacPherson or Lucy Lawless, who plays Xena). Mars, being Ms Aries' ruling planet, makes her more muscular, toned or streamlined in unusual places than the other zodiac signs. She often has strong eyebrows or very defined facial features. As mentioned earlier, she also often looks fantastic wearing brights, particularly red — which is the astrological colour for Aries, too!

She can be quite a head-turner (even in her older years) and men are often floored by her appearance. When she walks down the street she usually creates quite an impact. Even if she is dressed down, rather than up, she is still likely to be able to make her presence felt. However, no matter how pretty, sweet or beguiling she may appear outwardly (usually this applies when she is on her best behaviour), if you're dealing with an Aries woman, do not race in — instead, tread warily.

Like playing with a loaded pistol, it isn't wise to take chances or rely on your luck with her. She is unique in her ability to have her way, come hell or high water. Ms Aries definitely has a mind of her own and she can be so forceful at times (in both the hidden and obvious way) that those more fragile souls may find her overwhelming. Saying no to an Aries can be just like raising the red flag.

She sees weakness as a lack of character. And she won't tolerate or put up with weakness of her own or others in a compassionate manner. But this approach may not apply to her children, although she can be quite a chore-master for them, too, if that's what she thinks is good for them. She's definitely the strongest woman of the zodiac, in an up-front rather than manipulative way. Capricorn and Scorpio women may be stronger on some levels, but they are more secretive about their hidden strengths.

While her Aries forcefulness might be the first thing you notice about her, underneath that outward strength she is a lot more vulnerable than meets the eye. She has two distinct attitudes or appearances – the first where she is the iron glove that clothes a gentle, delicate hand; the second where she appears soft and vulnerable externally but then has the other side to her nature that could help her survive an atomic bomb blast, if she had to. She is unique in the way that she is the warrior woman of the zodiac, trying to express herself in modern terms.

If you want to delve into the depths of her soul and get to know her better, it may take you some time. Don't judge her by her initial actions, appearance or beliefs. Keep looking, watch her eyes and her body language instead of the performance, and you'll see an extremely feminine, sensitive, and sometimes insecure and complex woman!

If you look close enough and see the occasions when tears well up in her eyes, you'll know that she's also one of the most vulnerable women of the zodiac. But you won't see her tender side unless she really trusts you. She often doesn't even appreciate her more tender side herself. She prefers to be calm, cool and collected (and highly independent) and — while this isn't always easy for her — she skilfully conceals her true feelings with clever humour and hides her heart behind many different masks.

This lady is no doormat, although it sometimes happens that she falls in love or lust with Mr Wrong and acts temporarily like a doormat. This phase lasts for a while — but usually not for long. Once she has had enough of being put down she rallies, regains her confidence and gets back on track.

Generally, she's not afraid of living life to its fullest, and this gives her tremendous courage when she needs it.

This woman's strong belief in herself and complete confidence in miracles spurs her on to jump from one new experience to another. She seeks adventure and her impulsive nature urges her to take some whopper risks. She's daring, enthusiastic, dramatic and, on occasion, she's openly selfish.

She drives herself forwards, rather than looking back — secretly afraid of what she might see. She has a great attitude that the past and the future are two different things. She doesn't necessarily carry the burdens of the past on her shoulders — the way some other signs do.

The Aries woman is an idealist who values truth, fairness and justice. She's fiercely loyal and will take on any challenger to defend her family or friends or to fight for a worthy cause. And if she loves you, she will die for you if necessary — such is her devotion.

[How Aries women operate]

Social

She's good fun to be around. Naturally outgoing and friendly, Ms Aries is a great companion, friend and support person. The Aries woman is bright, lively (sometimes very, very funny) and entertaining in social settings. She likes a good gossip session as much as a philosophical discussion, and few other women or men, can match her skill for bantering.

She's usually well-informed, has lots to share and isn't afraid to ask questions that others might think are naive or foolish. Lots of Aries women enjoy the chance to visit cyberspace chat rooms and many have made international friendships through the Internet. But, don't expect her to be sitting by her computer waiting for your e-mail.

Most Aries — even if they love surfing the world-wide web — can only sit still for short periods of time, and before long she'll be racing out the door for some action adventure. Some Aries women have a reputation for having thick skin and being hard to get to know, but when they strip off their tough facade, they unleash a lacy, eyelash-batting temptress. She can be noticed when she wants to be, and she generally does want to be noticed.

At a party or outing, she's the one surrounded by a small troupe of select men and women eagerly listening to the tale of her latest (sometimes greatly exaggerated) adventure. She usually doesn't like to listen as much as she likes to talk, and she can have a hard time sitting through other people's stories. If you strike up a conversation with an Aries, be forewarned that if you pause for a breath, she may finish your sentence and keep right on talking. Don't take it personally, she doesn't mean to be rude; she's just impatient to keep the conversation moving.

Although she can be tough going at times, her disarming innocence combined with her frequent good deeds make up for any shortcomings and keep her in the good graces of her friends and neighbours. An Aries is often active in community affairs and she's probably some sort of volunteer and a member of at least one social reform committee.

She wants to be involved in helping people who are weak, and particularly loves to help sick animals and people who can't take care of themselves — especially small children — because she is truly a child at heart. She'll gladly help raise funds for the new community playground, and after it's built, she'll swing from the monkey bars and slip down the slide.

Love and family

She's warmhearted, alluring and generous and she's selfish, demanding and unpredictable. In a relationship, the Aries woman gives being possessive a new twist, since she has no intention of being possessed herself. It's not that she plans to stray, it's just that she can't be bothered to tell her lover everything she does and everywhere she goes. Naturally independent, she needs to have a life of her own, not just to orbit around her man.

If she kept him up-to-the-minute on what she thought, planned, or had happening in her life, the list would just tire him and she'd rather he save his energy for the whirlwind weekend she has planned. She's a big planner — how does hang gliding at sunrise followed by a picnic lunch, and water-skiing in the afternoon sound?

Keeping up with Ms Aries and living up to her expectations can be quite a demanding chore. If you're lucky, you'll have time for a short nap or a relaxing soak in the bath before dashing out to see the latest action film. If there are no new releases at the box-office, rent a classic James Bond, or Indiana Jones flick. Don't kid yourself by thinking she'd like to see one of your sentimental favourites. This woman of Mars can be the most innocent princess of selfishness. After all, she'll ask, 'Why wouldn't you want to watch a movie that you know I'll like?'

The Aries woman doesn't really have marriage on her mind and she may not have much interest in playing the mother role, either. Her ability to 'love them and leave them' is sometimes a good thing for her because she has an uncanny ability to fall madly in love — for a month or two at a time.

If she's interested in anything more than a fleeting romance, she'll let you know. Otherwise, hold on to your pride and refrain from whispering sweet nothings until after she proposes marriage. Open admiration and frequent praise go a lot further with this woman than a string of mushy clichés whispered in her ear. And do be wary of criticising her. Remember, she is the iron glove that clothes a gentle, delicate hand.

She prefers to keep her independence on all kinds of levels (she often loves to pay for herself, even though she may dream of being taken care of financially). She's wary of being bought or owned, so unless the relationship is really settled, resist showering her with expensive gifts or she may begin to feel she owes you something — or that you want something from her. She doesn't want to be indebted to anyone. She is a giver rather than a taker, and she can quickly spot, and sometimes resent, those who tend to give too much. Innately she knows that there is no such thing as a free lunch or a free ride in life.

An Aries friend who is the manager of a publishing house once called me from a plane to recount what she referred to as the 'most awful two days she had ever endured'. I sat spellbound as I heard her 'horrifying' tale (it all sounded like a dream come true to me). Anyway, apparently, she was on her way home from a reunion with an old college boyfriend.

She had planned to stay for a week but within hours of arriving, the enthusiastic suitor from out of her past bought her flowers, took her to an expensive restaurant, and gave her five different gifts, including a velvet box, which she noticed was small enough to hold a ring. This last gift, the ring-shaped box, she simply refused to open.

Instead of finding him charming and generous, she thought he was terribly forward, pushy, smothering and extremely self-assured. She booked the next flight out of town and never spoke to him again.

Apart from this encounter, I have found many Aries women prefer to give gifts than to receive them. (Naturally, not all of them!) Many Aries women love to buy themselves gifts. Other Aries women love being spoiled and pampered, but they usually want to know exactly what is expected from them in return before they can relax and enjoy any offerings.

When you are dealing with an Aries, remember that Aries' independent spirit makes them cautious, even wary, of commitment and involvement. Aries women love to be the boss on various levels of existence, and that naturally means they don't like to hand over the reins of control to others too quickly or easily.

Most Aries women eventually marry, but when Ms Aries allows that ring to be slid on to her finger, it's with a smile that says: 'I love you, but you will never own me, and I may not stay around as long as I have promised'. She needs a patient, persevering companion. Consequently, she's looking for a man who's very secure, loves her unconditionally and has a life of his own. At the same time, she wants him to be willing and able to drop everything when she needs him to. Tall order, isn't it?

As well, she's drawn to men who are strong, powerful and sensitive, but she wants you to let her be her own person. So, supporting her dreams and keeping the flames of passion burning will guarantee her enthusiastic return home after a day of enterprise or adventure.

As a mother, Aries initiates her children into the wonderful world of magic, mystery and miracles. She loves to point out nature's wonders on walks through the bush, and romps in the park. She freely gives credit to the fairies and the nature nymphs for work well done. She plays pirates and searches for sunken treasures in the backyard pool, and she gladly samples all the food at make-believe picnics and tea parties. She's a delight to her children and they're a pleasant reminder to her that age is a state of mind.

She really believes in magic and can be uncannily psychic. Her unwavering belief in the unseen universe seems to develop a strong set of eyes in the back of her head. Her children rarely stand a chance of deceiving her and she is a lovingly strict disciplinarian. Sometimes she is so powerful an influence over her children that even when they grow up they still think 'I couldn't do this, or say this or that, because my mother wouldn't like it'. She's a strong influence on all around her.

Career

As laziness doesn't become her at all, an Aries woman loves it when she finds her niche in a career or a way of earning income from her creative self-expression! Whether it's writing, sculpting or serious business like running a merchant bank, an Aries woman can succeed at whatever she chooses to do. But something she doesn't choose to do? That's a different story. If she's stuck doing something she doesn't want to do, it'll be torture to be around her. She's either the leader of her band or she's banging the cymbals out of time to protest that she's not.

She usually shows her true feelings or frustrations by fiery outbursts or sulky withdrawals when she's not happy. And while not all Aries are quite this bold, even the more reserved ones know how to get your attention. She makes a very successful business leader and she's a loyal supporter of idealistic causes and purposes. She loves to come up with new ideas, explain how they'll work, and then dash off to find the next challenge or hurdle.

She's exceptionally resourceful, makes a skilful coordinator and adds zest to a creative team of any sort. She sometimes has a difficult time working for conservative companies because rigid routines are not really her style. But given a bit of flexibility and some authority, she has the magic power within her to work wonders.

She hates dealing with adversity, however, and tends to squirm in positions that require gentle tact and diplomacy — like complaint departments — but she can be very smooth in public relations and sales positions when she puts her mind to it. There's a lot of the seductress in her nature and she can lure someone into a business deal just as successfully as she can lure someone into her love life.

Her independent 'hands off' attitude in business dealings means that at times Ms Aries gets more of a turn-on from her business success than she gets from her romps in the bedroom. She's nearly always a high achiever when she's doing what she loves. She thrives in careers that offer lots of variety and encourage spontaneity and physical expression.

Action-oriented positions often suit an Aries best. If she yearns to express her creativity, she might be fulfilled as an actress, writer, artist or gourmet chef (Joan Crawford, Bette Davis, Emmylou Harris, Loretta Lynn and Reba McEntire were all born in Aries). If she's chasing excitement above all else, she'll love the life of a ski instructor, private detective or, in extreme cases, a tightrope walker or lion tamer. (Bonnie Warner, Olympic luger, and Libby Riddles, champion dog sled racer are both Aries women!)

Financial

Aries impulsiveness can be a blessing, but it's just as often a curse when money is involved. Just because she plops her spare change into the piggy bank at the end of each day doesn't mean she won't race into a questionable get-rich-quick scheme. She's drawn to excitement and adventure and she frequently miscalculates financial risks.

Lots of Aries have lost more than their pocket money by playing the stock exchange and leaping before they really took a good look. She has to learn how to save money and keep it because building financial reserves for a rainy day doesn't come naturally to her.

Even when she's had a bad financial experience an Aries woman usually recovers her losses and her hope, sometimes as quickly as she dusts off the dirt from her financial fall.

She's willing to work hard but she likes to play hard, too, and she'd rather spend on self-indulgence than self-improvement. She's optimistic about money and doesn't waste time worrying about it. But she likes the freedom that a healthy bank balance provides and she's willing to do what's necessary to create enough income to satisfy her needs and whims. When she slows down and puts more thought into her finances she wises up and puts more money into her savings. Once this woman learns to save as much as she spends, her financial portfolio begins to grow and the smell of sweet financial success surrounds her.

Physical

An Aries woman is a dynamo of energy and her potential for impeccable health is excellent. She can sustain an intense level of activity without tiring and her strength is usually much greater than her size would suggest. Regular exercise moderates her extremely high energy levels. Aries women enjoy friendly competition and often get their workout on a tennis court, running a race, or attending aerobics classes. Burning up physical energy helps Aries to keep her temper in check and run her mind more smoothly and clearly.

But even as a strong Aries, she has her physical limits. If she burns the candle at both ends or pushes herself too hard, her emotional state goes haywire and her body rebels. She needs to slow down every now and again to catch her breath and nurture her body. A long winter's nap by the fire or a warm siesta in the backyard hammock will do the trick. If these activities are too stationary for her tastes, a leisurely bike ride or a stroll through the park will work, too.

She may have a tendency towards headaches, which a balance of work, play and rest may relieve. An Aries woman needs to drink lots of water when she's active to avoid heat exhaustion and dehydration. Her blazing energy keeps her body temperature on the high side of normal and when she gets sick, she can spike a fever hot enough to stir-fry vegetables.

She can also create accidents when she plunges head-first into action without enough preparation or caution. More than a few Aries bang their heads, or worse, on the bottoms of swimming pools they impulsively dive into from hotel balconies.

Aries women have a natural tendency towards a fit muscular torso atop strong, shapely legs. Even out-of-shape Aries tend to have great legs that faithfully help them jump back into top fitness whenever they choose. She has a strong bone structure and good posture. When she's walking quickly, she may lead with her head, a gait characteristic of Aries' impatience. This impatience fuels her frustration, ignites her anger and causes nearly all of her health problems. Learning to meditate or taking a yoga or tai chi class can help her stay healthy long past retirement.

Mental

She has a multidimensional outlook that expands her mental horizon beyond the norm and makes her creative and sometimes eccentric. In a mental race, if she reaches the same conclusion as some of her opponents, you can be pretty sure she didn't get there the same way. She has an in-built, almost metaphysical, capacity for making quantum leaps in her thinking process.

These brainstorms of quick thinking application can lead her from A to Z in one leap, rather than going through the thought process step by step. Ms Aries loves to solve difficult mysteries, but avoids facing her greatest mystery — which is herself. She goes on many journeys of the mind and is anxious to learn new philosophies and grasp innovative concepts. She's outspoken about her opinions and won't back down from a debate; the more heated, the more she likes it.

She's an avid learner and a seeker of wisdom and truth. She's almost impossible to reason with when she's impassioned and she'll scorch you with her wrath if you ever suggest she's lying. There's a big difference to Ms Aries between exaggerating or stretching the truth, and out-and-out lying. While she delights in the former, she abhors the latter. Her quick-thinking ability means she has the mental energy and prowess to make decisions on the spot, which helps her and hurts her interchangeably. But no matter what predicament she's in or what roadblocks she creates, an Aries woman will rise to the challenge, and she loves nothing better than triumphing over adversity.

Spiritual

The Aries woman believes in hopes, dreams, magic and the mysteries of life. She knows she's here for the rollercoaster ride of her life and she lives in a fearless and sometimes reckless manner, trusting the angels will rescue her if it's not her time to move on. She has an unshakeable belief in her special creator, expects miracles and takes leaps of faith with complete confidence. She's not a person with blind faith, though! She likes to push her chances and see just how far her convictions and trust will take her.

She's not much for tradition and ceremony, so church services and long sermons are sometimes traded for inspirational sunrise walks or moonlight meditations. She respects other people's religious choices and she may follow a particular belief system, but she also could explore a variety of religions.

Even though she loves life in the fast lane, she's inspired by nature and often seeks the solace of a quiet forest or the sound of a waterfall or babbling brook. She's fascinated by the miracle of living, the power of love and the infinite spiral of eternity. And she can be disappointed when others don't share her wonder at the marvellous universe and world we live in. An Aries woman can see the pot of gold at the rainbow's end and the fairies' magic dance, and she's not embarrassed to admit it.

The Aries Man

> He's honest, dashing, confident and very, very sexy. He won't tolerate injustice and he stands up for the underdog with a fearless, idealistic stance.

The Aries man flies through life like a cannon ball, picking up momentum as he goes and hitting a wall head-on every now and again. His daily schedule would make most people's heads spin off, and his friends constantly encourage him to slow down and take a break. But this strong-headed man of Mars scoffs at the unsolicited advice and merrily zooms off on his way.

The only thing that ever stands between an Aries and his next action adventure is his sometimes stressed out body, which occasionally will stubbornly refuse to cooperate until he gets some much needed rest. Still, he fantasises about being Hercules and has enough dramatic charisma to make you believe he really is.

He is usually very physically powerful, and although he may seem to have more accidents than most around him, he has a strong physical energy and resilience. He has great tone when he is younger and is often athletic; however, as he matures he can sometimes see his muscle tone turn into flab. He has a lot of charisma (when he wants to have). He's independent, impulsive and incredibly charming. He values honesty and lives his life by following his own set of complicated and irregular standards, which tend to change as he grows older. But he's always true to himself and, as with Aries woman, what you see is what you get. Sometimes, because of his desire to live in the fast lane, he gets involved with some of the seedier aspects of life, like shady characters, drugs, gambling, too much booze and the kind of women you can't take home to mother.

A mixture of hot and cold, passion and passivity, innocence and sophistication, Mr Aries can be temperamental, cranky and difficult to get along with one minute and then the very next moment all soft and sensitive and seeking attention. He has many facets to his sometimes wild-at-heart character and he only reveals his more sensitive side to those whom he completely trusts.

If he is extremely sensitive, as some Aries men are, he may never reveal this vulnerable side of himself at all. He may believe that real men don't cry — at least not in front of others — and he can hold a tremendous amount of emotion trapped up within himself. This pressure-cooker internalised energy is revealed frequently through the intensity of his gaze or his nervous activity.

He is often a natural athlete and he can live at a whirlwind pace. Part of this is because he loves sporting pastimes and a hectic lifestyle. The other reason, though, is because it helps him to release a lot of built-up inner energy. When an Aries man is lethargic and lacking vitality or runs around looking for dangerous pursuits to test his mettle, it often indicates he has something unsettling and restrictive occurring in his life.

When he's at a crisis type of crossroads or he's upset about a situation, he either extinguishes his brilliant inner spirit and fire, dimming his life-spark, or he goes to the opposite extreme and goes on a personal warpath, which often ends up in some kind of accident or legal repercussion. The Aries man can be self-destructive, particularly if he isn't living the life of his dreams or he doesn't feel appreciated. These are the cases where he can be his own worst critic and judge.

[How Aries men operate]

Social

While the Aries man delights in playing the 'bad boy' at times, he still manages to be the total charmer of the zodiac. Where Mr Aries falls short on diplomacy, he rises tall in spirit and boyish charm. He's honest, dashing, confident and incredibly sexy. He won't tolerate what he views as injustice, and he stands up for the underdog with a fearless, idealistic stance. His forceful aggression results in many victorious battles.

Though his intentions are pure, the Aries man has a talent for creating conflict, sometimes by giving his opinion in a loud and somewhat tactless way. He himself has paper-thin skin and will lash out like a burning whip at anyone who threatens his fragile ego. But he forgets his anger quickly, rarely holds grudges and means no real harm. His bark is often far worse than his bite and he can feel extremely unhappy if he realises after an outburst that he has unintentionally hurt someone's feelings.

He loves to take on the world in more ways than one. He enjoys action-packed outings like white-water rafting, surfing, bungee jumping and mountain biking. If he can't make it to the great outdoors, he'll probably settle for an action flick or watching one of his favourite sports teams on television — preferably with the volume cranked up! The Aries man who would rather play in the artistic arena will enjoy a controversial modern art show, listening to the latest electronic music, visiting a technology expo to check out the new inventions or surfing the Internet.

Love and family

If you're in hot pursuit of an Aries man as a prospective partner for the rest of your life, I hope you're ready for a bumpy ride. Having a relationship with an Aries man is like navigating a plane through fire and ice. This guy's passion is hot enough to turn your knees to rubber and melt the shirt right off your back. Among the long list of Aries heart-throbs are Warren Beatty, Dennis Quaid, Alec Baldwin and Matthew Broderick.

Mr Aries has enormous sex appeal and he usually knows it and uses it to his total (and sometimes unfair) advantage. This muscular male mixes a steamy love potion that women stand in line to taste. But be warned, Mr Ram has a short attention span and a tall desire for variety. If he sees someone else he'd like to warm up to, you may be left out in the cold.

However, as easy as it can be for an Aries man to skate away from his current love affair, ironically he may fall to pieces if she leaves him — especially if it's for another man. He'll be relentless in his pursuit to win her back even if he was losing interest before she left. 'How could anyone leave me?' he'll wonder.

To keep him interested, a woman needs to as unpredictable as he is, sometimes distant, sometimes passionate, but always on his side. She needs as much energy to burn as he has or she must be willing to actively support him in his adventures by experiencing them second-hand. But don't expect him home for dinner every night or you may be disappointed. Patience is indeed one of your most needed virtues when you are dealing with the up-and-down ego and unconventional and demanding lifestyle offered by an Aries man.

One of the things that makes this man so incredibly appealing is his obvious inability to be controlled or possessed. Even in his childhood, the Aries male has a distinct mind of his own and plays by his own rules, regardless of the consequences.

A well-known Aries comedian confided to me that when he was in Year Two at a private Catholic school, his teacher frequently embarrassed him in front of the entire class, sometimes grabbing him out of his seat to swat his behind with a ruler. One day when the teacher went into the supply cupboard for chalk, he slammed the door behind her and locked her in. He was promptly expelled from the private school but he still believes he made the right choice.

Aries men usually get you back for something you've done to them (real or imagined) in some form or fashion — not necessarily out of vengeance, but more as a form of meting out their own justice.

Be warned: any woman who believes she can change this guy is setting herself up for a grand lesson in life. He is what he is so you had better love him as he is or you're in for a hard lesson in relationships. He'll wear you out long before you'll wear him out because he has a spirit as big as eternity and nobody (particularly someone who wants to control him) is going to suppress this true spirit for long. He's going to want to think his own thoughts, too — not just listen quietly to yours.

The Aries man is as generous about giving his opinion as he is selfish about his own needs. He's also the hero figure. However, this same man will stop to help a lost child find his parents and donate a car full of food to the local shelter for the homeless. There's no question that he has a warm heart. In fact, he can actually be overly vulnerable sometimes.

He doesn't like being alone much so he might go from one relationship to the next, believing that some day his action adventure princess will arrive. If an Aries finds his true soulmate he will be hopelessly devoted to her. He won't let her run his life but his heart will be hers for keeps — as long as the fire is stoked and the heat is on. As for fatherhood, no one is a prouder father than a Ram. He adores his children. And while at times he's domineering, he's also playful.

Remember, though, that he must always be number one in your life. Ignoring his desires in favour of fawning over one of the children will surely cool his flame. He will always be a boy/child at heart, too, so he doesn't want you to forget his needs in favour of one of the 'other' children, even if he pretends he wants to take care of himself.

Career

He can be tough to work with and demanding to work for. Some say Mr Aries is better working by himself because his independent nature makes him a lone ranger. The Ram is a pioneer, an entrepreneur and a leader. He's not a good subordinate unless he has his own area to supervise, and he isn't cut out to be a follower. His high energy and bright intellect thrive on being in charge. He excels as his own boss, particularly if he has flexible and lucrative deadlines to meet. He can get great pleasure and satisfaction from his work and career as long as he is the one calling the shots.

Mr Aries also thrives on variety. He really dislikes routine and if he's working in a punch-the-clock setting he may be openly miserable and disagreeable. Routine can make him physically ill — if it's the type of routine that really has nothing new or exciting to offer. Especially in his younger days, the Aries man does much better in positions that have some unsupervised time and not too many restrictions. He has a touch of nomad in his soul that makes him a free spirit who loves to wander.

Aries men were no doubt some of the legendary bounty hunters and pony express riders in the wild west. In today's world, Aries men pursue — or dream about — careers as heroes, sports stars, movie stars, investors, private detectives, actors, comedians, talk-show hosts, stunt doubles, fighter pilots, magicians, progressive artists, professional athletes and fire fighters. Whether it's physical pressure or mental pressure, the Aries man thrives in cutting-edge positions. Think of David Letterman's spontaneous humour, Harry Houdini's mesmerising magic and Kareem Abdul Jabbar's outstanding basketball skills. But regardless of his job, this man does not live to work. He's not afraid to work hard, but he won't tolerate too much overtime and he gets irritable if his play time is cut short.

Financial

He can be super-combative and if he competes in the financial arena he can be a force in the big money games of the world. Luck and taking a chance often play a role in the way he makes his fortune. The Aries man is enterprising, optimistic, intuitive and impulsive when it comes to money. He can make a million and lose it again several times during his lifetime. (John D. Rockefeller, J. P. Morgan and Hugh Hefner were all Aries.)

He's also resilient and adaptable and just as willing to paddle a dinghy as he is to sail a yacht. If he doesn't yearn to be rich or fear being poor, he often ends up somewhere in the middle. But if he's driven to material wealth he can be super successful in his ventures.

His impulsive nature can put him in precarious financial positions. This man is sometimes accused of being penny wise and pound foolish. He consistently deposits a small portion of his income into his savings account but may part with a month's pay to gamble on a high-risk investment without doing a bit of research or consulting a single expert.

Hunches generally mean a lot to him. He can be extremely inconsistent and is extravagant when it suits him. He complains that lunch is overpriced but then pays top dollar for a house or a car because he doesn't have time to shop around.

Lady Luck likes him, though, and he often bounces back quickly after a major financial setback. He'll rarely end up penniless because he doesn't sit around waiting for opportunities to bang on his door, he goes out and tracks them down. An Aries man has the courage to transform an inspired idea into a profitable opportunity. If he goes after what he loves to do and creates a way to make money doing it, he's sure to succeed.

His love for excitement and drama often extend into his financial and career world, too. Although the Aries man daydreams about smooth financial sailing, the reality of living on easy street often bores him. He enjoys the financial challenges life offers and would rather be an independent gambler than a nine-to-five banker.

Physical

He's born with an inner-driven physical power of a most impressive and special type. The Ram is a whirlwind of activity and movement. He speeds through the universe leaving behind a shimmer of excitement and more than a sprinkling of chaos. Woe to anyone who stands in the way of this headstrong inferno. He moves so fast he can be extremely accident-prone (that is why his insurance premiums are so high — his past claims record often goes against him). He can break things (including limbs), lose things and end up at the wrong place simply because he has been travelling so fast that he can't keep up with himself.

He's a firebrand ball of energy. He needs to keep a careful watch on his inputs and outputs of physical expression. He can eat and drink far too much and then fall out of shape and find it tough to get back in shape again. He needs to be quite disciplined with respect to taking care of himself. Otherwise, he can turn to flab (sometimes even become obese) and then become quite irritable because he doesn't like himself too much.

No wonder most Aries men play one or more sports (which they try to continue throughout their lives) and jump at the chance to go rock-climbing, skydiving, skiing, surfing or anything else that gives a blast and helps keeps them in tiptop physical shape.

An Aries man needs to exercise, and often his desire to get fit encourages him to push himself beyond his body's comfort zones of operation.

When he overdoes it and is confined to his bed, he's depressed and moody and curses his body for interrupting his adventure. A more mature Aries will pout but silently thank his body for forcing him to take the rest when he should have had the sense to do so anyway.

This man's lust for speeding through life can also make him prone to injuries. A head injury might indicate he's travelling in the wrong direction and he may want to reconsider his present course before resuming his adventure. He benefits by learning to move more carefully and deliberately — like a Leo or a Capricorn — so he can avoid accidents like stepping on broken bottles and running into fences.

Accidents aside, the Aries man has the potential for excellent health. His optimistic outlook keeps him from harbouring negative emotions and helps him avoid diseases that are caused by chronic worry and negativity. His only real health enemy is his tendency to overdo things. He loves excess and may have a stronger taste for alcohol or some other type of indulgence than he will readily admit.

He's usually got a very impressive physical body and is well proportioned — in every way. The Ram is generally strong with well-developed legs and broad shoulders, much like his animal counterpart. He sometimes has thick eyebrows that nearly meet at the top of his nose, and he probably has some hair on his back (and occasionally he's extremely woolly and hairy). His straight back and poised posture show his self-confidence — and his agility and speed make him one of the most enjoyable athletes to watch.

Mental

Mr Aries doesn't sit around talking about doing things, he goes straight out and does them! The Aries man is bright, creative and daring. He doesn't like pondering a situation; he prefers to make a quick decision and move on.

He knows if he makes the wrong decision it will be obvious soon enough and he can usually reverse course and pull out before he crashes and burns. He would rather try something than think about it because the Ram is a 'doer' more than anything else. He believes experience offers far more than any theory and his fearless nature encourages him to overlook many potential risks and dangers.

He likes being the ideas man and he's great at coming up with new and innovative ways to accomplish goals. He's an inventor of sorts, though he's not the one to work out the finer details, preferring the big picture and wide horizon to the close-up, magnified view.

He's his own worst enemy when it comes to making and keeping friends because his mental speed combined with his impatience makes it difficult for him to put up with people who are slow and deliberate in their thinking and speaking. Even when he tries, he can't seem to stop himself from jumping to conclusions and playing 'fill in the blank' when someone else is talking.

Spiritual

He's a seeker on the pathway of life as much as an adventurer and explorer. An Aries man is just as adventurous about spirituality as he is about the other spheres of life. He has an open mind and is willing to learn about whatever interests him. He won't turn down the chance to experience a Native American sweat lodge and he may have studied with Christian missionaries or Tibetan monks. It's not uncommon for an Aries man to experience many belief systems throughout his life.

He enjoys spiritual initiations that require some sort of risk or challenge. An Aries man would love the chance to wind his way through an ancient maze of tunnels or search for the Holy Grail. He loves meeting the challenges of life by using his body, mind and spirit together.

He generally believes in a supreme creator, trusts in lady luck and also gives thanks to his many guardian angels. He trusts himself and has an inborn certainty that he'll be alive for as long as he's supposed to be here. He also has a strong inner voice that is always ready to help him out even though he sometimes ignores it until he's in some sort of trouble. It is through spirituality that Aries has a great chance to cultivate tranquillity and inner peace. If an Aries can teach himself to sit quietly in meditation, he can accomplish just about anything.

The Aries baby

Be prepared for some excitement, because this is the dramatic, gorgeous firebrand baby of the zodiac.

I hope you're ready for some action. Before this baby is born, it's probably making its presence felt by doing high kicks and tap dancing around in your womb like Aries Arthur Murray. The Aries infant wants to be free and is intent upon being born as quickly as it can (possibly ahead of schedule).

If its Aries nature is pronounced, this little mite isn't destined to be quiet. He or she is likely to have one of the loudest cries and screams in the neighbourhood. The Aries baby knows exactly what it wants, and the way it believes it can get what it wants is to scream for it, sometimes at shrill, ear-splitting levels.

Once this child can stand up on its own, it will shake, rattle and roll the sides of its play-pen in a strong and persistent fashion in an effort to get out and explore the world. And if you don't keep a close watch, the Aries baby probably will get out by hook or by crook.

For those of you who absolutely love your sleep, don't expect to be getting too much. It's most likely that this little bundle of energy doesn't need a lot of sleep. Ready to take on the world from the moment it can move, it's rearing to get out of its bassinet or crib and find some action.

You'll need to take extra precautions to ensure it doesn't manage to climb over the side of wherever it sleeps or is left to play, because an Aries baby has the ability to move furniture around in order to reach for a toy or something that it wants. And don't be misled by its tiny size. Your offspring is going to be a great deal stronger than it appears.

It's also astro-programmed to be athletic and active. Expect to get lots of exercise. It's likely that the baby Ram will be able to walk at an early age, and once it masters walking it will soon be running and flying with the wind beneath its baby wings.

With a strong, innate will and high desire level, your Aries infant is ruled by Mars — the planet of go-getter energy expression (the sign depicting sports people in astrology). Your Aries baby is likely to be a go-getter in a way all of its own. Consequently, before its entry into the world you're advised to get as fit as possible so you can keep up with this brand new little person.

You'll need to be super-patient to deal with this little bundle of volatile and bouncy joy. Cute and cuddly and everything you ever dreamed of, nevertheless your Aries baby is born with a knack for pushing you to your limits and doing whatever it can to attract full-time attention.

From the day it's born, the tiny Aries not only loves, but demands, to be the centre of attention. And when you don't pay it plenty of attention, it will ingeniously think of many clever ways to get you to tune into it. The Aries baby's intense energy level can make it prone to high fevers, so do keep a close watch if you detect a higher than normal temperature.

Your Aries offspring is likely to be a trailblazer and leader in all kinds of ways. Some of his or her antics could even make it into the *Guinness Book of Records*. Have your video recorder handy and your camera full of film because you're likely to shoot plenty of amusing, entertaining and head-spinning baby footage to keep you enraptured in the future — some of it of the heart-stopping, close-to-the-edge variety, as this baby is born a natural risk taker.

And while you'll be kept busy, mentally, emotionally, and physically keeping up with your Aries, you'll get an abundance of love and delight back in return.

• • • • • • (The Aries toddler through teen

Your heart will stop a hundred times with this one, so fasten your seat belt for a wild ride and stock up on soothing bath oils and calming music so you can relax at the end of your action-packed days.

From the time Aries children are two or three years old it's clear they already have well-developed and opinionated minds of their own! These little ones are very assertive from the word go.

Rams will let you know what they want and how they want it, and while most two-year-olds like to say the word 'no', it can be an Aries' favourite.

Aries children are somewhat like wise old souls trapped in young and sometimes unmanageable bodies. They are easily frustrated by constraints that their parents or the school system place on them and they resent their freedom being curtailed in any way — especially without an ample explanation.

They begin wanting to know the whys and wherefores earlier than most children and continue to be interested in the answers to these types of questions for the rest of their lives.

Many Aries have a vivid imagination and while this may lead to some wild exaggerations it's also a valuable and safe way for them to escape from mundane situations that are forced upon them. So the next time your five-year-old Aries says he or she can't go to bed because there's a purple, orange-eyed monster in their bedroom, try playing along.

When my friend's four-year-old Aries son told her he couldn't put his toys back in the toy box because there was a giant striped dinosaur in the playroom, she suggested he polish his leadership skills by offering the dinosaur a chocolate chip biscuit if it would clean up the toys for him.

Aries love to play heroes and dragon tamers, so you might as well learn to enjoy these scenarios when they're young.

Since the wee Aries delights in imagination and mystery, they really get excited about Santa Claus, the Easter Bunny and even the Tooth Fairy, and it won't harm them to have some fantasy in their lives. The trick is to listen carefully to their questions and when they reach a point where they ask you to tell them the truth and they really want to hear it, tell them.

But remember to tell them, too, that many of the world's most wondrous and miraculous things are mysteries and every thing or idea that we can imagine could very possibly exist in some way, somewhere, whether we can see it or not.

Little Rams have an overabundance of energy, which is both highly entertaining and at the same time can lend itself to recklessness. Keep lots of kisses and band-aids stored up for this one's little cuts and bruises. It's also a good idea to be sure to invest in the proper safety equipment for his or her sports activities. Helmets, knee pads, elbow pads and face guards are required parts of an Aries wardrobe.

This youngster loves mayhem and mystery. He'll climb into dark cubbyholes just to explore them and she'll walk across the top of the jungle gym just to see if she can. Your heart will stop a hundred times with this one, so fasten your seat belt for a wild ride and stock up on soothing bath oils and calming music, so you can relax at the end of your action-packed days

Most Aries have a special place in their hearts for all of Earth's creatures and Aries can begin learning about caring and nurturing at an early age if given the pleasure and responsibility of taking care of a pet.

Start with something small like a fish or turtle, or maybe a guinea pig, and work your way up as your Aries shows readiness and desire. The younger Aries will need to be shown how to carefully and delicately touch or hold their pets and you will need to supervise these interactions until you are certain that your little animal-lover is capable of taking care of the pet in a careful and loving manner.

Aries, perhaps more than other Sun signs, really love great surprises. Bake his favourite cake, plan a surprise holiday and when you buy them presents be sure to hide them extremely well. Aries kids seem to have a psychic fix on where their presents are hidden. An Aries friend of mine once proudly told me that each year before his birthday, he would find his hidden presents, carefully unwrap them to see inside, and then meticulously re-wrap them so that no one ever knew. At the age of 43, he was still smiling about this clever accomplishment.

As the Aries youth grows older, he or she tends to become more competitive and more aggressive. These traits will generally level out again when they reach young adulthood. But in the meantime, it's important that they be encouraged to pursue healthy outlets of expression they like and are genuinely interested in.

Don't try to force your own favourites on an Aries youth. Let them tell you what really interests them and then support them to pursue it. Aries can get lots of satisfaction from expressing their personalities in all sorts of arenas from sports and gymnastics to painting, acting or making play models of some sort.

Do your best to designate a play area where he or she is permitted to really let loose and not have to worry about hurting anything or breaking anything. And do be careful of the criticism you dish out to this fragile young ego. He or she may act independent and even cocky at times, but no matter how much Rams insist that they don't need you, be assured that they need you much more than you think.

Loving encouragement, honest praise and frequent positive reinforcement are the magic building blocks for Aries youngsters and they continue to bolster their spirits throughout their lives. Aries has a dramatic reaction to parents, teachers and anyone who tries to run his or her life. You can count on your Aries teenager to show open defiance — not only to you, but also to teachers, police officers and the head of the local gang.

He or she has relatively little fear, and you will need to do your best to guide Aries with love and logic and resist trying to 'rule with an iron fist' type of approach. The more you demand and insist on something with an Aries, the less likely it is that you will end up getting it.

One of the most successful approaches in dealing with young Aries is to present them with choices that are within clear limits. 'Would he or she rather baby-sit little sister for a few hours or help Dad to wash and wax the car?' It's important to give your Aries options or he or she will make their own choices without involving you in them.

Some Aries, for all of their energy, may be a bit on the quiet side. These introspective types need to have their privacy respected — especially by their parents. Resist the temptation to read his or her diary, don't snoop around in their drawers, and learn to knock instead of barging in through a closed door.

If you suspect your Aries teen is in some type of trouble, calmly ask him or her to tell you what's happening. You will know whether they're hiding something or not. You will find an open, honest relationship with your Aries much more fulfilling and enduring than any type of controlling or dominating relationship.

Try to let go of your own judgments and just love your Aries for whoever he or she really is. And whatever you do, don't laugh at an Aries' dreams and don't repeat their secrets — no matter what.

If you can help a young adult Aries to see that their dreams really can come true, you're fanning a highly creative and ingenious spark of talent and inspiration. This young man or woman has a great deal of artistry and creativity just waiting to flow through and make something magnificent and breathtaking to add some zest to the world.

If the growing and developing Aries spends too much time in negative settings or if he or she is repeatedly put down, they begin to lose their inner drive and motivation to explore and experience life to its fullest.

An Aries will never have his or her spirit totally broken. No matter what the circumstance, if an Aries truly wants to win, he or she will triumph with flying colours.

If the Aries is nurtured with stardust and imagination as well as love and fair discipline, the Ram will grow to live the dream held most dear in his or her heart. And you will have the pleasure of seeing your Aries' brightest dreams come true.

TAURUS

[21 april — 21 may]

taurus taurus taurus taurus taurus
taurus taurus taurus taurus taurus taurus
taurus taurus taurus taurus taurus
taurus taurus taurus taurus taurus taurus

taurus taurus taurus taurus taurus
taurus taurus taurus taurus taurus taurus
taurus taurus taurus taurus taurus
taurus taurus taurus taurus taurus taurus
taurus taurus taurus taurus taurus
taurus taurus taurus taurus taurus taurus
taurus taurus taurus taurus taurus

element: earth

planetary ruler: venus

symbol: the bull

quality: fixed (= stability)

colours: earth tones, orange and yellow

gem: coral, emerald

best companions: virgo and capricorn

strongest virtues: strength, commitment

and determination

traits to improve: over-indulgences, lack of

flexibility and stubborn temperament

deepest desire: to be respected

for who you really are

Taurus celebrities

Cate Blanchett, Janet Jackson, Daniel Day-Lewis, Renee Zellweger,

Pierce Brosnan, Glen Campbell, William Shakespeare, Tony Danza,

Dennis Rodman, Uma Thurman, Tony Blair, Lee Majors, Shirley Temple,

Shirley MacLaine, Ella Fitzgerald, Natasha Richardson, Audrey Hepburn,

Willie Nelson, Rita Coolidge, Bianca Jagger, James Brown, Bill Crosby,

Burt Bacharach, Orson Welles, Rudolph Valentino, Sigmund Freud,

Eva Peron, Melissa Gilbert, Katharine Hepburn, Florence Nightingale,

Stevie Wonder, Harvey Keitel, Aaron Spelling, Tori Spelling, Liberace,

Dennis Hopper, Grace Jones, Cher, Barbra Streisand, Andie McDowell,

Billy Joel, Andre Agassi, George Lucas (movie director), George Clooney,

Jessica Lange, Hitler, Jerry Seinfeld, Queen Elizabeth II, Jack Nicholson,

Emilio Estevez, Debra Winger, Al Pacino, Joe Cocker, Michelle Pfeiffer,

Saddam Hussein, Shannon Doherty, Jana Wendt and Salvador Dali.

[General outlook]

Look out, Taureans! New millennium magic is coming your way, bringing with it a new brilliant planetary line-up to help you make your dreams come true. And it's really just as well. The last years of the twentieth century threw you the most amazing set of wildcards that you have ever in your life had to deal with, leaving many of you Bulls grappling to come to terms with a new lifestyle, work, health or financial situation.

The good news is that there's never been a better time to chase after your pot of gold at the end of the rainbow – because you are likely to find it! Armed with a new-found courage and enthusiasm (plus incredible support from others), it's time to make your dreams reality.

Be bold. Be brave. And keep firmly in your mind that until you pluck up the courage to try, you'll never know what's possible, and nothing is impossible under the sun, moon and stars for you now.

Romance

When you Taureans fall in love, your senses are arrested. A mere look, touch, taste or smell can mean more to you than simple words. And in this regard the new millennium is no different for you. When it comes to Bulls and their earthy passions, you will continue to be driven by your senses, but your attitudes to relationships are changing and you are ready to develop more independent pursuits. A part of you is no longer so caught up in chasing after romantic fantasies. Single Taureans will be attracted to independent partners, while married Bulls need to be careful that having different interests and tastes to your partner won't slow you down and deter you from doing what you want. Take special care that these differences of interest don't cause you and your loved one to start to drift apart.

Health

Good health is around you in the new millennium and where you may have suffered any illnesses recently (probably associated with stress and tension) your complete recovery is imminent. The majority of Taureans will be extremely healthy and as strong as an ox for most of the first five years of this important era, and as the new millennium dawns many Taureans will consider themselves invincible. Just remember that while it takes you longer to get sick than most, it can also take you longer to recuperate from illnessl. Don't forget that prevention is better than cure. Exercise regularly, eat healthily and rest frequently. And remain healthy and happy by doing the things you love.

Finance

The dawning of the new millennium signifies a prosperous era for Taureans where affairs of the wallet are concerned. It's highly likely that you'll be making more money than you have ever made before — but that doesn't necessarily mean you'll have more in your pocket to spend so don't rush off and book that Caribbean cruise just yet! There are mortgages, study responsibilities and other people's needs to consider when you divvy up your money now. Concentrate on clearing your debts and getting some savings stowed away for that proverbial rainy day. Choose tight budgeting over impulse spending and you'll set yourself up nicely for the future.

Career

Exploring new territory is a theme for Taureans in your new millennium astro-forecast. This is a wonderful time to break away from the safety and security of known areas and to test new talents and learn new skills. Many Taureans will start their own business while others will turn an interest or hobby into a new career. Remember always that when you do what you love, and love what you do, you can't fail! Opportunities are all around you in your career sector during the new millennium so keep an eye out for them!

[Millennium wildcards to watch for]

You Taureans can expect an enormous overload of possibilities and opportunities to surround you, which could very well bewilder and confuse you so that you are unable to take full advantage of them. This will almost be a case of 'too much, too soon', occurring around you. Planetary patterns indicate that this is a tremendously busy time for Taureans. Greater responsibilities fall on your shoulders where work, finance or home-renovating are concerned and you may even feel as though you're the only one who can solve the problems that arise. Learning to delegate is all important and will give you more time to spend with loved ones.

You're a creature of comfort and you love to surround yourself with life's treasures and pleasures.

Lucky you! You're one of the most fortunate signs of the zodiac, Taurus. You were born with a taste for the finer things in life and fortunately, usually you have the talent and creativity to satisfy that rich appetite you have to live life to its fullest — and even beyond. Many Taurus people are very successful and live opulent lifestyles. Your sign often lives longer than most others do, too! When it comes to being a star or person of note, many Taureans rate high on the ladder of success in various fields. George Clooney, Cher, Barbara Streisand, Jerry Seinfeld and Michelle Pfeiffer are all Taurus-born. However, it would not be fair to leave out Taureans, Saddam Hussein and Adolf Hitler. I mention Saddam Hussein and Hitler because it is interesting that such a creative, talented but fixed sign as Taurus can also occasionally be such a hard-nosed stirrer and a battler, too. I guess that when the contrasting flows of energy from Venus (your ruler) discordantly meet up with Mars (the male domination energy planet), if they aren't configured harmoniously in any Taureans' horoscope, this powerful combination can create an individual that rocks the foundations of the world.

Remember you are the zodiac's bull after all! That can make you sulky, stubborn and very petulant at times; it can also turn you into a force to be reckoned with! Your zodiac symbol, the Bull, is what really displays most prominently your character in many ways. It represents your strength and persistence as well as your stubborn and sometimes bull-headed nature. And since you're usually easygoing and patient, many people tend to underestimate your strong determination. But when you set your mind to something, you can rustle up enough energy to make the annual 'running of the bulls' look like a walk down easy street! If you want something (I mean really want something), it is far better for others to stand aside, than to stand in your way. Saying 'no' to a Taurus is like talking to the trees!

Now although the Bull symbolises your sign in astrology, you also have a celestial fairy godmother waving her magic wand over you. This heavenly fairy godmother is your ruling planet Venus, the Roman goddess of beauty, the arts, pleasure and emotions. Venus is the celestial entity that smiles on you and often makes you an incredible 'good-looker' (check out Taurus George Clooney for a most handsome example of how Venus can smile on someone). Even if you are not born good-looking under Venus (if the bull was more in control when you were born), there will still be something especially gorgeous about you in some way. Maybe it is your skin, your hair, your health, your vitality, and your glow. Venus will not let you miss out on inheriting some of her great physical gifts. These Venus gifts may just be in a little less abundant form for you than for those Taureans who were born when Venus was smiling on them. But whether you are born under Venus's influence or under the Bull influence, one thing is certain — you probably need to watch your weight as the years pass by. Taureans do have a tendency to pack on the pounds, and it is little wonder at times, because often you do love your second helpings! Plus many of you tend to forget exercise as the years go by and replace it with watching TV instead! Many a couch potato has been born under the sign of Taurus (so watch out for those bouts of partaking of soft drinks and potato chips. These are the types of indulgence that can undermine your potential for good looks or beauty quicker than anything else).

Usually because Venus rules you (and Venus is after all the goddess of good times and pleasure) you are a creature of comfort and if you have your druthers, you love nothing better than to surround yourself with life's treasures and pleasures! Those big-sized fridges were designed with someone like you in mind! These inborn characteristics that make you love to have 'more,' rather than less of anything, are what help you to start learning about the value of money at a very young age. And lots of Taurus-born people become extremely successful and wealthy — either through their own talents and skills, through associations with the right people, or through their marriages. Interestingly, too, many Taureans work in money-related industries, like banks, the stock market, investment organisations and insurance companies. Where the money (and comfort) are to be found that is often where you are to be found, too!

The famous line from the Jerry McGuire movie, 'Show me the money' is likely to have been written by a Taurus because to a Taurus money means a great deal. With it you are safe and secure; without it you are fearful and cranky. Until you are wealthy (if indeed you do make it to being wealthy), you can sometimes struggle with the temptation to live beyond your means and rely on credit and luck to see you through. This doesn't always work out well for you, or for those around you, and your way of handling money can become risky business at times. Fortunately, you place a high value on your own financial security, and this helps to stop you from going too far overboard on spending. Some of you work hard, others don't, but whatever you have earned, as much as you love to spend it, you want to keep it, too! You are the kind of sign that wants to have your cake and eat it. Money is often the prize and the torment of your existence. You don't want to spend it or give it away, but you don't want to go without anything either.

This temptation to have what you want, to live within your means, to make more money and to keep building up your savings often places you at some interesting crossroads in life. It can also take you on some extreme journeys and see you enter into unusual associations.

Now don't get me wrong, you can be one of the most generous signs of all, but money still holds a special place in your heart, even in the midst of your most generous spin cycle. You can be generous to the extreme about some things — like giving special gifts and donating your time, energy and knowledge to good causes (and possibly even giving blood), yet on other levels, you can hold on to your prized possessions with a death grip. You are probably one of those people that occasionally must admit to having the attitude that what's mine is mine, and what's yours is mine, too.

In fact, Taurus is the zodiac's collector, and your collections are never complete. Even if your outer appearance is low key and humble in terms of what you seem to have, you often have a lot more hidden away than others know about — for example Taurus Jerry Seinfeld has a fabulous and growing collection of cars. Owning real estate and expensive toys makes you feel safe and you even can have some expensive trinkets, too (Barbra Streisand is quite a renowned collector of antique jewellery, even if a vast part of that collection is costume jewellery). If you get into collecting you are usually good at it. You can have an almost psychic sense for knowing the true value of jewellery, antiques, and items other people would throw away with the trash. This trait really takes over when a Taurus goes shopping! If shopping were an Olympic event, you'd bring home the gold medals with no problem! It's as if you have 'shopping radar' and can detect bargains even before you see them. This Taurus trait can be helpful (and also a hindrance) in more ways than some people can imagine! Shop till you drop can take on a whole new deeper meaning when it is describing a Taurus. Many of you can actually wear yourselves out, or make yourselves ill, when you are a shopping mission that you wish to fulfil. You love to shop but shopping can take different forms. For a man, it may be not so much clothing or jewellery as much as acquiring shares or stock options, collecting stamps, or even choosing plants for the garden. Before you say that the Taurus you know is not a shopaholic, remember, shopping can mean different things to different people!

Shopping can even become a profession for some people born under this sign (as in those who find clothes for the stars of movies and so on, or who find the props to host parties and so on). In fact, for one of my Taurus friends, her shopping radar actually helped to pay off her exorbitant credit card debts. Sandy was on her way home from a meeting with her financial adviser. They calculated that at the interest rates she was paying it would take her nine years to pay off her credit card debts. She felt depressed by the reality of her situation and she was determined to turn her financial picture back around. She knew this wasn't the best time to spend money but something about a little antique store she drove by called her name and she decided to park her car and explore the shop. She said she had a feeling that something was in that shop that she was supposed to find. After looking around for only a minute or two she spotted a unique necklace among the costume jewellery. She bargained with the shop owner and purchased the necklace for $75, all the while feeling guilty for indulging her whim under her current circumstances. But the whim paid off big time. It turned out the necklace was an early, but less-known original from the Cartier collection and was worth thousands of dollars. She struck gold! And you Taureans often strike gold — gold in a variety of forms (courtesy of your fairy godmother, Venus) — sometimes when you least expect it. You can really make your own magic when you set your mind to something and listen to your intuition.

It is surprising that even though you are surrounded by magic (and often have incredible power to make wishes that do come true), you are one of the (usually) more balanced signs of the zodiac. That is because emotionally, Taurus, you're stable, strong, and grounded. You're a natural poker face (a terrific comedian — look at Jerry Seinfeld and how clever Cher was at delivering her funny lines, years ago (possibly, too far back for many readers of this book to remember — but I do!) when she used to do the Sonny and Cher show. You Taureans can be great listeners and thoughtful, considerate friends. Externally, you tend to be quiet, understanding and patient. But that's only half of the real Taurus story. You are sugar and spice and all things nice, when you are in tune with the moon, stars and other planets. However, when you are out of tune and if someone pushes you too hard, you can be as stubborn, as fearsome and as angry as a raging bull. When you are in this stirred up state, you may even stamp your feet and snort — just like the bull does when it is enraged.

Most times, you can be stubborn to a fault and you will resist change even when it is good for you. There is a joke in astrology that goes — 'How do you get a Taurus to move?' — the answer — yell out 'Bomb!' Generally, no one can make you do something that you don't want to do. This characteristic can be one of your greatest strengths, but it's also the one that drives your friends the most crazy, causes problems with your relationships and aggravates your parents the most when you are growing up! But remember you do have a fairy godmother, Venus, so not very many people can stay mad at a Taurus for long because you have a shining personality, a wonderful heart and people really appreciate and remember your kind words and special attention. Your unassuming nature makes you popular with all kinds of people and you can pick and choose your friends. However, you're too kind-hearted to turn anyone away, so you usually have more friends than you know what to do with. And what's more, some of these friends are possibly the last ones you really do need to have around you — but that is a whole other story!

Because of Venus's influence, you often have tons of creativity that can express itself on many different levels. It may show up in writing, your involvement with fashion, hosting parties, playing music, colour coordination, cooking, gardening, painting, or putting bits and pieces together in an appealing and unusual way. You would love to make a generous income from one of your artistic abilities but you may tend to think that work must be drudgery or somehow a sacrifice. In fact, those Taureans that do turn their hobbies or their love for coordinating things into a career, often become the top people in their fields. There are many famous chefs born under this sign.

Many Taureans have green thumbs, and take tremendous pride in their gardens. In fact, many landscape gardeners, plant and garden equipment suppliers and florists are Taureans. For a Taurus, doing what you love can be fun, rewarding and profitable.

Taurus is an Earth sign

To your advantage, you have a practical sense for survival that gets you through challenges and over roadblocks that might trip up others. You're organised and systematic in your planning and you can see the steps you need to take to prepare for your future goals. You also appreciate natural resources and respect the environment. And you take great care of everything you own because you can't stand to see anything damaged, wasted or broken.

You're incredibly understanding of other people's faults and are willing to give everyone from your best friend to a perfect stranger the benefit of the doubt. You also have the courage and the wisdom not to 'go along with the crowd.' When you see yourself as you truly are, you realise that the traits that bother you the most about other people are the parts of yourself that you haven't learned to acknowledge and love.

To your disadvantage, you sometimes act like you don't have much self-discipline and you can be apathetic when it comes to motivating yourself. Sometimes you're even apathetic about doing the things you really enjoy, especially if you're feeling depressed. You can be weak-willed at times, which is surprising because of the stubbornness you have within you. It can be a shame that you don't summon up that stubbornness and use it to break bad habits or change the things that are happening in your life that may be sabotaging your progress or interfering with your good health!

Because you're so connected to the Earth, it's easy for you to get weighed down with earthly pleasures and that means you might lean towards over-eating, over-drinking, over-working, over-shopping or overdoing it in some other way! You can sometimes stubbornly refuse to do the things you know are good for you and heaven help anyone who criticises you when you're having an emotional day!

[Insights into your sign]

The bright side: One of your greatest strengths is your patient determination and ability to stay focused on your carefully laid plans until you achieve your objectives.

The shadow: It's easy for your patience to melt into procrastination, especially when it comes to starting projects you don't want to do. You also resist change, sometimes even when it's for your own good.

[Looking beneath the surface of your sign]

Because Taurus' hidden traits are usually so well disguised, you can scare the hair off someone's head when you break into your bucking bronco routine. You sometimes give a warning glare, or lower your Taurus 'bull horns' before you charge, but you often take people totally by surprise.

You can appear to be calm and collected when your insides are actually rumbling with all sorts of energy. But most Taurus people don't like to make a fuss or cause other people trouble or hard feelings, so you put up with a lot of things that other people wouldn't tolerate. And this can do you more harm than good over the long run, especially where your health is concerned.

You rarely admit it when you're being stubborn, and there are times that you'd rather cut off your own arm than have someone else twist it. The sooner you begin to see yourself as you truly are — both good and bad — your life will use less effort and you will have more energy for creative and productive endeavours.

[How to tune into your sign's powers]

> As bamboo sways and bends with the breeze, your sign has the greatest power when you learn to be flexible, too.
>> Seize the moment.
>> Have more faith in your own instinct and intuition, instead of handing the power of your decisions over to others.

Characteristics >	Benefits >	Drawbacks >
Affectionate	Warm relationships	Can smother friends
Calm	Good in crises	Move in slow motion
Creative	Artistic self-expression	Go over the top
Determined	Eventually reach goals	Bloody-mindedness
Empathetic	Understand others well	Think they know how to advise others, even when they don't
Friendly	Show appreciation	Try too hard to be nice
Insecure	Humble them	Need constant reinforcement
Kind-hearted	Well-liked	Easy mark
Loyal	Trustworthy	Others take the praise
Materialistic	Have the best	Unrealistically big spender
Self-indulgent	Reward self	Excessive to a fault
Patient	Easygoing	Procrastinate
Persevering	Well-developed stamina	Stubborn as a bull
Possessive	Caring	Controlling
Quiet	Inner strength	Represses emotions
Sensible	Don't take silly risks	Miss a lot of fun
Stable	Grounded and focused	Lack spontaneity
Stubborn	Hold ground	Cut off nose to spite face
Sensual	Pleasure-seeking	Hard to satisfy, especially sexually
Systematic	Highly organised	Neurotic
Thoughtful	Show gratitude	Feel unappreciated

The Taurus woman

She can show you more about soft caresses, velvet lips and longer loving kisses than any other sign. Treat her like a goddess and she will treat you like a god.

The Taurus woman is as steady and strong as an ancient Redwood standing tall and firm through calm and storm. She has an A-plus reliability record and is probably your most loyal friend. Her steadfast nature adds up to a tall stack of great qualities like patience, understanding and thoughtfulness, just to name a few! She can also be the most one-eyed, stubborn person you've ever had to deal with, but you'll love her anyway because she is such a great and giving person. She is exceptionally kind-hearted and often entertains or takes care of people who she knows either need a good meal, a friendly gesture or some support. She's also the kind that rescues lost cats and dogs, adopts orphans, works for charity causes and probably volunteers for Meals on Wheels on her day off work.

She can truly be a great citizen of the world. Most people will agree that knowing her and having her in their lives (although wearing at times) is something they are truly grateful for. She is special, because she really does think of other people and cares about their contentment. She has a good heart. She is naturally a people person, even though she is not always an outgoing person. She may not be the most popular person on the social scene, but she is one of the most important and influential contributors behind the scenes — the one who really makes things happen.

She treats people with respect and remembers her friends' birthdays and anniversaries, and all their kids' names and favourite toys. She's honest, sincere and usually humble. She speaks her mind, but does it in a way that it doesn't look as if she's giving unsolicited advice. She's clever at saying what she wants to say without being direct and she can also say a lot by her silence.

Ms Taurus can be quite an expert at sulking and there are many times when she keeps her deepest thoughts to herself. This woman of Venus adores comfort and seeks fine, luxurious surroundings. Her home is often truly a reflection of Venus and can be one of the most comfortable and beautiful homes you ever have the luck to visit. Even though she has this strong connection to Venus (which would make you expect that she would be a fashion plate), she can be one of the worst dressed women in town. (However, note; this lack of fashion does not apply to all Taurus, but if it applies to the one you're reading about here, you'll relate!)

On her really off-target dressing occasions, she can look like she picked her clothes out in the dark and doesn't own a mirror. She can also be oblivious of the fact that she needs to lose weight. Even if she does admit that she could do with losing a couple of pounds, she tends to put off taking any action in this direction, indefinitely. Obviously, there are many gorgeously proportioned and fit Taurus women, and when a Taurus decides she wants to improve her personal style or fitness, she can be determined about reaching her goals. However, she does fight temptation more than most!

Ms Taurus also loves to be spoilt and prefers to do things easy, rather than tough. She's shamelessly self-indulgent at times and knows how to pamper herself quite royally. However, she also likes to be taken care of, and if she had her choice she would much rather be spoiled by her lover, rather than take care of herself. She is quite wilful and thick skinned when she needs to be, but she has her limits! She can stand up to criticism but if you're mean or cruel to her she can throw a pink fit that will knock you flat with surprise.

[How Taurus women operate]

Social

The Taurus woman is often the hostess with the mostest, even if it's not her party. She's genuinely interested in making sure others are having a good time and she's usually a great listener, whether someone is bragging about their success or lamenting over spilled milk. When a Taurus lady goes to a party she makes a dozen new friends and learns the names, careers, hobbies, future plans and a choice bit of gossip about nearly everyone there.

She loves to travel and is fabulous at planning trips for herself and others. Some Taurus women make a career in the travel business and seeing the world is one of the ways a Taurus can earn a great living and play at the same time. She gathers information and trivia like a bee gathers nectar, and she probably has a growing collection of art, memorabilia, antiques or collectibles of some sort. If you want to tease one of your Taurus friends, pick up one of her antique knick-knacks (carefully, of course), and walk around with it while you talk. I can almost guarantee she'll pace with the urge to rescue it from your hands, but she won't want to hurt your feelings, so she probably won't do anything but sigh with relief when you put it down.

She has champagne taste and she recognises top quality when she sees it — no matter how out of place it might be. A woman of Venus can spot the real gold buried in a pile of glitter from twenty feet away. She has her own built-in quality sensor, and she doesn't miss many bargains either! Her wardrobe is a mixed bag of classic elegance, showy glitter, department store bargains, and bits and pieces that may or may not match! Basically, if something trendy catches her eye, she'll buy it! (Look at Taurus, Cher, whose unique and mainly outrageous outfits — both on and off stage — have probably given the tabloids more interesting photos to print than most of the other flamboyantly dressed stars put together, apart from maybe Aquarian Dolly Parton.) She can have a conservative way of dressing, but she's also likely to have those times when a feather boa and sequins really tempt her Venus side to put on the Ritz.

In her everyday life, ideally, she prefers a regular routine. She resists change and is impossible to budge when she digs in her Taurus hooves. If you really want her to consider making a change you need to appeal to her practical senses and her emotional heart. If she can't see how a new opportunity will enhance and enrich her life, why would she bother? (A sense of adventure rarely inspires action or change in a Taurus.) If there's nothing really of value to be gained and the benefit to her isn't quickly obvious, you'll have to work hard to sell the idea or change to her. (Be warned, Ms Taurus is not an easy sell.)

So, who is this Taurus woman? She's the goddess Venus in human form. She is complex, she is social and she is friendly. She is also one of the zodiac's most popular women, making friends in every city, town and port she visits. She has an amazing amount of self-control (when she wants to), is a stable force and exudes comforting and soothing energy.

Love and family

Where it comes to love and family, Taurus can run hot and cold. Generally, she is warm, affectionate and sensitive and she wants a lover who can appreciate these qualities. When she is in this frame of mind, a man who complains that she hugs him too much or leaves without kissing her goodbye doesn't stand much of a long-term chance with this woman. When she is cold on romance, she can become extremely distant and very independent. Even though she might not admit it, she is a romantic. Her idea of romance is walking hand in hand through the park, slow dancing, making love to the tune of her favourite screenplay or Broadway musical and lots of cuddling and sharing. She loves great movies — old and new, all types of music from classical to rock, and if you really want to spoil her, pamper her with a trip to the salon or spa for facials, massages and body wraps. Another way of wooing a Taurus is to buy her chocolates, expensive jewellery and delicious dinners.

Planet Venus, the Roman goddess of beauty, art and pleasure, rules a Taurus woman so she likes a leisurely day at the art museum, a walk through the conservatory and a relaxing bubble bath complete with candlelight and champagne. If you dare to call her love of pleasure either vain or selfish she'll stomp you with her Taurus hooves, and poke you out of her life with her sharp bull horns! (But she'll keep the jewels!)

When it comes to marriage, usually a Taurus knows exactly what she wants. Although whether they get their ideal mate or not is another thing! A Taurus is looking for a strong handsome manly type of man, someone she can have a battle of the sexes with. She wants the kind of man who works hard, plays hard and doesn't mind her indulgent shopping habits! He should probably also be powerful enough to handle her strong-willed personality. If he's not strong enough and willing to stand up to her, like the 'bull', she will walk all over him in her metaphorical high heels!

While she can have all sorts of rules and regulations for him, for herself she insists on being treated with love and respect and is usually put off by rudeness. Some Taurus women decide not to walk down the aisle, because they like the peace and harmony of being on their own. Plus she often knows that 'you can't hurry love, you just have to wait', so where some signs of the zodiac tend to race out and marry the first man who asks (like the Fire signs, Aries, Leos and Sagittarians often do), Ms Taurus is quite prepared to wait, wait and wait, until someone she feels is the 'right one' comes along. Sure she may have some false starts along the way, but she learns quickly that selling yourself short, just to have a man in your life, usually ends up such a disaster or such an unhappy experience it just isn't worth it. Once she finds the man that suits her the best, she usually commits to a long-term relationship, settles into it, and makes the relationship work as much as she possibly can. She can be a terrific partner to the right fellow. She's normally not the jealous type and she welcomes her mate's male and female friends into her life. But she won't appreciate it if her man makes plans that don't include her! She probably won't want to go somewhere like the football game every week, or those really male dominated sporting pastimes like the Indianapolis 500 or on an ice-fishing trip, but she'll still be upset if she isn't invited.

One of the most important things to remember is that she has an inborn desire for finery, luxury, praise and pampering of all types. Anyone who treats her like a goddess will be rewarded like a god. This woman can teach you more about soft caresses, velvet lips and gentle loving kisses than any other sign. But you have to be prepared to do some things her way, all the way, after all she is still born under the sign of the Bull, and she can be extremely stubborn when she wants to be and can refuse to budge sometimes, even if she is being rather unreasonable!

As a mother, the Taurus can be one of the most devoted, attentive and patient and persevering mothers of all! A Taurus loves holding her babies and smiles when she washes their tiny fingers and toes. Her patience is a huge virtue in motherhood and she can calmly organise many children at the same time without becoming frustrated. But she's stubborn, too, and chances are that arguments will be heard throughout the household when her children begin cutting the apron strings. But her stubborn nature helps her children to grow stronger and sometimes stirs a drive in them to question what they've been told and decide what's right for themselves.

Career

A Taurus woman's combination of personality traits makes her well suited for a wide range of different career paths. Her patience makes her a thorough and sensitive teacher or instructor, her loyalty and stability make her solid in areas of security or finance, and her appreciation of beauty makes her a creative addition to any company or organisation that deals with the arts, make-up, hair styles and various sorts of fashion areas. A career as a tour guide or travel planner is often a great choice for a Taurus.

Her unswerving reliability makes her a trusted and reliable employee and as long as she knows she's appreciated there's not much she won't do for the good of the cause. Her comfortable ability to handle all types of people, no matter what mood they're in, approaches an art form. She excels in client services and public relations but she sometimes has a difficult time with sales.

Many Taureans are musical and most are gifted with creativity in some form. (Cher, Ella Fitzgerald, Janet Jackson, and Tammy Wynette are all Taurus women.) She can often make more money pursuing one of her creative talents than she can in a 9 to 5 job, but her fear of instability and insecurity make going out on her own seem risky. A profitable compromise for a Taurus woman is to keep her day job but devote some evenings and weekends to the pursuit of her creative dreams. She'll be surprised how quickly her moonlight income can catch up to and even surpass her payroll cheque. Once she develops the courage for entrepreneurial opportunities a Taurus is unstoppable.

Financial

This goddess of beauty and pleasure respects the power of money and is willing to work hard for most of her income — although many Taurus women would really rather not work at all. If she had her druthers, she'd marry money rather than work for it. Because comfort and security are up there with her top values she usually pursues careers that pay well and offer good job security and fringe benefits.

Most Taurus find money interesting by the time they're two or three years old. They love picking up and playing with shiny coins and if you give a three-year-old Taurus the choice between a fifty cent piece and a dollar, you can bet she'll pick the dollar. (Lots of Taurus swallowed at least one coin in their younger years, so keep a close eye on the little ones!) Most Taurus begin earning money before they're teenagers. A friend of mine's Taurus daughter set up a profitable Avon business when she was in Year Seven. She organised the door-to-door sales kit, filled out all the forms, and talked her younger Sagittarian sister into going out to make the sales. It was a successful venture, and in less than a year, they both made enough money to buy new bicycles!

A Taurus woman is usually careful about managing her finances, but she worries about money and she also loves to spend money. Her financial anxieties and spending habits can add great stress to her life. For that reason, many Taurus women are fabulous at negotiating and bargaining for lower prices or better interest rates. That is, unless she has some strong Aquarian or Pisces energy influencing her, in which case she can pay top dollar without even thinking about the fact that she might be overspending. She generally steers clear of plans that promise overnight riches, even though they tempt her. But she tends to believe that true and lasting wealth is built one day and dollar at a time.

Physical

Many of the most beautiful women in the world are born under this sign (Michelle Pfeiffer, Cher and Jana Wendt are good examples of the unusual feminine beauty that being born under this sign can create). Taurus women can be strikingly attractive and unusually beautiful. Their beauty originates on the inner level and if a Venus woman is fulfilled and healthy she practically glows. Unfortunately, if she's unhappy or depressed her body can soak up fat like a sponge and any criticism of how she looks will send her straight for the ice cream or chocolate chip biscuits. When she gets into her negative phase of her physical appearance, she can appear ground-bound and weighed down, as if something of the 'bull' energy is dragging her beauty onto a lower level.

A Taurus should do whatever it takes to stay motivated and physically active. If she really values her good looks and her beauty, she needs to 'think thin!' Part of the reason she puts on weight is because she tells herself that she is going to diet tomorrow and for her, tomorrow never comes when it comes to dieting

She may not like to exercise but that's exactly what she needs to boost her body's slower metabolism. It can seem to take her an eternity to burn a single calorie without vigorous exercise, and she enjoys bread and sweets too much to stop eating them. However, if she practises moderation in her diet and does just a little bit of exercise, such as walking or going to the gym once a week, it can truly make a huge difference. Also, she can change her eating patterns, where she still eats a good amount but chooses healthier, less fat-creating foods (e.g. switching from ice cream to non-fat yoghurt).

Taurus women who take an interest in eating healthy and low-fat foods can become gourmets of natural nourishment and have the bodies to show for it! They can also become fabulous healthy food preparers and could actually become talented enough in this area to write a book and share their ideas and insights with other women who might be wanting to beat the bulge.

Most Taurus women avoid physical exertion; they don't really like to get sweaty, unless it's in the bedroom in a moment of passion (which is actually excellent exercise). She may have suffered from some type of childhood illness that kept her from running, playing sports or doing other types of vigorous exercise and that lack of interest in exercise has remained with her in later years. But she's incredibly determined when she wants, so if she sets her mind to using exercise to keep slim and trim, she can become a dedicated fitness princess. And when she truly wants to get into top shape she surprises everyone, including herself, with her inner strength and power.

There are lots of fun activities that Taurus can do to get the exercise she needs. She can have a tomboy hidden inside and that part of her enjoys some types of outdoor adventures like hiking, canoeing or camping. She can be surprisingly physically resilient and tough for such a feminine person, but if she does get injured, it can take a while for her body to heal because she is running on a slow metabolic clock.

Her emotions can also affect her physical health and energy levels. A word of caution for Taurus is to avoid situations and people that frustrate her unless she's willing to confront them. The bottling up of Taurus' strong emotions within her body can turn into high blood pressure, respiratory infections and her dreaded enemy — putting on lots of extra weight.

When a Taurus is stressed out or on the verge of getting sick, one of the first signs is often a sore throat or laryngitis. When she keeps in what she wants to say, her body expresses her frustration in the form of some type of sickness like a cold or cough or an upset stomach. Learning to speak her mind can be a great form of preventative medicine for a Taurus, and laughing and singing are great stress busters for her.

One of a Taurus woman's greatest beauty assets is her smooth, healthy-looking skin that resists wrinkles for the greater part of her life. Naturally if she eats too many sweets (which she sometimes does), that can mean her skin lacks some of the glow and lustre that it normally would provide for her beauty.

Mental

She's deliberate in her thinking, practical in her reasoning and creative in her solutions. She respects other people's opinions and admires people who are well read and full of information. She's great at memorising all sorts of information from telephone numbers and addresses to important dates and once she's logged a bit of information into her memory bank it's there for good! She gets a kick out of trivia and is often impressed with people who can spurt facts off the top of their heads.

She has a fertile imagination but she tends to limit it to her hobbies, using her sensibility to make most decisions. She also refuses to be pushed or intimidated into doing anything she believes is wrong. And this can create a dilemma, because she also believes in respecting and obeying authority — especially her parents and her employer. So if her parents or her boss ask her to do something that she doesn't think is right to do, she will probably feel like she's stuck between a rock and a hard place.

A Taurus is a practical thinker, and she usually keeps her focus and attention on issues and decisions that affect her personally. She isn't motivated by strictly mental goals and she'd rather hear the bottom line than all of the theories.

She has a natural ability to learn several languages and she loves to travel to other countries and see how the people in other cultures live, work, play and raise their children. The Taurus who don't have the time or the money to globe-trot enjoy books and movies that take them on mental journeys and adventures.

Spiritual

Many Taurus women like to have clear-cut rules, and obvious boundaries between right and wrong, and this can be true in their spirituality as well. They're often happy to follow the rules and do what's expected of them in exchange for eternal life in the promised land. This isn't to say that a Taurus with her down-to-earth practicality doesn't sometimes wonder about the origins of her belief system or religion, but she doesn't waste time asking questions unless she thinks she can find a concrete answer.

Most Taurus women stick with their original religion or belief system throughout their lives. Their loyalty and obedience to authority makes it easy for them to stay on whatever path they were put on by their parents and they seem to know that all paths lead to the heavens eventually! They generally don't balk at fulfilling religious requirements and they often enjoy the parties and socialising that originate in their place of worship.

She probably believes in the afterlife and hopes it's as dreamy and heavenly as the oil paintings she's seen with people lounging around on clouds eating grapes and listening to great music. And while she tends to stay on the track of tradition, she sometimes takes an interest in a public fad. For example, the popularity of angels may catch her interest but a stereotypical Taurus will be more interested in adding angels to her decorating scheme than in trying to communicate with them. She's intrigued by mystics, palm readers, and handwriting analysis and she might even still have her childhood ouja board. She likes mystery so she's probably had at least one or two psychic readings predicting her future and she thinks it's fun to find out whether the prophecies will come true.

The Taurus man

> *He makes new friends everywhere he goes but he has a special place in his heart for his childhood buddies. He loves spoiling himself and his friends and he is definitely rated the host with the most!*

There are generally two clearly different types of Taurus men. The first is the friendly Bull, and the second is the raging Bull! The friendly Bull is everyone's best friend and probably exudes enormous charm and charisma (most of the time). He's soft and gentle, buys presents and flowers for his women friends, but amazingly, not all women respond to his 'nice guy' image. In fact, it's the second

Bull — the raging Bull — who has the greatest success and power with women. This Taurus often has the external appearance of the friendly Bull, but when he loses his temper or his cool, he turns into the kind of Bull you meet in a bullfight — and when he is mad, you had better run for cover. Naturally, there are plenty of Taurus men born with a bit of both the friendly and the raging Bull in them, so you'll have to use your discernment to determine whether your Taurus is really easygoing or trouble. Of course, being born under Venus, whether he's nice or sometimes rather nasty, he is likely to be extremely charming or possibly even devastatingly good-looking. But for Mr Taurus especially, handsome is as handsome does! So, if he does tend to have some of the bad temper aspect of Taurus, it might be wise to keep him aware of his bad moods or selfish outbursts at times. Throughout his life, and even when he is a small child, it isn't advisable to allow him to get away with his negative (or darker) side, simply because of his good looks and charms.

One thing that troubles or unsettles Mr Taurus is that he doesn't like to be fenced in (and neither does the bull). He knows he needs his boundaries but most times it is difficult for him to accept the boundaries that other people put around him. For a sign that is generally conservative, hates change and expects life to flow with continuity, Mr Taurus is often a contradiction. He is the one who makes things change by the way he either refuses to face reality, or the way he pretends everything is fine when it isn't. He can (without sometimes knowing it) set in motion and instigate conditions or events that stir up his personal and professional existence and bring about incredible disruption and change. He can be something of an underhanded operator — the kind of person who looks like they are headed in one direction, but is actually going somewhere different.

When it comes to money, that can sometimes be the greatest love affair of his life. Taurus men are good at business and many of them amass great fortunes. He will make money from a wide range of hobbies, involvements and industries. He can be found in the arts, the stock market, medicine and even in the movies (look at heart throb George Clooney, a Taurus). Taurean men also can get into unusual careers because they love the money it brings them. In fact, for many Taurus men money makes their world go round. The Taurus man likes to build up his financial security early in his life so he can look forward to sitting back, relaxing and feeling comfortable. He begins planning his empire at a young age and doesn't believe in cutting corners. He's willing to work hard to lay a firm financial foundation and he takes his time and takes each step carefully and deliberately. Time is his friend and if he uses it wisely he becomes more sensible and more responsible as he grows older.

He has a ton of charisma, even as a child, and many Taurus men have strong, earthy good looks that improve with age. Lots of Taurus men have great bodies with broad shoulders, big chests and muscular legs. They have plenty of natural sex appeal and a smooth way with women. He uses this to great advantage and can often be quite an effective Don Juan. He also enjoys his conquests because it proves to him that he hasn't lost his touch. Don't be surprised to find that, like his ruling planet Venus, Mr Taurus can have quite a high opinion of himself. He can also, in his bachelor days, be a total heart-breaker and often extremely sexually active with multiple partners, just like the Bull in the bullpen.

Both the friendly Bull and the raging Bull can be masters of overindulgence. But they're hardly ever greedy and they like to share good fortune with friends and strangers alike. Taurus is a man of Venus and his early passions and pleasure-seeking are what drive his determination to create a stable, comfortable life.

[How Taurus men operate]

Social

Friendship is important to Taurus men. In fact, some prefer the company of their guy mates more than their girl friends. (And yes, due to the Venus influence there are quite a number of Taurus men who prefer men sexually as well.) Regardless of their sexual preferences, friendship is a stabilising influence in the Taurus social world. In fact, many a Taurus man is probably still good friends with the kid he sat next to in Year One. This guy makes friends everywhere he goes but he has a special place in his heart for his family and his earliest buddies. He looks forward to going home for the holidays and counts down the days until his next school or family reunion.

He's a strong, gentle man who loves to be content and problem-free! He likes a little excitement every now and again but he's not a huge risk-taker and he doesn't always like surprises. Chances are he's happy to spend his free time taking a hike through the woods, sitting on the back porch or balcony reading a good book or checking out the sports pages, and playing with the dog. He might have a garden or some other outdoor hobby but he doesn't need to have an activity planned to enjoy a Sunday afternoon. In fact, he'd probably rather not have plans so he can do — or not do — whatever he wants.

He usually likes any kind of party, depending on his mood, because he loves to eat, drink and be merry. He usually has a pretty hefty appetite, and like the stocky bull, most Taurus men can eat nearly anything! Just as well that most Taurus men seem to have been blessed with an iron stomach. And if you meet a Taurus who has an interest in fine wines or beer, buy him a drink and maybe you'll be buddies for life! He loves spoiling himself and his family and friends, usually to excess, and he is definitely a generous host.

Some Taurus men (but certainly not all) are so easygoing they can lull a baby to sleep, but don't mistake his outside for what's within. The Taurus man is a tower of strength and determination. When he sets his sights on something he perseveres until he gets it. He has the strong will to push ahead through all sorts of roadblocks and the patience to bide his time and wait for the right moment. And if he can curl up on an overstuffed leather recliner, turn on the TV, have a beer and watch the sport shows, he's practically in heaven.

Love and family

When it comes to matters that touch his heart, this is where Mr Taurus probably meets his greatest challenge. If he could have his cake (have freedom and emotional ties) and eat it, too (be untouched by those around him), he would. But with love and family, he normally has to commit himself in ways that he finds unsettling and possibly even confronting. Leaving himself vulnerable, especially emotionally, is not a pleasant state for him. Many Taurus men wait a long time before they choose to marry.

It can be difficult for the woman who wants a Taurus man to get him to make the plunge. However, once he makes the plunge, he usually gives the partnership or marriage everything he's got, or at least the best he is capable of. He is often greatly sought after by those around him. A Taurus man has an appealing appearance and enough charisma to charm a mall full of holiday shoppers.

When this guy wants to smooth something out or be the peacemaker, he can summon up some powerful magic and create some amazing results. His practical determination doesn't stifle his sensitivity and he has a warm and kind heart.

He makes a really great and loyal friend and he keeps in touch with his neighbourhood pals, his uni roommates and the little girl he met in the Year Ten biology class who set all the grasshoppers free before they could be dissected. Chances are he's hoping for the day when she — or someone like her — becomes his wife. Unlike some signs of the zodiac, a Taurus male puts a high value on the stability and security of marriage and he gives himself plenty of time to carefully choose the 'right one'.

He's romantic in a homespun way and will enjoy taking you to out to dinner and to the movies. He's really sweet about doing the sorts of things that his date or girlfriend likes, so if you like chocolate he'll buy you imported chocolates by the pound and if you like flowers he'll either send them or pick them himself. But be careful not to scratch a piece of his antique furniture, get fingerprints on his photographs, or set a water glass down on his polished woodwork. There are some things a Taurus just can't stand and he's a stickler for keeping his possessions in tip-top condition.

Once he gets past a certain age, don't expect him to look forward to loud nights in crowded nightclubs, even if he has fun when he goes out with you every now and again. He's happier in the woods, at the beach or at a boat or car show and his favourite place is almost always home sweet home.

He'll usually marry a woman who is just like dear old mum! His ideal companion is someone who is well bred, attractive, polite, classy and down-to-earth. She definitely is not likely to be the type who his mother and friends would disapprove of, wouldn't embarrass him in public, or argue with him or put him down in front of his family, friends or co-workers.

Naturally, you can cross out the last two sentences if he falls under a woman's sexual spell. When this occurs, he forgets his rules of relationships and flaunts a side of himself that is most unusual. However, after a short time, this relationship is likely to hit the rocks and he reverts back to his old self. When he is with his life-long partner, and not just chasing skirts, he makes a devoted husband who will give everything for the woman he loves as long as she's loyal and madly in love with him. He's a great listener and does his best to take care of his wife's desires and his family's needs. As a father, he's a patient role-model and a firm disciplinarian. He enjoys wrestling and playing football with his sons and carrying his daughters on his shoulders. He's committed to spending quality time with his kids and will happily teach them how to tie their shoes, ride a bike and drive a car.

Many Taurus men spoil their children with an abundance of gifts and toys though they stubbornly refuse to believe this is true. A Taurus friend of mine was shocked and hurt when he came home from a long business trip and his kids greeted him with 'What did you bring me?' instead of 'Hi Daddy, we missed you.' He really didn't see the part he played in their behaviour.

Career

There's the hard-working Taurus and the lazy one (and naturally lots that move between and in and out of these two work-related phases). Some Taurus men never stop working, while others need a bomb put under them to get them out of bed and off to their job. However, most Taurus men are reliable, determined and willing to do whatever it takes to get the job done right. They have amazing endurance and they can easily complete projects and meet deadlines that seem impossible to the mere mortal. A Taurus combination of traits — if he chooses to put them all to use — power him on to be a huge success in any occupation he pursues.

A Taurus likes careers or jobs that he can keep doing well into his seventies and eighties. He doesn't want to change his lifestyle in his older years and his financial security means more to him than retirement. His loyalty and reliability make him a perfect trustee or guardian. Taurus men make great contractors, architects and managers. They're strong construction workers and have green thumbs when it comes to growing crops, tending orchards or making just about anything grow. Lots of Taurus guys work on or manage properties or farms and many of them have a dream to buy land and real estate. He also might have a soft spot in his heart for fine art, precious metals, gemstones and old relics like coins and stamps. He appreciates good music and can become a successful musician or composer, such as Taureans Stevie Wonder and Billy Joel, not to mention Johannes Brahms. If he doesn't become some sort of singer or musician he'll at least have a great stereo system and a wide variety of music to suit his every mood.

Financial

He naturally desires all the finest things in life, and that desire often inspires him to become a successful money manager. At his best, a Taurus can manage his money and property to build a rock-solid financial empire. And if he has a lofty goal of some sort — one that's bigger and more enduring than himself — he can be unstoppable! Many Taurus men realise philanthropic dreams by donating a gymnasium to an orphanage or building a museum or a library for their home town. They like to set up scholarships and many leave money to their school or their community when they die.

But, there's another side to this story, Mr Taurus can also be one of the worst money-managers of all. He is the type that can let money slip through his fingers. If Mr Bull gets greedy and stops listening to his own good money sense he can slide into some pretty deep debt, too. Fortunately, most Taurus men value security and stability so much that they curb their expensive appetite until their wallets can afford it.

Because he likes the finer things that life can provide (if you have the money to afford them, anyway!) — chances are the Taurus nest egg will be well padded and he'll enjoy his later years doing all the hobbies and interests that he put off when he was younger. One of a Taurus's greatest dreams is to save enough money early in life to some day live like a king on the interest alone.

Physical

A Taurus man usually has a strong neck, a broad muscular chest and a 'reach out and touch me' kind of body. But in spite of his 'hunk' status he's sometimes self-conscious about some part of his anatomy, which isn't as well-built, or in proportion as the rest of him. He is firmly connected with the physical world, and he often has a heavy down-to-earth kind of tread, so if you see a guy who is walking with steady, smooth and deliberate steps, it could be a Taurus. Like Nature, he has his seasons for doing things, and he takes his time with whatever he's doing and won't be rushed in any way. (And that's just another reason why a Taurus is a great bedroom companion.) Athletically, Taurus men make tough full-backs, strong distance swimmers and fantastic long-distance runners.

Most Taurus men have deep, soothing voices that sound great on the radio and even better across the dinner table. They usually have some natural musical ability and singing is one way they let off steam, reduce stress and heal their minds and hearts when they need it. But a Taurus doesn't really fret about too many things. He usually has some concerns or worries about the future or some anxiety about the ways things are changing, but he doesn't waste much energy worrying because he's practical enough to know it doesn't do any good.

He works hard, plays hard and needs a lot of rest to stay healthy and strong. Lots of Taurus guys love to get up with the sun and get in an early morning work-out before they tackle the rest of the day. If it's a weekend or holiday, he likes to take care of his end of the responsibilities early so he can sit back, relax and enjoy the rest of the day! And if he's a sports lover, he'll probably have some favourite teams that he likes to follow.

Mr Taurus can be healthy and strong his whole life if he remains physically active, gets some exercise and doesn't eat or drink his way to obesity. An overweight Bull is an unhappy Bull, and it's easier for him to keep fat off than lose it once it's wrapped around his waist. A Taurus carrying extra pounds ups his chances for ankle and leg injuries and puts an added strain on his heart and lungs. His body usually tells him it's time for less fun and more rest by turning a cold into a sore throat or an ache into a big pain!

Moderation is the Taurean's key to good health and he's usually sensible enough to begin learning self-discipline by the time he's in his twenties. Plenty of Taurus men learn about moderation the hard way, but once they learn it they do live a long and healthy life.

Mental

Mr Taurus can have a mind like a metal trap. Once he's made up his mind on something or has fixed his opinion, it can take a magical key to change his outlook. That magical key that can make him change his mind often involves money, sex or power. Generally, a Taurus man's creativity and practicality add up to wise and resourceful thinking and bright solutions. Reading and travelling fire his imagination and he loves to see how different people or cultures solve the same problems. He likes options and he likes fresh ideas that work.

One of the reasons Taurus is such a great problem solver is that he usually doesn't get ruffled by impatient people or high pressure situations. He stays calm so he can come up with a plan of action and take over the leadership role if necessary. And Taurus can come up with some ingenious ideas! They might defy logic, but they usually work! He doesn't talk fancy but he has lots of valuable ideas and insights and he admires inventors and entrepreneurs.

Mr Taurus is perfectly capable when it comes to recognising what's going on under the surface and behind the scenes but sometimes he stubbornly refuses to see what's going on under his own nose. He likes a good discussion but he doesn't like looking stupid or being manipulated. He hates being contradicted and embarrassing him is the equivalent of stepping into a bullfight ring and waving a bright red flag in front of his face.

Spiritual

He's a land lover and his spirit is lifted by a sunny day and soothed by a warm breeze. The forest is his cathedral and he feels closest to his creator when big trees, birds and animals surround him.

He probably has his mind made up about religion and there's a good chance he's consistent about his beliefs. He doesn't seek change so he's not interested in shopping around for a new or different religion and he seems to know that many religions have some basic things in common. He may not attend regular church services, but he probably likes the sound of an old pipe organ and if the choir sounds good he might join in.

He believes in some sort of afterlife, but doesn't torment himself wondering what it's like or if everyone makes it to Heaven or not (possibly because he has an inner fear, conflict or doubt that he might not make it to Heaven himself). He goes about his life trying to do what's right and leaves the rest up to his maker. When he feels like he could use some extra support, he's not too embarrassed to pray for it or, too proud to be grateful when he receives it.

The Taurus baby

> *Ruled by Venus, Taurus is the 'pretty baby' of the zodiac and often seems aglow with a special radiance. But along with all that charm this baby has all the stubbornness you could expect of a fully grown Taurus Bull!*

While the actual birth of your Taurus baby should be relatively simple (compared to some), the hours of labour you go through before the birth can be quite exhausting. But while these hours can take a toll on you, they are generally not painful and the reward of this beautiful star baby will soon erase all memories of your own personal sacrifices.

During the course of your pregnancy you may experience some false labour pains when you think the little one is going to be born and it isn't. Time plays a big role in the Taurean infant's destiny, therefore times of birth, the amount of time it takes during labour, and times of conception are likely to somehow be important and may be topics of great interest and conversation, especially with other parents or expectant parents of a Taurus.

But whether it's a speedy delivery or extremely slow, the birth of this child will have something special and very calming and wonderful about it. If there are any dramas associated with the birth of this new baby they will most likely occur in an organised sort of way, rather than a chaotic one. It is often the destiny of the Taurus baby to have a sense of time, structure and order surrounding its birth, rather than upheaval. This tiny little mite innately loves order and it will attempt to come into the world as artistically and harmoniously as possible. Its birth however may be slow, because it likes to make sure that everything is ready and prepared before it makes its appearance (a characteristic that will continue to be shown throughout its childhood and adulthood). Therefore, you may have all kinds of delays getting to the hospital or other forms of false starts before this child actually comes into the world. Taureans often run behind schedule and are known for being late to appointments, therefore even for its own birth this little soul tends to be fashionably late.

From the moment it emerges this baby is likely to have something special about it. The Taurus newborn is often extremely attractive and has a special radiance and almost 'Mona Lisa' type angelic expression, whether it's a boy or a girl. And you can count on this little one having distinctive features and a refinement surrounding it.

After the birth, once it is in your care there's wisdom in setting up yourself and your Taurus baby with a rhythm and schedule for feeding, bathing, playing and sleeping. You need some rules and guidelines that you can stick to for this bub. It loves order and will flow harmoniously with you if you keep your end of the bargain. However, if you abruptly change around routines without providing smooth transitions, the little Bull can become surprisingly petulant, disruptive in behaviour and refuse to cooperate.

But even if little Taurus already knows how to drum up its own form of temper tantrum from day one, this soft, smiling bundle of baby will appeal to everyone who sees it and will have a talent for encouraging plenty of attention. And attention and love shouldn't be too tough for this littlie to attract because of its warmth and beautiful radiance. People will naturally be drawn to this baby because he or she has tons of magnetism to spare.

When it comes to learning to talk, this infant is likely to not only talk but to sing or gurgle – and probably gurgle in tune. And once Taurus babies learn to walk they quickly learn to dance or jig around, too. This little one has a depth of musical and harmonious rhythm waiting for a chance to express itself within its soul.

But because Taurus is so attuned to its refined senses, this small person won't take kindly to being around noisy, rowdy conditions. Even before it's born, this baby is likely to sense musical vibrations and during your pregnancy it's best to seek out harmonious types of music and atmospheres. The way it may let you know it isn't attuned to the racket surrounding it is by rolling up into a tight ball so you can feel its knees or feet sticking out. Even the tiniest Taurus usually knows exactly what's required to communicate its displeasure.

From the moment it's born this child will let you know how it's feeling. He or she will ooze with pleasure and seethe with red-faced fury! Expect to have the noise equivalent of a drum and bugle corps when this wee one is upset or frustrated. Even the typical experiences of wet nappies, gas or teething pains can be distressing for a Taurus and he or she is sure to tell you about it, generally in a loud and clear manner. Taurean babies usually have good lungs and know how to use them! But at least your Taurus baby will only complain when it has good reason to — not necessarily for simple attention-grabbing (although it can be extremely appreciative of lots of cuddling).

Since baby Bulls are so attuned to all their senses, Taurus will love its food and have strong preferences about what it eats and when it eats. The times this infant will be most upset is when it's hungry. Regular feeding is important because if you run late this baby will kick up its heels. And don't bother trying to make a little Bull eat something that he or she doesn't want or you may end up with mashed potatoes stuck to the ceiling and peas flying across the room.

When a Taurus baby gets mad at you, it will stiffen up and show its discontent by becoming red in the face, glaring at you, possibly even stomping — somewhat similar to the Bull that is the ruler of its zodiac sign. Good luck getting the little Bull to do anything that he or she doesn't want to do. Better put on your thinking cap, because it will takes brains rather than force to get this one to comply with your wishes!

The Taurus toddler through teen

They love to love and be loved and praise works better than criticism with children of Venus!

By the time a Taurus reaches the toddler stage, it's become undeniably obvious that there's no point in trying to rush this little soul. They're on their own time schedule and even when their minds are racing their bodies tend to move in a deliberate and slow motion. Any attempt to rush them will slow them down instead and as these children grow older they will often slow down even more — on purpose — just to passively assert themselves. I remember asking a five-year old Taurus boy what he did when he wanted to make his mummy mad. 'I go slow,' he whispered. 'And,' I asked, 'what do you do if you want to make her really mad?' He smiled sheepishly, and said, 'I go slower.'

But aside from the inborn bull-headedness that is deep within a Taurus' soul, these children are affectionate, cuddly and lovable. They love to love and be loved and they are often one of the most popular children in the family. They will gladly give their aunts and uncles hugs and kisses and look forward to going to their grandparents' houses. Little boy Bulls tend to be 'all boy', expressing whatever the stereotypical images are for the culture in which they're growing up. And the same holds true for little girl Bulls. The boys like to pretend they are just like their dads, and the girls will want to dress up in their mummy's clothes, make-up and jewellery.

Many Taurus children actually enjoy being neat and tidy and even at an early age show an interest in running the carpet sweeper or washing the dinner dishes. I once watched a little Taurus pick up all of the family shoes that were next to the front door and one-by-one deliver them to their appropriate bedrooms, all the while humming while he worked. And while this trait is often wonderful it can also be a mixed blessing. Parents are encouraged to permit the little ones to help when time and safety allows. If there isn't time for them to help — or if they will truly be too much in the way — set them up with some art supplies and put on some happy music and they can amuse themselves for at least an hour.

Many Taurus youngsters have a natural talent for music so it's not a bad idea to begin introducing them to a variety of music and instruments at an early age. Just remember not to force anything upon them because this is sure to eventually fail. The Taureans who put up with being forced to play and practise an instrument in their youth often rebel later in life by refusing to play again even if they are really talented!

Taurus children have a good bit of built-in self-discipline, so encouraging them and praising them goes much further than giving them ultimatums, criticising them or making lots of demands. When it's time for them to start kindergarten, they may resist and even claim to hate it at first, but once they make the transition they will do quite well and make some new friends, too. It's just that Tauruses are not fond of any sort of change and it takes them longer than most children to adjust and feel secure. Going off to school is a big step and the more you help them to look forward to it and prepare for it, the better off you both will be.

Overall, Taurus young ones tend to be good students and they're often willing to exert the effort it takes to get high scores even when that means putting in extra time and working harder than their friends. Because of their dedication and efforts, they may take great pride in making it on to the school's honour roll and it would be a great idea for you to celebrate these successes with them.

As your Taurus child grows up through adolescence and into the teenage years your patience is sure to be tested. This young person will be honest, reliable and good natured, but he or she will also occasionally dig in the Taurus Bull hooves so deeply that nothing or no one can budge them. Once they make up their minds about something they will tolerate any form of punishment to stick to their guns. Do yourself a favour and try to avoid these stand-offs altogether by negotiating and really tuning in to your child's needs, desires and sensitive feelings! It won't pay to badger them or embarrass them in front of their friends and you can nag them until you're blue in the face with little or no result. Think of these years as your opportunity to develop your own patience, creativity and resourcefulness.

Most parents of Taurus children are pleased with the level of responsibility that their Bulls demonstrate by the time they are in high school. They can usually be trusted to follow the rules even when you're not around to enforce them. It's a rare Taurus who would take the family car without permission or throw a wild party when you're out of town. But remember the strength of peer pressure, and a Taurus desire to be liked and fit in. There will be times when they will go against their own better judgment and your rules so they can go along with the crowd. Dish out the expected punishment, but stop short of ridiculing or demeaning them. They already know what they've done wrong and they probably already regret it. You will probably approve of and like most of the friends your Taurus teen has chosen. You may have trouble remembering them all though. Taurus is known for having a ton of friends and acquaintances and even a shy Bull will have a relatively easy time making friends.

Remember that the adolescent and teen years can be difficult for a Taurus. They like stability and these years are filled with one change after another — not only externally, but internally as well. Changing hormones can really play havoc with a Taurus and these kids can go from happy and smiling one minute, to crying their eyes out the next. And don't be surprised if you ask them what's wrong and they say they don't know. They really might not know the root of their discomfort or sadness. They might just be releasing some of the pent-up emotional stress that goes hand-in-hand with these bumpy years!

The most reliable advice concerning the youth of a Taurus is to treat them with respect, truly listen to their ideas and their thoughts and give them an abundance of hugs, kisses, pats on the back, praise and compliments. They also need gentle, non-emotional reprimands and wise, well-thought-out guidance. Make the time to talk with them and share with them and try not to let your disappointments and expectations tarnish their hopes and dreams. Your young Bull can go far in the world but you are an important stepping stone to their success. If you doubt them and second-guess them they will doubt themselves. If you show them you believe in them, they will believe in themselves.

GEMINI

[22 may — 21 june]

gemini gemini gemini gemini gemini
gemini gemini gemini gemini gemini
gemini gemini gemini gemini gemini gemini
gemini gemini gemini gemini gemini

element: air

planetary ruler: mercury

symbol: the twins

quality: mutable (= flexibility)

colours: yellow, blue

gem: agate, aquamarine

best companions: libra and aquarius

strongest virtues: creativity, curiosity, sharing

your dreams or visions with others

traits to improve: self-doubts,

fear of the future, mood inconsistencies

deepest desire: to be understood

for who you are

Gemini celebrities

Jo-Beth Taylor, Kylie Minogue, Naomi Campbell, Jewel, Joan Collins,

Germaine Greer, Lauryn Hill, Nicole Kidman, Anne Heche, Drew Carey,

Prince William (born on the cusp of Gemini/Cancer), Courtney Cox,

Priscilla Presley, Annette Bening, Brooke Shields, Stevie Nicks,

Melissa Etheridge, Lenny Kravitz, Joseph Fiennes, Alanis Morissette,

Morgan Freeman, Noah Wyle, Liam Neeson, Mike Myers, Bjorn Borg,

Anna Kournikova, Tom Jones, Natalie Portman, Michael J. Fox,

Elizabeth Hurley, Tom Allen, Steffi Graf, Boy George, Helen Hunt,

Juliette Lewis, Isabella Rossellini, Wynonna Judd, Marilyn Monroe,

Henry Kissinger, Prince Rainier of Monaco, LaToya Jackson, Bob Dylan,

Prince Philip, the artist formerly known as Prince, Johnny Depp,

Donald Trump, Paul McCartney, Salman Rushdie, Clint Eastwood,

Pat Cash, Kathleen Turner, Gary Sweet and Angelina Jolie.

[General outlook]

Vibrant cosmic energy and exciting astrological aspects affect your sign throughout the new millennium. Twins enter the brand new cosmic age with an abundance of vitality, creativity and hope for the future.

The truth is you've plenty to be excited about. The end of the millennium proved to be a traumatic time for the Twins. Life showed you that nothing is etched in stone and, like a serpent shedding its skin, circumstances forced you to cast away an old or outdated lifestyle, habit, career or love relationship.

Just as well, your astro-trademarks include curiosity, adaptability and strong survival instincts. Armed with renewed inspiration and all-important support from close friends and family, there's nothing stopping you from making your dreams come true.

Start making your cosmic 'wish list' for the next five, ten and twenty years. Think big, think love and think abundance. If you want something or someone, you can have it or them; however, you must believe more in yourself (totally believe) to ensure that you do fulfil your secret dreams, wishes and hopes.

Romance

It is about time that you had some breakthroughs in romance after having some disillusionment recently. Fortunately, the new millennium magic shines on Twins in the romantic arena. Single Geminis are armed with a new-found sense of confidence that makes them extremely attractive to the opposite sex. Also you are much more independent now and this appeals, too! Married Twins and those in long-term relationships are lucky in love, as well. Mutual respect, trust and a healthy dose of passion are the astro-keys to a happy and long-lasting union and you know this now, so will not settle for anything less and that is what will make the new millennium a breakthrough time for you romantically.

Health

Many of your most heartfelt aches and pains were self-inflicted in the past, but throughout the new millennium, you (thankfully) feel motivated to look after yourself. And, particularly, you go out of your way to relax, laugh and enjoy every day. You can waste an awful lot of time worrying perpetually over what tomorrow may, or may not hold for you and yours! Eating healthily and kicking bad habits (such as smoking, partaking in too many alcoholic drinks in an attempt to cheer yourself up, or late nights out partying) will have incredible benefits on your physical, mental and emotional wellbeing.

Finance

Money is around you, and coming to you from unexpected quarters in the new millennium. However, as though you are caught in a financial revolving door, just as it comes in, money does seem to be going out. Additional financial responsibilities might seem daunting in 2000 and beyond, but rest assured that wise planning now will reap wonderful rewards in the future.

The clue to improving money matters is to proceed with caution, avoid hasty financial decision-making and, where necessary, take advice from professionals. With a little bit of savvy financial guidance, your new millennium bank account is destined to rocket to new heights.

Career

The new millennium is going to be a prime time for your career. Windows of opportunity are waiting to be pushed open throughout the new millennium and Twins surprise themselves (and others) by making a sudden career change or leaping up the work ladder two, even three, steps at a time. Problems or necessity will work for you now as they will force you to come up with creative solutions. Be willing to go out on a limb and dare to be different and try something different in your work arena, and you will discover your own hidden talents in the process.

[Millennium wildcards to watch for]

While it's true that Geminis greet the new millennium with enthusiasm and confidence, don't worry if you experience occasional moments of self-doubt. Keep in mind that mistakes merely give you opportunities to learn, grow and get back on track. Don't be too hard on yourself if you do not kick a winning goal every time you try to make a score now; this is your astro-era to reach for the stars and beyond! Although the new millennium still requires that you master the two traits you most love to ignore, patience and perseverance, if you keep on, success, and the entire fulfilment you have dreamed about, will be yours.

> *You love drama, intrigue and confusion*
> *(although you say you don't), and this*
> *affection you have for mental thrills and*
> *spills, and generally creating mayhem when*
> *it suits you, is what makes you one of the*
> *most talked about signs of the zodiac.*

Who can figure out a Gemini? Not me. Your sign is a unique (and contradictory) blend of neediness and independence, devotion and indifference, high minded ideals which are often undermined by your lower minded responses, and on and on. Plus, you can say one thing one moment (and really mean it when you say it), and then you turn around and do exactly the opposite the next.

You are a potpourri of unusual and different feelings, energies, expressions, talents and attitudes. Even looking at Geminis through the cosmic mirror of astrology does not make describing a Gemini easy. Because of the twin-nature of your sign, you Gemini are the zodiac sign that is hardest to pin down. You have the greatest of all tick-tocks of personality swings and outer image. Also you go through many incarnations in one lifetime which have you tapping into a new set of personal and professional desires and drives. Keeping up with your state of mind, your beliefs or your views, can be like chasing mythical rainbows.

And you can be something of an illusionist and trickster, too! Just when others think they have found the keys to your personality or thought patterns, you Geminis switch mental gears and leave those around you needing to take the time and energy to get to understand you all over again. You probably like to keep others guessing, and you do! But you are not all flights of fancy and illusion all the time.

When you truly set your mind to some pursuit, plan or project, you can be one of the most determined of all signs. If you want something, you can be determined about getting it, or hang onto it in a way that would make a bulldog on the rampage look passive. Your mind is your magic wand, and the saying 'you are what you think' really holds true for your sign. Your thoughts, Gemini, decide whether you play the game of life as a winner or a loser. Or, as a victor or victim over circumstance. That is why it is so vital for you to master your thoughts and think positively.

You use a tremendous amount of energy on thinking, too. You are the mental athlete of the zodiac, and your mind seldom stops ticking over. Even when you're asleep, your mental wheels turn continuously. And, it comes quite naturally for you to play mind-games with others. But the worst thing you do is play mind games on yourself.

Many of your sign have made a profession out of being actors or entertainers because you do well playing roles (or talking on radio or appearing in front of the camera) because it comes so naturally for you to perform. Look at the Gemini formerly known as Prince. He has played successful mind games with the media and the public over recent years. His latest Gemini twin trick was to inform us that he has decided to have no name at all! But the laugh is probably on him because trying to get through everyday life without a name is likely to be very draining and demanding on him. So who is playing with whom?

Through the clothes you wear, you strive to create mixed messages or give out strange signals. The artist formerly known as Prince is also an expert at presenting an interesting and changing appearance. In fact, most Geminis love to present a variety of images to the world. Because you are a Gemini, your looks and the way you present yourself visually are often unusual, too. You can be a head turner and change your appearance in a way that sometimes causes others (who know you well) not to recognise you. Your moods can also alter your look quite dramatically, and what you have on your mind (happy or sad thoughts) can make you seem bigger (happy), or smaller (sad) in stature.

Your moods can also have a pronounced effect on your behaviour and the flow of your relationships. Although you are often most charming and accommodating, you can be incredibly contrary when it suits you. You have times when you are calm, easygoing and give the impression of being an extremely uncomplicated individual. But should something occur that puts you under pressure or worries you, you can move from calm to chaotic extremely quickly.

Your twin nature (remember that your sign is ruled by the Twins) is responsible for making you the master of inconsistency (at times). Because you are so mercurial in nature, you can be a tremendously exciting, mysterious and alluring companion. Anyone who thrives on being around someone who is creative, changeable and something of a chameleon will love being around you. You have great ideas, moments of great insight, even genius, and an incredible ability to excite and inspire others with your concepts.

You are usually far from boring company. You love drama, intrigue and confusion (although you say you don't), and occasionally you do like to go for a walk on the wilder side of life. As much as you say you love peace, harmony and quiet, you also can be an expert at creating mayhem when it suits you. Because you are unpredictable (as a group and as individuals), you are one of the most talked about signs of the zodiac. The saying that 'there's only one thing worse than people talking about you, and that is people not talking about you' . . . was certain to have been intended for a Gemini.

Because your ruling planet Mercury is the planet of communication and mind powers, you also can be the zodiac's greatest genius thinker and analyst (at times). You can also be the greatest of business people (look at Gemini Donald Trump). You can be incredibly psychic if you learn to tap into the enormous unlimited resources accessible through your own mind. And when you are creative and tap into that magical higher zone of creativity, you can be in a league of your own.

When you are on track, you can quickly carve out a living legacy in anything you desire, especially music (Bob Dylan), acting (Marilyn Monroe), real estate (like Donald Trump) and combining business with show business (ex-Beatle, Gemini Paul McCartney). Or you may go into politics like Geminis Henry Kissinger and President John F. Kennedy. If you rise and shine, you often stand in a league of your own. You can be a trendsetter (Kylie Minogue), a trail blazer in your field (like Clint Eastwood who turned the spaghetti western into an art form) and become a fashion statement or a cult figure as well (like Stevie Nicks and Judy Garland in their day).

You pursue your dreams with a strange kind of driven tenacity, and also with an amazing vulnerability or ingenuity. You seem to have an innate knack for turning your desires or dreams into realities (look at Nicole Kidman, who went to America and married Hollywood's crown prince, Tom Cruise). Naturally, like all dreams or wishes, living them once they come true can differ from dreaming or wishing them. These desires usually turn out to be good ideas or bad ideas once you begin to live them, but at least you get to give your dreams or wishes a test run in reality, which is more than many other signs of the zodiac do.

Never underestimate the power of your thoughts, dreams or wishes Geminis. Your thoughts are far more potent than you possibly ever appreciate or realise, and can be used to either build your life, or sabotage your life, according to the way you think about things.

In your everyday existence you are generally found upfront and centre, rather than waiting in the wings or hovering backstage. You do have a special brand of confidence or self-assurance when it comes to your own talents, abilities or skills. Self-promotion comes easily to you (because you often derive great pleasure from talking about yourself, your opinions and your conquests or trials and tribulations).

Nevertheless talk is not necessarily cheap with you, although sometimes you talk out of both sides of your mouth. Usually, however, you do live up to your words, promises or arrangements.

When you don't have a secret agenda, you can be the most up-front person. You are like an open book at moments like these, and this is when you can keep nothing secret and delight in spilling the beans, even when you know you should hold back on sharing what you know. At other times you keep long-running secrets, schemes, dreams and desires locked away safely in the sacred garden of your powerful mind. This habit of keeping secrets or thoughts all to yourself is something that usually works best for you. By holding the mental imagery or thoughts about exactly what you want or desire within you, they gain and grow in strength.

Talking about things (or sharing your dreams, hopes and wishes) sometimes dissipates your focus and weakens the magical powers of your mind. Taking your thoughts out to play only when you know nobody can sense or tune into them is often one of your greatest powers of all. This is when you are at your highest level of scheming, manipulating and conniving and when you do this inner-dialogue or brain churning activity you are the mind-master of the zodiac. Nobody does it better!

You can be a big fan of your own abilities, too. Modesty is often much more of an affectation that you assume than an honest characteristic. You love praise and often sing your own praises to those you wish to impress (and to yourself). Though you are shy when caught up in certain situations (especially where you may feel out of your depth), within your comfort zones of operation you are a mental giant. If you want to win someone over, or impress them with your charms, you can open up their heart and mind to you in a moment. You have the wise person and the ingénue within you, to call upon. And you have a talent for knowing when to assume a certain role or say the thing that needs to be said to break the ice. But while you are extremely adept at promoting your own best interests when needed, to be fair to you, you often loudly sing the praises of others as well.

You are a fantastic promoter of yourself and a wonderful promoter of those you believe in or care about. If you want something, or someone, you usually get the results you desire (even if it is a hard row to hoe to get things connected and signed, sealed and delivered). You have an enormous range of viewpoints, personality traits, secret and open schemes, dreams, hopes and wishes. You are a mind-smith, a negotiator and a natural manipulator. You can also be complacent and lazy on occasions.

Too often, you want the doors of opportunity just to spring open for you, rather than to go knocking on them. Your mind is strong enough for you to think of something and to make it happen, so you often do believe or feel opportunity appears magically before you. However, there are seldom enough opportunities to keep you content. Because generally one thing, one project, sometimes even one true love, is seldom sufficient for you. You would love to have it all and more, and to take it all with you as well wherever you go. You are the writer, the teacher, the media person, the entrepreneur, the performer, the computer buff and the occasional (and sometimes more frequent) totally highly strung (Prozac-taking) neurotic, too.

You live not just in the moment, but in the past, present and future all combined and this is what makes you so amazing. There are fewer boundaries around you than most, and while this opens up your horizons, it also confuses you. Your mind zips and zots all over the place like a human computer entering in its own form of specialised and random data at a rapid pace. You are like a human jigsaw puzzle, using your mind overtime, as you attempt to analyse each and everyone around you, and also at the same time put all the bits and pieces of existence and beyond all neatly into place. No wonder you become highly strung or a little irrational at times.

Although you are usually a wonderful communicator, you have the propensity to confuse yourself and those around you. Your great plan, scheme, dream or commitment of today can turn into a forgotten or abandoned cause tomorrow. But maybe it's just as well. Some of your concepts, plans, ideas and beliefs come straight out of left field.

You can also express yourself not in straight talk but in riddles. When spoken by you the words, phrases and language of any country can take on an entirely new meaning. In your finest form, many of you frame and combine your words like catching fish in a net in the ocean (you have to think about this to imagine how flapping around your words can be at times). You can be a poet, a writer or a song-writer. You have the ability to be a magician, a mathematician or a mental gymnast with your thoughts.

Your mind does not operate on wheels of thought, or cycles of thoughts, it runs on a system that creates thoughts that come out of you more like geometric shapes, the magic of languages, of mental and physical energy flow. You are always the child, the student, the teacher, the innocent and the master of destiny all rolled into one. That is why you are unique and it is something (this uniqueness) that somehow you intuitively (but not necessarily consciously) sense. This uniqueness is also the same thing that means that others will seldom ever understand you, nor will you truly ever really understand them either. In some ways, you live on another mental plane or planet from the rest of us.

By some amazing good luck, your mental preoccupations don't stop you from being a social success. People usually love being around you, because you are so delightfully different, entertaining and stimulating. You are friendly, curious and passionate and you're ambitious, resourceful and restless. You get others involved in your mission to find answers to all sorts of questions. The way you go about this undertaking sometimes seems chaotic to others, but you always have a creative sense of where you're going and you're usually busy getting there.

Your symbol, the Twins, represents your ability to see and appreciate at least two sides of every story, and this can sometimes make you quite a diplomat. You're more than what you seem to be and no matter what part of yourself you're showing, there's always another side of you waiting for its turn.

Your ruling planet is none other than Mercury — the ancient messenger of the gods. Mercury's influence makes you a natural communicator and it also gives you a yearning to travel. Your abundance of energy (mental and physical) is a gift from Mercury and so is your ability to think fast! But Mercury has two sides just like you do. This planet can intensify mood swings and put a new twist on decision-making; that's why you sometimes find yourself changing your mind back and forth before you reach a decision.

You have a lively and versatile personality and your two-sided outlook on life creates some interesting and exciting challenges. You know you'd have a more pleasant journey through life if you were a little less critical of yourself and others. Your keen and observant eyes see every imperfection and you sometimes blurt out your opinions before you consider whether or not you should.

You have a gift to see at least two sides to every situation and when you take the time to see the big picture you make smart and creative choices. But when you're feeling holier than thou, you sometimes believe your way is the only way — seeing the other person's point of view can be almost impossible when you're in a self-righteous frame of mind. Tact can sometimes be a thing that you forget to apply when required. However, because you're the champion of smooth talk when you need to be, you can usually talk yourself out of any hot water you get into! Which is just as well.

If you don't have something going on to occupy your busy mind, you'll create a drama or conflict to stir up the pot. That is why there is usually plenty of excitement surrounding you, much of it spur of the moment and unexpected. You thrive on spontaneous fun and you're always ready to try anything new and different. You seek out variety in life. No matter what challenges come up you handle them or find a way around them. Your versatility makes you compatible with all sorts of people. You're attracted to quick minds and you're almost always in the mood to learn something new. You're ambitious and adaptable so you can succeed in any project that you have the patience and persistence to complete. You may totally immerse yourself in a project for days, only to decide you don't like the way it's going and abandon it for something completely new. Chances are though that your inquiring mind won't let you rest until you return to the abandoned project and find a way to make it work!

You have a genuine and contagious form of enthusiasm and you can easily open the same doors that get slammed shut in other people's faces. It's amazing to watch a Gemini charm his or her way into an off-limits area. Your wide-eyed curiosity is sometimes misread as naiveté or foolishness but in most situations you can turn the tables in your favour. You have an uncommon capacity to take in and understand a huge amount of information and you can switch mental gears in the blink of an eye.

Your emotional gears may not be so easy to shift but you do your best to keep your feelings from interfering with your thoughts. You're a fast-learning student of life — except when it comes to learning how to secure your emotional desires and needs. It is hard to feel happy at heart when your feelings are constantly disrupted by the never-ending spinning wheels of your over-active mind.

Gemini is an Air sign

To your advantage, you have an abundance of creative ability and a flair for originality. It's as if you pick some of your greatest ideas out of thin air and the uniqueness of your thinking makes others respect you and want to hear what you have to say.

Your curiosity about life and your desire to learn about all sorts of things fires your enthusiasm for living and learning. When you wonder about something you often take the time to investigate it and you're well rewarded for your quests! Your insights can be shared in a variety of ways but artistic expression and creative inventions are two of your strong points.

To your disadvantage, you're interested in so many different things that it can be hard for you to focus on just one or two at a time. Consequently, you can be easily side-tracked and suddenly find yourself heading in the opposite direction from your goal. (But even these side trips are interesting and educational.)

You sometimes feel overburdened by your responsibilities, however, you continue to take on more rather than delegate some work or admit you're human. You push yourself to sprint in a race that has no end and your mind crackles with anxious energy.

[Insights into your sign]

The bright side: One of your greatest strengths is your ability to think quickly and adapt easily to new situations and circumstances. You take accurate leaps of logic that leave others scratching their heads in amazement and you're resourceful enough to transform a shipwreck into Fantasy Island.

Characteristics >	Benefits >	Drawbacks >
Adaptable	Free spirit	Lose interest quickly
Ambitious	Strong self-starter	Take on too much
Charming	Hold others spellbound	Misleading
Clever	Think quickly	Smarty pants
Curious	Great student	Go off on tangents
Exuberant	Uninhibited	Show off
Expressive	Clear communicator	Exaggerate the truth
Fickle	Open to new possibilities	Don't live up to promises
Friendly	Meet people easily	Vulnerable
Intelligent	Apply knowledge	Mind clutter
Inventive	Insightful vision	Tell white lies
Mischievous	Playful	Downright annoying
Moody	Time for introspection	Self-absorbed
Nervous	Energy to burn	Highly strung
Passionate	Enthusiastic	One-eyed
Restless	Productive	Complaining
Romantic	Steamy fantasies	Rose-coloured glasses
Sentimental	Open-hearted	Can get depressed
Talkative	Opens doors	Won't let others get a word in
Versatile	Many options	Too much going on
Youthful	Wide-eyed wonder	Spoilt brat

The shadow: You're so focused on the mental aspects of life that you sometimes overlook your emotional, spiritual and physical needs. Your quick wit can be sharp and stinging and when you're emotionally wounded your sarcasm bites like the teeth of an angry dog.

[Looking beneath the surface of your sign]

You definitely like some parts of your personality more than you like others, Gemini. But the parts you don't like — the ones you try to hide — aren't nearly as bad as you think they are! It's true that you can get into more than your share of mischief and it's also true that you sometimes act like you know it all — when you really only know it a little. But what a great combination that can be! You can convince a room full of scientists (and sometimes yourself) that up is down. Your mental wheels whirl round and round until you're exhausted, but your mind rarely stops to rest.

You can worry until you make yourself sick and you can also make yourself sick by not taking time for rest. The next time you're on a roll and you're tempted to keep going without a break, stop and take a deep breath. You can really overwork yourself and when you're focused on a project or goal the other parts of your life — including your health — tend to suffer unless you plan holiday and rest time into your busy schedule. When you push yourself too close to the edge you can be distracted, irritable and detached. You secretly want someone to care enough to rescue you but you act like that's the last thing you want.

Do yourself a favour and get some fresh air and a little exercise. A walk a day keeps stress at bay. You need to get your blood circulating and your body moving to release your mind and give it a break. Plus, the more you exercise, the less you eat and the better you sleep!

[How to tune into your sign's powers]

> *When your mind is centred, nothing is impossible for you.*
> *Be grateful for your ability to be anything you want to be and you will attract the opportunities you seek.*
> *Always look on the bright side of life.*

The Gemini woman

> A Gemini woman has an innocently seductive
> ability to charm the pants off a man —
> sometimes before she's introduced herself.

She's a temptress, yet also that cute girl next door type and a drama queen all rolled up into one (as Marilyn Monroe — Gemini — so aptly personified). You are wise to never judge a Gemini woman by her appearance because a woman of Mercury is everything she doesn't appear to be, and nothing like she seems. She's a walking, talking puzzle, and she can solve a riddle, paint her nails, and talk on her cell phone while she changes her flat tyre.

She's invigorated by doing at least two things at a time, and impatient with people who can't seem to do more than one thing at a time. She doesn't like to wait for others, but tends to love to have others wait on her — or for her. Not that she is unpunctual by nature, it is just that on special moments or occasions, she does like to make her entrance in a way that creates the most impact. She is often spoilt by her father, doted on by her brothers, and has had the claim to fame of being her teacher's pet.

Ms Gemini frequently prefers the company of men to women and sometimes has very few, really trusted, women friends. She knows she has a better chance to wrap men around her little finger than women, and she likes it that way. Women are often those she sees as students or teachers of whatever it is that she needs to teach or learn, but she doesn't like to have too much feminine competition around her, unless she knows it is competition she can outsmart or outshine. The Gemini woman is often far better equipped for bringing up a boy child than a girl child.

Because she burns up so much energy with her often unstoppable thoughts, this woman of the zodiac is the one who suffers from energy burnout and mental exhaustion. She puts herself into mind-overdrive and even if she has little activity happening around her, can wonder why she runs out of energy and needs to give herself lots of time to recuperate and recover again. If her mind is really going full bore, she can experience minor accidents or illnesses. These are frequently her consciousness' way of making sure that she slows herself down for a while. Her desire to live every minute to its fullest, or to make the best of every opportunity, is often what most tests her ability to keep up a hectic pace.

As much as she loves drama, change and adventure, she also needs to make the time and give herself the mental space to have a good night's sleep and take time out from all the goings on around her. She innately hates to live a predictable existence (although that is often what she claims to desire the most). She thrives on mental challenges and likes to hide behind her mind. She is one of those people that get going the best when the going is tough. She often falls apart when she has too much time to think and doesn't feel her most creative when times are easy or comfortable. If she has something to prove to herself, or to the world, she is a human dynamo.

The in-between times in the chapters of her life are the most frustrating for her. She needs some challenge or pressure to improve her performance, otherwise she goes rusty. She seeks variety in all areas of her life and yawns at repetition and routine.

Ms Gemini can't stand to be bored and is seldom boring. In fact, she probably has plenty of interesting things to talk about and enough interests and hobbies to have something in common with everyone. Unfortunately, she often settles on a partner for all the wrong reasons and frequently has problems in her relationship because she has ended up with a man who isn't really suited to her tastes in life, desires or mind levels at all.

She is often quite beautiful and unique in her appearance. She can be the person who possesses both brains and beauty. Her Mercurial winged sandals can lift her like an angel. But insult the Gemini woman or hurt her feelings and you'd better have on armour to shield yourself from her sharp claws. Gemini Judy Garland was once called an angel with spurs.

The Gemini woman makes a wonderful friend but also a tough foe and the same applies to the way she treats herself. She can be super tough on herself and extremely giving to herself. She is the Isis of the zodiac, the zodiac woman who lives and exists with many veils.

Yet as many layers as you unravel, you still seldom get to truly know her. Even when you spend magical moments or share heart-to-heart times, be prepared to discover that there are still more layers to lift underneath the person you thought you had got to know.

She is only going to be prepared to allow you to look beyond these veils if she believes that she can trust you with her life, soul and heart's desires. And there are not going to be many people in her lifetime that she feels this way about (except perhaps her mother, or a special sister). If you are ever lucky enough for her to share her true soul and self's secret deepest side with you, count yourself among the chosen few.

[How Gemini women operate]

Social

She is usually a great person to know and those around her often benefit greatly from having her in their lives. Ms Gemini brings colour and invaluable resources on many different levels into other people's lives and that's just one of the reasons she's fun company. This woman believes in experiencing and appreciating all life's gifts and diversions and her actions inspire other people to do the same. You can find her where the action is because she's usually the one generating it or is somehow in the middle of the stir.

She's seldom short of words and she loves to exchange ideas, test the waters and check out people's opinions and backgrounds. She can discuss every aspect of an issue with you and yet when the conversation is over you probably have no more idea where she really stands than before you asked her. However, your time wasn't wasted. You've probably learned a tremendous amount about everything and nothing along the way.

She's nearly impossible to pin down, she's mischievous and she's often fickle. But if you're looking for action, she can spin you off the planet. Beware! If you bore her, she may spin you out of her life. Of course, she'll probably do it with so much charm you'll feel almost as if she's done you a great favour.

Gemini women indulge themselves by gossiping, running up gigantic telephone bills and going on spur-of-the-moment shopping sprees. Don't ever expect her to rush home after work when there's a hot sale in the area. She is also quite self-centred, often wants to talk about herself (but at least her stories are interesting) and, quite frankly, often doesn't really want to listen to what you have to say. In fact, if you have a deep dark secret or concern you want to share, that doesn't interest your Gemini friend in any way. Tell it to someone else, rather than Ms Gemini, because it's likely to go in one ear and out the other where she is concerned. She's usually only interested in solving her own concerns or problems — not yours — unless she's being paid for her advice.

Compassion is not normally one of her finest qualities unless she's feeling compassion for herself. Nevertheless, she is one of the people you will learn more from, have the greatest fun with, and will end up gaining something valuable and tangible from knowing. Being around a Gemini is like receiving an invisible charge of cosmic electricity. Once you have been in their presence, you are likely to be somewhat transformed and consequently (without even knowing it) suddenly begin to see, feel and inculcate things differently than you did before.

Love and family

A Gemini woman has so many hobbies and interests that it's difficult for her to find one man who wants to do them all. However, this creates a problem. Being a woman of many parts and interests does not so much apply to the mating and dating areas of life. If ever there's one woman of the zodiac who wants stability in her love and family areas, it is Ms Gemini.

Because the rest of her world moves so statically, she wants home, love and family to be her rock of Gibraltar. However, as much as this is what she desires, she often has a very strange way of going about making it a reality. Ms Gemini tends to go after romantic interests who are often the least interested in having a solid, safe home and romantic base. It is almost as if she likes to chase after the clouds and try to bring them down to earth in some of her fantasies about living happily ever after. Fortunately for her, Ms Gemini is normally not lacking in suitors.

She's entertaining, clever and exciting, and she has brilliant humour, silken diplomacy and an insatiable taste for variety. A Gemini woman has an innocently seductive ability to charm the pants off a man, sometimes before she's formally introduced herself. She is quite a captivating siren when she wants to be and she can also be a man's best friend as well. If he wants to have a woman who can give him every aspect of femininity, plus a touch of child and genius as well, he is certainly going to find it in Ms Gemini.

However, when it comes to fidelity, she can have double standards. What's good for the goose is good for the gander, but she will rewrite this exchange any way it suits her. While she will be totally possessive about who and what matters to her, she won't tolerate much jealousy herself. Heaven help the Mr who comes between her and her sister, and Lord help the sister that comes between her and her man.

Her relationships are often very complicated and occasionally there are past partners involved. Ex-partners, or memories of them, play a big role in forming the new relationships that the Gemini is attracted towards. Ms Gemini is often on the rebound if she hasn't yet found her Mr Right. Her man had better be emotionally secure because she has a cool head and a distant heart and she keeps all of her innermost thoughts to herself. It wouldn't help much to hear them anyway — her inner dialogue tends to be an ongoing internal debate with neither side winning.

When it comes to romance, a Gemini can seem fickle but she's probably just looking for her true love, and her fickleness is a result of her quest for the ideal man. She knows what she doesn't want, but she may not know what she does want. She has every possibility of finding a soulmate, but she might not recognise him right away, so he needs to be swift and breathtaking in his pursuit. Otherwise, she'll be off on another adventure before he can sweep her off her feet.

When a Gemini woman considers marriage she's interested in an intellectual equal. She wants a man who can keep up with her as easily as he can watch her go off on her own. Anyone who attempts to clip the wings of a Gemini will be left holding his scissors in one hand and her wedding band in the other. Love her and appreciate her many different faces and she'll return that love in creatively inventive, steamy shows of affection that you can't even imagine. You'll also have the pleasure and the headaches of being married to a multitude of women in one.

Gemini women make great mothers and many of them play the role of single parent better than two separate adults. She's fun and imaginative and she enjoys making crafts and doing art projects with her kids. She lets them make their own gingerbread people and she joins in when they want to paint their faces. She encourages and respects her children's thoughts and dreams. She can be a bit on the inconsistent side, sometimes even flaky, but her children grow up with wings of their own and fly home to visit her often.

Career

This woman cut her baby teeth on a copy of How to Win Friends and Influence People. She's persuasive enough to land any job she wants and has the smarts to do it well. She gravitates to positions that offer a variety of responsibilities, a chance to travel and a pool of diversity.

Careers in sales or promotions, advertising or public relations are a breeze for a Gemini. She also can be a successful author, popular talk show host and charismatic politician. Many Geminis enjoy successful acting careers (Courtney Cox, Joan Collins and Brooke Shields are all Gemini-born), serve as super-organised secretaries and hostesses, and are vibrant leaders and professional speakers.

The bright, sunny disposition many Geminis show on the job may be the opposite of what shows up when she's home, but she's an inspiration to her colleagues none the less. She usually enjoys her work and even on a bad day she tells lively jokes and plays office pranks to keep morale high.

Financial

The typical Gemini deposits her pay cheque with one hand while she's signing for a credit card purchase with the other. She views money as the trade beads of our time and can easily talk herself into buying her latest whim or fancy. To a Gemini, money is a token in the game of life and she knows that money is something that she can attract simply by thinking about attracting it into her life. She does this by associating with clever money-making people or through reading about ways of making money. She knows if we apply ourselves, we all have a key to opening up the bank of Wall Street if we're serious contenders in the money-making game. If she's interested in money, she'll accumulate a great deal of it. If she isn't, she will probably still get by better than most financially.

She doesn't mind taking risks and the sound of a profitable investment scheme is music to her ears. She jumps into opportunities that look too hot to miss, and sometimes gets burned. But she has some very accurate hunches and she usually thinks things over before she embarks on a financial enterprise. Once a Gemini learns that the better she manages the money she has, the more she gets to manage, she makes big strides up the financial pyramid. But no matter how much money she has, she's always her same old Twin self.

Physical

Because Geminis are so multi-dimensional, they come in every shape and size imaginable. However, most women of Mercury are blessed with tall, lean bodies and slender arms and legs. But a Gemini of any height stands tall and she may have the look of a flighty bird just before it takes to the sky. She likes to stay at least one step ahead of everyone else.

She nearly always defies her age and manages to stay youthful in mind and body long into her life. Her prospects for good health are very strong but she can literally run herself into the sick bed if she doesn't get the right amount of physical exercise and rest. She lives on a mental tangent and she frequently forgets to take care of her physical needs.

Under stress, she can lose weight overnight because her mind never stops thinking and burning up energy. She can suffer from over-tiredness even though she claims she didn't do anything to cause it. She disregards that her mind runs through a twisting maze of possibilities all day long. She needs to sleep but she often suffers from restlessness or insomnia.

Her circulatory system holds the key to her physical wellbeing and she needs regular exercise, sunshine and fresh air to regulate her nervous energy. A moderate level of physical exertion converts her stress into activity and gives her some peace of mind.

Being born in Gemini also means that she should begin building her physical stamina early in life. She may have a delicate constitution that needs strengthening and she should avoid living in areas with polluted air and water supplies. The Gemini's best health friend is her adaptability because she sees life as a series of transitions. Her worst health enemy is her nervous nature which can create countless physical problems.

A Gemini is susceptible to accidents involving her hands and arms. Sometimes this is her body's way of telling her she's about to make a poor choice. Gemini also are prone to allergies and bronchial problems but these will often correct themselves when she maintains a moderate aerobic exercise routine.

Mental

She's a quick thinking, smooth talking mental trapeze artist and she can prove it. The Gemini Twins illustrate that two heads are better than one. The only trouble is she doesn't always know which one of her Twin selves to listen to and they rarely agree.

She's exceptional at noticing a need for improvement and figuring out the best way to proceed. She enjoys intellectual puzzles and visualises new inventions. When she follows through with her inspired ideas she dramatically increases her opportunity for fame and fortune.

Her keen desire for intellectual satisfaction is her driving force and she should be left free to follow her dreams no matter how unusual her dreams may look. She can be very determined when it comes to following her inspirations. Getting in her way doesn't even slow her down, so don't bother.

Geminis have open minds and are willing to change their opinions as new evidence and findings reveal themselves. They can be good listeners — if they practise — but many Geminis have a tendency to interrupt. And while they're quick to offer advice they won't appreciate this trait in others. Even with all that talking, a Gemini won't divulge her deepest feelings to anyone, and she may disguise her true motives as well.

Spiritual

Gemini explores spirituality with her mind. She reads book after book and theorises about spirituality but she may overlook her heart's ability to truly understand what she reads. Her dualistic nature encourages her to experience and appreciate the perfection and balance of the universe. It helps her to learn that every person and event has as many positives as it does negatives. It sounds simple, but she knows the implications are profound.

Her creative mind visualises all sorts of afterlife possibilities including a galaxy teeming with angelic hosts. Of course, her version of heaven includes artists and musicians and her imagination can run wild with ideas. She suspects she has to wait to find out the answers but she has a hunch that whatever she can imagine has been, is, or will be in existence somewhere. She rarely discusses her own spiritual beliefs though she's interested in hearing yours and she's willing to theorise with you in an objective manner.

The Gemini man

He can take your breath away with a longing glance and melt your heart with a passionate kiss. But you'd better love exciting chase scenes if you plan to pursue him.

The Gemini male is as curious and playful as a puppy chasing a butterfly. He's also as restless as a squirrel in springtime and probably as quick, too. The moment you're certain about him he changes into someone else, and just when you're beginning to feel comfortable with the change he transforms again.

He's the zodiac's magician and young or old he always has a few tricks up his sleeve, including a disappearing act. He's creative, inventive and clever and he's charming, expressive and sentimental. But remember, this man of Mercury is in a perpetual state of internal mental debate and his moody, restless side may be lurking just on the other side of the moment.

Still, he's more likely to be showing his ambitious, versatile side in public and he's quite possibly the most exciting man you know. There's no question that a Gemini man is full of life and bursting with energy. He is also the person who is likely to surprise, delight and disappoint you in the space of an instant. Attempting to anticipate how Mr Gemini is going to handle anything that occurs in his life is like trying to anticipate when the Saints will win the next Grand Final. You never know!

Women seem to like his boyish qualities and he plays them like a musician plays a violin to get all the applause and attention he can from the fairer sex. The problem with Mr Gemini is he tends to like to play the field and has been accredited in astrology as being one of the zodiac's most prolific heart-breakers. Naturally, sooner or later, he settles down and when he does, he often becomes one of the best partners of all. But, it takes time for him to really adjust to a solid, ongoing existence, rather than living moment to moment. He likes every day to have some variety and uncertainties and if he doesn't get this adrenaline rush from his work or hobbies, he often ends up looking for it in all the wrong places.

Mr Gemini often gets into hot water because he likes to sizzle, even if it means sabotaging areas of his life that he truly values. He is a man who often finds he's in a position where he has created his own nemesis. However, regrets, or saying he's sorry, rarely cross his mind. He knows that if he had his life to live over, he probably would never do anything different anyway. At least he is usually man enough to stand up to the music of life and dance with it, rather than hide from it or pretend he's something that he isn't. For a somewhat devious man, in his own way, he is one of the most blatantly honest and up-front people of all.

Is it only coincidence that three modern-day princes were born under Gemini: Prince Rainier of Monaco, Prince Philip, husband of Queen Elizabeth, and Prince William, destined one day to be the King of England? Each one of these three has been influential in his own way, even Prince William who, although still a teenager, shows signs of having a mind of his own and a future as an interesting and charismatic leader.

And of course, another Gemini is that prince of music, the artist formerly known as Prince — and hasn't he picked himself a mouthful of a new name?

[How Gemini men operate]

Social

He loves his times alone and he loves the time he spends with others. He needs both. His inner world is also another realm of social experience. However, the company he keeps within himself is the many different facets of his own personality. Some of the best conversations he'll ever have in his entire life (and the most creative ones) he'll have with himself. He loves to share ideas, see what's going on around him and explore all kinds of social structures.

It is the Gemini man's curiosity which determines most of his social activities. It leads him around the block one week and around the world the next. Usually he's a blur of activity and can create the somewhat eerie illusion that he can be in more than one place at the same time. He thinks learning is fun (he may even be a teacher himself), and thoroughly enjoys a morning at the science museum followed by an afternoon lecture explaining how humans can adapt to live on Mars. (And many Geminis actually do read science fiction, too.)

He's a genuine people person and the more offbeat others are the more interesting he finds them. He loves to travel to remote areas and meet people whose lives are totally different from his own. When he's at home, he's in front of the television channel surfing between a *National Geographic* special and the football, or he's talking to a new friend on the Internet, possibly even playing chess via the Internet.

He may be someone who is creating things for the current technological era, as he loves to be involved in merging mind, technology and business.

Yet, as much as Mr Gemini loves anything that stretches his mind, let us be realistic — he also loves anything that tantalises the senses of his body. He can actually be quite a sensualist and should get into the pursuit of physical pleasures, too. He needs to get into enough physical things so that he removes himself from his over-active mind now and again. Too much thinking and not enough sex or fun times makes his body rusty.

It is important for Mr Gemini to live, not just through his thoughts, but by way of his mind and spirit as well. He is often a person who lives vicariously through watching others do things rather than doing them himself. He may also be a writer, who writes stories, rather than living the fullest of life himself. Whatever it is he does (or that is his thing), he wants to make sure he isn't accepting less than he deserves or could have, simply because he has taken the easy way out.

He's often smarter than most people and he can even be a genius at times. He probably only has a few people he would regard as close friends, but he has loads of acquaintances. He can be an entertaining companion and witty and interesting but can be a little brutal in the comments he makes. He's clever in the way he tells his tales, leaving the best bit for the punch line, but he can be put off by anyone who doesn't listen when he's talking. He's an information highway and a source of entertaining trivia, but he also has a talent for spreading juicy information that might be better left unsaid.

Love and family

It's hard not to fall head over heels with the boyish good looks and charming smile of a Gemini. He can take your breath away with a longing glance and melt your heart with a passionate kiss. But, you'd better be invigorated by exciting chase scenes if you plan to pursue him. He's often sought after by a bevy of eager beauties who think they can catch him.

When he wants to, especially romantically, he can become the road runner of the zodiac. 'Catch me if you can', takes on a new meaning when a Gemini man wants to have his fling, and avoid any form of committed relationship. Many women, after dating a Gemini man for years but getting nowhere, say they'll never go out with a Gemini man again, but they always end up doing so.

He is often your doctor, your lawyer or your brother's best friend, and what's worse, your mother probably likes him. He's one of those guys that just seems to fit in with the things that interest you or that you want to get interested in. Because he is a chameleon of sorts, he is one of those people that can go anywhere or meet anyone and have something to offer. He is a great person to have around and he usually provides some sort of special service by being in your life. He generally doesn't waste your time; he's got lots to offer. He can be both your pain and your pleasure, but he's usually never boring.

He makes a fabulous friend and there's rarely a dull moment when he's around. His intolerance for boredom motivates him to turn ordinary events into new and exciting experiences. An ordinary date like dinner and a show is an entirely new experience with a Gemini. He'll take you to dinner at restaurants with lots of atmosphere and character and whether you dine in a gourmet four-star restaurant or have a meat pie and mashed potatoes at the local pie shop, it will be an evening to remember and relish. Whatever you end up doing, you're likely to remember it as a special occasion, and when it's time for the show, don't be surprised if he's scored front row seats and possibly even backstage passes.

The Gemini man is a skilful flirt and enjoys a variety of women. He typically prefers clever, energetic women to quiet, passive ones and he provokes a heated argument every now and again followed by a passionate make-up session in the bedroom. He is accurately accused of being fickle but it's less because he can't make up his mind and more because his mind has so many complicated facets and opposing thoughts.

He craves diversity, so if you have a set routine you like to follow you might consider the Capricorn man instead. But, anything's possible, so if you have your heart set on a Gemini, toss your day planner out the window and go for it. You'll have to move quickly and pounce unexpectedly. And remember, there are no guaranteed results.

A Gemini man is capable of being a faithful marriage partner but his wife is living on fantasy lane if she thinks she can keep his restless spirit on the home front. He probably stays home about as much as he goes out. But one way to make him want to stay home is to throw a party or create a great party atmosphere at home all the time. He'll gladly stay home to host a party or social event because he enjoys the chance to show off his home and talk to his friends at the same time.

If you allow him his space, support his need for variety, and honestly trust him because he is committed, he usually has a good record for fidelity. But that doesn't mean he's always on time or remembers every special plan, promise or occasion. It does mean he can show you he loves you in more ways than you thought were humanly possible and you'll never have a dull day again.

As a father, he can truly go dotty over his children. In fact, he can turn into someone who is totally different from the person he used to be (when he was without children), if fatherhood really hits home with him. He will start to teach his son chess at age three (and be sure his son is a genius), or give his daughter diamond earrings for her fifth birthday.

He can go totally over the top when children open up his often tightly locked heartstrings. With his children, he's a daddy, a friend, a counsellor and a stand-up comedian but surprisingly he's often not a disciplinarian and he may not see the value in having as many rules as you think are necessary. He does, however, insist that his children learn polite manners and social graces and he may expect you to be the one to teach them.

His favourite way to teach is by example and his children learn a great deal just by spending time with him. However, he often puts the main responsibility of bringing up the children on his partner, and instead of being the main teacher or role model for them, he puts this on his partner, too. He likes to take the credit when the children excel or are good but if they misbehave he tends to look to his partner for the reasons why.

Career

He can be one of the people who are listed in the *Guinness Book of Records* for some high achievement or other. He may have sold more fridges to Eskimos than anyone else alive for example! I've yet to meet a Gemini man who's not a natural born salesman. But his bright and versatile mind makes him a strong candidate for lots of different career positions. He can be an organiser, a performer, a sports player or even an analyst. One thing is certain though, his work needs to let him express his creative and inventive energy. He suffers in a job or career that's laden with guidelines and lacking in ingenuity. (He's not always cordial enough to suffer in silence either.)

He loves to use his sharp mind to solve problems, unravel puzzles and mysteries and invent new products and methods. He laughs in the face of tradition and may have a clock that runs counter-clockwise just to keep people on their toes. His almost frantic desire to learn a little about everything makes him a bona fide Jack of all trades.

When it comes to choosing a job, his curiosity spurs him onward and he's a natural explorer and an interesting philosopher. He's also a captivating politician, a fascinating orator, a winning corporate spokesman and an enchanting performer (Errol Flynn, Tasmania's first Hollywood star, was Gemini-born). He can be a dramatic and exciting writer, too. Advertising appeals to him, as well as all the hospitality areas of employment. He may also work two jobs to get some variety throughout the working week.

Financial

The Gemini man is both a prince and a pauper when it comes to his finances. He's amused by money and enjoys the power it wields but he finds reading the stock reports tiring and managing his mutual funds monotonous. It's amazing how much Mr Gemini loves to test his financial luck. He will get into business deals, go to the casino or invest money in long-shot schemes, almost as if he wants to test his fate and fortune. Somehow he generally lands happily on his financial feet, but not before he has several near-to-bankrupt type experiences. He is the kind who will put his shirt on a horse, not necessarily because he has great faith in the horse, but because he feels like doing something to test his luck.

He's wise to hire a financial adviser or two to review his assets and help him decide how to invest before he spends everything he has on a whirlwind weekend. His advisers can also help him stay on top of trends and determine if an investment opportunity is stable. But if he has his mind set on something, he generally does what he wants no matter what advice anyone gives.

His thirst for entertainment and his fascination with novelty can cause a Gemini man to shirk routine responsibilities like paying his bills and balancing his chequebook. He probably has the money, but he finds paperwork so dull that he sometimes pays late charges and may even end up with a bad credit rating.

Fortunately that's not too much of a problem for him because he can talk his way into or out of just about anything he wants, big or small. But if he has his own company, he's wise to hire a manager or executive secretary who can stay on top of the tedious details of running the business while he births new ideas and wines and dines his clients in classic Gemini style.

Physical

Surprisingly, some Gemini men really have problems moderating their weight. It is as if because they have so much going on in their minds they allow their bodies to become run down or neglected. However, in the main, Mr Gemini is usually agile, flexible and youthful. Generally, he has the appearance of being tall and limber even when he's short and brawny. His movements are quick and he may startle you by springing forwards to answer the phone or jumping up to look out the window.

This guy isn't really interested in long gruelling work-outs (but he should be), and usually doesn't have the drive to follow an intensive daily exercise routine. His busy life and the chattering that goes on perpetually in his own mind generally comes first where his interests are concerned and he prefers to burn calories by running his brain around in circles. If he were a dog he could probably catch his own tail.

He'd rather play sports to stay in shape and he loves competition and rarely can resist a challenge. Boxing can actually be something that he might even find an interesting example of learning how to protect himself and also stay in shape. Those who know Geminis may need to be as versatile as he is to keep up with him because he may invite you for a game of football and show up at the field with a soccer ball or tennis racquet instead. This is usually okay with most of his friends but some of them don't appreciate the unannounced change in plans.

A tour of his home is like a walk through a department store because he usually owns a variety of sports equipment, numerous gadgets, a large collection of books and movies and a wide selection of games. He probably also has a great selection of art and music. Expect him to have the biggest TV on the block. And at a Gemini's house, you have a good chance of spotting a magic hat and you might even see a rabbit hop out of it.

He needs to watch when he's driving or in a hurry doing something. He tends to be distracted quite easily and this leaves him physically vulnerable. He's sometimes prone to accidents, especially when he's thinking of one thing and doing another. He can also attract aggression sometimes (another good reason for learning boxing). His tendency to play devil's advocate can stir anger in people who don't realise he means no harm and he's probably been punched or slapped at least once.

He needs to take care of his hands and arms and he can do this by paying more attention to his actions. Learning to be present in the moment will help the Gemini man more than he wishes to admit or believe.

Mental

He lives in his thoughts. The world around him is a distant place because his real home and his real connections are all within him. He is the person who truly does fit into the saying, 'Still waters run deep'. His mind is his own form of magic wand.

Not very many people can win a mental contest with a Gemini. His mind is his most treasured asset and his deep desire to decode the meaning of life is his motivating force for researching and learning.

A Gemini man wonders about everything. His mental quest begins before he can even walk and as he grows up he asks questions like 'Why does the sky look blue?' and 'How do the bees know how to make honey?' By the time he's an adult, he's moved to a more complex line of questioning, but his childlike curiosity will forever serve him on his journey through life.

His mind never stops, even when he's sleeping, and he can exhaust himself with questions that he's not yet able to answer. A favourite pastime is to take a situation and consider every possible outcome using his mental sharpness together with his imagination. This game can go on for days if he permits it and ironically, while he's running through all the imaginable alternatives, he sometimes misses the actual outcome.

He has a brilliant sense of humour and is such a quick-thinking smooth talker he can convince you to change your lifelong political convictions while you're standing in line to vote.

Spiritual

The Gemini man's spiritual nature is captured by the vision of an angel on one shoulder and a devil on the other. At no time is his dual nature more perplexing than when it comes to making decisions concerning his spiritual belief system. After all, he's not a rule follower, but that doesn't mean he won't go to church on Sunday or if he's of a different faith, synagogue on Saturday.

For a non-conformist, he sometimes is a surprise package, especially when it comes to spiritual matters. He can be spiritual, but mock established religions because the two sides of his mind tell him that it's best to keep a foot in all camps.

He believes in heaven as much as he believes in hell and he's probably had a taste of both already. He likes to think of the afterlife as an opportunity to be many places at the same time and if it's true that angels can appear and disappear whenever they choose he respects and envies them as role models. He's fascinated by the utter devotion of those who belong to religious sects and admires their faith but he needs a storehouse of concrete evidence before he completely embraces anything that can't be seen, touched and tested.

His spiritual mission is to understand why he's here, where he's from and precisely where he's going. But his human nature is so good at controlling him that when he begins to make spiritual progress with these questions he's generally side-tracked. Still, if a Gemini directs his journey with the help of a wise mentor or teacher of truth he can rise beyond his mental constraints and see the light of his own soul.

•·•••••(The Gemini baby

This is the very busy, pushing, prodding cute baby of the zodiac. Its curious nature will keep you entertained and on the go.

Expect the unexpected with this baby while it is on its way into the world and after you take him or her home! There is nearly always some mystery or serendipitous situation surrounding the birth and babyhood of a Gemini. And you can't plan ahead with this birth or newborn because its whole destiny runs on a day-to-day approach to just about everything in life. Therefore 'Whatever happens, happens' is the no-rule rule with this baby at its birth.

While this infant loves everything to happen in a hurry, that doesn't mean it will necessarily make a speedy entry into this world. Therefore, you can't rely on calendars or other people's experiences when it comes to the birth of a little Gemini. It lives in its own unique realm and time frame.

This tiny one could delay its birth a little as though it is weighing up its options. Or it may start to be born in an absolute rush and then halfway through getting things in motion suddenly change its mind and seem to want to go back from where it came. You need to be prepared to be kept constantly in a state of vigilance with this birth and baby because it delights in surprises.

The Gemini baby is a natural communicator. Even while in the womb this baby is already going to be expressing itself in a Morse code, dots and dashes, kicks and wriggles, no straight line kind of way. Look for its messages and you'll find them in many forms and fashions. But also be prepared because this child will be masterful at giving out mixed messages. Its birth could even be the subject of headlines in the local papers in some way because the unusual destiny of this little soul naturally seems to attract conversation or interest from outside its own family group. This is an interesting baby and unusual or exciting conditions seem to occur when it's born.

As Gemini is the sign of the natural student in astrology, from the moment it is born the Gemini baby has a natural desire for exploration, adventure and for every possible kind of experience. This curious little bundle is always on the lookout for something new. He or she is likely to be very observant and notice things that other people don't even see. Its awareness is quite awesome and many parents of Geminis swear that their children seem to operate on a highly psychic level.

From the day it is born (and possibly well before), the Gemini baby is usually a fast learner. On all kinds of levels of perception, it has an ability to take everything in. Now I want to make it clear that this isn't meant to declare that the Gemini baby's aptitude or ability for fast learning or multi-level observation will always be apparent to you or to others. In fact, numerous Geminis who turned out to be geniuses in intelligence were actually thought to be a bit slow as infants and toddlers.

This baby has a unique mind and its intake and perceptions or reaction responses can be hidden from external view or from other people's senses. For all kinds of reasons the Gemini baby can be extremely difficult to analyse, understand or interpret. Remember this is the child that is masterful with mixed messages. Therefore when it has picked something up totally, it can still hold things back within itself. Apples are not always apples where the miniature Gemini is concerned.

Because of its curious nature, once this baby is mobile it will take off on one exploration after another — first crawling under the coffee table, then behind the china cabinet and off across the kitchen floor to retrieve one of the cat's toy mice, all in a matter of minutes. Therefore, as its caretaker you are going to need to consider carefully how you can do whatever it takes to protect this bundle of speedy curiosity from dangerous situations. This baby is a real hand-and-finger, push-and-pull type of explorer, and because it's a button pusher and a wire puller you need to pay special attention to taking every manner of safety precautions.

Born under Gemini this little one is the zodiac's mind-star and communicator (if it chooses to share this part of its internalised thinking side of its personality with you). As a baby, usually the Gemini will babble and gurgle to itself all the time and quickly learn to talk and once it can talk you can say goodbye to your cherished silent moments!

This baby — with or without a big vocabulary — tends to be a very active conversationalist. And as he or she grows into toddler and pre-school age this baby or child can often sleep best with soft music playing or some kind of soothing noise around it, meditative style (and it may feel more relaxed with the night-light left on). Being highly psychic, this baby is always tuned into the world around it and even when you're sure your little one is asleep they probably have one eye and one ear half open.

(The Gemini toddler through teen

> *Gemini children constantly wonder about things most people don't question in their entire lives! These kids are like miniature scientists with giant desires to test things and run experiments.*

The Gemini toddler is clearly in a class of his or her own, especially when it comes to curiosity and mischief. Parents of these children will tell you jokingly that they feel as if they 'got two kids in the shape of one'. That's not surprising, really, when you consider that Gemini's zodiac symbol is the Twins. Double the trouble and double the fun; your Gemini toddler will certainly entertain you and put you to the test on every level.

And once these kids are truly mobile — look out! This is a great time to take all of the little treasures and knick-knacks that you value and lock them up somewhere out of reach until Mr or Miss Curiosity is old enough to obey the 'look but don't touch' rule. This advice goes for all appliances and other household items that can prove to be dangerous in the hands of an exploring tot. While it's a bit of an effort, it's also extremely worthwhile for peace of mind to move anything that your child cannot safely play with so it's well out of his or her reach. If it's not under lock and key, it's considered fair game by a small, inquisitive Gemini.

Households with Gemini children are notorious for having special toddler gates to block off rooms, contraptions to child-proof the cabinets, safety plugs in all the electrical outlets and not a breakable item in sight! Otherwise, the parents of these adventurers spend the entire day saying 'No', 'Don't touch', and 'Be careful'.

At the same time, Gemini youngsters are wondering about things their parents may have never questioned in their entire life! These kids are like miniature scientists with giant desires to test things and run experiments.

'I wonder what the dog would look like in Mummy's high heels?' and 'I wonder if Daddy's new leather jacket will float, if I fill the bathtub the whole way to the top?' are on the list of less harmful questions — at least when it comes to personal safety. But the Gemini child doesn't exclude dangerous questions from his or her experimenting. These young would-be scientists want to know where the loose wire leads to, why the blender blades look invisible when they're moving at top speed and how the chain saw in the garage works. In other words, don't let a Gemini child out of your sight.

Once the Gemini child begins to talk it will be a bit easier to explain safety precautions and then you can enjoy safe explorations together. You'll also truly enjoy the talks you have with your young Gemini offspring and you have a rare opportunity to take a fresh look at the world through his or her wide eyes. And when this little one begins to expand its vocabulary you may be surprised at how quickly it learns and how much it loves to keep on talking.

Young Geminis adore playing with telephones, pretending they are talk show hosts and hostesses and carrying on both sides of their own conversations. They also have a natural ability to begin to learn a second language at an early age. And by the way, if you have a computer and are hooked up with one of the world-wide systems of communications, be sure you keep it a secret from your little Gemini or they may learn the facts of life in a computer 'chat room'.

Gemini children, even when they're sleeping, seem to almost buzz with nervous energy. The more they can channel and burn up this energy during the day the better they will sleep at night and the more even-tempered they will be. Otherwise, these kids can be very high strung and nervous.

They also appear to have shorter than average attention spans although this is not actually the case. If a Gemini is truly interested in something, it can occupy his or her mind and actions for a long time. But otherwise, it's on to make the next discovery or find the next new thing to touch, turn on, bang on or take apart.

When it's time for kindergarten or Year One, the Gemini generally adapts well, even if the teacher doesn't! But don't worry, any teacher with a few years' experience has dealt with plenty of Gemini children whether they realise it or not. The wise teacher will be sure to give the Gemini plenty to do and lots of things to think about so that his or her mind and body are occupied at all times.

So-called quiet time can be like torture to a young Gemini unless you give them a thought problem or riddle to silently work out while they are supposed to be silent. Quiet play things like modelling clay, crayons, construction paper and kaleidoscopes are lifesavers for the parents and teachers of Gemini children who desperately need some peace and quiet.

As the Gemini youngster discovers more creative outlets of expression, the incessant talking will slow down a bit and more energy will be channelled into other forms of activities. This is when you will really begin to see how very bright, artistic, alert and creative your child truly can be. Gemini children love to visit the 'hands-on' science museum and get a huge kick out of science kits complete with measuring devices, test tubes and stuff that bubbles and fizzes. Lots of Geminis really enjoy looking through microscopes and telescopes, and are really turned on by the idea of the microscopic world and far-reaching space with all its stars and planets.

As your Gemini child nears adolescence and the teenage years, be prepared for some long bouts with moodiness and sometimes sullen and uncooperative behaviour. The same person who used to want to know everything may go through a phase where they find almost nothing interesting. This is a sure sign of overload. The Gemini is most frustrated by having too much going on, or too little. The sometimes delicate nerves and emotions of the Gemini operate best on an even keel.

And don't be surprised or disappointed if your Gemini teenager is reluctant to make decisions or frequently changes his or her mind. Keep in mind that trying to force the issue rarely helps. And while it may be difficult for you as a parent to watch your son or daughter pass up a great opportunity because they can't make up their mind, or put it off so long that they miss a deadline, just remember these are the learning years and sometimes missing out on an opportunity early in life leads to a commitment on the part of the Gemini not to miss the boat somewhere down the road.

A Gemini on the verge of young adulthood is at the most likely age to show their rebellious side and make a statement of their own. They may choose a style of dressing that's off-the-wall or they may cut or dye their hair a shocking colour or get their nose pierced. It's pretty hard to predict with a Gemini.

Whatever they choose to do, the pleasure they receive from their rebellion will definitely be enhanced if they can upset your apple cart at the same time. Try to resist the urge to react to them in an emotional way and keep a level head so you can be on the lookout for more full-on signs of rebellion — like breaking the law in some fashion — that could lead to serious trouble.

The best advice for the parents of Gemini youth is to practise the art of loving them unconditionally no matter how far they stray from your own set of morals, ethics and life choices. Treat them with respect and show them genuine affection, especially when they act like they don't need you in any way, shape or form.

Basically, the more you love them as they are, the sooner they tend to swing back to some sort of middle ground where you can all truly enjoy each other again. Plus, it helps to remember that the Gemini growing pains and rebellion are important things for them to experience and will benefit them greatly as they begin to discover and pursue their inspired purpose in life.

CANCER

[22 june — 23 july]

cancer cancer cancer cancer cancer
cancer cancer cancer cancer cancer
cancer cancer cancer cancer cancer
cancer cancer cancer cancer cancer
cancer cancer cancer cancer cancer
cancer cancer cancer cancer cancer
cancer cancer cancer cancer cancer
cancer cancer cancer cancer cancer
cancer cancer cancer cancer cancer
cancer cancer cancer cancer cancer
cancer cancer cancer cancer cancer

element: water

planetary ruler: the moon

symbol: the crab

quality: cardinal (= activity)

colours: silver, blue

gem: pearl, moonstone

best companions: pisces and scorpio

strongest virtues: inner soul power,

intuition, open heart

traits to improve: negative thinking,

cynical attitude, lack of focus on important

everyday matters

deepest desire: to be loved, and to love in return

Cancer celebrities

John Farnham, Pamela Anderson Lee, the Dalai Lama, Tom Cruise, Lisa Rinna, Cat Stevens, Princess Diana, Camilla Parker-Bowles, Imelda Marcos, Harrison Ford, Tom Hanks, Meryl Streep, Carly Simon, Mel Brooks, Mike Tyson, O.J. Simpson, Dan Akroyd, Linda Ronstadt, the Sultan of Brunei, Sir Edmund Hillary, Nancy Reagan, Kevin Bacon, Donald Sutherland, Sylvester Stallone, Robin Williams, Bert Newton, Chris O'Donnell, Bryan Brown, Clyde Packer, Hermann Hesse (author), R. Buckminster Fuller, Cyndi Lauper, George Michael, John Cusack, Nelson Rockefeller, Liv Tyler, Deborah Harry, George W. Bush, Courtney Love, Giorgio Armani, Michael Flatley, David Hasselhoff, Nelson Mandela, Terence Stamp, Gina Lollobrigida, Yul Brynner, Brigitte Nielsen (ex-wife of Sylvester Stallone), Anthony Edwards, Anjelica Houston, Janet Leigh, Ringo Starr and Athena Starwoman.

[General outlook]

Life keeps getting better (even if more demanding) for your sign well into the millennium future. Like greeting an old friend, Cancers reach out and welcome the new millennium because intuitively you already sense that it is going to be an extremely educational, rewarding and fulfilling time for you. Your stars are on an upswing now, and new millennium magic is shining brightly upon your dreams, hopes and wishes. You are beginning a new cycle and a professional or personal win early into the new millennium will kick start this new and uplifting astrological phase.

New passions, interests and ideas compete for your attention throughout the new millennium. You are undergoing a type of emotional and psychological spring-cleaning and life is leading you on an exciting new journey. Remember that to make way for the new, it's necessary to sort through the old. Trust your instincts. Try not to hold on to outdated connections now. You have a tendency for sabotaging your own progress, simply because you attempt to take situations, attitudes, beliefs, attachments, relationships or possessions with you, to places in the future where they do not fit or belong! Your ideals and priorities are changing in the new millennium and what was once important to you is likely to seem trivial now. Be open to everything and let love, light and laughter seep into your life. The new millennium magic will bring you more happiness than you ever thought possible, if you believe in it and do not try to outsmart, outwit or out scheme it. Thinking you know better than the flow of fate and destiny will hold you back and sabotage your potential now.

Romance

Love and romance continue to be important for romantic Cancers as the new millennium dawns and takes on its continuing flow. The difference is, a recent break-up, reunion or change in the status or conditions surrounding your relationship has left you older, wiser and more mature (yet, hopefully not more cynical) concerning affairs of the heart.

You have learned that true happiness comes from within yourself, and to look for it elsewhere is unrealistic. Whatever path your heart has taken you down, you now benefit from the experience. Marriages blossom while single Cancers are hit by Cupid's arrow. Get ready to give and receive love in abundance, but love of a more healthy, independent and unique type than the love you had in the past.

Health

The idea of putting the past behind you and starting afresh applies also to your health and fitness. Many Cancers kick their cosmic health goal by giving up smoking or another bad lifestyle habit. Remember, too, the wisdom of listening to your instinct in matters of health and wellbeing. Muster your self-discipline – with little effort you can make leaps and bounds in your wellbeing and physical fitness and quickly be on the road to shining good health in the new millennium.

Finance

With all kinds of expansion surrounding you (and plenty of dreams that you wish to fulfil), the stars reveal that cash flow is your biggest challenge as the new millennium gets underway. It's possible that when you most need cash on hand, you'll discover that your money is tied up in a fund, trust or other investment program. The key to dealing with your topsy-turvy financial life is patience and planning. Plan your budget carefully and ensure that you have some cash available readily on hand for that unexpected 'rainy day'.

Career

The new millennium ushers in fresh energy on the professional front. Many career opportunities are coming your way and happily you now receive recognition for your hard (and often unseen) work of the past. The first few years of the new millennium are an ideal time for promotion or to ask for a raise or promotion. Be bold. Remember, until you ask you may not receive. Also do be prepared to put yourself up front in your career sector. It is possible you have invested a great deal of time recently grooming others rather than focusing on your own advancement.

[Millennium wildcards to watch for]

You are one of the most resilient signs of the zodiac. Although your staying power is legendary, as the new millennium dawns you have less patience for people and projects not in line with your true path. Cancers undergo enormous inner changes, and this can be confusing for themselves and others. In many respects, what served you before is no longer right (possibly your job, relationship, financial or health situation). Let your heart — not your head — guide you now. There's never been a better time to make your dreams come true than the new millennium, but this will only occur where you hold your faith, and remain true to your dreams, too.

Understanding Cancer

Operating under the powerful ever-changing ebbs, flows, phases and faces of the moon, you Cancers are the most sensitive, changeable and, therefore, unpredictable sign of the zodiac.

You are one of the zodiac's greatest mysteries because your ever-changing thoughts and moods keep everyone guessing, even you! Even those who have known you for your entire life can't quite figure you out, and most Cancers (although they may not admit it) quite enjoy having things that way. While you may sometimes complain, 'no one understands me', you enjoy being a little eccentric. You like being unpredictable and the mere idea of behaving the same way, day in and day out, doesn't really appeal too much to your highly imaginative nature.

The world is truly your stage and you are great at playing many different roles. You can be an enchanting and alluring sex pot one moment, an elusive, detached hermit the next, a show-off, a shy type or an intimidating, powerful force to be reckoned with — all in the same day.

I am a Cancer and when I was a child, my mother (who was also an astrologer) used to recite a poem to me, which she believed summed up my moon-guided nature, usually when I was behaving like a spoiled brat. Mum used to say, 'There was a little girl who had a little curl, right in the middle of her forehead. When she was nice, she was very, very nice, but when she was bad she was horrid.'

Now just as the moon can be jolly when it is full, and rather intimidating when it is at its lowest ebb, I think Cancers can run hot and cold too (and be nice and not so nice at times as well). As a Cancer, most times you are nice; however there are certain emotional or other buttons within you, that when pushed, can switch you from nice to mean in an instant. Anything and everything can affect you, for both better or worse, because you are one of the more sensitive and easily affected signs of the entire zodiac.

Why are you so super-sensitive? Well, your actions and feelings revolve around and are affected by everything and anything. It may be the position of the moon, the planets, the weather, the novel you're currently reading, the movie you just saw, and possibly something as obscure as what side of the bed you happened to get out of this morning. It may be something grand or small that hits your emotional chords. However, because you are like a supersonic emotional laser, a whole conglomeration of worldly and intangible situations sometimes need to be in specific places for you to resonate in harmony with everything within and around you.

If one little butterfly flaps its wings in the wrong direction, that can set you spinning. When the cosmic pieces do not fit together well, that is when you can read the riot act and stir up all kinds of trouble.

Don't kid yourself, Cancers, that you are such a softy either (as many astrology books do tend to make you out to be something of a passive, shy sign). For a somewhat timid sign, it is amazing how much magnificent power resides within you. You Cancers accomplish some remarkable goals and accomplishments throughout the course of your lives and many Cancers make a global impact. Just look at Cancers Princess Diana, Imelda Marcos, Sir Edmund Hillary, Nelson Mandela, and the Dalai Lama as examples. These Cancer individuals certainly have made their imprint on the world.

When you want something, you usually get it and your sign has the strength, conviction and passion to surmount the insurmountable and achieve remarkable success. However, your path is not necessarily an easy one because there is always a multitude of factors influencing you at every moment. Your ruling planet, the moon, ensures that your emotional world is kept in a constant state of flux and for that reason your feelings can sometimes take over and run your life. However, those Cancers who learn to balance their emotions and rely upon their instincts and intuition to guide their daily decisions often leave a lasting legacy.

As you are such a complex and unusual personality this generally provides you with enormous insights into what makes other people tick. Because you are intimately familiar with the hidden aspects of yourself, you know that most people and situations are not what they appear to be on the surface, but ironically, few people know this about you! In fact, your Crab sign of the zodiac is often misunderstood and thought of as a thick-shelled, side-stepping loner, although nothing could be further from the truth.

You actually care tremendously about others and are one of the zodiac's most nurturing of signs. It is just that your tender heart needs a tough shell to protect it. Your outer (sometimes hard to penetrate) shell protects many things about and within you — like your vulnerabilities, your strengths and all of your secret desires, plans and ambitions. You have a very private side to yourself (just like the hidden side of the moon that rules your sign) that you keep tucked safely inside and hidden from popular view.

Nevertheless, when you aren't wearing one of your many masks, or keeping your distance from the world around you, usually your eyes or your facial expressions can be read by anyone watching you. Cancers can say an awful lot without saying a word — they say it with the flash of a smile, the hint of a frown, or the glare of indignity — just think of Cancer Princess Diana's incredibly expressive presence.

Whether you realise it or not, you reveal the most about yourself by your posture, moods, attitudes and levels of confidence. But since you operate under the powerful ever-changing ebbs, flows, phases and faces of the moon, your feelings fluctuate constantly. Even if someone catches a glimpse of your emotions from your facial expression or body language, very few people know what the next minute will bring, and no one knows what's really going on beneath your surface.

For that reason, many people are surprised when they read astrology books to actually find out that Cancers are the most sensitive of all the zodiac signs. Probably when you are dealing with superstar type Cancers like Tom Cruise, Harrison Ford, Robin Williams, Courtney Love or Pamela Anderson Lee it is hard to realise just what a vulnerable, sensitive person you are dealing with, because Cancers are quite magnificent when it comes to putting on a bold front.

Not every Cancer is cut out to be a superstar (usually these ones are born closer to a full moon than a new moon) but when you are you shine brightly (most of the time anyway). Because you are so sensitive, some of you Cancers attempt to lead quiet, reflective lives, but this is usually not what the universe has in store for you.

Whether you are in the spotlight, or hiding from it, a Cancer's life is often filled with drama, emotion, jealousy, temptation, turmoil and triumph. You attract extremes because you are quite naturally an extremist yourself. Because of your ups and downs, dealing with you or getting to know you can sometimes be a true test of patience for others. In fact, you can be one of the more difficult of the zodiac signs to truly get to know.

As much as your powerful emotional connections to the world around you and to your inner churnings can be a trial to you (and to others around you), this inner ocean of emotion is also your great gift and sometimes source of pleasure. Being so attuned to your feelings gives you the power to explore every range or spectrum of emotions and feelings.

Your feelings make you highly creative and super-imaginative. If you are an artist, a writer or an actor, you can have a powerful ability to express the depths of feelings or expression through your craft.

And, where you can manage it, tapping into your inner world is time well spent because once you have tapped into it, your ability to sense things in the air and delve deep inside your own inner resources, highlights and shows you your innate psychic abilities. You are one of the most tuned into, psychic and intuitive signs of the zodiac. Many of you Cancers take your intuition and psychic senses for granted. You do this because you mistakenly assume that everybody else feels things as intensely and as deeply as you do, but this is not the case.

Because you have so much wealth of feeling to call upon, you are usually highly creative in unusual ways and often project the confident appearance that you're right on top of things, when in fact, you aren't. You are much more vulnerable and sensitive than you often seem. Most people would be surprised to know that behind your confident smile or demeanour there's a little voice shouting 'help!'

You rarely ask anyone for help. Surprisingly you Cancers can be a very independent sign, when you choose to be. However, if and when you need a helping hand, a shoulder to lean on (or even cry on), or a tender word from others, somehow whatever you need seems to magically manifest for you. Others are powerfully attracted to you, and your projects or causes in life, because there is something magical about you — and this serves you in your moments of need.

Usually, life does tend to pick you up and dust you off when you need it, possibly because like the moon you are a reflection of everything and everyone around you, and if you are allowed to lose your lustre, it isn't a great reflection of the world at all. Others like to make you happy, because when you are happy, somehow this makes other people happy, too! Your moods are infectious in more ways than one.

Every day and night, in all kinds of ways, is truly a multi-dimensional emotional experience for you. However, not all of your emotional moods, rides or experiences are enjoyable. You can go through enormous anxieties, apprehensions and pain, because you tend to swing back and forth like a pendulum. This 'tick-tock' behaviour, affects the way you feel about yourself, others and the world around you. It also means you start things, and then do not get to finish them. There are times when you feel higher than the clouds and other times when you feel lower than the furthest depths of the ocean. Therefore, you do go through more than your fair share of good and bad days, but just as the moon renews itself, given some time you eventually return to your brightest side again.

You complete this process by filling yourself up with positive feelings after you have been through the blues for a while. Because of the extreme nature of your sign, you spend a lot of time feeling totally happy, or completely sad. Your true self exists within the emotional realm that rules within you. Your emotions are always your life's greatest teachers. Through the extreme range of your feelings, you learn about life, love, yourself, others and destiny.

Tuning into your inner depths and expressing it outwardly can be quite a task. It is also likely to involve you in some self-reflection and soul-searching. This inward journeying (and attempting to express what you have discovered on this journey outwardly), can consume a great deal of your time.

Every now and again (possibly when the moon is full and the universal flow of emotions is running rampant) you Cancers sometimes surprise yourselves and others with your volatility. When this occurs, your weird and wonderful ways can be unleashed without limits or boundaries.

On certain earth-tingling moments like these, your 'off the wall' behaviour can be quite an amazing experience to behold and go through. This is when you knowingly or unconsciously turn up the cosmic volume on your multi-levelled personality gauge; throw your abundant personalities into unlimited high gear, express your shadow-side and dance the wild fandango with your eccentric moods or fantasies.

When you go through this kind of 'living the wild life' experience, you have the courage to become anyone you want to be, say anything you want, and act any way you desire (often this is something that can be quite a turnaround from your usual behaviour). You can be a true adventurer or out-of-control person during these times. You often do things that are actually more out of line than in line now. Great creativity is born from this inner, somewhat wild-child, creative side to your character. On the negative side, some highly destructive or self-sabotaging behaviour may come, too.

Whether you are being creative or destructive, playing out all of the roles that you have within you is part of your destiny in life. As a child and even when you are grown-up, you Cancers usually love dressing up, and playing different parts. Clothes can often become costumes to you, and what you wear can affect your behaviour quite dramatically.

Wearing certain colours can sometimes noticeably affect your moods and many Cancers have shoes, underwear or outfits that they consider lucky pieces of clothing. This can be confusing to others because since your external appearance is something you tend to put together to create a certain effect, your image or look can be a huge misrepresentation of who you truly are.

I remember years ago, a long-haired Pisces surfer boyfriend of mine said that what I looked like was absolutely different from who I really was. I got what he meant when one night when I was all 'put together' in one of my more seductive styled outfits (in my younger days I wore the shortest mini-skirt, combined with a brief top), my boyfriend claimed that I was false advertising because of the way I was dressed. It may sound like he was being mean-spirited, but, in reality, he was pointing out something that was quite enlightening to me. He was right. We Cancers do tend to falsely advertise ourselves in all kinds of ways. We give out many mixed messages with our appearance, emotions, changing opinions and our actions, too. In addition, we can tend to be star dramatists and performers when we want to get our point across, or the full moon is stirring up our inner emotional ocean.

Underneath the self-confident exterior you usually display, you still need the biggest pats on the back and the most loving reassurance. You get tired of lots of things but you never get tired of true appreciation and genuine affection. And when you're not getting enough reassurance or when you're feeling pushed beyond your limits, you really can be quite a crabby mean-spirited Crab.

No one can send a chill through the room quite like a Cancer who is having a bad day. But, by the same token, you can do the reverse. On a good day, you can turn the world on with a smile. No wonder those around you can hold their breaths in anticipation, as they wait to see whether you are going to smile or snarl at them.

You don't mean to be tough with others, as you actually have a gentle and kindly heart, it is just that sometimes you do tend to get lost in your own mind-space and forget that by being in a bad mood (or being withdrawn) you are affecting others. You've been gifted with the ability to appreciate the peaks and valleys of human experience and this can make you too connected to others at times, and also make them too connected to you.

Your life is coloured with an emotional richness and you're strongly affected by all the various vibrations and energy in your environment. You can enjoy more pleasure and endure more pain in a month than some people feel in a lifetime. You do try to be good and to rise above your moon-ruled unsteady emotions but often this is no easy task because the moon has such a powerful, magnetic hold on Cancers that it's not easily broken. Remember that like the moon in its spiral dance across the sky, you must circle through darkness and light, thunderstorms and rainbows before you reflect your fullest, brightest light. One of the greatest things you can do is love yourself for who you are, and realise you are meant to be a contrary type of person. It is the way you learn and go through your life's lessons.

When you feel gloomy or unloved, you often go on shopping sprees. For some Cancers buying shoes can be one of your biggest indulgences. Some say shoes are so important to you because you are so up in the air with your head filled with fantasies and dreams that shoes are the item of adornment that keep you firmly connected to planet Earth.

Like Cancer Imelda Marcos, I had so many pairs of shoes at one time that my husband, John, said I must have been a centipede in my past life and still thought I had a hundred pairs of feet to buy shoes for. But your shoes only represent a fragment of your prized possessions in life.

Whether you collect dolls, costume jewellery, antiques, stuffed bears or porcelain pieces you love your possessions and your closets are often brimming over with various treasures and bits and pieces. Some of you are such avid collectors that you are always looking for more storage space to hold your treasured acquisitions.

When it comes to possessions, relationships and memories, you tend to be a clinger at times. As your astrological symbol the Crab so admirably and stubbornly demonstrates, you'll gladly sacrifice one of your pincers before you'll let go of one of your treasures. But remember Cancer, a real crab grows a new pincer to replace the one it lost, and you won't, so choose your battles (and your possessions) carefully.

Making careful decisions can be one of your greatest challenges because your head and your heart are often in conflict with each other.

I believe that the degree to which you experience this conflict, as well as your temperament, personality and emotional tendencies stem from, or are birthed from, the phase the moon was in when you were born. That is why a Cancer born at full moon is quite different from one born on a new moon, or the phases in between.

The moon phase and whether the moon was harmoniously or discordantly connected to other planets at the time of your birth, all influence your emotional range and the degree of your mood swings. If you were born under a more discordant moon aspect, you are one of the more emotionally charged up, over-reactive types of Cancer and your mood swings can spin and twist you around in crazy circles.

However, if you were born on a more favourable moon phase, your feelings are generally more balanced and harmonious and you experience less dramatic emotional 'tick-tocks'.

Many Cancers fit in somewhere between the two extremes, in which case you have fluctuating emotional energy flows. Because you operate under different emotional chords, your reactions and responses are often the opposite of those around you. Sometimes, when others laugh, you cry. Or, when others feel sad about something, you can only see the bright side.

Nearly all you Cancers love the extroverted side to yourselves and are somewhat afraid of your own inner demons or shadows. You often wish to be brave and fearless, but when things are really tough going, you love to retreat (and hide in your shell) rather than face problems. While living on an emotional edge can be fun, it is also extremely draining. That's why one of your favourite pastimes and means of escape is sleep. And sleep is very good for you, too. It helps you release many of your deepest emotions and relaxes your troubled mind. Sleeping and daydreaming can help you with your day-to-day decision-making because they allow your mind to catch up with your emotions and provide you with a little more consistency in your thoughts and feelings.

When operating on everyday levels, consistency is often one of your major problems. For many Cancers, making plans in advance can be difficult because you cannot be certain that a plan or arrangement you make today, will feel comfortable or sit well with you when the time to live up to that plan or arrangement comes around. Having ongoing relationships can also be testing for Cancers. You are always worried others are going to see through you and that they won't like what they see. You often undervalue yourself and underestimate your own special brand of sex appeal.

Confidence can be something you have in short supply, but in truth, you have many reasons to feel confident. Most Cancers have warm and loyal hearts and you are all operating under the magical lunar forces of the moon, so you are among the world's greatest and most mysterious magicians. After all, your ruler, the moon, is the most sung about, talked about, creativity inspiring and mysterious heavenly body of all.

On the other hand, all that sparkling moon magic has its dark side and you can be extremely stormy and headstrong, too (for such a mild type of sign). When you don't like what is happening, feel hurt, misused or don't trust someone, you can break all the polite rules of your sign, stomp the expectations others have of you into the ground and grind them into dust.

Amazingly, you throw out your psychic thunderbolts in such a way that you can almost make the sound of a thunderclap with your mind. Like Scarlett O'Hara in *Gone with the Wind*, you stamp your foot, say 'La-De-Dah', and without warning you either close up your heart's drawbridge on those around you, or wage some other form of psychic or emotional war. Many times when you throw one of your tizzy fits you leave others puzzled.

Even when you rock the boat and shake things up, you still generally manage to get away with it somehow. Like the moon moves through its phases so comfortably and easily, you can do the same. Others often come to expect strange or unusual behaviour from you — as if it is okay for you to act oddly or inappropriately, even thought it's not okay for others!

The way you can change your own life and the lives of those around you on a whim is really quite extraordinary. Should others try to get away with some of the things you do on a regular basis they would never succeed. And no one can make a fuss or throw a tantrum like you can when you're really upset or passionate about something or someone.

When you are upset, jealous, overloaded, feel used, or are on the psychic warpath, Attila the Hun would turn and run from you. And when you flex your psychic muscles, you often get what you want from others.

Your psychic senses together with your emotions make you a powerful negotiator (and manipulator), whether you admit it to yourself or not. As far as using emotional blackmail goes, you Cancers are generally the true experts of the zodiac, beginning from your day of birth. Little wonder that whatever Cancer wants, Cancer usually gets! You are the zodiac's most successful weaver of invisible magic. But also you do need to be most careful when it comes to choosing what you wish for, because you just might get it!

Cancer is a Water sign

To your advantage, you have great emotional understanding and intellectual comprehension beyond the realm of many people. You tune into whatever is important to you when discussing things with others, or when sensing what they are feeling (or not saying). When you look like you're politely listening, you are actually filing away the bits and pieces of information that you think you can use in the future. You're also more insightful than people give you credit for being and this often works well to your advantage.

Others feel a little off-guard when you are around, and this gives you a kind of mysterious or intriguing energy field. You have an off-the-planet kind of feel about you and a deep sense of cosmic awareness even if it's on the inner or subconscious levels. You understand that true love is a state of being, not just an emotion, and you believe it's possible to find true love in every lifetime.

To your disadvantage, you sometimes overreact to emotional issues and lose your temper big time, and this can cause more problems than it solves. You have such powerful emotions that they can take over your better judgment at times and literally run your life. When you feel depressed, you're really miserable and your dark mood can spread like a rain cloud over everyone who is around you. On your worst days even strangers a block away can feel your gloomy outlook and reach for their umbrellas to weather the internal storm.

[Insights into your sign]

The bright side: You have fantastic fantasies, and you have the go-getter nature and savvy to turn these fantasies into realities. One of your greatest strengths is your deep understanding of human nature. You know what other people are thinking (or intending), sometimes even before they have had the conscious thought themselves.

The shadow: You can get so caught up in your emotions that they sway and even dominate your decision-making. At times, you're so physically overwhelmed by your own feelings (or the strong vibrations of the people around you) that you walk away from unique opportunities.

Characteristics >	Benefits >	Drawbacks >
Charming	Well-liked	Manipulative
Competitive	Successful	Attract rivals
Confident	Self-assured style	Intimidating
Crabby	Powerful self-defence	Unfairly lash out
Creative	Unique expression	Too much going on
Emotional	Intense feelings	Wild mood swings
Imaginative	Creative vision	Over-reactive
Insecure	Strong outer shell	Fear being unloved
Intuitive	Active inner voice	Irrational
Moody	Mysterious	Hard to live with
Motherly	Generous nurturing	Controlling
Naive	Wide-eyed wonder	Easy target
Patient	Hard working	Procrastinate
Protective	Warrior's inner strength	Won't let go
Receptive	Open to new ideas	Brain noise
Sensitive	Depth of emotions	Often feel sad
Shy	Beguiling	Appear aloof
Sympathetic	Soft heart	Take on others' pain
Tenacious	Staying power	Fight unnecessary battles
Understanding	Learn from others	Take on others' dramas
Vulnerable	Others help you	Become dependent

[Looking beneath the surface of your sign]

You often pretend to feel one way, when you feel quite different, but you cannot keep up the performance forever. You are one of those people whose eyes reveal their moods, secrets, and fears. You are enormously overly sensitive. Like the elephant, you never forgive or forget, and if anyone does you wrong, generally you extract your revenge, one way or another.

When you feel all alone, misunderstood or unloved, Cancer, you can throw yourself the most melancholy pity party in the zodiac. You can have a tendency to wallow in your own gloom, reliving the events that wounded your sensitive heart and exaggerating them with each passing day. You can hide away for days on end, building your fortress instead of reaching out and asking for a lift from a friend.

Your intuition knows you're over-reacting but when your emotions override your intuition you can quickly get carried down the river of darkness. It's true that you have more of an emotional battle to wage than most, but you also have more awareness.

You focus on all the things that could or may go wrong and generally tend to think too much and make mountains out of molehills.

[How to tune into your sign's powers]

> *Explore and expand upon your fantasies because your fantasies are what make you so unique.*
>> *Love your emotions, they provide you with a wonderful window through which to view the world.*
> *Trust your intuitive voice.*

· · • • • • (The Cancer woman

Grab your parachute because this woman will fly you to the peak of ecstasy and drive you crazy enough to make you jump off.

She is one of the most feminine signs of all the zodiac women. Her ability to be so naturally feminine is often her most special and unique power. With the feminine wiles to support and drive her, no wonder the Cancer woman often leads a charmed life. From the day she's born she has 'something special' about her. She rules over her family like a little princess expressing her heart's desires with her dancing eyes and accepting her attention and gifts with gracious smiles. (Princess Diana gave the world a splendid example of the regal opportunities that Cancer females can attract — for better and for worse.)

Because Ms Cancer draws from the most feminine of instincts, she can also be complex, stubborn, wilful and manipulative. She is capable of being quite ruthless when she has her own fixed agenda (even as a child). However, it is this diversity of personal, powerful (and often hidden) charms that make her a force to be reckoned with. It goes without saying that as she navigates her way through life Ms Cancer often becomes a good businesswoman and a skilled negotiator (on many different levels) as well.

In her own quiet fashion, she soaks up the limelight. She doesn't necessarily wear red or put on glitz or glitter, but she manages to somehow look like she is standing out in the crowd anyway (look at Cancer Meryl Streep as an example). Her mysterious deeper side intrigues people and captivates those around her. It also lands her loads of attention. She knows how to make others feel loved and appreciated, too. Because she tunes into others, this reflects back on to her. Once touched by her, others frequently go out of their way to help and assist her. She makes a great friend, a terrific psychologist and a good listener. Her sensitivity and patient understanding helps others to open up and discover more of themselves.

She sometimes doesn't operate too well in the everyday world, so she relies heavily on her fantasies to carry her through life. She is a moon goddess and her feelings and confidence can rise and fall with the tides. Her emotional swings can drain her and she often feels like invisible strings are yanking her around.

Modesty aside though, Ms Cancer is often tougher than she gives herself credit for. When put to a test or challenge it is amazing how she can rally and triumph over any difficulty. When she needs to be, she is the weaver of magic spells, the heart stirrer, the ingénue and the wise one all rolled up into one. She is also the great zodiac seductress who, when she wants to, can make men surrender their good sense, their hearts (even when their hearts are promised to someone else) and their souls to her.

Having two Cancer women in love with him, Prince Charles (Scorpio) was moonstruck. Princess Diana and Camilla Parker Bowles are both Cancers — moon maidens. When it comes to feminine wiles, romance, love and seduction, Cancer women are brilliant strategists. They flex their emotional muscles in the fields of romantic exchanges. And often they win the man of their dreams (even if he later turns out to be the man in their nightmares).

When love goes wrong, her fragile ego suddenly appears. Nobody beats herself up as much as a Cancer woman with a broken heart. The only cure for her broken heart is to replace an old love with a new love. The men Ms Cancer is involved with at any given time often separate the different chapters of her life. Cancer women sometimes have several children by different fathers, as the chapters of life unfold.

When it comes to relationships, Ms Cancer doesn't have ones that are usual in any way. In fact, love and sex don't necessarily go together for Ms Cancer. Being a complicated woman, she can sometimes feel physically attracted to someone she isn't in love with, and fall in love with someone she doesn't necessarily want to make love to all the time. Monica Lewinsky was born right on the cusp of Cancer and Leo. Although technically a Leo, she has a lot of Cancerian characteristics, and a romantic, soft, clingy side to her that is definitely Cancerian.

Naturally Ms Cancer's ideal relationship is a combination of love as well as sex, but life often turns topsy-turvy for her, where relationships are concerned. Even though she can be quite seductive when she wants to be, the role of femme fatale or seductress is usually something she only conjures up if on stage or for rare, special, magical meetings and occasions.

While she can be the great goddess of sex now and again, don't ask her to play that role consistently because she usually can't. Seduction is part of a magical feminine chemistry that she can tap into. However, being the seductress is not a role that she can easily portray all the time. It takes a number of special ingredients for her to be a sexual magnet — like the right partner combined with the right moon phase, the right sexual chemistry and the right environment. She also has to think that she looks pretty and be in the right mood to take on this role.

There are too many parts and sides to her multi-dimensional character to allow this one role of seductress the chance to rise and shine above all the others in a consistent form. Therefore, as much as Ms Cancer loves to have men worshipping at her sexual altar (Cancer Pamela Anderson is a great example of this), she only has fleeting insights, or access, to the possibilities this sexual charisma affords her. That is why playing the seductress (although she has this seductive aspect strongly within her and may even make a living out of it in some form or fashion) possibly does not happen as frequently in her life as Ms Cancer would love it to.

[How Cancer women operate]

Social

Sometimes she's the earth mother, sometimes she's the caretaker of others and other times she's the dreamweaver. She loves to have people around her, but only the right people. She is the kind who comes to your door to visit carrying gifts and probably a gift that you really love, as well. She'll play baby-sitter to your kids and she'll maybe even help with your housework.

She won't want to do this if she doesn't feel like it. Only ask for something from Ms Cancer after you've found out in advance what space or mood she's in. Remember her moods rule her. So as long as you're in tune with her emotions you are certain to remain friends indefinitely. Step out of tune with her moods and you could face the wrath of Medusa. If anyone could turn you to stone with a flash of her eyes, it's Ms Cancer on a bad day. But on a good day, no one can make as many people smile and feel good about themselves as a Cancer.

When she's happy and looking forward to a night on the town she can be absolutely radiant in her splendour, especially when she's looking for love or is in love. She can slip into a dream, colour it with feminine softness and tie it all together with a moonbeam. Ms Cancer can dress like a kaleidoscope. She'll put on every colour at once. Baubles, bangles and beads were made for her (and if she can afford it, diamonds can truly be this girl's best friend).

Being an extremist, she'll either dress in her 'cleaning the house clothes' or in all-out head-to-toe style. She often owns wardrobes crammed with clothes and shoes, but still has nothing to wear. As I pointed out before, Cancer women adore shoes and collect them. It's no surprise that Imelda Marcos is a Cancer. But we can't be too hard on the female Crab, after all — in her mind — she has eight feet.

Keep in mind that no matter what she's wearing, it is no indication of who she truly is. Ms Cancer is certainly one person you cannot judge by her appearance. If you really want to get to know her, it takes time, but eventually you'll see that she has a long list of wonderful qualities. A Cancer woman is patient, understanding and loyal. She probably still has at least one friend from her childhood, collects people like treasures and has a hard time letting go. She gives a lot of herself to her friends and she generally expects a lot in return.

For all her independence, the Cancer woman still likes to be spoiled and she can be strongly affected by her circle of friends. She's easily influenced by her associates' habits and moods and often reflects whatever they're feeling. She simply can't stand to be criticised, ridiculed or rejected and she doesn't like to see those things happen to anyone else either. A Cancer will courageously come to the rescue of someone who she thinks is being hurt or picked on. She's one of the biggest 'rescuers' of the zodiac.

But as helpful as she can be, she can also be very distant, petty and aloof at times. When she's really tired she can be crabby and irritable and nearly impossible to deal with. Don't take it personally; she just needs a short break or a mini-retreat. When she's overworked herself or when her sensitive emotions have been trampled on she withdraws into herself for a while. Give her a little time before you rush in to cheer her up. Then, after a day or two, show up at her door with her favourite flowers and a big saucepan of homemade soup.

Love and family

Grab your parachute because this woman will fly you to the peaks of ecstasy and drive you crazy enough to make you consider jumping off. The steamy and dreamy rewards you receive will make up for your occasional skydiving adventures though. She follows the moon through its cycles, keeping all of her secrets — and those of lots of other people — in the dark.

If you can give her true emotional security by promising to love her forever and meaning it, she'll take you on a mystical, magical carpet ride of your wildest fantasies and dreams. But be warned, a Cancer woman has high expectations and she has a tendency to put the man she's infatuated with on a pedestal. If he eventually falls off the pedestal, then he discovers that the old adage, 'Hell hath no fury like a woman scorned', was certainly written about a Cancerian.

She needs a mate who is secure, tolerant and has an understanding sense of humour. She won't tolerate criticism or cruelty and if you reject or embarrass her she'll fade out of your life like a falling star. And once that happens you will be hard pressed to convince her that you're worth a second chance.

To win her heart, wine and dine her, entertain her, make her laugh and walk with her hand in hand in the full moon's light. That's when you'll really see her shine as she translates the messages written in the stars. Her heart is most open when the moon is full and her radiance will take your breath away.

When it comes to relationships, the most beloved word in a Cancer woman's vocabulary is 'Mrs'. She doesn't like to be single and if she is single, every new man she meets under any conditions at all (to repair the phone, to visit the people next door, to sell insurance), opens up the possibility that she could be meeting Mr Right. She spends most of her single days in anticipation of 'Him' showing up.

When Mr Right does turn up (sooner or later she settles for someone who seems to love her the way she wants to be loved) Ms Cancer (now Mrs Cancer) is most fulfilled by a mate who has vision, inspiration, wisdom and purpose. He needs to be strong in his convictions and beliefs and secure enough to accept her potential rejection of both. It takes a genius to understand her every mood and a speed reader to scan her changing emotions. But if you're willing to shower her with your love and devotion and wrap her in soft, fluffy clouds of frequent reassurance, she may let you slide on some of the other requirements. She will insist, however, that you learn her moon dance and you'll be glad you did.

She's not always the easiest person to live with but she gives a great performance and is never boring. She can be as naive as Little Red Riding Hood on her way to her grandmother's house, innocently stopping to talk to a strange wolf or two along the way. And she can be as wise as a prophet, looking deeply into your eyes to read your heart.

If she reads loyalty and devotion, she won't mind when you go off to do your own thing. She knows you'll be back. A Cancer woman can't help but nurture people. If she's a mother, she's Supermum, always a loving intuitive step ahead of her children. If she doesn't have kids, she's superwoman flying about taking care of her lover and her friends.

Career

A Cancer woman's imagination and creativity blossom in her work. She loves positions that encourage self-expression and offer a variety of responsibilities. She works well in a relaxed atmosphere, either alone or with a small number of people who are charged with creative energy. She thrives on novelty but knows that constant change rocks even the biggest of boats. She is motivated by her desire to polish her talents and she also enjoys making and spending money. She expects to be appreciated in her work and her pay cheque will need to adequately reflect her worth. She can handle pressure for short spurts but she's better off in a career that's moderate to low stress. A Cancer makes a wonderful writer, actress, singer, painter, teacher or anything else that gives her an outlet for the depth of her expression. Cancers make great counsellors and advice-givers. Being a Water sign, some Cancers are drawn to professions that are on or near the sea. Ms Cancer also excels in occupations that focus on women or women's products, particularly the world of high fashion. And nearly all moon children are fascinated with the sciences of astrology and stargazing.

Financial

Ms Cancer has a good chance to make a lot of money throughout her life, but first she'll have to believe she can. Once she believes in her money-making powers, money will practically roll in with the tide and land at her feet. Some Cancer women are so financially blessed they can easily save or invest half of their income. At least a quarter of a financially successful Cancer's wealth will probably come from high interest investments and from the stock exchange. She has an ability to accurately predict coming trends and fads and she often makes a small fortune by marketing one of her inspired ideas or products.

Regardless of where she makes her money, she's better off hiring someone to manage her accounts and book-keeping because she usually considers this work tedious and sometimes ignores it altogether. Once a Cancer discovers the pleasures and comforts of wealth, she seeks more and more of this green-spun security blanket. She wants to make enough to save for a rainy day and have plenty left over to indulge herself by taking exotic holidays, checking into the finest luxury spas and chatting with her long distance friends for hours. She also loves to lavish on those she adores all the best that money can buy.

Physical

She alters her appearance as frequently as she changes her expression. One minute she's a wide-eyed innocent, the next she's an eyelash-batting flirt. But she's always mesmerising and like fine wine, age improves her.

Cancers are very sensitive to the environment and can suffer from stress-related health conditions that are often difficult to diagnose. She burns up a lot of energy worrying and processing her emotional dramas and it takes her longer to refill her energy reserves then it takes most people. When she's unhappy, her weight will either go up or down depending on her individual personality and the moon's position in its cycle.

Getting into tiptop shape can be difficult for a Cancer and pushing herself too hard can lead to serious health problems. Instead, she might consider making gentle activity a part of her day to help maintain her strength and boost her immunity. She's probably not much for hard-core fitness training but there's a good chance she loves to swim, likes to ice skate or fancies dancing. She also benefits from short, brisk walks, deep massages and stress-reducing yoga sessions.

As for potential health problems, her stomach and breasts are the most sensitive parts of her body. She should avoid heavy foods when under stress or shortly before going to bed. Meals should be small and frequent and she shouldn't combine more than three or four different foods at one sitting. She also should make it a habit to drink at least half a gallon of pure water every day.

When a Cancer woman is experiencing a physical low she can allow herself to sleep as long as she needs to, but she should also listen to classical music, watch a funny movie and spend time in meditation. Moderate exercise, light eating, adequate sleep and sweet dreams help keep a Cancer feeling her best.

Mental

The moon heightens Cancer's dual nature and gives her the pain and the pleasure of seeing the world from her emotional side and her intellectual side — sometimes at the same time. When a Cancer woman realises her emotional response is clouding an issue, she can usually take a step back and analyse the situation with her head. That's when she makes her most intelligent decisions, but sometimes her emotions overrule.

She's charmingly clever in her thinking and imaginative in her solutions and ideas. Many Cancers are finding success through the Internet; selling their creativity on-line and making worldwide connections without having to leave the comforts of home. She also has a wicked sense of humour based on her keen observation of human nature. If Cancer can avoid self pity when things don't work out the way she expects and resist blaming life for her problems and stress, she's a step ahead of herself and that's exactly where she likes to be.

She faces her biggest mental challenges in life at times when she buys into her own vulnerable act. She may start to believe that she really is helpless and worry that she can't make it on her own. But the truth is she has solar systems more going for her than she thinks.

Spiritual

She worships the oceans, the skies and all of nature's wonders. Religion and spirituality are part and parcel of her cosmic connection to the moon and the stars. She often becomes involved in metaphysical hobbies, groups or studies. This might even include a wicca group or other cult following. Cancers look for connections to the universe in all the usual and unusual places.

Many Cancer women have a fine-tuned sense of intuition and a natural talent to tap into the messages from above. Sometimes she feels like she's more in touch with the gods and goddesses who rule the moon and stars than she is with the earth and she often believes in some sort of universal consciousness.

She loves to go to church of any denomination, not necessarily for the service, but for the sense of peace that reverent environment provides. However, she doesn't need to go to a building to get in touch with her spiritual side. When the moon is full, she might even hear the music of the spheres or feel the presence of her guardian angel.

The moon is her gateway to the realms beyond earth and the vastness of the sea reminds her that Earth is her temporary playground and schoolhouse. These forces combine to give her special insights. She has incredible wisdom and she might even have a psychic ability to communicate through the cosmic Internet.

The Cancer man

> He's as changeable as the ocean, churning up the sands of your insecurities one minute and kissing your tears away with his sunny smile the next.

He's the man who keeps you guessing even if you live with him for fifty years. He's the person who loves nothing better than to make plans, then break them, then make them all over again, exactly the same way as they were originally. If you don't mind taking one step forwards, two steps back and then a couple to the side, this is your man. But if you want your life to run on a straight highway, you would probably be wise to find yourself another sign of the zodiac. Many women consider Mr Cancer to be one of the hottest tickets of the zodiac. After all, look at the unique mass sex appeal guys like Cancers Harrison Ford, Tom Cruise, Tom Hanks, Bryan Brown and John Cusack have to offer.

There is something cute and cuddly about most Cancer men. They bring out the mothering, nurturing protective instincts in others. But, cute and cuddly or not, Cancer men are often quite a task to live with, especially those who were born when the moon was out of phase. You may ask, how do you know if they were born when the moon was either in or out of phase? Just stay in their company for a while, and you'll find out!

Mr Cancer is likely to be good-looking, easygoing and open-minded (at least on the surface). As much as he appears the regular guy next door type when you first meet him, be warned, he isn't. The word complex takes on a deeper meaning when it's used to describe a Cancer man. He doesn't have as much consistency as other men, especially when it comes to his feelings and emotions. While he may be a great businessman, an incredible athlete or even a brilliant brain surgeon, he has his extreme vulnerabilities and insecurities, which often are deeply hidden within him. Because he has many tugs and pulls occurring within him, one day this guy is strong and patient and the next day he's lost, confused and vulnerable. His real world is the world within himself and this means he often experiences emotions, dreams, hopes, wishes and thoughts he cannot share with others.

When he's on track (and some are much more on track than others), the Cancer man is sexy, charmingly confident, competitive and fiercely protective of his family, friends and prized possessions. He's understanding, generally open-minded, and a great friend to the underdog. In relationships, he can be passionate, needy at times, aloof when it suits him, and he also can be unreasonably jealous (as Cancer O. J. Simpson revealed).

Passion can rule his life, but often his passion conflicts with his emotions and commonsense. And when he's angry or hurt, he can say and do things that he truly regrets in hindsight. If he is truly emotionally scarred, he's likely to disappear from life for a while and hide out until he has healed his broken heart or other emotional wounds and he feels better again.

Look out if his feelings are hurt and he decides to stay and fight instead of fleeing for cover. The male Crab can deliver a piece of his mind charged with enough emotion to send ripples through the universe. But when he kisses and makes up it is so, so easy to forget and forgive him.

[How Cancer men operate]

Social

The Cancer man can be the life of a party, telling jokes, showing off and encouraging everyone to step into the limelight with their own talents and stories. He likes being in the spotlight but he doesn't have to star in every show.

He's a good listener and he may be an expert on human nature and personal dynamics. He often has a knack for impersonating his friends and can sometimes imitate a few famous people, too. Because of his acute perception, he sometimes knows people better than they know themselves. But people rarely realise this and the Cancer can appear so vulnerable that people are compelled to offer encouraging words and free advice — most of it off the mark.

The male Crab loves social occasions that mix sports with food. He might be up for a challenging tennis match or golf game followed by a pizza or watching his favourite football team with a Foster's in one hand and a meat pie in the other. He also likes funny movies and probably has a hobby or two like painting or photography. Many Cancers who formerly spent most of their social time in the confines of their own shells are now blossoming with friendships and new acquaintances made via the world-wide web. Mr Cancer can be one of the most popular men in his neighbourhood.

Love and family

If you're serious about falling in love with a Cancer man, before you hand him the keys to your heart, take the time to find out how he feels about his mother. If he's on great terms with her, you've got an excellent chance of having a fantastic relationship as long as she approves of you. If he has nothing good to say about his mother, then you could be in for a rocky romantic ride.

No matter what he says about his mum, however, when your heart's set on a Cancer, the old petal-pulling test of 'he loves me, he loves me not' will work as well as any other. In fact, it probably works better than most because this guy can love you and love you not, several times in the course of a day; or at least that's how it may feel. The truth is that if he loves you he always loves you but his moods have a mind of their own.

A Cancer man's creative thoughts will inspire you and his success will motivate you. But don't go anywhere without your own sunshine because this guy's pessimism can cast a shadow the size of Texas. The good news is that it won't be long before a different mood comes marching in! One minute he's reciting poetry and the next he's reading the riot act. He's as changeable as the Pacific Ocean, churning up the sands of your insecurities one minute and kissing your tears away with his sunny smile the next.

If you've already fallen for a Cancer, take note, his heart is as soft and delicate as a moon shadow and he protects it carefully. You may have to make the first move because even if he knows you're interested, his fear of rejection might hold him back. Appeal to his senses by inviting him to a romantic candlelight dinner complete with atmosphere and fresh flowers. Wear your softest skirt, and a sheer blouse that stops just short of being wicked. And don't order the crab claws.

When it comes to marriage, a Cancer will look for a woman who's affectionate, nurturing and understanding. He'll never admit it, but he really loves to be pampered, spoiled and handled gently. Bring him breakfast in bed, fluff his pillows, and massage his weary feet and he'll fly you to the moon so you can play among the stars. But if you treat him like he's less than number one in your life, or if you stray, be warned that Cancer will not put up with it! Lest you're tempted to do either of these things just think of Cancer Henry VIII who divorced three of his six wives, and had two of them beheaded.

As a father, he's gentle, caring, sympathetic and easy to talk to. On most days, he has infinite patience and genuine fun playing with his kids. He loves his children unconditionally and is willing to do whatever it takes to provide them with the best possible education. He's a proud father who can't help but get tears in his eyes when his son brings home a good report card or when his daughter gets a role in the school play. He's also a protective father and when his children begin reaching the age where they want to take care of themselves he often feels gloomy and may even go through an identity crisis of sorts.

Career

The lunar man is ambitious and has an intense drive for security and success. He may not look like he's heading for the top, but all that fancy footwork can be deceiving. You can bet his objective will always be in view and once he's close enough to snatch it, he'll hold on for dear life.

He isn't crazy about routine, but he can handle it if there's some variety from day to day. Cancer men make wonderful teachers and professors. Their topics are different each day, their schedules change throughout the year and their classroom sets the stage for their expressive and captivating performances.

For the most part, Cancer can select any profession he desires but he seems most content in an atmosphere that promotes creativity and celebrates imagination. He has his own steady pace so a high pressure, fast deadline position could challenge him considerably and may take its toll on his health.

Many Cancers are ship captains, fishermen and sailors. Quite a few work on cruise lines as hosts and entertainers. You'll also find numerous Crabs serving in the coast guard or working jobs that allow them to live near the beach. Other occupations that suit them include acting, writing, designing, hotel management, antique appraising and any type of art form or handicraft under the moon. Actors Bill Cosby, Tom Cruise, Tom Hanks, Harrison Ford, Sylvester Stallone and Robin Williams are Cancers. So are writers Ernest Hemingway and Neil Simon.

Financial

A male Crab learns about money early in life, and he probably plopped at least a hundred dollars worth of change into peanut butter jars by the time he was ten or eleven years old. He won't turn down paper money but he loves the shiny reflection of a brand new dollar coin and the jingle jangle of a pocketful of change.

The lunar man has faith in silver and gold and considers them to be two of the safest investments. He's not one to take chances with his money because money means security to him and he rarely takes chances with security. He does everything he can to plan for a stable retirement filled with warm relaxing days and cool moonlit nights.

If Cancer isn't making as much as he'd like in his profession he's sometimes motivated to start a side business that allows him to pursue a hobby that he loves. This is often the turning point in a Cancer's financial picture. When a Cancer does what he loves, his inspiration is imprinted on his work and his imagination brings his work to life. And sometimes that adds up to more profit than even he can imagine.

Physical

The Cancer man is known for his broad shoulders, flexible arms and strong, sometimes large hands and feet. He probably has sensitive looking eyes, a shy smile and great legs. Cancers have excellent balance and their hand-eye coordination is unsurpassed. They excel in sports that combine coordination, quick thinking and competition. Cancers can totally dominate in ball sports like baseball, basketball, soccer, handball and football. They make great kickers and talented receivers because they can hold on to an object as if it's a matter of life and death.

Unfortunately, this same trait of 'holding on' also applies to a Cancer's fondness for old habits, particularly the unhealthy ones. His stomach and chest are susceptible to stress-related problems including muscle spasms, ulcers and indigestion. Many of the Cancer's health problems would disappear if he began eating more fruits and vegetables and less meat and cheese. He's wise to increase his water intake and avoid excessive alcohol. Talking of alcohol, that can be the greatest undoing for a Cancer man. Combined with gambling, it can drive his health right into the ground in a very short space of time.

He should also learn to be more careful when he's depressed. A Cancer man can be prone to small, but painful accidents like dropping a knife on his foot or shutting a door on his hand. Examining the events or thoughts that corresponded with the injuries might show a pattern or reveal a message that the Cancer has been ignoring.

Still, for a Cancer male, stress plus pessimism equals sickness and he can suffer from one little irritating illness after another. He should consider learning some self-relaxation techniques and increasing the number of days he exercises each week. But he shouldn't go overboard because pushing himself to the limit can break down his immune system. A sick Crab's best friend is his bed and after several days of peace and quiet he'll be back on all eight feet again.

Mental

This man of the moon swings on a pendulum back and forth between his intellect and his emotions. When he's swinging out on the positive side of the pendulum life seems to flow along in perfect harmony and balance. When he's swinging out on the negative side of the pendulum he can be Mr Doom and Gloom himself.

A good hard laugh is one of the most potent therapies when his pessimism persona takes over, and singing and dancing work almost as well. If he's really under a dark cloud, a brisk walk or short drive to the travel agency is always an exciting way for a Cancer to get motivated again. He doesn't have to book a flight; just picking up the brochures can be enough to stimulate his mind back to a centred position.

A Cancer man gets tons of benefits from healthy outlets that help balance his fluctuating moods. Without a variety of ways to vent his emotions, he may abuse prescription or illegal drugs. But most Cancers have a good bit of self-control and can moderate their vices. And all of them know that when they take time for exercise and deep relaxation they have a lot more energy.

Spiritual

Mr Cancer is usually filled with questions of eternity, creation and existence. His mind can turn round and round with imaginative scenarios, creative theories and visionary possibilities. He knows he's somehow connected to the moon and the tides and on some level he knows we're all stars in the making.

A clear summer day with puffy white clouds and the scent of honeysuckle wafting on a breeze can bring a tear of gratitude to his eyes. He appreciates beauty and his spirit is refreshed by nature's wonders. He knows there's some sort of cosmic or divine design and he trusts the universe to steer him in enlightening directions.

He's intrigued by ancient observatories and is quite possibly convinced that the past, present and future are written in the stars. His greatest thrill would be to catch a glimpse of eternity and he thinks the sky is the best place to look. And who knows, maybe some moonlight night, as he is walking back from a surf along the beach, he'll catch a wave of inspiration and see a flash of his infinite soul.

The Cancer baby

Cancer is the cry and cuddle baby of the zodiac. This baby instinctively knows how to touch your heart and will do whatever it takes to wrap you around its cute little finger.

No wonder Cancer babies, whether pretty or not, are often the most adored, cooed over and cherished of the zodiac.

There is such a special invisible form of vulnerability about them that goes beyond the fact that they're infants. It's almost as if you can sense — for no really explicable reason — that these little babes have just arrived straight from the soul-realms and are not quite ready for dealing with the physical demands of life on planet Earth.

Ruled by the moon astrologically, Cancer is the zodiac sign which represents the need to nurture and be nurtured, the act of mothering and the protective domain of dealing with babies. If you have a little Cancer baby, you're opening yourself up to a complete and total mothering or fathering type of experience.

This newborn introduces you, whether you think you're ready or not, to a new level of nurturing and presents you with an opportunity to experience true unconditional love with all of its shades and hues of pains and pleasures. Destiny is certain to decree that you will have a very special experience with this child's birth, babyhood, childhood and adulthood.

This is going to be a heart-filled and sometimes heart-wrenching experience. There's something so vulnerable about the Cancer infant that you will probably feel that even when this individual is in middle age — he or she is still your baby.

Your Cancer child operates on all levels of consciousness because he or she operates from the depth of truest feelings and intuitions. This little moon baby can clearly communicate with you through thoughts and feelings. And take note that it can hear your thoughts and feel your emotions as well. Therefore, in some fashion or another before and after its birth, this baby will be expressing itself to and through you and will be affected by your expressions as well.

The baby Crab is also likely to possess some type of mysteries or unknowns. Even during your pregnancy you will probably be faced with some questions that you can't answer regarding this new life. Some, but certainly not all, women who are carrying a Cancer may suffer from some unusual or unpredictable types of pregnancy upsets which occur for no apparent reason and may disappear as unexpectedly as they arose.

This is the little soul that keeps doctors scratching their heads. There are lots of reasons for these happenings with a Cancer. One reason is that because the Cancer baby is more closely connected to the ethereal levels of existence than the physical ones it has all kinds of different resonance and vibrations surrounding it that can affect you in mysterious ways. Also this one is not likely to be born early and could very likely be late unless your doctor decides to provide a helping hand (and that is also a high possibility with this baby).

Ruled by the ever-changing moon, it is very difficult to analyse little Cancer because it is so multi-dimensional and goes through so many phases and stages in just one day. Like its ruler the moon, this infant transits through many different personality and emotional phases and stages and its personality is constantly evolving. But one thing is very possible — this baby is likely to have a delicate, sensitive nature and may be prone to crying (mainly because it wants to know it is loved and because it wants its mummy).

There will be times you worry a lot about your baby Cancer because it has a very vulnerable and delicate aura surrounding it. But as much as this infant is a sensitive soul, it can be stronger and more resilient than it shows. But it is easily hurt and upset so be sure to cuddle him or her frequently and treat them with loving tenderness. This child is more impressionable than most and an upsetting drama that occurs around it can leave a lasting mark. And when it comes to sleep, this baby will love its sleep and will get very cranky if anything upsets its sleeping pattern or restful times.

For all its sensitivity, the Cancer baby can be tough and even forceful when it needs to be. He or she is likely to emerge into this world wailing loudly and demanding to be loved immediately. Cancer babies have a reputation for crying more than most babies and they do cry an awful lot (just ask my Mum!).

Sometimes their tears are no more than an outpouring of expression. The crying process is important to its development. Experienced care-givers of Cancers quickly go through the typical checklist for tears — check the nappy, try feeding it, pick it up, check for a fever, and so on. But many times, what's most puzzling and frustrating for the parents of these babies is that even when they appear to be perfectly comfortable they may still cry. Once you've ruled out a medical problem just resign yourself to the fact that this little one is sometimes just talking to itself or expressing its inner doubts and fears, hopes and dreams in the form of tears. Plus, for an infant who cannot yet talk one of the greatest ways of releasing emotions is to cry. And the Cancer baby is so emotionally oriented that it could be crying for memories of past lives or things that are unseen or hidden in other realms of consciousness. But regardless of the underlying emotional reason, one of the best things you can do is cuddle this little one snugly in your safe, protective arms and sing a soothing melody.

Another thing that can work wonders is gently lowering the wee one into a warm bath. Most Cancer babies love warm baths and if you snugly wrap the babe in a warm, fluffy towel when you lift it out of its bath it will coo with delight. Because of its unpredictable development and nature it isn't wise to base your expectations of this baby's development or physical progress on the stages of growth you have observed in other babies — or even in your own earlier children. This little one will have a growth and development cycle all of its own and it may also be a late developer in both walking and talking.

The Cancer toddler through teen

Like real crabs, Cancer children tend to feel safer inside their shells; at least until they've checked out the area and decide it's okay to come out and play.

Unlike many toddlers, the little Cancer child will generally think and use caution before he or she acts. These children tend to be extremely tentative about their actions and trying something new may involve a good bit of watching others before Cancers decide whether they want to try it or not. And it's best not to push them. For a Cancer tot, something like riding a swing for the first time or going down a slippery dip can be a big and scary event, even if they decide on their own that they'd like to give it a go.

Of course, this doesn't mean Cancers can be left unattended. Like all children, Cancers have their share of curiosity — especially about water — including swimming pools, ponds, lakes and creeks. So no matter how cautious these little people normally are, don't underestimate their pull to water, as this is their astrological element and it has a great attraction for them.

More than one little Crab has crawled to the water's edge before Mum or Dad could scoop them safely up into their arms. This act may be met with screams and cries on the Cancer's part, but most Cancer children love to be held even more than they love water! When other youngsters are no longer interested in being confined to their parents' arms, the Cancer children still relish it and often demand it.

Like real Crabs, Cancer children tend to feel safer inside their shells; at least until they've checked out the area and decide it's okay to come out and play. They will, no doubt, have all types of secret hiding places and if you build or buy them a little playhouse all their own they'll squeal with delight. You might as well give them a 'Do Not Disturb' sign to hang on the playhouse door because Cancers need and enjoy their privacy. And considering how moody these children can sometimes be, you may enjoy their privacy more than they do at times.

Most of the time though, the little Crabs are very affectionate, considerate and loving. They learn to respect other people's things — including yours — at an early age because they have an inborn care for their own toys, clothes and treasured possessions. In fact, it wouldn't be out of character for a Cancer child to carefully place a new doll or special toy up on a shelf for safekeeping instead of playing with it.

Cancers generally prefer things to stay the same. Don't surprise him or her by painting their bedroom without asking first or you could end up painting it back to the original colour just to stop the Cancer's crying! The old adage, 'If it's not broken, don't fix it,' could have been written for the developing Cancer — and actually for Cancers of any age.

Don't be surprised or upset if your Cancer child seems to prefer playing alone over playing with other children. The young Crabs tend to be more introspective than extroverted and they rarely run out of imaginary games or imaginary friends. Cancers are well known in the zodiac for developing friendships with the fairies who live in the flower garden or the leprechaun who sleeps in the wood shed. This is all part of the mystery that lies deeply inside each Cancer's heart and soul.

For a Cancer, the thought or image in their mind can seem nearly as real as the things he or she can taste and touch. Don't worry, by the time the Cancer is ready to go off to school they'll begin to show more independence, less shyness and more of a willingness to interact with people you can see! That doesn't mean your little one will get voted 'most outgoing,' but it does mean that in time they'll make friends — just like all the other kids. But your Cancer child may still prefer your company or the company of other adults to that of kids his or her own age because adults tend to behave in a more polite manner than other children and Cancers like to be treated well.

By the way, don't feel slighted if you overhear your Cancer offspring telling a friend that his or her real mother is a queen, or real father is a knight in shining armour. The truth is that for Cancers their homes are their castles and the rock or foundation upon which every other aspect of their lives is formed. Upsets and turmoil in the home can be very difficult for a Cancer to take and even if his or her parents stage their fights quietly behind closed doors a Cancer will pick up on the emotional imbalance and most assuredly be affected by it.

One of the ways a Cancer shows that he or she is hurting emotionally is to internalise their emotional pain and create a physical illness. Upset and nervous stomachs are a common ailment among Cancers, especially as they enter adolescence and their turbulent teenage years. These are also the years when Cancers feel most awkward and out-of-sorts.

Considering how little they want to stand out or be different at this age, they tend to wildly exaggerate each and every one of their self-perceived flaws. And for heaven's sake, don't tease them about the things they are absolutely dreading about themselves. Calling a Cancer who thinks he has a big nose by the nickname Pinocchio can send him into solitary confinement for days.

Teenage Cancers seldom do things openly they fear will result in their parents disapproval — a steady flow of love is their most valued treasure. For that reason it is very, very important to find ways to discipline the Cancer that don't involve withdrawing or withholding your love in any way. You can send a Cancer to her room without dessert, but don't send her there without a hug.

Even if she stiffens her entire body when you try to embrace her, a Cancer will be grateful and feel reassured by your gesture of love. And the same goes for the boys. No matter how cool he may want to look in front of his friends, he will rely on family hugs and kisses in the privacy of his own home.

Most Cancer teens are relatively good students but they will excel much more in the subjects that have relevance in their daily lives or can support their plans for the future. And while they can retain a good bit of information from reading and listening to lectures, a Cancer learns best by experiencing lessons in life and then processing his or her own feedback — particularly emotional feedback— and sorting out the data after the experience is over.

To support your Cancer at this stage of young adulthood continue to encourage him or her as consistently as you did throughout the growing years. It is usually a good idea to increase the amount of praise you give to them at this age because as they near high school graduation and the impending changes it brings, they may become preoccupied with their fears, rather than focusing on their future hopes and dreams.

And remember all that daydreaming you've watched your Cancer do throughout his or her life? Well, now is the time the young Crab will truly begin to blossom and, with your loving reassurance, make those dreams come true.

LEO

[24 july — 23 august]

leo leo leo leo leo leo leo leo leo leo
leo leo leo leo leo leo leo leo leo leo
leo leo leo leo leo leo leo leo leo leo
leo leo leo leo leo leo leo leo leo leo

leo leo leo leo leo leo leo leo leo leo
leo leo leo leo leo leo leo leo leo leo
leo leo leo leo leo leo leo leo leo leo
leo leo leo leo leo leo leo leo leo leo
leo leo leo leo leo leo leo leo leo leo
leo leo leo leo leo leo leo leo leo leo
leo leo leo leo leo leo leo leo leo leo

element: fire

planetary ruler: the sun

symbol: the lion

quality: fixed (= stability)

colours: gold

gem: amber, chrysolite, neroli

best companions: aries and sagittarius

strongest virtues: bravery, loyalty and

big-picture attitude to life, love and

everything else

traits to improve: bossiness, vanity, arrogance

deepest desire: to live all your dreams

and more

Leo celebrities

John Howard, John Laws, Anna Paquin, Matt Le Blanc, Kevin Spacey,

Madonna, Stanley Kubrick, Neil Armstrong, Dean Cain, Magic Johnson,

Whitney Houston, Geri Halliwell, Gillian Anderson, Antonio Banderas,

Mick Jagger, Dustin Hoffman, James Cameron (director of *Titanic*),

Arnold Schwarzenegger, Daryl Somers, Lisa Kudrow, Bill Clinton,

Monica Lewinsky (on the cusp of Cancer), Jacqueline Kennedy Onassis,

Robert De Niro, Melanie Griffith, Sandra Bullock, Charlize Theron,

David Duchovny, Roman Polanski, Hulk Hogan, Jennifer Lopez,

George Hamilton, Pete Sampras, Wesley Snipes, Julian McMahon,

Sean Penn, Michael Richards, Robert Redford, Patrick Swayze,

Matthew Perry, Melissa George, Fidel Castro, Halle Berry, Ben Affleck,

Billy Bob Thornton, Susie O'Neill, Michael Klim, Christian Slater and

Peter Weir.

······ (Leo in the new millennium

[General outlook]

After being swept away by uncertainty and confusion in recent times, like a Lion waiting eagerly to pounce, Leos are poised and ready for the right path to reveal itself to ensure your success in the new millennium. You've recently learned the values of patience and humility and while many Leos have undergone periods of self-doubt, the good news is that the new millennium brings you great rewards — rewards that you have certainly earned for yourself, and have long been waiting to receive! Shortly into the new millennium, your noble Lion's path becomes clearer and the right people, places and projects are revealed to you. This encourages you to do things (take on new careers, relationships and attitudes) that you never believed possible before. Overall, positive astrological aspects are affecting you and this helps you grow. You attract positive and creative people and situations into your sphere. Your creativity, genius and generosity are recognised and your desires to love and be loved are fulfilled. Start focusing on what you want in every area of your life. Write it down, think about it every day and you'll soon see your dreams become a reality.

Romance

Love and romance make up the cornerstones of your existence. Without them, your world crumbles. With them, your world is safe, secure and stable. Because you now know how important love is to your life's structure, you are not prepared to put up with love that isn't true. You do not want to compromise yourself in relationships any more. You understand how much love and romance are your greatest source of energy and you can't live without them. You are naturally ruled by your heart — not your head — and as the new millennium dawns, this will not change. More than ever, you want to feel loved, secure and safe. Now you set yourself on a romantic mission. You won't stop looking for love until you find the emotional security you have not had recently. The great news is that you will find it in the new millennium. Love is in the air, and you've never been happier than you will be in relationships in the new millennium.

Health

Many of the end-of-century health problems faced by Leos fall by the wayside soon after the new millennium begins, because you remove yourself from past stressful conditions. You enter the new millennium robust and strong, and ready for the many challenges coming up. Watching your weight is a must, as the possibility of over-eating combined with sedentary habits are your biggest downfall. Try to incorporate a healthy eating plan and regular exercise into your everyday life. Remember, too, that spending time with loyal friends and family will always recharge your batteries.

Finance

It is time to play it safe financially, rather than take any kind of speculative or risky action with your hard-earned money. You cannot take chances with money now, even though your financial outlook looks positive during the first few years of the new millennium and beyond. Finances remain a sensitive issue, especially where you are in joint enterprises with others, and where you have taken big risks with your money recently, too. Particularly where others have control of your purse strings, you need to be extremely watchful.

Career

Ambitious and dynamic Leos find themselves facing new frontiers in their professional world. Many of you receive surprising offers of work because of the good reputation you have built up in the past. The truth is, when you combine your creative spirit and love of people you realise your full ambition. Working as a team, however, is all-important. Be creative, be communicative and there'll be nothing stopping you! Also do choose your trusted work associates wisely. You learned in the past how the wrong associates can cause you all kinds of career upset or problems.

[Millennium wildcards to watch for]

Keep away from drama and overloading yourself with other people's problems. You could also become overwhelmed by having too many options to choose from. Take some time to think over your choices rather than making an impulsive decision. Keep in mind also that your decisions are going to affect other people (i.e. your partner, children, other family members). Learning to meditate or reflect about things in silence will work wonders for Leos. It will be far better for you to take on one thing and do it well in the new millennium than take on a variety of things and find yourself unable to give them all your best efforts or attention.

> *You Leos truly can show courage under fire, and will risk all to save the day, not just for yourself but to protect, nurture or assist those you truly love.*

Even for an astrology amateur your sign is one of the easiest to recognise. It isn't so much your 'look,' your status, your many talents or your remarkable energy levels. It's you! When you're not trying to stand out, or are in your quiet mode, you somehow still have the ability to make an impact and leave a lasting impression. However, when you are high in confidence, you are quite bedazzling.

Like your ruling star in astrology, which is our solar system's golden god the sun, you light up our lives. And you also give us plenty to talk about! Often we find ourselves wittingly or unwittingly revolving or gravitating around you, your whims or wishes without really knowing why we are doing it. Your star quality (and talent for self-promotion) turns acquaintances into devoted followers.

Of course, the sun doesn't shine every day, and neither do you! On your dark days or nights, your power to propel others and the world around you into darkness is the downside to this field of personal power. It is fortunate for all of us that your doom and gloom phases don't usually last too long. Just as the sun and the light returns eventually at dawn, most of you know inherently that even after disappointment, disaster or heartbreak, you will rise and shine again. Most of the time however, you somehow manage to remain the king or queen of your world.

Your stamina is generally amazing. Your energy levels and endurance often impress others because you seem to move in perpetual motion. Plenty of physical exercise fanatics are born under this sign (like Madonna, Arnold Schwarzenegger and Mick Jagger). Then you have the other extreme, Leos who let themselves go to flab. You live an exciting life, often because you couldn't stand to lead a boring one. You live for your dreams and you're highly motivated by your clear picture of success.

Your dreams often do come true in a huge way, because you have the capacity to really think big. Unfortunately, you think so big that you over-extend yourself. Your thinking big attitude is one reason Leos figure so high in bankruptcy statistics. But when you play the game of life and win, which so many of you do, your list of successful personal and professional achievements can be astounding to tally up.

It is not uncommon for a Leo to be running big companies in a position which includes a comfortable penthouse office and a title so big and impressive it barely fits on a business card. Of course, not all Leos get to rise and shine by the fair and square way. Some Leos try to climb to the top by other means and, as Leo Monica Lewinsky revealed, Leos will do anything and go to any lengths to be noticed. All's fair in love and war was probably written with Leo in mind.

For a great example of a Leo who has worked the way up the ladder of success (at least until now), look at Larry Ellison, business executive, billionaire and original thinker behind Oracle. At the time of writing this book, Larry is a billionaire, and also the richest man in California (but not richer than Bill Gates, Scorpio, who lives in Seattle, Washington, of course). Larry certainly has big dreams, plans and ideals, and has seen many of them happen already.

His journey to success (revealed in his biography entitled *What's the difference between God and Larry Ellison? God doesn't think he's Larry Ellison*) has involved a run of calamities and legal challenges. Nevertheless, Larry is the epitome of a Leo! He drives Ferraris, dates tall gorgeous Swedish models and races his yacht in the Sydney to Hobart yacht race. Over-the-top extravagance, showbiz hype, razzmatazz style, fame and fortune often appeal to this sign. If they have it, they often flaunt it. And even if all Leos do not want to live in penthouses and live the high life, many Leos do gravitate towards starring roles. Like rock stars (Leos Madonna, Mick Jagger, Whitney Houston), or superheros (Leos Arnold Schwarzenegger, and television's Superman, Dean Cain) Leos are up front, centre-stage in many areas of life.

Leos also love to be the first to do something, and this includes space travel. Astronaut Neil Armstrong is a Leo. Like politically ambitious Leos John Howard and Bill Clinton, they also love running countries. Throw in a dictator or two (Leos Fidel Castro, and Benito Mussolini) and a conqueror like Napoleon Bonaparte. Leos often become legends in their own lifetimes (for the best and worst reasons).

You Leos have the ability to take command. And as a fixed sign of the zodiac, you generally know what you want, whom you want, and what it will take to get it. You have your eye fixed on specific, earmarked, targeted prizes, expectations, relationships and financial goals, too. Your list of basic requirements for happiness include status and financial success, love in abundance, attention, applause, respect, access to the fountain of youth, power, lots of friends, scores of fans and money to burn.

As well, you dream about a devoted mate who praises and adores you, cheerfully caters to you and never complains or criticises you. And you can be quite a wild child. Sex, drugs and rock 'n' roll can be your idea of inspiration and relaxation (although often you get over your drug or pill-popping at an early age and become a health guru). You will go to extremes to get what you want and stubbornness and one-eyed attitudes help you on your go-getter quest for glory.

When you have your heart set on something (or someone), you permit no one or nothing to stand in the way for long. Not even your family, religion, financial highs and lows, your politics and particularly not your boss or supervisor can dominate or redirect your quest for fulfilment for long. This quest to fulfil your desires is often propelled along by an incredible support team of fate, fortune and destiny as much as your good works. Some think you have a particularly lucky star shining on you, throughout much of your life Leos, but every now and again, your luck deserts you, usually exactly when you feel you need it the most.

Lucky or not, you are a stickler for taking command of your life, and doing things your way. That is possibly why your guardian angel sometimes abandons you to your own devices. You hate to have anyone (even the forces of nature) telling you what to do. No wonder you are not one of the easiest children, teens, marriage partners or employees to manage, instruct or direct! You Lions only like to follow the rules that suit you or better yet, rules that you have decreed. Your golden rule can be: 'I am right, everyone else is wrong and I will never see it any way differently'.

Hell has no fury like a Leo when your boss, your partner, your audience or anyone else tries to tell you how to do your job! You delight in and dare to be different and you're proud to take risks and break records. And you want to succeed or win each prize your own way, not someone else's way. That is why you don't handle unasked-for advice, reprimands or criticism very well and your pride can be like a prickly pear at times. But then who said that just because you're a Leo you have to be perfect?

What's so terrific about you Leos is that you usually end up winning (sooner or later), and best of all for you, winning by doing things your way. You earn your success because you put your heart and soul into just about everything you do and that kind of dedication and focus brings its own form of reward.

Where others have tried to thwart you along your journey towards success, when you do triumph by doing things your own way, you often have the last laugh. You know from experience that there is great truth in the saying 'the best form of revenge is success'. And on many diverse levels, because you know how to take care of yourselves, life takes care of you! In fact, you Leos are exceptional at taking care of yourselves in all sorts of challenging and even threatening situations and it's a rare occasion when you don't get your way by hook or by crook.

This story is such a wonderful example of the Leo field of power that I laugh even as I remember it. It also points out that one should never be fooled by the physical size of a Leo (with Napoleon being a good example of this), because it is their gigantic spirit that counts. One of my more petite Leo girlfriends — who only stands 157 cm (5 feet 2 inches) tall and who looks as sweet as apple pie — showed her real Leo power when dealing with a dilemma recently. She wielded her Lion's roar with tenacity and amazing courage when she had to deal with what she took to be a group of rough and ready-for-trouble guys in her local shopping mall car park. She said that when she was returning to her sports car after shopping, four young guys were sitting in it drinking cans of beer. Not only were they drinking in her car, but they had the radio turned up full blast. Furious, she ran full pelt towards her car shouting, 'Get out of the car! Get out of the car!' Caught off guard, all four leapt out of the car, spilling their beer all over the place in their shock. At almost the exact moment that the four uninvited car-revellers sprang clear of the vehicle, my Leo friend caught sight of her car (one similar in colour and style) parked three spaces away in the other direction. The car she was so charged up about was not even hers! The point is this little Leo was so fierce that her growl alone scared a handful of rowdy guys into taking immediate action without even questioning why they should get out of their own car! It says something, doesn't it?

Whether it is warranted or not, you Leos truly can show courage under fire, and will risk all to save the day, not just for yourself but to protect, nurture or assist those you truly love. Whether facing the pressure of saving the day or simply getting along in everyday life, you have incredible resilience and survival instincts, too. After a setback, you somehow manage to rally yourself again. Even if you lose the lot financially (which many of you do several times over) you start again, and make your fortune all over again.

Even family or childhood tragedies or ill health don't stop you for long. You have your own form of Eveready battery — and this is your inner belief and faith in yourself. However, the problem with your inbuilt Eveready battery is that it doesn't know when to stop and recharge! Moderation isn't one of your stronger virtues and overdoing everything can take its toll, particularly when you overeat, overwork, overexercise, overspend or party too much.

Your 'enough is not enough' attitude leads you into a good bit of adventure and a fair share of trouble as well. And Hallelujah for the Leo and the credit card. 'Just charge it!' has a close to religious meaning for you. Your bills can make your accountant weep and many others rich. Nevertheless, even with your extravagances, money seems to gravitate nicely around you. Seemingly out of thin air you often manage to find enough funds to cover your crazy, zany, wonderful and often most generous (sometimes to a fault) indulgences.

Your extravagance arises because you like to spoil yourself and to pay for things for others – you have a generous nature. Spending money often has a lot to do with your pride, too. You take pride in being able to buy and acquire all the things that you love. You also spend a lot on your family. They are generally dressed in the best, live in a great place and attend the right schools and so on. It is interesting to note that a Lion's family is called its pride.

To a Leo, pride is more important than most things and praise ranks right up there, too, because you Leos are always trying to prove yourselves. It is strange that other people's opinions matter so much to you. Underneath that fame, charm and smooth-talking, often beats a nervous heart. Many of you are afraid that people (or the world) will eventually wake up to you, or see through your bravado. That is why it is so important to praise you, and if there are genuine criticisms to share with you, to remember how delicate and thin skinned you can be.

You are only vulnerable to certain people, and at certain times. When you are operating under full steam, you can be insatiable and so caught up in your own momentum that you don't even hear what others have to say. But whatever phase of your life you are going through, you don't take kindly to any type of put-down or joke at your expense and you dread criticism even when it's humorous or well intended. In fact, at the first hint of a reprimand or an insensitive comment from others, you either turn on your sunny charm and change the subject, or you go super nova with that famous fiery and very scary Leo temper.

Leo is a Fire sign

Astrologically, you are one of the zodiac's three fire signs — the other two being Aries and Sagittarius. This is the good news. As spirit and energy (the base sources of the fire element in astrology) are the true forces of your Leo make-up and everyday existence, you are in a prime position to lead, speed and exceed in and at anything and everything you tackle.

Whether you want to overcome obstacles or upsets, or heal a time of ill health or bad luck, you have the tenacity, true grit and power to do it. You're great at staying focused on your most important objectives and when you set out for something you generally get it, one way or another.

Your fire sign connection also creates that easy to replenish fiery type of exciting and resplendent energy you are famous for and provides the courage and determination to follow your own path and accomplish the most heavenly goals. You're not afraid of facing adversity or difficulties along your way in life. In fact, you expect them as part of the plan.

Being born under the fire signs means that you were born to rise and shine and be the guiding light to others along the pathway of life. It encourages you to be a leader, a lover and a loyal friend. Your inspiration is designed to encourage others to follow their dreams and your certainty in miracles sees you through all manner of difficulties.

Now the bad news. To your disadvantage, your competitive nature can be narrow-minded in its approach and your desire to control the events and sometimes the people in your life causes you considerable stress and frustration. You have a 'do as I say, not as I do' approach to life, where you value your own free will and resent others telling you what to do. But you have a hard time stopping yourself from telling others what to do, even when it's not your place to do so.

You can be one-sided and fixed about situations to the degree that you cause chaos when bending a little would create harmony. You sometimes live under the heading of 'I'm right, no matter what'. And there are definitely times when you can assume the unattractive role of 'the bully'.

[Insights into your sign]

The bright side: You have an ability to inspire and motivate other people. Your talents, together with your enthusiasm and organisational skills, make you a strong and inspiring leader.

The shadow side: You have a tendency to believe that no one is running their life as well as you could run it — and you don't hesitate to tell them so. You can be a 'know-it-all' and sometimes you can even talk yourself into believing your own tall stories.

[Looking beneath the surface of your sign]

You are your own toughest critic and you never feel you are good enough or have done enough, even when you know you have performed miracles or broken records. You would rather swim in shark-infested oceans than reveal any part of yourself that you don't think is worthy of broadcasting on the evening news. You tend to compare yourself to people who have incredible talent or abilities and this comparison sets you up for feeling inadequate or lacking.

Characteristics >	Benefits >	Drawbacks >
Adventurous	Develops character	Foolhardy
Ambitious	Strong self-starter	Self-interested
Aristocratic	Distinguished	Stuck up
Authoritative	Respected opinions	Know-it-all attitude
Capable	Go-getter	Bossy
Confident	Brave	Show-off
Courageous	Willing to face adversity	Foolhardy and reckless
Determined	Lots of willpower	Headstrong and wilful
Domineering	Quick results	Bullying
Energetic	Healthy vigour	Trouble relaxing
Enthusiastic	Others support you	Overwhelming
Extravagant	Good lifestyle	Bankruptcy
Generous	Charitable	Expect appreciation
Honest	Straight shooter	Tactless
Opinionated	Strong convictions	Unrelenting
Optimistic	See the bright side	Foolishly overconfident
Organised	Efficient	Petty
Proud	Independent	Conceited
Selfish	Focused attention	Insensitive
Temperamental	Express feelings	Drama king or queen
Vibrant	Radiant personality	Look for trouble

Like a castle surrounded by a drawbridge and moat, you have the capacity to be receptive or closed off to others (or the world at large) on a momentary whim. When you're honest with yourself, you see that you do your biggest boasting when you feel the smallest. And watch out that you don't become your own worst enemy. When you really feel out of your depth, overwhelmed or under siege, you can eat your way through a crisis and then suffer all kinds of pangs of regrets because you can gain weight so rapidly and have a terrible time trying to shake it off. Weight can be a form of protection for a Leo. It can provide a physical barrier to the world and others, but in some cases the protective barrier turns into an enormous suit of armour that few can penetrate.

But Leos, also remember that you're blessed, and a star of stars. When you begin to see that you really are as capable and courageous as you act, you begin to understand why people are drawn to you — and you begin to truly love yourself. To get yourself centred and empower your Leo outreach, try starting your day with a mental list of three things you feel really grateful about in your life!

[How to tune into your sign's powers]

> *Sometimes wait a little before you take the lead.*
> *> No matter how famous, successful or praised*
> *you may be, remain humble, act with integrity, open*
> *up your heart.*
> *> Accept criticism as openly as you accept praise.*
> *> Follow the messages of the heart, but not your*
> *emotions — there is a big difference.*
> *> Consider the welfare of all, rather than just your own.*

The Leo woman

> *Being born with a talent to portray the most powerful female personalities of the zodiac, through the changing and different stages of her life the Leo woman switches easily between the roles of glamour girl, heroine, shrew, goddess, virgin and temptress, not to mention the enchantress.*

Never underestimate the Leo woman because if you do . . . you're likely to make a huge mistake. Ms Leo is probably one of the most formidable feminine forces of the zodiac and she comes in a very appealing package — herself. The Leo woman has the courage, pride and feline grace of a Lioness, and often the natural poise, power and regalia of a queen. It doesn't matter if she's overweight, feels way past her prime or seems down on her luck.

Never write her off, she will bounce back. Ms Leo has the ability to rise, shine and recover any lost ground, many times over. She can tap into a special type of magic within her at any time, because her magic is the unique faith she has in herself.

Her toughest times are when she loses her confidence, and then she had better take a long hard look at the circumstances or people around her and work out what it is in her current situation that is stopping her from being her true self — a shining, energetic go-getter.

Most of the time, when her confidence is intact, she has an innate sense of dignity and an air of authority, which she deftly reinforces with brilliant style. Royalty or not, if Ms Leo donned a crown people would bow before her without giving it a second thought.

A natural actress, this woman throughout the different stages of her life has the capacity to play the roles of superstar, glamour girl, goddess and enchantress. And when she plays any of these roles (or all at the same time), she does it super well. Usually she has her support group gathered around her (made up of close friends, family members, or associates), because just as the Lion needs the pride, so the Lioness needs her group to reflect back to her her progress, nurturing energy and accomplishments.

When she is in the flow, she exudes vitality. She's alight with enthusiasm, sparkling with animation and glowing with energy. She has the ability to enchant and inspire, and people are drawn to her magnetic charisma. She's a wonderful organiser, a strong leader and an optimistic friend. The Leo woman has just as much fun with people her own age as she does with children and their great-grandparents. She's a master at seizing the moment and transforming it into an award-winning snapshot in time.

The Leo woman can turn an ordinary gathering into a festive party just by attending! She knows everyone needs a party now and then and she can turn up the intensity of the party mood whenever she chooses.

She can also pull the plug on the party atmosphere without warning if she's in one of her dark moods or if she feels slighted or left out. When a Leo decides to be mean, or feels justified to be cranky, just like the angry Lion, they can be scary energy to be around.

Others do sometimes need to keep a clear distance between themselves and Ms Leo's claws. If she doesn't like you she can be a formidable opponent (and often a hidden one, too).

[How Leo women operate]

Social

When it comes to socialising or making her presence felt, she is quite a brilliant strategist to say the least. The Lioness glides into a room on a fresh breeze of confidence, surveys the situation and selects her position. She wants to give herself the best vantage point for observation and for stepping into the spotlight if the opportunity arises.

When she's in full swing, you're wise to listen carefully. If she's attending a conference she's probably one of the speakers. But if she's not, she's the one sitting directly in front of the speaker, probably close enough to make eye contact. She's not (usually) attempting to move in on anyone's turf, or to outshine her colleagues, as people often mistakenly believe. Generally she's just giving herself the best advantage and reinforcing her vulnerable Leo ego at the same time. But be warned. If she wants something, she goes after it — no holds barred.

One of her favourite places to be is on the stage — or in the box seats at the theatre. She loves movies, too, and theme parties that require dressing in costume. She also loves to welcome her friends into her home for great conversation, lots of laughs and mouth-watering meals (which most times she whips up herself). She always invites the most interesting mix of people and her parties create warm memories and lasting friendships.

Being nice doesn't mean much to her. She tries to be nice sometimes, but she fails at pleasantries. The reality is, Ms Leo is only interested in you if you are truly interesting to her. Of course on some social occasions she is forced into situations that are unavoidable, where she has to be on her best behaviour, but usually she avoids places where this is likely to arise.

She does not tolerate fools or play the nice person, unless you have lots of money or a social position — then you can be boring and she will still like you. She doesn't waste her time, and she usually has places to go, people to meet and sights to see. So if you are wasting her time she is likely to quickly (sometimes even rudely) withdraw her attention. Thereafter she will avoid you as much as she possibly can manage. She also is very good at forgetting names, yet at the same time, excellent at dropping them.

Love and family

Many love stories and movies are based upon the real life romances of Leos. The Leo woman is a natural romantic (after all the part of her anatomy ruled by her star sign is — the heart). She usually has no shortage of suitors. She has a great deal of magnetism when it comes to relating to others. Being a vibrant combination of every goddess in the mythological world all rolled up into one she has a huge appeal.

In manner she has both girlishness and womanhood thrown in as well, and this creates a unique aura around a Leo woman that intrigues men and yet somehow threatens them at the same time. Born to be loved, this woman usually knows how to look good with what she's got and she's hot enough to have what it takes. A flash of her bright smile says she's interested, but her regal manner holds suitors at arm's length unless she chooses to invite them into her inner circle of friends. She also is very selective about who she lets into her heart.

Heartache or romantic turmoil can turn her world upside down more than anything else. From her first teenage crush that goes wrong, Ms Leo quickly learns to protect herself from anyone who may hurt her delicate feelings. However, this doesn't mean that she is always so sensitive where other people's feelings are concerned! Ms Leo can be quite a heartbreaker herself.

Ms Leo is usually extremely attractive and she has the ability to turn men's heads as she walks down the street — if she wants to. While not dainty in her movements, her fluid, yet deliberate (sometimes even bold) movements make her enchanting to watch and if she takes to the dance floor, watch out! When this lady strips off her royal robe and struts her stuff she can make the dancing professionals look like rookies.

It's no coincidence that Madonna is a Leo. Madonna breaks the rules and taboos (a very Leo approach) but always (and in a most subtle way) really stops just short of going too far, knowing it's best to leave her audiences begging for more. She aims to shock and tease and she succeeds. Playing the game well is what life's all about and Leos have one real wish — to win the game.

Leos are frequently fashion trendsetters. Jackie O. (Leo) really was a true Leo princess who set all the fashion trends in her day and became a living legend. Madonna also has set many styles in motion. And Madonna's earlier counterpart in those days now past, when Hollywood was brand new, was Mae West. Her name stood for sex appeal in her time. Mae West was quite a Leo! Anyone who could say 'Is that a pistol in your pocket or are you just glad to see me?' or 'I like two types of men, domestic and foreign,' as Mae did, has certainly got a handle on the shock-a-thon and thrill value of saying the unsayable, just like Leo Madonna does today.

But Leo women have their fair share of 'man' problems and Mae, Madonna and Jackie are examples of this as well. Because they're such leaders, trendsetters and go-getters, men are frequently intimidated by them. Their men can go off with women who are less daunting, simply because the Leo Goddess is often just too much of a bright light (someone with the potential to outshine them) for the man to handle. That is why hunting for a real mate (their equal) can be tough for a Leo because the Lioness is looking for a man who's as powerful, intelligent and captivating as she is.

She often finds it difficult to meet men who fit her detailed list of requirements. And sometimes she chooses unwisely and sets her romantic Lioness pounce upon someone who causes her a lot of grief and heartache. Sometimes, sex is the real attraction, rather than other more long-lasting relationship components. Leos look for sexual chemistry — kind of like in the jungle — but what they really want is someone who is adept at real love, and love takes on many faces on planet Earth, with sex-love often being one of the less sustaining kinds of love.

Leos are often attracted to forbidden fruit, too, and go after someone romantically who they know is not going to be a great companion or even come close to a match made in heaven. Many Leos love a challenge more than anything else, especially in the love, sex and emotionally charged departments of life. Often it's a sexual zing that sets the romance into full flight and when she thinks that someone is her match (even if it is more lust than love she is feeling) Cupid's little arrows do a big number on her heart and her hormones.

She can go through every phase of infatuation and resentment imaginable. She can experience an anguish of the ultimate 'achy-breaky-heart' kind and also the spiritual elation of the highest love connections — sometimes at the same time. But if and when her heart is wounded a Leo woman suffers more than most; usually on the deep levels within herself so that others often don't know just how much she's really hurting.

When she's infatuated by love she sometimes neglects the other areas of her life and her health, wealth, career and general success can suffer. She showers her lover with thoughtful gifts, frequent praise and hot romance. But her royal demands are heavy and she's not easy to keep happy and fulfilled. She's a handful, she's complex and she needs a strong and gentle lion-tamer type of man to win her respect and keep her content. (And we all know there aren't too many of these around.)

The man who loves a Leo needs to be very, very secure within himself because she will press all of his most sensitive buttons to find out if he truly is the one. Sometimes she does this without even knowing. He also needs to trust her completely as no true Leo woman ever gives up flirting. She needs to see herself as attractive and alluring. Rejection or a lack of attention and affection isn't easy for her to handle. She has to shine brightly and sometimes she chooses ways of doing this that some men find competitive, confrontational or even hurtful.

Love hits them so deeply and means so much that many Leos put marriage on the back burner until they're well into their thirties or forties. But that doesn't mean they lead celibate lives. She's probably refused or returned at least one engagement ring, and broken twice as many hearts. Love keeps a Leo sparkling, but just because it's good, great, or even fabulous doesn't mean it's worthy of a walk down the aisle.

To remain meaningful, the sex must be great, otherwise Ms Leo loses her lust-light. The Leo woman doesn't need a man, but she loves to have one. She knows she can make it on her own and any man she marries had better know it, too. She doesn't tolerate disrespect, vulgarity or rude manners and she certainly won't take orders from you. She barely managed to take them from her parents, and that only lasted until she learned the word 'no'.

If you love her, want her and value her, treat her with warm love and gentle kindness and she'll treat you like her king. Flatter her and adorn her with gifts and glittering gemstones and she'll purr with delight. She's no ordinary lady, and if she's chosen you, you're no ordinary man. As long as equality and fairness prevail in your relationship and the fires of passion are frequently kindled, she'll keep finding her way back home.

A Leo woman makes an award-winning mother, delighting her children with her animated performances and disciplining them with a generous but firm heart. The Leo mother gives her children plenty of space to romp and expects them to do the same for her. She encourages them to ask questions and she values their opinions. She understands her role is to help prepare them for their own journey. And that is what she courageously does. Never mind that she cries as her five-year-old son picks up his lunch box and heads out the door for his first day of school. She's allowed to be sentimental, too!

Career

The sky is truly the limit in terms of what direction or career a Leo woman can choose to fulfil her ambitions and earn her income. A Leo can be anything she wants to be and more. She always has several enterprising talents and frequently finds it challenging to choose one over another. For that reason and because of her leadership ability the Leo might create her own unique position combining her skills and talents, or even start her own company.

She's probably very adept at expressing herself and generally has a low pleasing voice so public speaking, radio or television might appeal to her. Many Leos enjoy careers in acting, singing, or hosting talk shows, sales, teaching, counselling or consulting. But whatever she chooses, she'll do her absolute best, no matter what the circumstances.

She'll also expect her supervisor to notice and applaud her performance. She doesn't expect people to gush over her (although she loves it when they do). But a little praise and appreciation go a long way for a Leo and there's ample proof she's worth every compliment she gets. Like the sun, she can keep nine balls spinning at the same time without ever dropping a single one. When she's hot on the job she's worth at least two people and when she leaves a position it sometimes takes three to replace her. A wise employer will pay a Leo well, compliment her frequently and promote her consistently.

If a Leo woman is after your job and you are one step or more up the corporate ladder before her, you would be wise to watch your back! She is highly competitive, ruthless and covert in her ability to stalk her way towards getting what she wants professionally — by fair means or otherwise.

Financial

Often referred to as lucky in the financial arena, a Leo woman creates her own good fortune with hard work, persistence and positive thinking. She knows the value of having a good credit rating and making wise investments. She also knows she has to spend money and save money to make money, and she usually strikes a good balance and reaps a profit.

She has the potential to amass at least a small fortune throughout her lifetime and quite possibly a good bit more. But money won't make a Leo snobbish. She already flaunts a royal persona that all the money in the world can't buy. She believes in earning her pleasures so if she comes into a large inheritance, chances are she'll invest it rather than spend it.

She's generous, almost to a fault, when it comes to supporting social service organisations and public radio and television. And she leaps to the aid of a friend who needs a loan to pursue his or her own dreams. Leo knows that what goes around comes around. After all, the planets have been doing it for light years.

Physical

The Lioness can win a best-dressed contest wearing little more than her thick mane of hair. It's often her crowning glory. When it's short, it's classy in a sassy sort of way and when it's long and loose it gives her something to toss around, especially when she's angry. Ms Leo was designed to wear every colour in the rainbow and she leaves other women wondering how anyone can look perfectly regal in deep violet, dreamy in sky blue and electrifying in bright red. Brunette or blonde, she can look rich and famous in a pair of hospital pyjamas. Melanie Griffith, Sandra Bullock, Jennifer Lopez and Whitney Houston are great examples of extraordinary Leo knock-outs!

Ms Leo walks with light steps and graceful poise that make her look taller than she actually is. She is either strong and healthy or frail and sickly — there's no in-between with the sun-ruled. Since the sun affects health and is the life-force of the zodiac, most Leos are healthy and those who aren't generally have astrological aspects negatively influencing their Sun sign. Most Leos are bursting with vitality and the harnessed energy of just one Lion could heat a small town.

If she does get sick (apart from other astrological aspects interfering with her Leo radiance), it's probably from taking on more than is humanly possible. But she argues that humans have such limiting conditions and she can't be bothered with restrictions. Still, she would be wise to balance the demands she places on herself with some well deserved pampering like a soak in a hot tub, a soothing massage or a centring chiropractic adjustment.

Stress and fatigue can affect a Leo's back muscles, spine and heart. She needs to pay more attention to what she eats and when she eats it. Being on the go can play havoc with her food choices and some Lions eat at least one meal a day standing up or while they're driving. A Leo also should avoid sugar, smoking and putting on excess weight. Some Leos' think-big attitudes show up on their waistlines. Grazing on whole grains and fresh fruits and vegetables can help keep a Lioness healthy. She should make time in her busy day to walk, run or do aerobics. Stationary Leos build up frustration quickly and need to burn it up to stay in balance.

Mental

The Leo woman is intelligent, practical and rational. She can handle a bundle of complicated and delicate situations all at once without becoming flustered (unless she's really stressed out about something emotional in her life). She's skilled at mentally dissecting situations and tasks and delegating the work to her subordinates with a sincere and cheerful smile. If she doesn't have assistants, she schedules the time in her own calendar and takes care of it herself.

She tends to be an extrovert and her friends and associates think they know her well. But there's a solar system of thoughts and dreams spinning in her mind that most people never hear about. The Leo woman can be amazingly secretive when she wants to be — and can operate with a hidden agenda. She's generous in helping others, but her friends do get a bit of unsolicited advice every now and again. And the Lioness is one of the zodiac's greatest storytellers, although she sometimes goes a little overboard on the details and exaggerates a bit. But she's never boring and if she starts to spin you one of her famous tales, never mind, she's just playing her dramatic self.

She has a quick wit and a dry sense of humour. Ms Leo also has a great memory for birthdays, anniversaries and special occasions. She picks up thoughtful gifts and artistic tokens for her family and friends along her travels and many Leos travel quite a bit. A Leo is a student of life and she seeks all forms of education and experience.

Spiritual

Most women of the sun are spiritually awakened, whether they show it or not. Watch her eyes light up when she hears beautiful harmonic music and see them fill with tears at the sight of a magnificent sunrise. She feels a deep connection with her creator and yearns to be in the splendour of the light.

She sometimes goes overboard with religions and may turn rather pious if she gets connected to a religion that has a holier than thou approach to life. Some Leo women are attracted to Buddhism or the more exotic religions, too, because they love to explore the different side of everything, including spiritual and religious matters. But whether she is involved in an organised religion or a more exotic one she usually is a devoted follower. This woman 'walks the walk' in spiritual and religious areas as well. She makes a concerted effort to exemplify her beliefs in the way she lives her life and she does a better job than most. She's probably read more books on spirituality (or even metaphysics) than most people have heard of and may know or even study with some of the most advanced meditation, yoga and other spiritual teachers and experts.

She's proud of what she knows about the mysteries of life and the way she applies it, but she's humble enough to realise there's a long way to go and she's always anxious to learn more. Her face can reflect light like a thousand diamonds when she's inspired and feeling grateful. She probably even prays a lot, too. When she taps into her spiritual inner side, it's in these moments that her true spiritual nature is revealed and her earthly fears melts away leaving nothing but pure radiant love.

> *The Leo man ranks among the top Romeos of the zodiac. When your romance is hot and happening, he'll spoil you with gifts, wine you, dine you and serve breakfast in bed the next morning.*

If you are dealing with a Leo man, in any areas of life, think of yourself as a lion-tamer in training. Most Leo men require special handling or treatment (especially if your desire is to get them to toe the line with you). However, naturally, there are many types of Leo men, just like there are many types of hunting and passive type lions in the jungle.

Some Leo men resemble the proud Lion in many ways. It is their arrogant stance, their roar, their hunting tactics when it comes to mating and the way that they love to flaunt their fiercely strong personality. An example of this Leo presence is Leo Mick Jagger, who has made a fortune out of strutting around, shaking his mane and roaring his lyrics. Then there are Leos without such a loud roar or powerful personality, someone like Leo John Howard. Because this latter example of Leo is not really the archetypal Lion, this chapter relates more to the full-on Lion — the one with the roar and the attitude.

So, if you are dating or thinking of dating or dealing with a Leo, get ready for a few tests and trials. Your Leo man is likely to give you a romantic run for your money in more ways than one. He will sometimes keep you on edge, often look like he's got somewhere else to go and may not remember your birthday (even when you've reminded him twice).

That doesn't mean he doesn't love you. It's just that he's so busy taking care of number one, which is probably not you. You may be very close to being number one, but he's likely every day to have many pulls and tugs at his loyalty and attention going on. He is a man who has many things to do, places to go and people to meet. If you're the type of gal who must have constant reassurance, attention and affection, you may find Mr Leo a little bit distressing.

Naturally, in our feminine quest for love, many of us star-gals run into a Leo charmer along the way. This is often our love affair to remember, and also one that we don't necessarily want to repeat. Often these fiery relationships fizzle after a very passionate start.

Most of us never regret the fact that we once loved a Leo. But being with a Leo man forever after, if he is the Mick Jagger roaring Lion type, takes a special kind of devotion. You either have it or you don't, and anyway you won't be the one to choose whether or not you stay with a Leo man indefinitely; he'll be the one to decide.

Look at Sean Penn with Madonna. They are both Leos and they certainly had passion between them, but this passion became their relationship nemesis. In their case, it is interesting to think of two Leo Lions together. Can you imagine two Lions struggling for supremacy and snarling at each other when things are tense? It could be quite a noisy and volatile relationship.

However, if the ongoing love affair does work out and you both sign on the dotted line, surprisingly after an initial power struggle the ongoing relationship usually settles into (surprise, surprise) — domestic bliss (but not always of course). Amazingly, Mr Leo once he has sown his wild oats turns out to be quite a wonderful husband (just hope he's sown his wild oats before he meets you).

Remember that in the Leo male you're dealing with a man who has an enormous ego (I should mention here that if he has other planets affecting his sun sign, he can be very different from a true Leo, even if he is born during Leo birthday time).

But if he is a true Leo, while he may not be wearing a crown or carrying a sceptre, he probably thinks he is a king nonetheless. When Mr Leo is in true form he stands tall, walks with pride and speaks with certainty. His home is his castle, his leather chair is his throne and his family and friends are his loyal subjects. He's intensely ambitious, deeply determined and practically glowing with energy. And his aristocratic demeanour gracefully masks his fiery drive and highlights his confidence and generosity.

A Leo's mind is brilliant; he can be generous to a fault, and his ego can be insufferable. But everyone loves him anyway because his boasting roar is just a cover-up for his secret fear that he's not as brave and capable as he behaves. The irony is this man has more true courage and inner strength than he can even imagine. Still, a king who isn't ruling isn't a king.

So a Lion without an important mission to fulfil has no other choice but to don his crown and patrol the kingdom, graciously offering unsolicited advice as he goes. He tells his neighbour where she should have her new swimming pool and spa installed; informs the paper boy that he could save five minutes on his route if he cut through the alley; and shows his gardener the fastest way to plant a bulb.

[How Leo men operate]

Social

No one loves to party like a Leo! He saunters in like a big graceful cat with his mane perfectly combed, his whiskers straight and his sharp claws politely sheathed. And don't worry; just because he sharpens his claws every day doesn't mean he'll actually use them. They're primarily for show, and 'Show and Tell' is one of Leo's favourite games.

A Leo man will almost always buy the best quality he can afford. He's willing to save for something he really wants and he's sometimes willing to go into debt for it as well. The typical Leo is a living example of someone who only buys the products that earn the highest ratings — and he's got a desk full of lifetime guarantees to prove it.

Leo likes to be the centre of attention so his appearance is very important to him. He also likes to be understood so his speech is often simple and straightforward. And he likes to be heard, so he has a practised way of raising his voice just over the din of the room when he speaks.

The Lion enjoys a variety of sports, good music and action-packed movies. (Remember, Arnold Schwarzenegger is a Leo.) He likes to teach and to learn and he might do some of his socialising at meetings and seminars. And he loves to travel, visiting museums and historic sites and appreciating the natural scenery and architecture along the way.

Love and family

Leo has the male zodiac personality of the mythological Prince who got turned into a toad, or in some cases the real toad who pretends he's a handsome prince in disguise. And while romance can be his middle name he can also be a true heartbreaker of the here today, gone tomorrow variety. At times in his life Leo can perfectly portray the role of both the prince and the toad.

(I should know, I've dated and fallen in love with several Leos who fall neatly into both categories.) That's why, if you're not living happily ever after with a Leo, he may be the ex-partner you don't talk to any more or the affair you'd love to forget. But always something turns up to make you remember. Whether you win him or lose him, love him or hate him, Leo is ranked high among the top Romeos of the zodiac.

And talk about a romantic. When it's hot and happening, he'll pick you up in a limousine complete with roses and champagne, treat you to a romantic dinner, surprise you with ruby earrings for dessert and serve you breakfast in bed the next morning. But when it isn't happening or when it's happening with someone else, you won't see him for dust. And it's no good sending out panic signals or a search party. Once he's gone, he's usually gone for good and some say he doesn't look back.

But he has no shortage of takers as few can resist the strength, power and sunny good looks of a Lion! And if he truly falls in love with you, you're in for something mighty big. He was born with a sense of romance and all good kings know how to treat a queen. He'll buy you the biggest brightest diamond ring for your engagement and the most regal house on the market for your wedding. He'll also buy you the highest quality vacuum cleaner and oven and expect you to use them both well.

He's looking for a goddess, a princess, a showpiece, a trophy, a cook, a lover, a mother and a healer all in one. He has some pretty high expectations (sometimes quite unrealistic ones), so he's great at helping you to grow and keep on growing. You can count on him to keep you on your toes and he's usually quite a challenge. If you love him and want to keep him, you have to keep the romance alive despite the arduous demands of everyday life.

But when it happens and it happens right, this man can be the best catch. He adores a wife who loves to take care of him. He doesn't want her to fawn all over him in public, he just wants her to love him, love him and love him again, and to efficiently meet his needs in a joyful manner. He also wants her to look good, even on Saturdays at home and he expects her to stay in reasonably good shape because in his mind she's a reflection on him, and he must always look good. Even so, he doesn't want her to out-do, out-shine, out-think, or out-smart him in any way.

But vanity aside, a Leo makes a wonderful mate and companion. And if you keep him happy with lots of loving passionate sex, hot meals, warm longing kisses (and remember, not a single put-down), he'll occasionally neglect his rounds through the kingdom and stay home to play Crown the King instead. But this honour can be dubious if he starts to give you one of his helpful lectures on how you should organise the pantry or how you could better manage your time.

You have to play communication games with the king — cut him off at the pass, side-step around sensitive issues, interrupt him with a warm smile and tell him his hair looks great and he smells wonderful. That will work most of the time, but remember that a king is convinced he has a royal obligation to rule his own family and possibly yours, too. And he's deeply wounded when his wisdom isn't both heeded and respected. Should he give you advice, he will expect you to follow it, whether you truly want to or not.

All Leos love cubs and he makes a playful, affectionate father. He's probably not too big on discipline although he talks as though he is. He enforces etiquette rules and table manners but he leaves the rest up to fate, or his wife, whichever is stronger. The typical Lion hopes his mate will control the children so he can focus on spoiling them. Diamonds for his daughter and gold for his son; nothing is too good for the children of a king.

Career

The Leo man is ambitious, determined and enterprising. He wants the best, the most luxurious and the most extravagant. That's why he usually seeks an office with a view. He's perfectly willing to work his way up through the ranks but his aim is always the highest paid or most prestigious position in the company. In the meantime, he's a loyal and conscientious employee. But always remember he was born to lead, not to follow.

He sometimes gets a bit too caught up in office politics though, and has a tendency to play teacher's pet with the boss. (That is, of course, if he's not the boss himself. Then he'll be hanging around with the stars, the celebrities and politicians, or the other big names that mean a lot to him.)

It's not so much that he wants to be seen hanging out with the top dogs, it's more that he likes to be in the right company, rub shoulders with success, be in the know and glean any advice or insights on how to succeed or improve company operations. He's a man's man, a woman's man, a friend and a confidant and he can get exactly what he wants, when he wants it. He often charms himself into a contract or choice situation, and he gets his way most of the time.

Any position of authority brings out the king's best qualities and his aristocratic air makes him a natural leader. His career is extremely important to him, as a Leo man believes he is whatever he does. He carefully selects a field that is creative enough to allow personal expression and profitable enough to support his opulent lifestyle.

Many Leos pursue careers in politics (John Howard, Bill Clinton, Napoleon Bonaparte, Fidel Castro, Herbert Hoover, and Benito Mussolini); the media, writing or journalism (Ray Bradbury, Alex Haley, Aldous Huxley); movies, theatre, acting or entertainment (Cecil B. De Mille, Robert De Niro, Dustin Hoffman, Sean Penn, Matthew Perry, Robert Redford, Martin Sheen, and Patrick Swayze); education, sports (Pete Sampras), law, sales or promotions, financial planning and professional speaking (John Laws).

Financial

Money often makes the Leo man's world go round and for some of them their greatest love affair can be with banknotes. Many Leos love lavish lifestyles, spending cash like water, driving big flashy cars and enjoying all the trappings of success. That's why a Leo man's first wish is to be filthy rich and his second is for everyone to know it. And after all, what kind of a kingdom has no treasures locked within its castle walls. As the fairytale goes, 'The king (the Leo) was in the counting house, counting out his money, the queen was in the parlour eating bread and honey . . .' He likes to be where the money is.

He's also very lucky in all kinds of ways. At an extreme, he's probably rehearsed his response to landing an unexpected million-dollar contract and made a list of things he'd do if he won the lottery. But the Leo knows full well that his best chance of having a million is to go out make it himself. He's willing to do what it takes and he often starts by learning as much as he can about investments, tax shelters and tax havens.

Some Leos become so fascinated with the world of finance that they pursue careers as investment counsellors or stockbrokers. He makes all kinds of financial gains through building excellent contacts with others and often through the fanfare of various assortments of women (from his secretary to the boss's daughter) who admire and seek his attention. Many women seem anxious to point him in the right financial direction and share their contacts or information with him.

To a Leo, money itself is less important than the pleasures, options and opportunity it brings and the doors it can nudge open. A Leo needs to keep a clear head when the temptation to take financial risks or a go-for-broke type enterprise strikes. He can dig himself into debt in an attempt to impress people with his success. But the tendency to spend beyond his means is usually a trait of a young Leo and once he's felt the pressures of being in over his head financially or been burned by a bad business deal, he won't make the same mistake again.

Physical

A male Lion is known for his strong build and his straight posture. His stately presence, gallant manners and flashing smile confirm that he's a child of the sun. Consequently, his energy level and potential for good health is excellent. He has the ability to achieve twice as much as anyone else simply on energy and enthusiasm but this abundance must be physically spent. If it's not, Leo will turn into a finger tapping, leg bouncing prisoner in his own body and the results can be temperamental outbursts and an occasional explosive barrage of hot air.

Some Leo men are quite hyper-active (especially as children). But most Leos learn this about themselves early in life and seek work and play that fully expends their energy reserves. However, many Leos need to play sport to keep their energy in flow right throughout their lives, and in this quest, many of them are runners! Meditation, yoga and other relaxation pursuits often suit them very well and help to calm them down.

Like the Lion in the jungle, good health is vital to his survival and his peace of mind. That is why it is so surprising that some Leos neglect their body's need for nourishment and rest until they have the wind knocked out of them by getting sick.

A sick Leo is a pathetic sight. Staunchly proud, he takes to his bed pretending not to need any help from anyone. But the king can't bear discomfort of any sort for long and he'll soon be ringing the bell by his bedside for service. Leos can be very difficult patients. Piping hot homemade soup and his favourite herbal tea will make him feel loved, scratching his back will put him thankfully to sleep.

The Lion needs lots of fresh air, a low fat diet and a limited amount of responsibilities and stress to stay healthy and strong. He often tends to ignore his own health and his vitality permits him to get away with this in his youth. But as the Lion ages, the importance of taking care of himself increases dramatically. Leo might consider indulging himself by purchasing some high-tech exercise equipment or building a warm, sunny home gym complete with a spa.

All sports provide natural expression for his physical coordination and there are plenty of Leo men who rank among the top professional athletes.

Lots of Leos also like activities that combine exercise with nature. Hiking, canoeing, cross country skiing and basking in the sun on a sandy beach keep the Lion most content. But he's up for just about anything when it comes to sporting action — as long as he thinks he'll be good at it.

Mental

Whether he goes to Harvard or uses life experience alone as his university, the Leo places education and life-long learning near the top of his priority list. He understands that the more he knows, the better his chance of success. Many Leos earn advanced degrees or take extra training classes to give themselves an edge. If it's formal training he's seeking or he has an opportunity for a once in a lifetime experience, the cost is not an issue. He can always find a way to pay for his education. (Henry Ford, and Carl Jung are Leos who invested in their own education and made huge impacts on the world.)

Leo's a great talker, too. The male Lion enjoys a good debate and welcomes fiery intellectual sparring sessions. Self-expression is the name of his game and when he plays he generally wins. But watch him closely in a competition as the Lion isn't completely above taking an unfair advantage by making up a statistic every now and again. If he loses, don't extend your hand in sympathy unless you want him to bite it off.

His pride is his most sensitive area and he won't take kindly to coming second to anyone. He pats himself on the back for his decision-making skills, impresses others with his sparkling sense of humour and tends to be optimistic about the future. But he also may harbour a deep fear that people want to take advantage of him in all manner of ways and this can make him reserved, aloof or downright paranoid.

Spiritual

The Leo man is most complex when it comes to his spirituality. He's likely to explore a lot of different spiritual pathways which can take him from ashrams in India right through to looking into the Church of Scientology. This doesn't mean he's going to join up, just that he likes to know what his many options are.

By the time he's middle-aged, he is nearly always more devoted to a particular belief system (possibly one which is just his own belief, not a popular one) and he often wonders about the afterlife. He's intrigued by the idea of heavenly hosts and may even try to summon one, figuring it's at least worth a try.

Don't expect him to wax poetic about his beliefs unless he's strongly influenced by other astrological aspects. With certain planetary influences Leo can take the lead in religious reforms or become famous by expressing his beliefs. But most Leos stick to reciting from the volumes of facts they know.

Leo can entertain you with bits of trivia about the Vatican, Buddha's childhood and the history of the cross. But he generally likes to keep his spiritual options wide open. He has one main faith and that is in the power within himself. And for some Leos this is the truest spiritual form of religion. He has unity with the oneness of his expression, but that doesn't mean he won't humble himself to higher powers; often this is where his heartfelt humility finds its highest expression.

You'll probably find a copy of the Bible prominently located in the Leo's library. He is likely to also have the *Tibetan Book of the Dead* as well as books by obscure theosophical philosophers or books on other cultures' spiritual viewpoints. With the spiritual books to learn from, or without them, the strong connection with the heavenly sun of most Leos results in a degree of spiritual awakening and a stirring to go and explore beyond what his limited senses can perceive. Even a Leo who isn't sure if there's a divine creator or not usually acknowledges one — just in case.

The Leo baby

The Leo baby is the little star of the zodiac; the super-bright usually up-all-night rearing to go baby — a strong individual, even at birth.

Just as within our solar system everything looks to the sun or revolves around the sun, so this sun-ruled baby will manage to be the centre of attention with everything and everybody revolving around it. Astrologically, this focus of attention is the Leo baby's birthright and destiny.

The Leo newborn will have the focus or attention placed on it in many different ways. As the sun orchestrates this baby's grand entrance into the world you can expect some type of attention-getting event or super-drama to occur around the time this little one is born and often connected to the birth itself. It's not like the baby Lion to slip quietly into the world. These children of the sun are more likely to show up with trumpets sounding and lights flashing.

This child somehow manages to set itself up for a starring dramatic role. As an example, when you hear or read about the babies that are born in taxis or delivered unexpectedly (making a dramatic entrance to the world) — Leo is that type of baby. Whatever it is doing, this little bundle of joy generally succeeds in being noticed — big time. Even when Leo enters the world in a quieter manner, he or she is sure to possess a dramatic energy or presence.

There will be something about this babe that commands your total attention — something beyond the already super-magnetic bond between parents and their children. When speaking of their baby Leos, parents often say things like, 'I can't put my finger on it but there's something different about this baby'. It is born with star quality; something invisible and intangible that makes you pay it extra attention and makes it extra special or noteworthy in some way.

In astrology, Leo is the showbiz (leadership and leading-light oriented) sign of the zodiac so even on the most ordinary levels of expression your Leo offspring is going to be placing itself in the cosmic limelight. He or she is a natural performer and exhibitionist, being particularly skilful at putting on a great attention-attracting performance late at night just when you are tired, exhausted and want more than anything else to catch some shut-eye!

Life for you after the birth of your cute, cuddly and very demanding baby Leo will change rather dramatically. The old ways will be thrown out the cosmic window and you'll be learning all kinds of new tricks with your Leo babe being your expert teacher. You are about to learn the true meaning of the expression, 'From the mouths of babes'.

Don't expect your routine to flow anything like it used to before this baby took centre-stage in your life. What can you expect? After all, this babe is the Academy Award winner of the zodiac. It's a show-stealer and scene maker type of infant; a baby who is going to do everything it knows to ensure you devote one hundred per cent of whatever it is you have to give exclusively to it. But this devotion from your side will be a labour of love.

You will not mind giving this baby your all, because your little bundle of light and joy will be so fascinating, intelligent, loving, radiant, unique and adorable that you'll be happy to devote your total attention to taking care of its welfare, support, encouragement and entertainment. Nevertheless there will be many times when you'll be left in the dust with little chance to do or think of anything else but your star baby. Once this child comes into your world your own affairs could be forgotten and misplaced with other things altogether . . . like whatever baby wants baby gets (whether you are aware this is happening or not).

It's important for the parents of Leo babies to hire a baby-sitter at least once every week or two, so they can escape and spend some relaxing quality time with each other. In the meantime, it's best to prepare for the reality that you are going to be very busy playing mummy or daddy and devoting lots of your life to attending to this tiny person's multi-dimensional needs.

And by the way, you will need to be very strong with this little one. Whether you intend to give in to his or her whims or not, somehow this baby manages to get its own way. For example, the Leo baby does appear to have some kind of innate sense or knowing about what you're doing or thinking at any given time. And in particular it seems to know whether you are, or are not, thinking about it.

The instant you get on with your own concerns and start to think about your own needs . . . or sit down, or if you attempt to relax just for a minute, the baby — even if it is asleep — can innately sense your lack of focus upon it and will all of a sudden act like it needs you. Young Lions are notorious for waking up just as their parents are falling asleep. This ability to pull you into its energy field occurs because this baby is tuned into you in more ways than you can imagine and the moment you stop having its best interests filling your mind and think about yourself it subconsciously knows and it doesn't like it.

From the day it is born, subliminally, this is a baby looking for a party and it will find it with adoring grandparents and other fans which will gather around it with admiring and loving gazes. It needs all this adoration, too — this is the food of its soul just as mother's milk and formula are the fuel for its physical development.

Because it loves attention, it is going to be a natural performer. Your Leo will probably be walking, talking, reciting poetry, saying the alphabet, climbing, jumping and running around in circles far earlier than you expect. Prepare for excitement and continuous drama with this baby, not just during its baby years but throughout its entire life!

If you or your partner were used to being the centre of attention or one of your earlier children was the light of your life before this baby arrived, it is very possible that you or someone else in the family is about to be eclipsed, or will be playing second fiddle. If the sun influence is powerful in your Leo baby, you won't have much chance to do or think of anything else but your star baby.

It's amazing how many Leos find themselves in the public spotlight, even from a very early age. This baby may even find itself being placed in an ad for television (like a nappy commercial) or having some other public role before it is even a year or two old. So get ready for a new phase of your life filled with excitement and continuous drama with your little Lion cub, because from the moment this one is born its motto is: 'Look out world, here I come'.

The Leo toddler through teen

Your young Lion will have no problem refusing to meet your expectations, but they may have all the problems you can imagine when you refuse to meet theirs.

Say hello to Hollywood because your little Lion cub is guaranteed to provide you with hours of show-stopping entertainment, especially once he or she starts crawling around and talking!

By the way, I should warn you that some of the shows your Leo puts on will be more pleasing than others. Along with their ability to make you laugh and smile with pride and delight, Leo toddlers can make you hold your hands over your ears to block out their noisy outbursts when they don't get their own way. Even against your better judgment there are times when you find yourself giving in — just to keep the peace! But resist the urge to do this because when you give in to a tantrum you're teaching your Leo that such displays are an effective way to get what he or she wants.

By the time Leo children are only three or four years old they begin to have clear ideas of what they want and what they like and they're very good at informing you of their desires. And while they have absolutely no problem refusing to meet your expectations, they have all the problems you can imagine when you refuse to meet theirs.

Try not to let your own ego get involved in these little battles of will or you will spend a good bit of time frustrated and angry. Remember that no matter what these children say or how they say it, they are still children and need to be treated with a mixture of praise and reprimand to grow up with a healthy balance.

Because it's in a Leo's blood to rule over some sort of kingdom, create an area where Leo gets to be king or queen. Maybe he or she can be crowned as regal ruler of the toy chest, or emperor of the imperial refrigerator box playhouse. This technique gives Leos a safe place to throw their weight around and also begins to teach them that leaders have responsibilities that go along with their power and privileges.

A great regal ruler of the toy chest will most certainly want to be sure all of the toy soldiers, stuffed animals, games and other toys are safely locked up in the kingdom's toy chest each night! And considering the rambunctious way that little Lions play, tossing toys to and fro and making enough noise to scare away the mice, creating a fun way for them to put away their things will pay off big time for you.

As far as playing goes, hopefully you will live in a neighbourhood or area where there are other children your Leo's age, because Lions crave companionship and are not all that fond of playing alone. If you do live in an isolated area it's a good idea to enrol your pre-schooler in some type of day care or playtime atmosphere for at least a few hours each week so they can begin making friends and fill their need for social interaction. And you might be relieved to know that most Leos look forward to marching off to kindergarten or Year One.

Leos have far less trouble adjusting to changes than many of the other Sun signs and it's usually fairly easy for them to make friends. But I should mention that Leos who don't learn the down side to being bossy may have a harder time holding on to their friends. It's your job as a parent or caregiver to help him or her see that there are great benefits to getting to be the leader but there are lots of drawbacks, too.

The same goes for being a know-it-all. These two Leo tendencies will definitely pay off for them throughout their lives but they will also pay dearly for these characteristics if they do not learn how to temper them.

One way to help your Leo channel his or her need to be in charge is to add a pet to your family. Most Leos are animal lovers and a puppy or kitten entrusted to a young Leo can do wonders to bring out the more gentle and caring side of his or her personality. I should caution you that Leo will want to be involved in the selection, purchase and preparation for the new pet. So decide ahead of time which animals your Leo can choose from and stick to your guns when you get to the humane society or the pet store. Having a cute and cuddly friend to play with and talk to is guaranteed to make your little Lion roar with delight!

As Leos grow older they can begin to take on more and more of the household responsibilities and should be encouraged to do so. You might as well assign this child things to take care of because if you don't, he or she will begin to poke their nose where it doesn't belong and create more trouble than it's worth. The key with these kids is to be proactive instead of reactive, which means staying a block or two ahead of them at all times.

Don't be surprised if the smart remarks start flying from the lips of Leo children at an earlier age than most other kids. Remember that you have a miniature performer in your house who has a gigantic need to be dramatic. It's not uncommon for Leos to pick up lines they hear on television or in a favourite movie, or maybe something you've said and then pick the perfect moment to perform the line — intonation and all — back to you. This talent can be hilarious as well as frightening because Leos tend to have booming voices and you never know when or what your little Leo will come out with! So always try to be careful what you say, even when you think your young Leo isn't listening, and be sure to monitor his or her television and movie selections.

As your Leo grows into adolescence and becomes a teenager, all of his or her traits will tend to be exaggerated and overly dramatic. The most comforting thought I have for you is, 'This, too, shall pass'. In other words, this is the perfect time for you to find out how developed your strength and patience are and probably discover a handful of new ways that your Leo can push your buttons.

One of the ways is likely to have to do with his or her self-discipline when it comes to doing their homework and studying for exams. In fact, as bright as sun-ruled Leos are, they do not always excel when it comes to their report cards. Help Leo to be a bit more far-sighted about the future so the Lion can see how learning and getting good marks now will help to build their empire later on.

Young adult Leos tend to be social butterflies so you will need to reach a compromise with them about their 'free time', meaning the time they spend out of school. Encouraging a young Leo to take on some sort of job for a few hours a week can help to increase their sense of commitment and responsibility, provide them with a bit of spending money (Leos love to have money in their pockets), and fill up a bit of their time with a constructive activity.

Organised extracurricular activities like sports and club memberships are also ways a parent can help a Leo to organise his or her time. But resist the urge to encourage a full schedule because your Leo will want plenty of time to party and have fun with friends as well as dates as they get older. Leos tend to have younger romances than many in the zodiac so be prepared for the roller coaster ride of infatuations and broken hearts. Like everything in a Leo's life, their romances are more fiery and more dramatic than most and their emotions can swing like giant pendulums when they experience the elation and depression that 'young love' can bring about.

The best advice I can give to the parents of Leos is to keep your own ego in check and fill them up with your true love, praise and affection. Make sure they know that no matter what happens in life you will always love them and cherish them with all of your heart — even when you're angry with them. And remember that as bold as Leo the Lion can sometimes be, inside he has a soft, vulnerable and tender heart. In most cases the more he growls the more he needs to be petted and pampered.

VIRGO

[24 august — 23 september]

virgo virgo virgo virgo virgo virgo virgo
virgo virgo virgo virgo virgo virgo virgo
virgo virgo virgo virgo virgo virgo virgo
virgo virgo virgo virgo virgo virgo virgo
virgo virgo
virgo
virgo
virgo
virgo
virgo
virgo
virgo
virgo
virgo
virgo
virgo
virgo
virgo
virgo virgo virgo virgo virgo virgo virgo
virgo virgo virgo virgo virgo virgo virgo
virgo virgo virgo virgo virgo virgo virgo
virgo virgo virgo virgo virgo virgo virgo
virgo virgo virgo virgo virgo virgo virgo
virgo virgo virgo virgo virgo virgo virgo
virgo virgo virgo virgo virgo virgo virgo

element: earth

planetary ruler: mercury

symbol: the virgin

quality: mutable (= flexibility)

colours: earth colours, ochre, orange, yellow

gem: agate, hyacinth

best companions: capricorn and taurus

strongest virtues: creativity, tolerance,

determination

traits to improve: self-esteem,

worrying about everything, looking for

gold at the wrong end of the rainbow

deepest desire: to be perfect

Virgo celebrities

Rachel Hunter, Richard Attenborough, Hugh Grant, Claudia Schiffer,

Mother Theresa, Michael Jackson, Jimmy Connors, Gloria Estefan,

Richard Gere, Cameron Diaz, Keanu Reeves, Sam Neill, Shania Twain,

Macaulay Culkin, Ingrid Bergman, Jacqueline Bisset, Elvis Costello,

Jada Pinkett Smith, Mark Harmon, Corbin Bernsen, Jason Alexander,

Lily Tomlin, Charlie Sheen, Van Morrison, Buddy Holly, Peter Sellers,

Robin Leach, Elliott Gould, Raquel Welch, Rachel Ward, Oliver Stone,

David Copperfield, Sophia Loren, Freddie Mercury, Salma Hayek,

Lachlan Murdoch, Harry Connick Jnr, James Packer, Yasir Arafat,

Gene Simmons, Tommy Lee Jones, Sean Connery, Jason Priestley,

David Arquette, Mickey Rourke, Michael Keaton, Ryan Phillippe,

Ricki Lake, Prince Harry, Agatha Christie, Lauren Bacall, Jeremy Irons,

Bill Murray, Fiona Apple, Robert J. Shapiro (lawyer) and Stephen King.

[General outlook]

The first fifteen years of the new millennium will be a momentous time for Virgos. Your astrological outlook for the time ahead signifies one thing; your life is about to change. Many Virgos will soon feel a restlessness and a desire for adventure, excitement and challenges.

Don't worry, that's exactly what you are going to get and it is also exactly what you need. Planetary movements indicate that things are not going to stay the same around you for long. Your relationships, work, beliefs and attitudes to life are changing. It's time to commence a new chapter, one fuelled with a new, fresh and vital attitude.

Romance

Get ready Virgo! If you haven't already undergone a transformation in your love or romantic world, it's about to happen soon. If you are not with the right 'one' during the first years of the new millennium, you are likely to feel the repercussions of this situation.

However, many married Virgos will discover that after facing a few challenges or times of upheaval, a new and profound depth to their marriage occurs. Also during the first years of the new millennium single Virgos are distinctly looking for a different kind of partner; one who is as ready to grow and learn as you are. This is a wonderful time for upgrading your romantic expectations and dreams on to a higher level. It is also a time in which you won't take your partner for granted.

Health

Your sign actually governs the house of health and wellbeing in the horoscope, so any situation connected to health and wellbeing are of the highest importance to you. That is why it is so surprising that when it comes to maintaining health and wellbeing, you can often be your own worst enemy.

You Virgos have the habit of running yourselves ragged. There just don't seem to be enough hours in the day for most Virgos to complete their 'to do' list.

Fortunately for you, your new millennium outlook on life embodies mind, body and spirit fitness. You will develop an interest in holistic health and work from the assumption that prevention is better than cure. If you do suffer health problems they are likely to be the kind that can be corrected with greater understanding of yourself, and what makes you tick psychologically. This may also involve finding more health and wellbeing information from alternative medicine sources, or other kinds of unique medical or psychological research.

Finance

Although you might suffer an initial setback when the new millennium dawns, as it progresses, financial matters soon improve for Virgos. Be patient and also be strict with yourself in regard to budgeting, saving and investing your money. Financial partnerships will be offered to you, but you should consider the pros and cons of these offers carefully before you accept. Dealing with foreign sources of income or investment is also likely.

Career

When it comes to your career, in the new millennium there will certainly be times when you might feel that you are taking one step forwards and then two steps back. Be patient. All good things come to those who wait and this applies to you now.

Retraining or brushing up on old and new skills might be necessary, especially for those Virgos moving into a different profession. Even if you find adapting or learning things hard at first, don't worry. Virgos' knack for organising yourself (and everyone else) is your greatest weapon and will ensure that you lead the field in various sectors in the new millennium.

[Millennium wildcards to watch for]

Your expectations could be a source of disappointment to you. Many Virgos enter the new millennium with unrealistic goals or expectations for the future. There are positive influences occurring in your astrosphere, but some of the things you are counting on will take a little longer than planned. This is only because, before you can move ahead and take advantage of the wonderful things coming your way, you need to clear something from your past.

Psychologically you are sabotaging your own future because of some unfinished business. The sooner this is cleared up, the quicker will be your progress into the potential that the new millennium offers.

Understanding Virgo

[
*Virgos are the magic people of the zodiac,
with your mind providing you with a unique
box of tricks.*
]

Attempting to describe you, Virgo, is like throwing all the jumbled pieces of a jigsaw puzzle on a table and then trying to describe what picture these pieces make once they are put together, before you have seen the completed picture of the puzzle on the box. Like a jigsaw puzzle, you are a person of many parts, complex thoughts and intermingling structures. Not many can truly figure you out because you live so much through your inner being.

Because you derive a great deal of pleasure from thinking, you think about everything and nothing. Like a private treasure chest, your mind is a place you love to explore. The problem is that you can spend so much time dwelling on your thoughts, analysing and dissecting them with your unique form of logic, that you sometimes forget to be present in the outside world. Also you can seem pre-occupied. People often think of you as quiet, but they wouldn't think so if they could hear your inner thoughts. You also tend to be a worrier, because thinking so much sometimes makes you get concerned about things in a way that can be detrimental. You think, even when you sleep.

With so much going on in your mind most of the time, no wonder so many of you Virgos can sometimes be forgetful. If your mind isn't busy enough as it is, you also love crosswords, riddles, mystery novels and mind games. In addition, libraries, research groups and computer programming (and now the Internet) are often where you can be found working or playing.

Whether you are a housewife, a businessman, a student or a priest, you are one of the truly great magicians or magic people of the zodiac. Mind-magic is in your zodiac genes and many professional magicians are born under your sign. The most famous of these is Virgo David Copperfield.

Whether a professional or not, you almost need to be a trained magician to perform some of the amazing feats you do as a regular part of your everyday life, like taking care of the kids, running a business and also organising the local library in your spare time. These little tricks of making time to do everything, and doing it well, come naturally. Organisation is a talent you often have at your disposal. Moreover, you are a modest sign, too. You usually are not someone who shouts your accomplishments from the rooftops. When you don't want to be seen, there are times (like the magician) that you perform your home-making sleight of hand, your psychological games, or blend into your chosen surroundings so that you become almost invisible.

When you choose to work behind the scenes, you do a sterling job. However, even when you are hard at work, your invisibility often prevails. Many times, others don't have a clue what you are up to. They think you are just busy — doing whatever you are doing — when half of the time, even when attending to an important or precision-type task, your mind is elsewhere. The impression you give out and what is going on in your mind are often poles apart. No wonder most people really don't know you as well as they may believe they do.

Talented and often unique in the way you express those talents, you Virgos are generally extremely unusual people in all kinds of ways. Whether you're a songwriter and performer, like Virgos Gloria Estefan and Van Morrison, a bank teller, a homemaker, a nurse, a dentist — or even an altruist like Mother Theresa — there's generally a whole lot more happening around and within you than your public image or worldly reputation reveals.

Your sign keeps the secrets of who you really are deep inside. You manage to do this because you have a knack, where you yourself are concerned, of being a master of false advertising. By this, I mean that your image, clothes, attitude, body language, general appearance and your personality are often unrelated — in other words, what you see is not necessarily what you get with a Virgo. This skill helps you to fit and blend into most circumstances or places, too.

You are truly a champion chameleon who can attune to whoever or whatever is around you. One of the reasons behind this behaviour is that when you do it, nobody really interferes with you. In fact, although it may seem unlikely to some, you are probably one of the most secretive signs of all, so secretive you can even keep secrets from yourself (or pretend to yourself, or play the innocent to yourself very well at least). Conversely, should you want to be noticed, or desire to voice your opinion so that others take note of you, you put your point across, or get an individual's or group's attention in such a way that others don't even realise you deliberately sought attention in the first place.

You can make others turn to you and say 'what do you think?' because you prompt them to do this by your body language, your mood shift or your mind messages. It is also strange that for a sign that is so astrologically aligned with communication (your ruling planet Mercury actually rules communication) you are one of the more misunderstood signs of all. Possibly because what you say and what you really think often have little in common.

During your life, you Virgos go through quite noticeable phases and cycles of experience, almost as though you have your own independent form of karmic seasons. There are those times (or years) when you find yourself with no time to spare or, when the other extreme is in force, every day seems to drag. The seasons you experience can relate to levels of your popularity, too. You are either extraordinarily popular or else others seem to forget you exist. Especially if you are a Virgo in the entertainment business, you can find yourself up on the public pedestal one moment, and then down in the pits the next (look at Virgo Michael Jackson for example).

In fact, gaining favour and falling from grace, and going back and forth between the two, often seems to happen to you Virgos. One would guess this occurs to keep you humble and honest, because every time you think yourself safe, and secure, or on a winning ticket, generally some twist of fate arises to shake your tree and your confidence again. Astrologically you are often presented or written up as being a paragon of virtue — even when you are not! Indeed, moral issues seem to have a special importance when it comes to your sign. Possibly, we other zodiac signs expect some kind of purity from you that we know we cannot live up to ourselves. It is, therefore, interesting that many nuns and priests (according to statistics) are Virgos.

The holy, sometimes even celibate, life appeals to your sign. Holy or not, you may choose to follow some strange pathways in life, because you wish to avoid temptation. You usually have high standards when it comes to what you consider right or nice. You can also be a very tough critic of yourself. Wanting to be a perfect person, and pure of heart and spirit (however, not always necessarily body) may attract you towards prayer, meditation and surprisingly occult practices.

In astrology, you certainly find a strong connection between mind, spirit and body. However, because your mind is so analytical, usually you tell yourself you have a good head on your shoulders. Your logic often overrules the lower minded energies or basic desires or temptations of the body — but not all the time. That is why you can be such a surprise package to others. You seem to have all the pieces in place in your life, and others put you in a nice neat package in their view of you, then unexpectedly you go out and do the opposite of what anyone would expect.

Because you are quite a complicated individual, you go to great lengths to make yourself appear uncomplicated to the outside world (which often makes you a tidy person). But your attempts to keep everything in place, don't always work. Your dislike of disorder pushes you to be a perfectionist. But disorder is the stuff from which perfection is birthed, just like the egg and the chicken. You can be a cleanliness freak, too (as most astrology books reveal). Maybe you are not struck by cleaning mania all the time but there will be those moments when you may suddenly decide to clean out all the kitchen cupboards, including the oven, at midnight.

Alternatively, you may have your cupboards filled with the latest of cleaning solvents, gear and disinfectants. In some form or another, usually your Virgo perfectionist or organised mania plays a role in your existence. That is why, for such a nice seemingly normal sign, you can be a total eccentric.

Your 'off the wall' side can be revealed when you Virgos carry your obsessions to weird and wonderful extremes. These obsessions are not always to do with cleanliness either. Some Virgos are slobs. You may not be neat, tidy and organised in the usual ways. Somehow you will be untidy and tidy together, but you may need to look for where you are both.

Your untidiness or clutter may come through your scrambled mixed emotions, your disruptive thoughts, your focus on what may go wrong, or your tendency to hold on to everything and keep it crammed in drawers, boxes or wardrobes. On the other hand, you may clutter your life up with trivia and meaningless, time-consuming chores or conversations. When your perfectionist side does get a chance to shine in a healthy way, you can use it to great advantage creatively.

You can be one of the more talented, hardworking signs of the zodiac. From performing right through to leading the science field, you have an ability to be a leader in many varied professions. And because you love order, you are attracted to conditions or environments that create structure, ritual, austerity and routine. You are prepared to put in the time, energy and study to reach your goal. You also have a very kind heart. You are often the person who goes out of their way to make the world a better place in whatever way you can.

You can often be found working for 'meals on wheels', animal shelters or youth groups. Helping others who are facing tough times or who are under pressure matters a great deal to you. You are often found working as a healer, counsellor, lawyer or judge because you admire doing right and love to take care of the sick, the needy and the underdog. Although you love to walk the highest of paths as an individual, and while you want to stay away from the seedier sides of life, you are often drawn towards them.

Even with your best intentions, you frequently end up doing the things you swore you would never do, or become the person you said you never would become. I remember a Virgo girlfriend of mine, who just after she got married said 'I will never have an abortion or get a divorce' and lo and behold she did both within eighteen months. That is why it is so important that you pay attention to your thoughts. On both positive and negative levels, the things you say and think often do come back to you.

You will merrily go along your way without creating a ripple for years, then wham — you will do the most unexpected things. There will be times when you move between behaving like a saint and a sinner or a total giver and taker — in rapid succession. You don't like it when you shake the tree of life and end up holding the apple of temptations.

Some of your desire for perfection and cleanliness is born from your inherent desire to be sin free — or otherwise clean, sweet and unblemished. You may even scrub and rub away at the external levels of whatever you want to renew or make shine. However, often it is the inner you that you really want to purify. Even if you wouldn't admit it to your very best friend (or yourself) the unsavoury, seamier side to life, as much as you say you want no part of it, often fascinates you, even subliminally.

You may have an unusual way of looking for the seamier side of life. You can be the person who keeps three chains, bolts and other paraphernalia on your door dedicated to keeping out intruders, but simply by preparing for the intruder and keeping them in your thoughts you reveal your fascination with them. But not all Virgos take their fascination with the 'dark side of existence' into reality. And should you choose to go for a walk on the wild side you often get caught in a somewhat embarrassing situation (as Virgo actor Hugh Grant found to his dismay).

Even if temptation never surrounds you, or puts you to the test, nevertheless, fate, destiny and the cycles of good and back luck often play an enormous role in the unfolding of your life. There is a great deal of the 'old soul' quality, and the reincarnation powers of the universe, linked to your sign. It is interesting to note that Australia's two young media heirs, Lachlan Murdoch and James Packer, are both Virgos. By coincidence or design, both Lachlan and James were born on the same day, but in different years. As the years pass, it will be interesting to watch the parallel paths of their lives and see how much the lives of these two young entrepreneurs intertwine as they go through their ups and downs, and generally compete with each other in the business arena.

Although (according to most astrological write-ups on your sign) you are supposed to be obliging, compassionate towards others as well as eager to compromise, that self-sacrificing side to your character only holds true to a certain point. You have your breaking point, but it is usually a much more adaptable point than most.

When something or someone crosses your 'I'll be nice until you reach this point' border line, you can be a virtual and real pistol. Especially when you believe in something, have your standards set, or want something, you will often not take 'no' for an answer. While you may seem to be a pushover for the more forceful signs, you can usually be surprisingly strong when you need. But you are strong in a more hidden than obvious fashion.

While not by nature as competitive as say the fire signs (Aries, Leo and Sagittarius) you are far better than most at winning over others or getting what you want, although you play the scenes out in your mind, rather than in front of the world. This is the way that you Virgos are the magicians. You play your best cards so that others do not notice the clever way that you have outmanoeuvred them, even after you have won your hand.

Because you prefer understatement to overstatement, you particularly like to avoid showy displays. Not that you won't put on a good show, if you need to, but creating dramas or showdowns doesn't come naturally to you, so you only work this way when necessary. For example, Mother Theresa was a typical, by the book, kind of care-taking Virgo. She did many good deeds, served others, looked frail, delicate and was extremely humble. But if some of the stories published about her after her death are to be believed, Mother Theresa was a power person of note. She could outlast and outsmart just about any opponent or adversary and end up getting her way.

You can be strong-willed and weak-willed at various times of your life, depending upon the conditions and who you are involved with — and why! However, it is spontaneity or impulsiveness which are often the two things you lack the most. Letting go or stretching your boundaries is difficult for you, even when you know it's in your best interests. On the other hand, these same boundaries and self-set limits make you dependable, intellectual and sincere. Your conscientiousness is part of what makes you so charming, witty and at times irresistible.

Your irresistibility opens up many romantic and social doors to you. Because you have a quiet kind of charm, you're guaranteed to meet intriguing people throughout your life whether you want to or not. The funny thing is you can learn the most about yourself from some of the people you like the least. People don't arrive into your world by accident. You attract them. Your friends, lovers and enemies are your mirrors. They show you things about yourself that you might otherwise miss.

Virgo is an Earth sign

To your advantage, you're highly adept at dealing with things that you can touch, feel or perceive with your well-developed senses. You appreciate the feel of fine silk, the sound of rain and the aroma of great food. You don't take life's gifts for granted and the more you're grateful for what you have, the more you seem to get. Your logical and practical mind can identify potential challenges and create alternative solutions.

When a situation backs you into a corner, you enjoy the chance to find the best way out and you usually succeed. You also have a keen survival instinct that helps you to persevere when others might give up.

To your disadvantage, you sometimes have a difficult time grasping intangible concepts and you might believe that if you can't see it, it doesn't exist. You can become most frustrated by ideas or situations that defy scientific tests or methodical approaches because you really want life to make sense. You're so firmly grounded that you sometimes forget life is a cosmic mission.

[Insights into your sign]

The bright side: One of your greatest strengths is your extraordinary sense of discrimination. You industriously test all new information, sorting, filing, organising and cross-referencing as you go.

The shadow: Your discriminating ability comes with a sharply critical eye. You can be quick to notice faults in others and even faster to find fault with yourself.

[Looking beneath the surface of your sign]

You probably don't show it, but your fear of chasing pipe dreams and falling prey to foolishness is almost always lurking in the back of your mind. You usually have a clear sense of what you would love to do, be and have in your life, but if you fear your vision isn't attainable you can become depressed and even more critical of yourself.

Your quiet nature helps you to hide your concerns but people who know you well also know how much you worry. You can practically turn worrying into an art form and then worry about worrying too much. (On really nutty days you wonder if you should be more worried than you are.)

Characteristics >	Benefits >	Drawbacks >
Analytical	Able to tune in	Pick everything apart
Detail-oriented	Able to focus	Miss the big picture
Discriminating	Appreciate fine work	Find faults
Disciplined	Self-contained	Stuck
Eccentric	Unique	Misunderstood
Exact	Conscientious	Perfectionist
Industrious	High productivity	Workaholic
Intelligent	Grasp concepts quickly	Play mind games
Logical	Able to reason	Override emotions
Methodical	Highly efficient	Lack spontaneity
Modest	Humble	Get overlooked
Perfectionist	Do your best	Nothing is good enough
Practical	Apply knowledge	Don't believe in wishes
Punctual	Accountable	Time runs you
Quiet	Unobtrusive	Withhold information
Secretive	Mysterious	Mistrusted
Self-contained	Individual	Distant
Tense	Quick reactions	Neurotic
Worried	Cautious	Paranoid

Take a deep breath Virgo and look at how attainable even your wildest dreams really are. Then use some of your objectivity to open your eyes to the fact that worrying does little more than burn energy and fill your mind with smoke. If you ever find yourself chasing what looks like a pipe dream, look again. Some of life's most impossible dreams have a way of becoming reality for those who believe they can.

[How to tune into your sign's powers]

> *Stretch beyond your comfort zone.*
> *Adopt a grateful attitude towards life.*
> *Get out of your own way.*

The Virgo woman

[*A Virgo woman, being a perfectionist, will wait a long time before she relinquishes the key to her heart.*

Some of the most beautiful and talented women in the world are born under the sign of Virgo, but that's no guarantee that they are living the life of their dreams. There is often a big gap between the Virgo's ideal and what is really happening around her.

Many models (Claudia Schiffer), actresses (Sophia Loren, Rachel Ward, Jacqueline Bisset), and performers (Shania Twain) are Virgos. Virgo women, however, lead a most complicated existence. Their beauty and their talents are seldom enough to fulfil their desire. They are always trying to prove something, mainly to themselves. No wonder the Virgo woman is on a constant quest to excel. And even when she reaches the top of her selected field, often she still lacks self-confidence and needs more than usual reassurance from others. It is also surprising how often she looks for reassurance — and usually from those who do not intend to give it to her.

Naturally not all Virgo women walk the same romantic path, and there are those that truly do command a great reward and loving return from their relationship exchanges. However there are many who seem to go out of their way to find a man who is likely to give them a 'run for their romantic money'. When it comes to 'being a slave to love' Ms Virgo often becomes a perfect example of the woman who waits hand and foot upon her man (and forgives him for all his shortcomings).

Frequently in her romantic dealings with men Ms Virgo allows herself to become the most vulnerable. Many find themselves attracted to the type of man who is quite self-centred and self-absorbed. Some constantly find themselves in relationships that fall short of their heart's desires. That doesn't mean they don't marry the men they love. It does mean that sometimes they fall in love with some surprising choices.

No other sign tends to give more in relationships to others than Virgos. They can be (especially the women) the most self-sacrificing of all the zodiac signs. She is the kind that will hang in there even if any real bond has long been broken between her and her mate. It is amazing how resilient and persevering she can be in areas that involve her emotions and her heart. In most other areas, Ms Virgo is also a dedicated and committed person.

When she is deeply involved in a field of work, play or hobby, she is so driven to succeed that she won't rest, or even stop to take a breath, until she sees her goal in sight. Just as well she is capable, critical, detail-oriented and self-disciplined. These qualities serve her well. She's also industrious, intelligent, practical and far too modest to clearly see her own virtues. But she isn't interested in dwelling too long on her positive qualities anyway. She's a one-woman search party focusing on her own weaknesses and vulnerabilities.

No matter how much she may feel emotionally beat up by others at times, she always beats herself up more than anyone else ever could. She's committed to constant improvement so she courageously faces her fears. But she can get so caught up in self-improvement and personal development that she rarely acknowledges herself for the super accomplishments she's already achieved.

There's probably a tall stack of successes in her life. She has a brilliant talent for accurately appraising a project's potential for success and an equal amount of denial that she deserves the credit when she rings up another winner. She values facts and information and likes doing research, collecting data and organising her new-found knowledge into categories and files. She knows disorganised information creates chaos and she tries to avoid this at all costs, which makes it even more incredible that she attracts chaos in so many different forms.

[How Virgo women operate]

Social

Unless she's up on stage, like Gloria Estefan, a Virgo usually dresses demurely, speaks softly and gets many social invitations even if she doesn't really want them. She feels most comfortable at parties when she knows everyone but she sometimes has more fun at parties when she doesn't know anyone at all. That's when she lets the other side of herself come out a bit more. She can be anything but quiet and demure when she really lets loose. But in most cases she leans more towards being shy than outgoing and has a reputation for being somewhat quiet.

She likes to keep things to herself but every now and then she indulges herself by calling a close friend and confiding that something is worrying her. Worrying is actually one of her number one hobbies and she does it so well it might be classified under her long list of skills.

She likes giving more than taking and her friends can tell lots of stories about times she raced to their sides to comfort them or bail them out of some predicament. She's also a supporter of the underdog and will take up the fight for someone who can't win alone. (Again, it's no surprise that Mother Theresa was a Virgo.)

Ms Virgo is usually dependable, sincere and trustworthy and she won't tell your secrets to anyone for any reason. At the same time, she can feel uncomfortable showing her emotions and even if she thinks very highly of someone she's not the type to gush with compliments or praise. Consequently when she does offer a compliment you know she is completely sincere. She is usually very private about how she spends her time and her money but her closest friends know not to pry into her affairs unless she invites them in.

Love and family

Don't mess with a Virgo woman. She's a delicate person and she feels every little move you make and is hurt by each promise you don't keep. If you tell a Virgo you'll pick her up at 7:30, don't show up at 8 o'clock unless you like tension-filled evenings. She believes being on time is a common courtesy and anyone who keeps her waiting will probably be considered somewhere between disrespectful and rude depending on the circumstances.

You'll do better to arrive on time with a long-stemmed rose and a beautifully wrapped crystal bud vase. She has discriminating taste and simple elegance always pleases her. In fact, sincere thoughtfulness reaches right through her armour and touches her heart. She's actually a lot more delicate than she shows.

She needs affection showered on her by one devoted man and she'll faithfully return that affection along with a sweet smile and a loving touch. Virgos have great hands and if she gives you one of her renowned back massages all her critical remarks will melt away under her warm, healing strokes. If you want her to relax, return the favour. Virgos can have ridiculously tight muscles from holding all their tension inside all the time.

If you're looking for a fast commitment, you'd better look elsewhere. She doesn't jump into anything and if you pressure her she'll fade right out of your life. She also won't welcome a string of personal questions. She has plenty of secrets and while most of them are fairly innocent she prefers to keep things to herself. A Virgo woman will wait a long time before relinquishing the key to her heart — and she'll wait even longer to give up the key to her hope chest. She's looking for a man who is willing to go to the heights and depths of love with her and she won't rest until she finds him.

If you think you can meet her standards and you're patient enough to stick around, you might be in line for some of the sweetest love under the sun.

A Virgo woman's love is a pure flow of energy. It's rarely jealous or controlling. It's usually quiet, enduring and loyal. It's sensitive, thoughtful and sincere. And when she meets her soulmate they can spark the kind of true love that most people think only happens in fairytales. She may want to have a child or two but many Virgo women are perfectly happy without children. If she does have children she makes a very loving and efficient mother. She probably won't spoil her kids with constant praise and attention but they'll know she loves and cares deeply for them.

Career

Ms Virgo is one of the most accomplished workers of the zodiac. If there's a job to be done, and you want it done well, she's the one to ask. Virgo indulges herself by working too long and too hard. If she manages to complete ten more things each day than appeared possible, she's satisfied. This drive helps her to accomplish an awful lot but it can also keep her from enjoying life! She needs to keep her work in the proper perspective. Frequent overworking can catch up with her and stress her mental and physical health.

She is very critical of herself and some days it's a wonder she gets anything done because she isn't satisfied until a project is picture perfect. She'll actually rewrite a phone message — twice — if her handwriting could have been neater. She loves organisation and you can walk through an office at night and know where the Virgo sits by looking for the desk that's completely cleaned off with the exception of her telephone and maybe a framed photograph of a loved one or one of her pets.

Her intelligent and conscientious nature makes her a valuable contributor to any company but she tends to be most drawn to the arts, the entertainment field, literature and publishing. She can be a marvellous sculptor, a clear and passionate writer, or a talented actress. (There are lots of fabulous Virgo actresses, including Ingrid Bergman, Sophia Loren, and Lily Tomlin.) She also makes a natural critic in these areas, though her reviews can be brutal in their detailed assessment. She doesn't miss a thing. Her attention to fine details makes her a strong candidate for editing, working with statistics, accounting and scientific research.

She has a natural talent with her hands and often pursues one of the healing professions. Virgos make great doctors and nurses, talented dentists and surgeons and skilful chiropractors and massage therapists. She has a talent for knowing what people need and taking care of them the way she would want to be taken care of herself.

Financial

It's vital for a Virgo to feel financially secure but the amount of money needed for her to reach her security level varies greatly from person to person. Some Virgo women can barely sleep at night until they know they've saved enough for their distant retirement. Others feel perfectly secure with a few hundred dollars in the bank and a refrigerator full of food. But most Virgos are somewhere in between.

She probably has some strange quirks when it comes to how she spends and saves her money but whether it makes sense to you or not she makes her decisions with utmost care and will not take kindly to any criticism. She's a virtual whiz when it comes to statistics and managing money unless she lets her emotions get in the way of her intellect. In addition, the way she lives may not reflect the truth of her financial picture. Her choice to live frugally doesn't rule out the existence of a Swiss bank account.

Her air of wealth may not mean that she is actually well off — or at least not yet. However, most Virgos create the level of wealth that makes them feel safe and that usually means an abundant savings of some sort. Even the wealthiest Virgos don't throw their money around and they usually receive the full value of whatever they buy.

Physical

Many Virgo women have a youthful quality to their beauty. Ms Virgo is often on the tall and thin side but even an overweight Virgo is built with a frame of flexible strength. She has a glowing sort of natural radiance, she nearly always looks well put together and she rarely believes she's as attractive as other people think she is.

Her wardrobe is probably organised by colours, keeping the skirts with the skirts and the jackets with the jackets. She likes to know exactly where everything is so she can quickly see her options and make up her mind about the perfect outfit for the occasion. She puts together great looking outfits, sometimes in very imaginative ways, and she has a great passion for shoes, especially comfortable ones with a hint of sex appeal.

She probably gets a dozen catalogues and a handful of fashion magazines and loves to carefully look through them — one page at a time. She might even paper clip the pages that show items she is thinking of ordering. She's not one to dog-ear pages, even in catalogues, and I've met more than one Virgo who was disgusted by people who fold the pages of hardback books or, worse yet, write in them. Her metabolism is fine-tuned and what she eats has a lot to do with how she feels. There's a good chance she's a vegetarian and if she likes to cook she can probably prepare healthy meals that even a junk food addict will love.

Many Virgo women are health nuts, and it's just as well because she needs to keep her system moving with plenty of roughage and lots of water. She has great potential to be very healthy and probably has more than her share of physical strength and stamina. However, her nervous system is highly strung so she should practise relaxation techniques and stop worrying so much about things that may never happen.

Virgo is prone to illness caused by stress and nervous tension and has a tendency to develop ulcers. That's why so many Virgo women have medicine cabinets that are bulging with tonics and pills and syrups of every type. She probably has an enema bottle under the sink next to her hot water bottle, too. She's wise to find a wholesome outlet for her stress and steer clear of people and situations that create tension. She'd also benefit by learning to express herself in some sort of healthy way instead of keeping her emotions tightly locked inside.

Mental

In Greek mythology, Virgo's ruling planet Mercury was the fleet-footed messenger of the Gods. His winged feet represented speed of thought and the mind's ceaseless activity. Virgo may be sitting quietly but you can bet her analytical mind is racing from one thought to the next, and back again. Her mind rules over her emotions and that makes her much more of a thinker than a feeler.

Even when she does feel strongly about something or someone, her mind can confuse her and turn her emotions inside out. Ms Virgo is quite capable of living a lie, rather than listening to the truth of her heart. It can take her a long time to make changes that other people would make in an instant. This is because she tends to analyse and rationalise her feelings in such a way that these emotional messages become distorted.

Commonsense runs her and that is why she is often found doing the same things at the same time even when she would love to be somewhere else altogether. Ms Virgo has a tendency to follow routines and patterns, rather than do what she is truly inspired to do, and as a result she often misses some of the most wonderful opportunities that present themselves to her. She can be so caught up with the forest that she doesn't see the trees! Her brilliance comes from turning chaos into order. This is one of the things she does best and she's always thinking of new and better ways to do things she already does well.

She's logical and methodical in her thinking but she also has an intuitive voice that chimes in. She's a born philosopher who likes to look closely at life and understand its meaning. But her practical nature often stops her from pursuing this line of thinking. She seeks a broad perspective in all things and her quest for wisdom takes her on some amazing journeys.

Spiritual

When it comes to her beliefs and religious practices, the Virgo woman carefully walks a line between her analytical mind and her intuition. She is often involved in cults or metaphysical groups, but even when she does all this, she may still attend regular church services on Sundays. She likes to keep a foot in many different spiritual camps. She often also gets involved in the structure or running of spiritual organisations. She reads a lot about different religions, metaphysical or spiritual practices and she probably goes to yoga, meditation and prayer groups.

Even when it comes to the feeling levels of spirituality, she keeps her loyalty to research and critical reasoning and generally uses both to arrive at her spiritual conclusions. But she's objective enough to know her intuition often has information she can't find in the library. But that doesn't mean she's comfortable with her hunches and intuitions; some Virgos might even wish their psychic voice would stop talking altogether.

She's probably fascinated by the stories of prophets and saints and is open-minded enough to know that all religions are worthwhile and beneficial in their individual ways. If she practises a particular faith, she'll follow its guidelines and enjoy participating in its rituals and celebrations.

Nature is often her most uplifting spiritual force. Spending time out in nature brings her closer to the gods.

Her attention to the fine details in life helps her to notice the symmetry, proportion and order of nature more than most people. She often bases her belief in a higher power on the evidence that surrounds her in nature and on the orderly universe that she lives in. Often she is very connected to goddess energy and may even be involved in women's spiritual groups, magic or other cults that have a goddess base. Whether she feels her special connection is to either one god or goddess, or the gods or goddesses in general, she is more than most connected to and aware of the magic of the universe and its spiritual make-up. After all, she's a Virgo and she knows, recognises and appreciates good work when she sees it!

The Virgo man

> *The Virgo man shines with a quiet mystery that's incredibly attractive and seductive. But watch out, because he can also be a master of mixed messages.*

The Virgo man really is one of a kind. His external 'Mr Cool' outer image is often skilfully composed, constructed and calculated. He's as sexy as can be (think of Virgo 'Mr Cool' Richard Gere) especially when he's brooding or sulking. Intellectually, he's smart, intense about his thinking process and often very powerful in business. He's Mr Charisma when he needs to be, but even in the midst of social activity he manages to project a subtle undercurrent of melancholy or world-weariness. For someone who is often perceived as a humble person, he is quite an effective role-player or actor.

He often cultivates an adopted personality that isn't really 'him' at all. Many times he can have difficulty letting loose, and totally being himself. Probably because he is a conglomeration of feelings, thoughts, attitudes and energy flows, it is hard for him to mix and merge all of them into one complete, comfortable and coordinated package.

For a person who is often so jumbled up with mixed messages on the inside, Mr Virgo can be quite the control freak on the outside. His home may be picture perfect, or as close to perfect as possible. His desk is organised and his car clean inside and out. He even sometimes wears the right clothes, the right smile and the right attitude. He does his best to be considered one of the good guys and he is incredibly sensitive to how people (especially those he respects) view him.

He definitely wants to be taken seriously, and he probably goes out of his way to read the right books, meet the best contacts and know the 'in' places. He is also extremely sensitive about his manliness. The saying, 'real men don't eat quiche' was probably written by a Virgo who ate quiche and then thought he'd look more like a real man if he was chewing on a T-bone.

Sex, and projecting sex appeal, play a much bigger role in his everyday existence than even he will admit to himself. His sexuality is more of the internalised, brooding and clandestine type (he probably has back copies of *Playboy* under the bed). He often has sex-capades happening on the quiet or in his fantasies that are in no way hinted at when you view his external lifestyle, image or behaviour.

There is often a lot more to Mr Virgo than you could ever imagine. He may even be the type that your mother warned you about — you know when she used to say, 'It's the quiet, shy ones you have to watch' (Keanu Reaves, Sean Connery, Michael Jackson, Hugh Grant, and Charlie Sheen are all Virgos).

Even if he appears pre-occupied with the stock market, the football scores or doing his laundry, he is often pre-occupied for a reason. Mr Virgo is the zodiac man who usually is working to a plan. He has an analytical mind, a perfectionist's drive and a disciplined approach to life. Because of his preoccupation with his thoughts and concerns, he is frequently mistaken as distant or even cold. Of course this isn't always true. Usually he's just busy making his plans, and until they involve you he is unlikely to share them with you.

He is usually self-sufficient and has no desire to depend upon anyone other than himself. Even some of the most successful Virgo men sometimes have a hard time delegating to their assistants. He tends to work long hours and often exhausts himself because he wants to give his best to whatever he is doing. Sometimes he works hard to keep his mind busy and to escape from his emotional turmoil.

Many Virgo men have more than one skeleton hanging in their closet. I've met some who have experienced more than their share of personal tragedy and gone through some deep and wrenching sorrows and losses but they usually don't share this side of themselves, when possibly it would help them if they did.

He is the little boy, the teenager, the adult and the old man rolled into one person. He has both feet firmly on the ground, yet his head is often up in the stars. He has the wonderful vision of a philosopher, the mind of a scientist and the desires of a kinky and passionate lover — and he's usually in a perpetual tug-of-war between the three. No wonder he is hard to understand — other people struggle to understand him but he doesn't really understand himself.

[How Virgo men operate]

Social

A Virgo man looks like he just stepped out of the shower — and he probably did. He knows he's judged by his appearance and he wants to be sure he's presenting an image that says he's responsible and successful. He takes pride in his image and knows more about quality clothing than most men. But even in jeans and a T-shirt this guy has a way of looking like dirt and grime won't stick to him.

He can be a bit of a loner but that's mainly because he has a hard time meeting people he really clicks with. He looks forward to parties and outings, always hoping to connect with people who have similar values and beliefs. What's interesting and frustrating for him is that he makes the same mistake in assessing others as they make when they assess him. He tends to pursue conversations with people who look and dress like he does, but he doesn't usually dress the way he really feels. And so he attracts a lot of very attractive, well-maintained women who are perfect in their own ways, but not necessarily suited to him.

Most of his social life revolves around people he meets through his work and the Virgo spends an incredible amount of time working. The only time he really kicks back and enjoys socialising is when he's holidaying and feeling relaxed. His quest for learning and understanding takes him on some long journeys, many of them on foreign soil, and he's fascinated by ancient ruins and historical monuments.

Love and family

He is often the guy in the corner at a party, the one who attracts your attention without trying. The Virgo man shines with a quiet mystery and aloofness that's incredibly attractive and very seductive. He doesn't seek the limelight and he doesn't need to. His powerful magnetism attracts women and his charm and clever but dry humour whets their appetite for more. He's dependable, punctual and sincere and he's practical, deliberate and leery of personal commitments. In other words, any woman who pursues him with a vengeance is forfeiting her chance to be included in his future plans.

While he likes to do the initial pursuing, he then prefers to be met halfway if he is exploring the possibilities of a relationship. His ego is too delicate to handle a tough time or to deal with rejection. If you want to play romantic games, he will probably not handle your hijinks too well.

A woman with her eye on a Virgo needs to be bright, classy and extraordinarily patient or she doesn't stand a chance. He's quickly put off by ignorance and apathy, usually finds vulgarity somewhat offensive and won't tolerate sloppiness. He believes in discreet shows of affection so hanging all over him in public will probably make him edgy. And resist any urge to baby talk, or asking him to make promises to you. The higher a woman's expectations, the further he'll let her fall.

He values honesty, consistency and self-confidence and he's looking for a woman with whom he can develop a genuine, caring and intimate relationship. More than a few Virgo men are trying to find a woman who's a good girl in public and a very naughty girl behind closed doors. I should mention that Virgos have their own unique vibe when it comes to sexuality. Regardless of his sexual preferences, both men and women are sure to find him incredibly appealing.

In most cases, Mr Virgo manages to merge two unique male qualities — he can be extremely gentle and yet he's very strong. He's certain about everything and yet he's still filled with wondering. He's one of the most proficient lovers in the zodiac and yet he worries about his performance — sometimes enough to deflate his own excitement.

And when it comes to marriage, a Virgo will never be happy if he settles for anyone less than his true heart's desire. If a Virgo man does find a soulmate you can bet she's as put together and organised as he is. She won't be the type to leave coffee cups and half-filled glasses sitting around the house and she won't be extravagant or wasteful. A Virgo can tolerate a number of things but dusty furniture and dirty dishes are not among them. Thankfully, his soft voice and gentle touch can more than make up for the times when you feel like you're married to Mr Clean.

Virgo men find children amusing, joyful and somewhat tiring. He doesn't feel a burning desire to be a father, but if he does have children he's very devoted to them. He has long chats with his kids and encourages them to think for themselves. He may not lavish them with hugs or spoil them with toys (unless the toys are educational ones) but he secretly worries about them and begins saving for their education before they're born.

Career

The Virgo man is a dreamer but his dreams are practical and he knows he can achieve them. It may take months, years or decades of hard work and dedication but that only makes the fruits of his success more sweet.

He probably enjoys his work because a Virgo won't choose a career that doesn't have meaning for him. He doesn't want a job just to make money. He wants a profession that makes an impact and improves the lives of others. He usually chooses a profession he can practise well in his own way and prefers one that encourages his creativity and benefits from his personal touch.

There's also an artistic side to his nature and his attention to detail can make him good at architecture, drawing, painting, music, photography and designing. In addition, many Virgo men enjoy working as researchers, accountants, scientists, editors and publishers, actors, critics and teachers. His smooth hand-eye coordination makes him a skilled surgeon and magician, and a great athlete. (David Copperfield, Jimmy Conners and Arnold Palmer are all Virgos.)

Whatever profession a Virgo man chooses, he gives it one hundred per cent and probably even more. He can be a bit of a martyr when it comes to work and his perfectionist nature can make it difficult to delegate tasks to others. Many Virgo men believe the old adage, 'If you want something done right, do it yourself'. But when he has assistants he trusts, he can be the master of making lists, leaving notes with little cryptic messages on them or giving specific, detailed instructions.

Financial

Chances are a Virgo man's finances are as organised as his house. He probably keeps impeccable records, saves all his receipts and lives within his well-planned budget. If you ever have a chance to take a peek at his chequebook you'll see that he uses the same colour pen to write in his register, probably black or blue, and the entries are printed in small, neat letters with every i dotted and every t crossed.

His ambitious nature keeps money flowing in and if he works for himself he can literally make millions. His objective is probably to plan well for his retirement, have ample money to pay his bills and have enough left over to travel and enjoy some of life's finer pleasures. He's diligent about getting his money's worth; his charitable gifts are often made anonymously, and only after he's researched the organisation's overheads and efficiency.

He's not a big spender but he gladly buys gadgets designed to create more order in his life. He views these purchases as investments. He's impressed with the useful and creative things people have invented and built to make life more organised. He can spend hours in stores that sell drawer dividers, multiple size stackable containers, and elaborate shoeholders and he would love to have a clothing rack that rotates like the kind at the dry cleaners.

Physical

The male Virgo is usually stronger than he looks, more attractive than he believes and a bit heavier around the middle than he admits. He's known for having a wiry kind of strength that gives him an ability to keep going when others are falling down around him from exhaustion.

Just because he's capable of maximum exertion doesn't mean he should make it a habit. He needs to take care of himself and resist the urge to burn the candle at both ends. He's slower to display outward signs of illness and it also tends to take him longer to build up strength when he's been subjected to stress.

If he stays in touch with his body he can avoid long-term sickness by such simple solutions as taking a holiday when he really needs one.

His nervous system is highly strung so he needs to engage in physical activity on a regular basis to avoid upset stomachs, lingering headaches and ulcers. He tends to dwell on his imperfections and worry about the future but an hour at the gym or a game of hoops with his buddies can divert his attention and help him to channel his energy in a healthy direction. He also might be into body-building or strength training and he might like to use stationary exercise equipment that allows him to read or watch television while he works out.

Virgos tend to favour a natural, holistic and preventive approach to health and there's a chance he's a vegetarian or favours organic foods and produce. He's no doubt a believer in the power of vitamin supplements and herbal remedies. The Virgo's connection to the earth is a powerful one and he intuitively knows his body was designed to heal itself with the assistance of natural methods when necessary. A Virgo man can benefit tremendously by combining self-relaxation techniques and gentle stretching with soothing music. He also would be wise to take time out of his work day for a brisk walk around the block to clear his mind and recharge his batteries.

Mental

He's a puzzle to others and a mystery to himself. His logical mind likes definitive answers but his intuition says there are only theories and perspectives. And after much consideration he generally admits his intuition is right. It's maddening to a Virgo that science facts change from time to time and what is true today may be false tomorrow.

When he feels most frustrated his insecurity rises to the surface and he turns his attention to the imperfections of those around him. A Virgo can wield his sharp tongue like a whip, lashing out and striking with startling pain. Virgo men are unsurpassed in their ability to arouse anger and violence with their words. But fortunately they can avoid this by having a healthy outlet for that pent-up energy.

When a Virgo learns to quiet some of his worries and calm his anxieties his true inner voice, or his intuition, becomes a bit louder and easier to understand. This throws some Virgos back into the dilemma of which mind to follow but if he pays close attention he'll notice that his logical mind is capable of errors, while his intuitive mind is only capable of love. Virgos seem to tap into the astral Internet without even realising it. Take a poll and you'll find out that every Virgo you know gets phone calls from people they're thinking about just before the telephone rings. You might say it's the universe's way of giving their intuition a wake-up call.

Spiritual

Nobody likes to fight for a holy cause, the underdog or for a spiritual belief as much as a Virgo. That is why so many missionaries are born under this sign. Mr Virgo really aspires to live a holy and good life and you'll often find him involved in religious organisations. This doesn't mean that he isn't open to different spiritual beliefs, but usually he likes to explore several before he makes any kind of commitment.

Many Virgo men know they're on some sort of quest or journey but not all of them realise the journey is spiritual in nature. They are so practical, analytical and critical they sometimes scoff at the idea of spirituality, even if they're secretly curious. But many Virgos believe there's a master plan of some sort and a few even believe it's their job to figure it out. And they might just do it if they're willing to accept that logic may not be the way.

The Virgo baby

> *The adorable Virgo baby will have times when it's the perfect, smiling and peacefully sleeping baby; and other times when it becomes so cranky it's one of the most cantankerous of all.*

A Virgo baby can appear to be a tiny earth angel. It's almost as though it has a brilliant white light surrounding it. Observers sometimes can even see this white light type of aura as a halo around the Virgo newborn's head. And that's because there's a lot of the angel (and a dash of the fallen angel, too) in each Virgo — especially in the Virgo infant. Virgo is the sign of the zodiac that represents the care-taker, server or teacher of others. This is regarded as the most caring and considerate sign of the zodiac. So this practical and organised sign of the zodiac does whatever it can to be born in a way that creates as little trouble as possible.

Virgos of all ages and evolution of consciousness despair over upset and chaos, fuss and bother. Virgos have an inner compass that steers them naturally in the direction of seeking and creating harmony. Because of this inner compass they sometimes experience some disillusionment, as they desire the world to be picture perfect. Even before it is born, a Virgo baby already has an intention to come smoothly into the world and fit in comfortably and without much fuss. That's why they generally don't put up too much of a struggle when they're born — in fact, many are born right on time with a minimum of pain and bother (not all of course, but many).

Even though most Virgos are considered easy babies in temperament they often have sensitive type health issues to contend with at birth and sometimes throughout their lives. This is the sign that rules the house in the horoscope of health and wellbeing. Therefore, at birth it is likely that this one will enter the world either via natural childbirth or on the other end of the spectrum — with every medical procedure possible. Extremes often are in force regarding health and physical wellbeing with the Virgo baby and child.

The health or physical body aspect of Virgo, and in particular the Virgo baby, is often an indication that a doctor or specialist will be monitoring or controlling this birth in some way that is out of the ordinary. Virgos have been known to try out some of the latest procedures associated with childbirth and while they're not trying to resist their entrance to planet Earth they sometimes are born in a roomful of hospital technicians and doctors. And actually the Virgo baby will do what it can to ease the situation because it likes things to go by the book.

Some Virgo births attract all sorts of special attention from the doctors and then when the time comes they turn out to run completely smoothly with precision and utmost regularity, organisation and efficiency. And when this happens you know a powerful harmoniser is coming on board.

Virgo babies may be very cranky, too, because they are so sensitive on physical levels and suffer more than others with baby complaints like gas, teething and even allergies. So your Virgo offspring is likely to have reason to complain and it's possible you won't be getting too much sleep on some nights. Another thing to keep in mind is that often the Virgo baby is an extremely light and delicate sleeper.

The slightest little street noise or even the telephone ringing is likely to awaken it rudely and have it upset for quite some time and unable to settle down again. It's well worth it to organise a sleeping situation for your Virgo baby that is as quiet and removed from activity as possible to ensure that the least noise or external disturbance reaches this baby when it is resting. Also, because this baby remains a sensitive and somewhat psychic child for quite a long time after its birth, it can really suffer from things like bright lights and bad vibrations (like arguments between its parents, even when they keep them quiet). Remember your Virgo infant can pick up on things other babies wouldn't even notice, so if you're upset about something it is likely to sense it and become upset too.

Not all, but a number of Virgos have food sensitivities or are extremely selective about what they eat. You may have feeding problems with little Virgo. This baby (because of its heightened sensitivity) could develop allergies to certain milk intakes and if you're breast-feeding be very careful what you eat, making sure to get healthy, fresh and in some instances organic foods and produce. And when you wash your Virgo baby's clothes, be sure to use very gentle soaps and detergents, preferably with no artificial scents or colours. The more natural the better when it comes to a Virgo.

It's a good idea to pay close attention to the Virgo baby's delicate metabolism and physical sensitivities. The Virgo baby is an adept learner but you will notice that your little one observes and internalises before he or she will actually try something new. In some form it needs to take its time and develop slowly. It needs to gently adjust to the bojangling world around it. Consequently, it isn't wise to push this wee one into doing things it isn't ready to do — like attempting to get it to stand up before it shows an interest or putting him or her into a baby swing without first letting them see how it works, and then eventually working up to swinging.

Allow your little one the luxury of developing slowly and comfortably at its own pace. To attempt to speed up this process is to put this child through incredible and unnecessary stress. But that doesn't mean this baby isn't curious; Virgos love to learn. This baby does well with mobiles or entertaining moving toys around it. If it isn't pushed to walk or talk, it will probably be an early walker and talker. However, if you attempt to speed up the process it could rebel and put off walking and talking for a long while!

The Virgo toddler through teen

> They're curious in a very different sort of manner and often are intrigued by questions no one else would think to ask.

Virgo toddlers love toys they can manipulate — like balls they can squeeze and squeak and bells they can ring. They like toy trucks that have lights that flash and sirens that sound and they like dolls that eat, wet and cry. They like things that are useful and they like to keep their things organised and tidy.

In fact, these little ones will at a very young age assign special places for their different books and toys. You may not even know they do this until one day you set the pink, squeaky elephant on top of the toy chest and your three-year-old informs you that's not where it belongs and points to his bed explaining, 'George always sleeps on my bed'.

Virgos are some of the most thinking children of the zodiac. They are curious in a very different sort of manner and often are intrigued by things that no one else would think to ask or notice. I once overheard a young Virgo who was trailing behind her father in the Houston Galleria asking 'Where do these stores get all these clothes?' 'Who makes the clothes Dad?' 'Are they nice people?' 'What if people who are mean are making our clothes?', and on and on and on. Her father had sort of a glazed, bewildered expression and I saw him stop to scratch his head in confusion as I turned into the card shop.

While the questions may befuddle you, their desire to stay clean will make laundry day a lot easier. Virgo children will actually request to change clothes if they accidentally spill something on themselves or get dirty somehow. And don't be surprised if your Virgo reacts very dramatically if someone else spills something messy on them. It's a good idea to always carry an extra set of clothing for your Virgo, especially if it's a special occasion and they have on one of their favourite 'grown-up' outfits. It's not that these kids are proud peacocks, it's more that they don't want to call negative attention to themselves and a big Fanta spot on a white shirt is definitely considered negative attention by a Virgo.

These youngsters really thrive in an atmosphere of gentle organisation and efficiency. They like routines so long as there is some built-in flexibility — and they like to know what's coming up and what's going to happen after that. Your Virgo will feel much better about greeting the day if they know what they can expect. And it really helps to break activities and events into steps for these kids so they can piece it all together instead of trying to swallow one big gulp of information all at once.

Rather than announce to your little Virgo that you will not be home tonight and they will have a baby-sitter whom they have never met, explain the bigger picture in more detail. You might say, 'Remember the award Daddy won? Well, tonight the people who are giving the award are having a grown-up dinner and Daddy and I are going to it.' Then, gently ease into the part about making his or her favourite dinner before you leave, and the fact that a very nice young woman (or man) who loves to play his favourite games is coming over to play with him tonight until Mummy and Daddy come home. You still may meet with resistance, but in time your Virgo will learn that you do come back home and that baby-sitters are sort of fun.

Make sure you have lots of challenging and thinking types of games and activities in your home for the Virgo child. These little ones enjoy putting together puzzles, solving simple riddles, telling secrets and following instructions that lead to a surprise, a treasure, or just winning a game! Virgos love treasure hunts, where they need to figure out the answers to clues and follow instructions to make it from one point to the next.

They are extremely observant, too, so if you ever plan an indoor scavenger hunt for the young Virgo on a rainy day they may find some things in addition to the ones you put on their list, like that high school trophy you thought you had lost, the Christmas albums you thought your sister snuck away with last year, and maybe even some loose change and your misplaced library card.

I should mention that if you have a particularly quiet or seemingly shy Virgo this will probably shift and change a bit as he or she gets older and begins school. Some Virgos make almost amazing transformations around the age of six or seven and go from being the silent observer to the non-stop talker. It's as if they have suddenly synthesised and processed all of the information they've been collecting for the past six years and they're ready to share it all — one bit after another. This phase will level out when they reach nine or ten, about the time they tend to rediscover the art and fun of listening.

One of the most difficult and challenging times that Virgos and their parents face comes during the adolescent transition. The ages of ten through thirteen are much more stressful to Virgo youth than many others because this time period is filled with change and transition and the Virgo cherishes the *status quo*. This is the youngster who will protest when you rearrange your furniture and who is visibly saddened when the family trades in the old car for a new one. There's not much you can say to a Virgo who's undergoing one change after another both inside and out.

The best advice I can give is to try to maintain the basic routine in your family that the Virgo is accustomed to so they have a stable place to return to where they feel safe and comfortable. Any large family-oriented changes at this time in a Virgo's life can really rock the boat. So if you're planning to move to a new home or new location, or if your hours at work are changing and you will no longer be there to greet them when they arrive home from school, you will need to carefully prepare them and ease them through these transitions using the softest of kid gloves.

Virgo adolescents and teenagers are extremely critical of themselves and of others, including you and the rest of the family! Their ability to survey, sum up, analyse and appraise people and circumstances begins to really blossom at this age and unfortunately it tends to grow much faster than their ability to be tactful. Just look at this as the perfect opportunity for you to thicken your own skin and practise the unconditional love you have in your heart for your Virgo — especially on those days when they are acting like everything but the little angel you remember bringing into this world.

Count to ten before you blurt out what you're thinking when you're angry at your Virgo. Words wound them more deeply than just about all other forms of reprimand and punishment and if they think you're withdrawing from them they can become truly distressed and frightened. Besides, in almost every case a Virgo is much harder on himself or herself than anyone else could possibly be. These young adults spend so much of their energy criticising themselves that the best you can do is help to balance their negative self-programming with positive and encouraging statements focusing on their abilities, talents and strengths and on how much you love and appreciate them.

LIBRA

[24 september — 23 october]

libra libra libra libra libra libra libra
libra libra libra libra libra libra libra
libra libra libra libra libra libra libra
libra libra libra libra libra libra libra
libra li

libra libra libra libra libra libra libra
libra libra libra libra libra libra libra
libra libra libra libra libra libra libra
libra libra libra libra libra libra libra
libra libra libra libra libra libra libra
libra libra libra libra libra libra libra
libra libra libra libra libra libra libra

element: air

planetary ruler: venus

symbol: the scales

quality: cardinal (= activity)

colours: blue and turquoise

gem: diamonds and opals

best companions: gemini and aquarius

strongest virtues: eye for design, social

charm and diplomacy

traits to improve: feeling helpless, lacking

direction and handing your power over

to others

deepest desire: a life filled with romance

Libra celebrities

Jean-Claude Van Damme, Heather Locklear, Catherine Zeta-Jones,

Olivia Newton-John, Paul Hogan, Bruce Springsteen, Michael Douglas,

Martina Navratilova, Sting, Meatloaf, Ralph Lauren, Serena Williams,

Gwynneth Paltrow, Mira Sorvino, Margaret Thatcher, Martina Hingis,

Julie Andrews, Mahatma Gandhi, Neve Campbell, Alicia Silverstone,

Angie Dickinson, Fran Drescher, Susan Sarandon, Sarah Ferguson,

Kate Winslet, Bob Geldof, Penny Marshall, Matt Damon, Randy Quaid,

Luciano Pavarotti, Donna Karan, Sigourney Weaver, Angela Lansbury,

Will Smith, Roger Moore, Julio Iglesias, Joan Cusack, Barbara Walters,

Brigitte Bardot, Linda McCartney, Marie Osmond, Mickey Rooney,

Evander Holyfield, Cheryl Tiegs, John Lennon, Deepak Chopra,

Britt Ekland, Shaun Cassidy, Mario Puzo, Luke Perry, Elisabeth Shue,

Ian Thorpe and Dannii Minogue.

[General outlook]

After feeling as if they are dragging themselves out of the old year, the good news is that Libras enter into the new millennium with their trademark 'happy-go-lucky' attitude renewed. A newfound confidence, combined with a desire for adventure, lead you to broaden your horizons in all areas of your life during the first years of the new millennium. Travelling, studying, starting a family or creating your dream home are just some of the areas that you delve into with renewed enthusiasm and passion now. Other people are attracted to your 'anything is possible' attitude and this entices new friendships, business associates and opportunities your way. This new millennium is an ideal time for you to start making your dreams come true. Celebrate life, love and good health. Things are getting better all the time.

Romance

For quite some time, many Librans have felt restless, confused and torn with uncertainty because of their romantic connections, or through their lack of them. Added to this, you have been receiving mixed messages from others regarding commitment — and the future, too. Not knowing if you were 'in' a relationship or 'out' of it (or about to be either way) has kept you off-balance. Libra is the sign of human relationships, marriage and companionship so it's no wonder you enter the new millennium with love and romance fixed firmly on your mind. Mutual goals (parenting, a family business, home renovation or travel plans) bring married Libras together while single Libras find themselves attracted to a different kind of partner, and with good results. Open your heart and mind where relationships are concerned, believe in 'happy ever after' and anything will be possible.

Health

Your health is optimum as the new millennium gets underway and a long term health problem can be controlled through learning new methods of relaxation and prevention. Make taking care of yourself your number one priority, as stress related to a new job, relationship or financial situation may cause you to skip meals or forget to exercise. Your saving grace is your love of sleep! A good night's sleep works wonders for you as this new millennium begins to make your everyday pace even more hectic than those of the past.

Finance

You may have made your new millennium financial resolutions with enthusiasm and the strong belief that you can truly make your fortune in the new millennium. But as time goes by your financial schemes, dreams and plans are likely to become little more than a hazy memory. Self-discipline concerning money matters is all-important for Libras. Stick to a budget and start a sensible savings plan. Be prepared to let other people foot the bill some of the time, as others sometimes take advantage of your generous and sociable nature. Be wise in the new millennium (and particularly penny wise, not pound foolish), and you'll end up wealthy. Also you would be most ill-advised now to lack attention when it comes to dealing with your financial matters. This is not the right time to leave the management of your funds for others to handle — certainly not without lots of supervision or revision. Instead, this is your time to become much more of a financial wheeler-dealer and financial planner than you have ever been in the past. You may even need to take on extra studies or training to accomplish this, but it will be well worth it!

Career

Your relationships with colleagues, associates and employers indelibly mark your professional experiences and your success depends on others during the first five years of the new millennium. Working as a team (your favourite way to work) will bring you wonderful rewards. New experiences to learn and teach arise, too. Keep in mind that entering new technical territory will be highly rewarding. Have confidence in yourself, be prepared to learn new skills and business techniques, and you'll move mountains.

[Millennium wildcards to watch for]

The stars and planets combine to blow the winds of good fortune over your life, allowing your dreams and visions to flourish. Several of your long-held aspirations start to come true. Although it's easy to get swept up in the magic of the moment, be careful that your feet remain planted on solid ground. You could become side-tracked from the things that are truly valuable now, chasing castles in the sky. Striving for your dreams (but in the most practical of ways) will ensure your continued success. Avoid going after short-term thrills at the expense of longer term dedication and planning.

[*Nothing or no-one can surprise you as much*
as you frequently surprise yourself.

Understanding and defining you Librans is a complicated issue because your sign operates in a league of its own. Even symbolically, you are unique. While the other signs have people or animals representing them (i.e. Aries the Ram, Taurus the Bull, Gemini the Twins, Cancer the Crab), you don't — instead you have the scales ruling you.

And there is more! Your ruling planet, the usually totally feminine energy planet Venus (who I consider to be your guardian angel and a wonderful goddess influence) is actually operating under her male expressive output when she rules you. With Venus effectively crossing over (or going into the closet in a roundabout astrological way) you are unique in the way that you are constantly receiving a weird blend of mixed and jumbled signals about who you are, what you want and what you should aim for in life. No wonder astrologers deem you the most undecided sign of the zodiac. There are said to be times when you Librans feel like you don't know whether you are coming or going. You have also earned a reputation for being a fence sitter.

Also, from observation, the altered energy-force coming from Venus can play some weird tricks on your will-power or sexual role-playing. I have sometimes seen this unusual flow of astrological output from Venus make Libran women stronger in will and attitude than most of the men they are surrounded by. Indeed, strong-willed women like Librans Eleanor Roosevelt, Margaret Thatcher, Susan Sarandon and Martina Navratilova are powerful examples of the Libran will — when it comes to the fair but also forceful maidens who are born under its sign.

With Venus flexing her more masculine muscles as she rules over your sign, some Libran women can be the ones who truly do wear the pants. Surprisingly, when it comes to the men of this sign, Libran men can turn out to be ruled by women (or run by sex, other men or women) and some Libran men can be extremely passive and even more gentle than their female counterparts. Sex appeal and sexuality often takes on a whole new dimension where your sign is concerned.

Now let's look at your unique and strange inanimate symbol of the scales. We use scales in our everyday life when we weigh things up. In most areas of life there is often a need to balance one thing, one situation, one choice against another. For example, we might ask ourselves 'should I go to sleep now, or stay up?' 'Should I eat a second piece of cake, or say no?' . . . and on, and on.

Choice-making, whether it relates to major or minor situations, is a constant process of our existence. For you Librans this everyday type of selection process can be something that puts you through unusual tests. You can take weighing things up and going overboard one way or another to extremes at times. This applies where you are all excited about something or someone one day, then the next wonder what on earth you saw in the situation. No other signs of the zodiac run the gamut of changing attitudes or responses as you do.

When it comes to dealing with situations or other people, 'I love you, I love you not' can take on a completely new significance and meaning for you. However, what is truly amazing about this selection process is when you really change your mind — where other signs alter their course and take off in a new direction — you Librans often continue with your original course. There is a part of your character that feels that once you have set certain wheels in motion you don't like to stop — even if you don't want to be there doing whatever it is any more. In these conditions you Librans become your own worst enemies because you often find yourself living lives which do not even slightly resemble the life you dream about for yourself. You can then be something like a robot walking around, running through your every day existence operating on automatic pilot.

In this automaton state you can go about your everyday business switched off internally and carry on as usual, simply because this is your routine. You don't even stop to think that you have the choice of changing your status quo and do what you love to do. So is this ability to switch off from your true heart's desires right or wrong? There is no right or wrong for you, there is simply an incredible message in your stars to love where you are right now. 'Be here now', really was written with a Libran in mind, because too often you are caught up in dilemmas concerning where you should be.

And you do have a tremendous amount to be grateful for astrologically. The unique and unusual input you receive direct from Venus helps you to gather a constant wealth of valuable experience to draw upon. Venus, in the way it affects you, opens you Librans up to both your right- and left-brain channels (the feminine/intuitive and masculine/practical side). This gives you a tremendous wavelength or bandwidth of conscious and unconscious thoughts.

You have the capacity to both give out and receive an abundance of information and this can make you extremely talented and creative. On physical levels, some of you may even be able to write well with both hands or otherwise be more right and left brain integrated than the other Sun signs. However, as mentioned earlier, this same aspect can contribute to making your decision-making turn into a dilemma. Because you can see so many varied points of view (like his, hers, theirs and mine), it can be tough for you to come up with the best decision. In addition, it makes it very easy to change your mind, because you have more aspects of your mind to change.

It's also interesting to note that in the horoscope your sign governs relationships and affects the house of marriage, partnerships, and relations to all other individuals. Relationships provide a unique mirror for us to view ourselves in. You Librans often have a greater need than most to capture a glimpse of yourself in the external mirror that a relationship can provide. Because relationships take on many areas of importance to you psychologically, emotionally and otherwise, you often spend a great deal of your life looking for the relationship mirror.

In addition, with relationships, sex can turn out to be something that complicates your existence. Your sexuality (or how you choose to express yourself as a sexual being and within a relationship) can become a major issue, both in a relationship and out of it.

Your life is constantly a work in progress because you are so multi-dimensional. This multi-dimensional side to you also complicates things; because it is these churnings that confuse you. Even where you give an impression that you are on top of everything and your own person, nevertheless quite frequently it is your teacher, your religion, society at large, your parents, peer group pressures or close others who are defining who you are, rather than you.

Even this situation, that puts you into unusual realms of sex expression that are often not truly representative of who you 'really' are, which includes sexual and morality issues, this still serves you. Because you are always looking for answers about who you are and what makes you and others tick, through being all things to all kinds of situations you learn the most about yourself, others and destiny.

Destiny teaches you some of your most incredible lessons. Many times life becomes quite a winding road for your sign, because the universe can tip your scales (through circumstances beyond your control) in unusual directions. It can place a challenge on one scale and lift a burden from the other, or put burdens on both scales sometimes. Yet no matter how often destiny pulls the rug from under you or takes you on a magic carpet ride during the course of your earthly existence, although what occurs in your life frequently takes you by surprise, nothing or no-one can surprise you as much as you frequently surprise yourself.

If your fairy godmother could grant you one wish, it is likely that wish would be for something that gave you 'peace of mind'. You love harmony (since you are sometimes operating under inner disharmony). Creating an ordered, organised existence means a lot to you. Chaotic conditions wear you down very quickly. When you manage to attain a state of harmony and order in your life (even if only briefly), you feel a euphoric sense of contentment.

Conversely, when the scales of life are unexpectedly tipped against you, your emotions and your existence bounce around like a rubber ball. You can lose your connection to your confidence or faith in the future in an instant when things go wrong. That is why you will do whatever it takes to maintain balance and harmony, sometimes even being prepared (for peace sake) to settle for less than you desired, planned on or deserve! Putting on a happy face often goes hand in hand with being born under your sign. After all, you don't want to rock the boat of life, so you will do whatever you can to stop any disturbances — even if it might mean continuing to live in hell when you are only one step away from heaven.

Now just because you will put yourself in an unhappy position to conserve peace or keep yourself safely distanced from confrontation does not mean that you have a tendency to play the martyr. Because you have two sides to you (something like Geminis), even though you love peace, you also like to stand up for yourself. Moreover, not too many signs have such a strong desire to dangle their world on a string as you do.

Your wish list usually includes a fine life, happy marriage to your soulmate, great friendships, and luxury living as well as having an all round lifetime party type of good time. After all, when it is all said and done you are ruled by pleasure seeking, Venus and her indulgent and frivolous qualities and desires make up a foundation stone of your character. You have a great love for the good life and hard times are not something you think of kindly. Indeed, your Venusian connection enhances your artistic abilities and magnifies your desire for pleasure and your dislike for discomfort or ugliness.

Life is often a bittersweet multi-dimensional experience for you. Another secret wish of yours is to find a way that you can have your cake and eat it, too — and sometimes you are lucky enough to manage to do just this. However, at other times you pay a high price for your desire to have everything you wish for — and more. Some of you will even go as far as to sell your soul for the easy life. This is when you find yourself walking a self-sabotaging pathway, a pathway that can lead towards moral, emotional and even spiritual bankruptcy. Yours is the sign that often learns the hard way that there rarely is such thing as a free lunch. And the expression, 'the piper must be paid', holds a special insight and significance to you.

When you lose your way, you can get yourself into all kinds of messes. Your weakness can be that you sometimes can't say no, even when you really want to say it. However, these tough-time experiences are seldom wasted on you. Through them, you learn who and what you do not want out of life. When you change your desires, your life can instantly move from one extreme to the other — like from the feast to the famine.

However, usually you do not consciously go looking for trouble or argument; you prefer to drive down the safer highways of life, rather than race down the fast track. While your opposite sign, Aries, is reputed to race in where angels fear to tread, your sign likes to check that you have a safety net in place, before you leap into unknown territory. While leaping may not come naturally to you, just knowing where you want to go next can be just as tough to decide upon as choosing where you want to be right now.

Throughout much of your life you can be like Alice in Wonderland asking the Cheshire Cat which road to take. As he tells Alice, it all depends upon exactly where you want to go and often Librans are not too sure about planning for their futures. There can be periods of your life when you spend a lot of time waiting for others to make up their minds, so you can make up yours.

Or you may wait at a crossroad expecting a breakthrough or an omen to appear or for an act of fate to do something that changes your life, instead of taking definite steps yourself to decide on something or someone. In the extreme, some Librans can wait their entire lives for their ships to come in, or the wind to change. They often also wonder why they stay stuck. I always remember a psychiatrist friend of mine who said so many Librans came to him wanting to change their lives but never did anything to make the change happen. He said it was his opinion that the only way to get Librans to take immediate action was to tell them they had 24 hours to live!

Apart from my psychiatrist friend, others tell funny stories about Librans. My girlfriend who runs a dress shop in Sydney, Australia, said she always knows when a Libran comes to shop because they try on a whole hotchpotch of different clothes. Then they ask what she thinks about each garment. If other shoppers are in the store they sometimes ask their opinion, too.

After they have tried everything on they usually end up with two items they want to buy (because they can't choose between them). But the instant my friend starts to write up the bill — and she waits for this part — they suddenly say, 'No, I won't buy it now, I'll come back tomorrow'. She always laughs and says, 'Thank you Ms or Mr Libran' and when she says this the customer almost keels over, because usually she is spot on.

Because you can be such an 'in the door one moment and out the door the next' type, it is just as well that your charm and your silken diplomacy can smooth the ruffled feathers of others. You tend to step on some toes and sometimes even the authority or the law with your ability to change your mind at a moment's notice or because of your flights of fancy. My friend Camilla, who is married to Trevor, a

Libran, says instead of having a treadmill they should instal a revolving door at their home. That way he can get all the exercise he needs, going round and round in the door, while he is deciding whether he is staying in or going out.

You are popular with people because you are a natural charmer. You also have quite magical powers of persuasion. You are usually well liked by others and especially become most likable when you need to be. When you are in fine form you can be the smooth talker of the zodiac. After all, diplomacy (and sometimes flattery of others) can be one of your greatest selling points. Your polished charm and appearance of inner peace is very comforting to others and your capacity to patiently listen and seem to understand them, attracts people from all walks of life.

Your right brain-left brain integration makes your outlook and your viewpoint usually extremely open-ended so you have some interesting ideas, views and concepts to offer up. You can often be extremely entertaining and witty. Sometimes you can even be quite a raconteur as well.

Being able to see both sides of most situations also gives you a great deal of innate wisdom. You can immediately grasp the concept that the experience of life is something that affects us all differently. For example, a rainy Saturday may be a good thing for the farmer but for the bride about to walk out into the storm the rain is a hassle and maybe even a big disappointment. To you Librans, however, the rain itself is just rain. Others bring their concept of rain to the picture.

You Librans are good at shifting your own viewpoint so that even when things look bad you can keep them in perspective. For this reason you're able to function with a sense of detachment that other people often mistake as indifference. However, indifference is not what you feel. The truth is you are exceptionally empathetic of others' trials and tribulations. However, you don't like to get caught up in dramas, and your philosophical outlook makes you more tolerant or easygoing about most things that bother other people.

Even when you present yourself in the most cool, calm and collected light, this doesn't always mean that you aren't brimming over with concerns or anxieties. Your feelings and senses run deeply and are so complicated, even for you, that you can rarely lay all your cards out at once. Sometimes your efficiency in hiding your true feelings works both to your benefit and to your disadvantage. The fact that very few people can fathom what's going on in your mind is a comfortable defence for you, but it also makes it more difficult to develop the honest, intimate relationships you desire.

No matter how popular or appreciated you may appear to be in your friendships, your career, your family circle or in everyday exchanges with others, there's a place within you that is very private and separate from all around you.

But your private fortress can't protect you from yourself Libra! And sometimes closing yourself off from the world just makes your internal battles more intense.

The good news is that when you really truly do want something, or make a decision, you go for it big time and nothing or nobody can hold you back. Just look at Libran trendsetters and trailblazers Sting, Margaret Thatcher, John Lennon and Mahatma Gandhi, for example. These Librans took decisive actions and stood their ground. But strangely, when it comes to choosing between a vanilla or a chocolate ice cream, you can deliberate long enough for both of them to melt before you decide. Yes and no are still two of the most difficult words in your vocabulary. Even so, you Librans definitely have the alert mind, the inner fortitude and honourable heart to follow your dreams, but only once you figure out what they are.

You can be very sociable in nature, too. Another plus to your character is your talent for discovering something nice or honourable in everyone you meet. Nevertheless, this openhearted ability is also responsible for some of your most distressing friendships and unhappy circumstances. When your generous nature goes overboard you send your better judgment on a holiday and invite your predators in for lunch.

Fortunately, your gentle manner and genuine interest in their dreams enchants even the most villainous characters — most of the time. But every now and again when you offer someone refuge from a storm, you let in a blast of trouble that darkens your clear blue skies.

Perhaps it's your own ability to be shrewdly devious (at certain times) that attracts these 'darkened' people and situations. They may serve as a reminder that as clever as you are, honesty and integrity are still the best policy. Your sense of justice already knows that even when deceit appears beneficial, it rings up an exorbitant price tag somewhere in the future. You Librans seldom escape from the cosmic justice system, because you are so closely aligned to it and with it.

• • • • • (Libra is an Air sign

To your advantage, you have an ethereal quality that is sometimes described as 'out of this world' or evolved. You're a seeker of light and a believer in true love and you have the potential to create the most beautiful and harmonious art, music and relationships.

You also have a greater ability than most to achieve a balance among all the areas of your life. Where some signs go overboard focusing on just the physical or just the mental part of life, you understand that all areas of your life run most smoothly when they're in balance with each other. Besides, all work and no play makes Libra miserable, grumpy and generally very unhappy!

To your disadvantage, you're a bit of a dream cloud and people sometimes hesitate to tell you the truth for fear of shattering your carefully created illusions. You also have a tendency to jump to conclusions and make some huge assumptions without always checking your facts before you share them with others.

You seek love above all else but your fear of exposing your vulnerable side can keep you drifting from one relationship to another. You tell yourself you want your freedom and in a way that's true. But what's also true is you may be going out of your way to avoid an intimate, one-on-one long-term relationship.

[Insights into your sign]

The bright side: One of your greatest strengths is your ability to achieve a balance in your emotions and in all the areas of your life.

The shadow: You sometimes become so preoccupied with trying to keep your life in balance that you overlook the messages, gifts and opportunities that are offered to you along the way.

[Looking beneath the surface of your sign]

When the Scales are tipped way out of balance, Libra, you reveal the sides of yourself you generally keep well under wraps. It's during these times that your diplomacy can turn to deceit and your appreciation of beauty can swell up into vanity.

You are always on a quest and seldom happy with 'being here now'. Whatever you think is most missing in your life tends to become your biggest goal. When you're lonely and depressed, you live in the illusion that your life is incomplete without a mate or perhaps without the type of mate you want. Therefore, the most painful moments for you are those in which you fear or despair that you will never find your true heart's desire.

You can fall into the trap of believing you will somehow be magically transformed if Prince Charming or Princess Grace would only appear. You're looking for your missing piece. The irony is that you're perfect as is, you just don't know it. Interestingly, your chances of finding your soulmate or appreciating the qualities in the mate you currently have increase with your own sense of completeness. You also may have a tendency to 'fall madly in love' with people who live on the other side of the world or people who are in some way unavailable. You feel comfortable getting intimate when you know the relationship has a predetermined end. I think it must have been a Libran who coined the terms spring fling, and holiday romance!

Characteristics >	Benefits >	Drawbacks >
Active	Many friends	Restless
Affectionate	Warm heart	Lead people on
Alert	Keen observation	Worry/constant analysis
Appealing	Magnetic aura	Give off the wrong messages
Artistic	Talented	Flighty
Balanced	Stable	Afraid of change
Beguiling	Enchanting	Deceitful
Charming	Alluring	Conniving
Creative	Inventive	Too much on your plate
Diplomatic	Smooth operator	Self-serving
Easygoing	Relaxed	Lack motivation
Generous	Unselfish	Unwise/extravagant
Gentle	Soft touch	Weak-willed
Honourable	Respected	Big-headed
Just	Fair	Self-righteous
Painstaking	Thorough	Perfectionist
Peaceable	Calm	Flee when you should fight
Petty	Detail-oriented	Trifling
Polished	Refined	Affected
Sympathetic	Deep understanding	Waste time on lost causes
Vain	Pleasing appearance	Arrogant

[How to tune into your sign's powers]

> *Instead of talking about your plans, do them.*

> *Live every day as if it were your last.*

> *Make everything important to you a high priority.*

The Libra woman

Her contrary nature stems from the fact that she has a lot of the traits of the little girl and the wise woman intermingling within her.

She may appear to be one of the truly feminine women of the zodiac — yet she is also one of the strongest women of the zodiac. Usually her physical exterior does not give a hint of just how powerful she can be (although Libran Margaret Thatcher is an exception to this rule). Ms Libra is a forceful personality and she generally has a way about her that makes her stand out in the crowd (even without trying).

She loves to be creative so Ms Libra may be found upon the silver screen (actresses Susan Sarandon, Catherine Zeta-Jones, Heather Locklear, Fran Drescher, Angela Lansbury, Sigourney Weaver and Gwynneth Paltrow); running a business or a country; modelling clothes on the catwalk; or designing clothes or houses.

She's naturally stylish and often a trendsetter and whatever she's doing it's likely that she's doing it in her own way, and operating under her own terms or rules. She's much more than meets the eye (and usually what meets the eye is nice to behold, too). However, the most interesting sides to her character, i.e. her inner dialogue, secret desires, musings or romances, usually are kept to herself. She tends to live her real existence in the world of fantasy, the world that exists within her own psyche, a world that no one else can ever glimpse or enter.

Though her mind is frequently spinning and dwelling on many things, she still manages to look as if she is only focused on one thing at a time. This ability to veil her inner processing is how the Libran woman can sometimes appear to be as cute as a kitten but can then turn around with power and pounce like the lion.

There are many times she thinks she is opening up and truly sharing her real heart and soul with others or when others believe they are communicating clearly with her. But sometimes these moments are more fleeting than lasting. She is constantly looking for the man who will love the real her, not the visible or superficial side to her. She has a warm smile, a sincere heart, a strong will and a stubborn nature. She is also very good at pretending and saying yes when she really means no — and vice versa.

Her contrary nature stems from the fact that she has a lot of the traits of the little girl and the wise woman intermingling within her. She can be intelligent, sensitive, honourable and affectionate then, right before your eyes, she will suddenly do an about-turn. That's when she can become childishly petulant, abhorrently self-centred, tactless, emotionally flippant or unreliable.

When she is in her 'humour me' phase, she wants to be pleased, adored and spoilt. And every time you believe that she is settling into a nice easygoing phase, something will occur that reminds you that she is a will o' the wisp Air sign. It is as though a sudden shift in the wind's direction can carry her off to the land of faraway thoughts. Sometimes in this state of mind she involves herself in outrageous forms of self-indulgence or self-pity.

When she stays in a negative mind frame for too long, she can be complex, argumentative, restless, depressed, irrational and confused. Then, just when you think you can't watch her despair for one more day, a blast of fresh air will blow her back to a balanced perspective again. With her mind back on positive track again, amazingly, she'll wonder what on earth you are talking about when you say 'it is good to have you back on planet Earth again'. As far as she is concerned, nothing happened, so what was there to fuss about?

Generally there isn't too much to fuss about, either. Fate and fortune do smile kindly upon her, and she usually lands merrily upon her pretty feet. She has a knack for being at the right place at the right time — and for meeting the right people as well. Life prepares Ms Libra brilliantly for the world at large. Being ruled by Venus, she naturally values beauty, harmony and equality, and she expresses these qualities through her appearance, voice and actions. She appreciates the fine gifts the earth offers and is truly grateful she can enjoy them. She loves everything connected to beauty and nature, but most of all she loves her peace of mind.

[How Libra women operate]

Social

Ms Libra is often a hostess with a flair for fabulous entertaining. She's gracious by nature and her life usually includes lots of successful friends and associates. She likes to see what is happening in the social scene, and she likes to be seen in all the right places. Because she has a social disposition, she frequently has to decide between several great social offers. Whether she is attending a black-tie high society affair, a footy game with her friends or the neighbour's barbecue, she'll have fun no matter which one she chooses. However, she'll still wonder what she missed at the other ones.

If Ms Libra could find the magic spell that could position her at two places at once, she would use it frequently. On occasion, she really enjoys getting all dressed up in her finery for a romantic candlelight dinner featuring gourmet fare and fine wines. Gorgeous clothes and fashion in general can be her great indulgence. However, even when she is most figure- or weight-conscious, sometimes ice-cream sundaes, chocolate fudge pie or New York cheesecake will make a smashing grand finale for this luscious lady's sweet tooth (but not always).

No matter what age she is, most Libran women have an alert eye for recognising quality and beauty. I had the fun of watching a friend's Libran daughter demonstrate her fine taste for the best just after her second birthday party. Her mother had given her a handful of different spoons to play with in her high chair. The little girl surveyed the spoons with a critical eye, then swept all the stainless steel ones onto the floor and reached for the engraved silver ones. Now that's a true blue Libra!

Like the fable of the princess with the pea, from birth most Libra gals know what they like and how things should feel. You can sometimes even see Libran children knowing how to dress to impress or having a strong attraction for wearing certain colours well before other signs have thought about such things.

Ms Libra is also a people person. She has many friends, male and female, heterosexual, bi-sexual and sometimes homosexual. She treats them all generously and they enjoy her bright mind and charming personality. She also has an ability to mix with different age groups and feel comfortable among those whose ages are far different from her own. She exhibits an appealing mixture of social graces and creative flair and she thoroughly enjoys all art forms that reflect symmetry and harmony, particularly beautiful people, beautiful scenes of nature, paintings, sculptures and music.

Love and family

Romance for her can be a bittersweet experience. She wants real love, craves love, but often goes looking for it in all the wrong places. For her, romance and love are essential if she wants to live the life of her dreams. She adores love letters and whispering sweet nothings in the still of the night. Librans, who are normally cautious in most areas of their existence, can completely lose their heads and go Gaga over some most unsuited affairs of the heart.

Because Venus smiles on her this Lady has no trouble initially winning hearts. Alas, she sometimes does have trouble holding on to them. Many Libran women seem to attract men who are a lot less driven or powerful than themselves. Libra has a weakness for finding the underdog attractive.

Because of her strong will and nature, she can be something of an 'overwhelm' even for strong men. Some find her to be demanding or filled with so many expectations that they feel like she's placing them under a continuous magnifying glass. She likes to subliminally call the shots, and a lot of men don't like that. Some, but certainly not all, Libran women surround themselves with men who unquestioningly follow their lead or bow to their directions — rather than those who challenge or conflict with their attitudes or desires.

You can learn a lot about her innermost yearnings by asking about her childhood and how closely connected — or emotionally disconnected — she and her father were. If she felt that he ignored her, or didn't find her beautiful, she may be most attracted to guys who play hard to get. She may also ask, 'Do you think I'm beautiful?' or 'Do you love me?' more than once or twice. If she holds fond memories of being the apple of daddy's eye then she will probably want to be courted and romanced by a similar type of man to dear old dad.

Even when she is up on top of the world in her career she'll be looking for lots of reassurance, sometimes through what appears to be the most peculiar run of relationships. For many diverse and complex reasons she has a bit of trouble turning away an enthusiastic suitor, even when she knows he doesn't meet her soulmate requirements. The truth is she delights in the attention, doesn't want to hurt anyone's feelings and often can't say the word no.

Consequently, she tends to allow her string of admirers to dangle when it might be more kind to cut them loose. But she doesn't like to be alone and as far as she is concerned having a troupe of mediocre beaus is better than not having any.

Libran woman can be in love more with the dream of romance than with the reality of romance. She also may create her perfect romances in her mind or live them vicariously through the leading ladies in steamy romance novels or films. She often resists making commitments but once she makes one, she generally sticks with it as long as there's a chance of making it work.

If she comes to the conclusion that her relationship will never be what she truly wants (sometimes after a lot of hard knocks and heart-ache) she kicks up her heels and begins her search again. She does this sometimes even while her current relationship is still in force.

As a mother, a Libra will tenderly care for her children, giving little thought to the sacrifices she cheerfully makes on their behalf. However, she insists they follow the rules and behave, especially when their father is home, and she rarely takes their side against him. She understands how to balance her children's needs with her husband's desires and she enjoys the structure and security she feels being part of a family.

Career

Once she has found a career she loves, there is not much that will stop her from turning her career into a highly successful one. Work and career mean a lot to the Libran woman, but she's most fulfilled when she uses her creativity to combine work with pleasure. The perfect position for her is one that allows her to do what she has talent for, and make money at the same time.

She has the ability to concentrate her focus on the task or question at hand, moving towards her goal like a jet and gaining momentum as she goes. She can keep up this pace for quite a while and generally maintains it until she reaches her objective. Once the goal is scored, she's on the next flight to 'paradise island' — whether that's a resort, a beach house, or her own couch — for total rest and pampering. She's extremely sociable and enjoys the company of others so much that she's wise to select an occupation that doesn't confine her to an office. She needs space to fluff her feathers and room to spread her wings and fly.

Many Libran women are strongly affected by music. It can excite and exhilarate them or it can soothe and relax them. For this reason, lots of Librans are drawn to professions in the music industry. Her artistic nature also makes her a natural for careers in writing, stage and film, drawing and designing, fashion and textiles, interior decorating and window and set dressing. Librans also succeed in public relations, the legal profession, antiques and antiquities, beauty and cosmetology, and research positions that require going out into the field for information.

Financial

Although she is probably the first to deny it, money and wealth do mean a lot to her. That is because her Venus nature makes her want the best that money can buy. Fortunately, her combination of personality traits places her in a position where she is capable of earning significant financial rewards. Of course she needs to apply herself but the Libran woman can work smarter than most (and she has been known to marry smart, too).

She has the ability to magnetise the people, resources and the money she needs to fulfil her purpose. Often her attitude to her own self-worth is the pivot point of her financial position. She sets her own value in the market place, and often she can make as much money as she believes she's worth.

She can be quite a savvy investor, too. Librans are known for owning original pieces of art and sometimes entire art collections. Their love for beauty encourages them to display their treasures, so visiting one of their homes can have the aesthetic feel of walking through an art gallery or museum.

Physical

Librans can be one of the best-looking signs of the zodiac (both the men and the women). They're known for their gentle, reassuring smiles and their tendency towards having dimples. In general, Ms Libra projects an attitude of peaceful contentment. Of course, that's not always the way she feels, but she tries to conceal her darker side with her charming smile and musical laugh.

When a Libra woman keeps her emotions and thoughts bottled up inside, her health will suffer. That's why it's so important for her to have some stress-releasing activities built into her daily routine. One of her first signs that she needs some exercise is pain or discomfort in her lower back or shoulders. When she holds on to stress, her body reacts to the burden and her back and kidneys sometimes act up to let her know she needs to take care of herself.

She knows she would feel better if she walked a mile or so every day, but she has a difficult time convincing herself that the benefits are worth the inconvenience. As an Air sign, her circulatory system is key to her physical wellbeing and aerobic exercise can boost her immune system considerably. She might try dance aerobics, or even jazz or ballet, so she can combine music with movement, which is a special talent of hers.

She also has a tendency to get terribly run down before she does anything about it. And she occasionally relies on other people to get her back on the road to good health again. She sometimes needs a coach, a trainer or a supportive group of friends to get her up and moving towards exercise and better health — especially if she has slipped into the doldrums or ill health.

She benefits from eating four or five very light meals throughout the day so her system only has a small amount to digest at a time. She also is wise to eat plenty of fresh fruits and vegetables and a variety of whole grains. Librans love gravies and sauces and cakes and biscuits, and these all have the ability to slow down and gum up her metabolism. But out of her desire to keep her system on an even keel, she tries to make healthy choices.

When she's out of sorts, she leans towards naturopathic remedies and she sometimes takes an interest in aromatherapy, flower essences or herbs. Chances are she believes in taking at least one or two vitamins every day and I've seen more than one Libran take a handful at each meal.

Mental

A Libran woman is a perpetual student. She has an ongoing curiosity about many things and she's not satisfied with abbreviated answers. She probably grimaces at the thought of a *Reader's Digest* condensed book and feels incomplete without her unabridged dictionary and a full set or computer disk of encyclopedias. Her mind urges her to probe ever deeper into her questions and interests.

Her emotions are her greatest fear because she worries they cloud her perceptions and distort the truth. The truth is very important to her and she seeks it through logic, research and observation. She sometimes feels frustrated when she looks back in retrospect and sees how her entire life has been about trading one idea or illusion for another. But she senses she's on the right track. She truly believes there are answers, if she asks the right questions, but she sometimes has trouble figuring out what the right questions are.

She honours fairness but she isn't above acting weak, beguiling and defenceless to encourage others to help fight her battle or support her cause. And people are generally willing to rush to her charming side. Still, if you ever have the chance to watch this woman in action when she's forced to stand her ground alone, you'll see a mighty contender. In fact, not many people can actually do battle with her and win. She's much stronger and well equipped on many more levels of existence than most would ever expect from experiencing a casual encounter with her. Like still waters, her strengths run deep.

Spiritual

The Libran woman can be very strong in her religious or spiritual convictions — once she's figured out what they are. As a seeker of balance, she often has a difficult time accepting doctrines that are male-dominated or one-sided in their approach. She probably has more of a leaning towards the goddess than the god, and she often gets involved in metaphysics and offshoots of mainstream religions — even some that may involve celibacy or other challenges such as going vegetarian as a proof of her faith.

Often she only stays on this pathway of self-sacrifice for a limited time. The world at large pulls her away from her spiritual path, but she always remembers how good she felt when she travelled on the path of higher spiritual thinking and she tends to return to this journey after being away from it for a while.

Ms Libran generally doesn't believe in or support religious wars, and she's probably repulsed by bloodshed that takes place in the name of God. Her alert mind (on an unconscious level, if not on a conscious one) knows God is in everything and everyone. She generally has a strong notion about the afterlife and is prepared to be accountable for all of her thoughts, choices and actions. Her sense of justice tells her that some sort of judgment must take place and she toys with the idea that the cosmic courtroom is within her own mind or soul.

> *He has quiet charisma that attracts women from all directions and he's charming enough to balance several relationships at the same time.*

He is 007, a small dash of Austin Powers, plus Superman and Clark Kent rolled into one. He can seem demure, shy and introverted, but when he wants to make his presence felt he knows how to do it on cue. He can sometimes be the quiet type, but do not think he's a wallflower! He is more the quiet type that your mother warned you about when you first started dating.

He often has adoring sisters, mothers (his own and other people's), aunties, nieces or female work associates who adore and dote over him. No matter what age he is, or what age his admirers are, he has a natural way with the ladies. With a little help from Venus, Mr Libra has the ability and the natural tendencies to become something of a heart-throb and sometimes even a heart-breaker. He can be sexy, dashing, charismatic, cute and cuddly, also petulant, sulky and self-absorbed. At his worst, he can be focused only on his own sense of self-importance.

Because he is a complex personality, when it comes to the Libran man the old saying, 'Don't judge a book by its cover' is great advice. He can be hard to read even after you've known him for years. He seems to live a life that contradicts his beliefs at times, or he does the opposite of what he says he intends to do. However, he's actually very logical when it comes to making his decisions, and changing his plans, but his brand of logic may not be obvious to anyone but him.

His reasoning is affected by the state of mind he's in at any given moment, so he may enjoy socialising today and dread it tomorrow! He tends to be the same way in his self-expression. You can get down on your knees and beg him for his opinion with no success at all — unless he feels like telling you what he thinks

On the other hand, if he feels compelled to share something with you, there's no stopping him. He also doesn't like to be pinned down or made responsible in any way, especially for the way he spends his money, or for his beliefs, actions or deeds. He doesn't want any of the bad headachy stuff that careers, business matters, relationships might entail, or that life in general may offer up. He likes to live in something of a vacuum at times and he prefers to escape from pressure, rather than thrive on it. If he had his druthers, everything would run like clockwork to plan — his plan of course.

When he's in balance, he's absolutely charming and very smooth. He's diplomatic, honourable, affectionate and sympathetic. He listens well and has a good batting average for helping his family, friends and co-workers. However, he's still far from perfect. And at burnout or pressure-point times he can be downright mean and nasty. But his friends, family or co-workers usually understand his foibles and give him a lot of leeway.

He has great charm that melts any ice very quickly even if he has been a heartless kind of rascal and somehow dropped the ball on others. Everybody quickly acknowledges that he didn't mean it, so all is quickly forgotten and forgiven. Some say however, that there are times when Mr Libra does sometimes get himself off the hook a bit too easily for his own good.

[How Libra men operate]

Social

The Libran male is born with social skills. He's one of the zodiac's natural networkers both in business and pleasure. This man would have had business cards printed by the time he was five if he knew they existed. He enjoys spending time with his friends and looks forward to meeting new people. He probably has a few favourite places, but he's willing to try something new if it's highly recommended.

However, if you're out with your Libra friend and you're really hungry, don't ask him to choose the restaurant. That type of decision could take longer than your stomach is willing to wait. (Librans are always at the heart of these indecision jokes, but they're quite capable of making a decision when they must.)

The Libran man likes socialising in interesting and sometimes offbeat atmospheres with great food, artistic appeal and cultural diversity. But as sociable as he is, he's not a guy who talks much about his own thoughts and opinions unless his passion for justice is sparked by an opinion based on ignorance. In that situation he can make the most stinging remarks and spur-of-the-moment speeches!

In most cases, though, the Libran man hesitates to express himself openly, and as unsettling as this may be for others, it benefits him in a number of ways. He's always learning about himself, and in the process he serves as the perfect mirror for others to see reflections of themselves.

Love and family

He has a distinct need for companionship and he's frequently driven by an urge to find his ultimate partner. But while many Libran men realise they have a deep need to share their love with a special mate, few of them admit it, especially to themselves. In the meantime, he can appear rather fickle as he floats (sometimes joyfully, other times lacking lustre) from one relationship to another, logically weighing the pluses and minuses as he goes.

Any woman who believes romance should remain unhindered by rational thought processes is in for quite a see-saw ride with a Libran. He has the capacity to talk himself into and out of just about anything, including love and romance.

He has quiet charisma that attracts women from all cardinal directions and he's charming enough to keep several revolving around him at the same time. He's bright, has an easygoing sense of humour and a warm sincere affection for just about everyone he meets. He's honest in a gentle (sometimes evasive) sort of way, meaning that he may think it's better to tell a white lie than to hurt your feelings.

Consequently, he has a tendency to lead women on when he does not intend to have a long-term relationship with them. But no matter how insensitive this sounds, his actions are innocently motivated by his misguided attempt at kindness. He has a warm heart and it can get him into all sorts of hot water in relationships because his intentions, though pure, often are mistaken as something other than what they were meant to be.

The Libran man is attracted to women who reflect the qualities he likes about himself, plus a few others that he thinks he's missing — like light-heartedness and playfulness. He generally seeks women who are physically appealing, socially adept and sympathetic to his needs and desires. He is especially swayed by a woman who attends to his every need. The Libran man enjoys being indulged and sometimes spoiled to an extreme.

His chosen mate will need to have a sense of humour, a generous heart and an active mind of her own and he hopes money in the bank, too. And even then Libra may not be able to make up his mind whether she's the one or not. Many Libran men place themselves in a dilemma by thinking there's a better relationship out there somewhere. So instead of having a real relationship with a real person, they daydream about the perfect relationship with a fantasy date. There's nothing wrong with a good fantasy, but it's hard to cuddle up with a daydream.

When he does meet a woman he believes is 'it', he's in seventh heaven. Many Libran men, once they settle down, can become very lazy and be tough to get moving. Here's a typical example: A Libran husband lounging in a recliner reading the newspaper says to his wife, 'I'll think about cleaning the garage in a little while, hon. Right now I'm thinking about mowing the lawn.'

The Libra man loves to have a family and while he might not seem very excited when he hears he's going to be a father — he is touched deeply on the inside. And when the little one arrives he will greet it with love and blossom with the experience of raising a child. (He may not bloom abundantly — but he will open up a bit more and let one of his emotional walls down a brick or two.)

He'll brag of his children's accomplishments and he may even develop his sentimental side. He treats his children with love, kindness and justice above all else. He probably doesn't tolerate loud rough-housing throughout the house, but in the yard, or in the playroom, he joins in the fun and has a better time than the kids!

Career

All work and no fun makes Libra a dull man. He likes to have an even blend of business and pleasure in his life and when he enjoys his work he's in his finest element. Most Libran men create well-established careers and many of them are involved in highly specialised and creative enterprises. The Libran man is a marvel to watch, both when he's in action and when he's not.

He may work diligently for days and nights, weekends and holidays until he's finally in a state of exhaustion. Then, poof!; he collapses into 'couch potato king', reigning over the remote control, a cool drink and a stack of take-away menus. There are Librans who manage to balance work and relaxation less dramatically, but many of them are content with the swing back and forth.

Many Libran men excel as actors and singers and they do very well managing theatres or the careers of entertainers. He's well suited for any profession that surrounds him with beauty and harmony and his artistic abilities shine in these environments. His refined social skills and his diplomacy combine to make him a smooth politician, attorney, corporate spokesman, negotiator or director of public relations. Many Librans also find satisfaction as artists, designers, tailors, sculptors, writers and reporters.

Financial

He's often chasing money and frequently gets himself into debt because he does have a tendency to live beyond his means. Those Libran men who are good financial operators do make their fortunes and when they do, they're generally wise in financial management. But these are the rare Librans — the ones who watch their money come in and then go out just as quickly are in the majority.

He often gets talked into investments, businesses, or indulgences that aren't as good as they sound. Or, he is the person selling something that isn't really what it's cracked up to be. He often has dubious financial dealings with other people and this can sometimes turn into rifts in long-standing friendships, in-law problems, legal hassles and also upsets with family members. He often spends his money on the last thing that he truly needs; he can be a person who is pound wise and penny foolish.

He has such a deep appreciation for inspired art and music that he probably owns some original paintings or sculptures and possibly has an extensive collection of music. He enjoys investing in the arts and one of his fantasies might be to amass his fortune through the purchases of exquisite pieces of beauty that are alive with the artists' spirit.

Even Librans without a lot of money have the ability to increase their income if they can increase their sense of self-worth. But money or no money, a Libran man can have a polished air of class that money just can't buy.

Physical

He can be strikingly good-looking in a special kind of way and there is usually a youthful quality surrounding him, even in his older years. Even if they're not striking, most Libran men have good looks, graceful mannerisms and brilliant smiles that are sometimes accompanied by a dimple or two. Mr Libra has pleasing features and there's symmetry about the way he's built. He usually dresses fabulously even if he doesn't dress in the clothes that are predictable — because he often has his own unique style.

He frequently is gifted with a pleasant voice and when he laughs people laugh with him. Unlike some signs — such as the Ram, who is known for his broad chest and shoulders — the Libran man's strong point is his lack of any unusually striking physical aspects. Instead, he is known for his overall pleasing appearance. Mr Libra often stands out in the crowd, but seldom in a flashy attention-grabbing way. He is cool, rather than loud, in presence, look and behaviour.

As an Air sign, his health is dependent upon the strength and conditioning of his circulatory system. Fresh air is Libra's best friend and he can really help his health by taking a walk every day. He's wise to skip the city streets and head for some pleasing suburban avenues and country lanes. The peacefulness of more pleasant surroundings is always worth the drive for a Libra. If he can't locate a quiet area, he might consider wearing a walkman to tune out the barrage of sounds. Librans also make good runners — they're light on their feet and they like the way the wind feels blowing through their hair.

His biggest health threat is his tendency to overindulge, particularly if he has a Taurus ascendant, in which case he has an over-stocked refrigerator and a hefty biscuit jar. But most Librans don't make gluttony a daily habit; they prefer occasional binges instead. Some Librans suffer from stomach upsets and frayed nerves from their constant effort to achieve or maintain a sense of balance throughout all areas of their lives. Librans can also suffer from discomfort in their lower backs and should invest in a desk chair and car seat that offer lumbar support. They also benefit from gentle stretching and deep breathing exercises.

Mental

Even though he is one of the more complex thinkers of the zodiac, the Libran man is still more of an open book than some. He is hard to pin down because he goes off on so many mental tangents. What he thinks or states today can differ from his assessments, beliefs or attitudes tomorrow.

Because he can swing between having a mind like a metal trap and acting as if he doesn't have an idea about what he thinks, many Libran men, for all their heightened capacity to use their minds and be geniuses at times, still come across as airheads every now and again.

The appearance of being vague or uninterested is generally the result of the Libran being lost in his own thoughts, and therefore only paying partial attention to the conversation in the room. He is the kind of man that sometimes says yes when he really means no, and his lack of attention can often cause all kinds of unusual disagreements, misunderstandings and poor communications.

This trait can be particularly annoying when you're attempting to get an important point through to him, because he can seem to be missing the point no matter how you frame or shape it. Some say that talking to a Libran man is like trying to talk to the trees if he doesn't want to hear you; but persistence usually works wonders with him. However, before you can get a Libran to agree, disagree or change his mind on something, you may need to give him time to mull things over. Just as this man cannot hurry love, he also cannot hurry his thought process at times.

Spiritual

He is usually quite knowledgeable about religions around the world. He may dabble in some of them (more than one) but usually he tends to avoid joining up (or if he does join up, it isn't for long). He knows that commitment to a religion or spiritual path is tempting because it provides a foundation to build on. But he isn't sure if he wants to assume any religious path or role in life that he may soon find tiresome or unsatisfactory.

Some Libran men, however, have no time at all for any organised religions (they may even refer to them as humbug). These types prefer to explore the path of the unusual spiritual beliefs rather than the accepted. He likes to follow his thoughts as much as his heart and this can sometimes make him rationalise his feelings, especially when it comes to spiritual matters. Often when he feels his strong connection to the universe he will talk himself out of his experience with logic or commonsense. However, he can be confused by his own logic and he often has a hard time choosing between his conscience and his head.

From day to day, he changes his feelings, beliefs and attitudes. It is not unusual for a Libran in later years to suddenly convert to a religion or take a solid stand in a religious organisation. However, it is often only when he is getting closer to meeting his Maker that he assumes any firm religious or spiritual commitments. As with most areas of his life, including his spirituality, Mr Libra prefers to keep his options open.

····● ● ● ● (The Libra baby

> *This baby is soft and beautiful on the outside and strong and determined on the inside. This 'model baby', even if shy, has a contrary side and a mind all its own.*

See the baby with the pretty pink lacy bow tied around her little head or the one wearing the tiny, hand-stitched romper that fits perfectly. This baby is likely to be a Libran (or have Libra located somewhere powerful in its horoscope).

Somehow Libra babies seem to attract the beautiful things in life. They often end up with the best of whatever is available. This is the child who has the hand-carved animal mobile swirling overhead, and the one whose room is filled with the best and brightest of toys, furniture and clothing. Libran babies are showered with all sorts of magnificent (sometimes extravagant) trappings of being a loved (sometimes spoiled), adored and well taken care of 'little darling'.

Unless other factors of the horoscope override its birth sign, a Libran baby is usually surrounded by magic because it's ruled and blessed by Venus. This wee one's attitude will be quite distinct. It will know it has something special to offer.

Even though Librans may cause trouble at various times, trouble isn't their intention. They just like to make their presence felt and they usually begin with some sort of grand and beautiful entrance into the world. Libran births are special or significant and are nearly always different from the normal or usual in some manner or form. At the same time, Librans have an innate desire to create harmony, so they will attempt to make their entrance into this world as harmonious as it is grand.

Libran births are sometimes slow and a bit complicated because Venus rules both pleasure and pain. It's also not unusual for a Libran to be born a bit late because this helps to ensure that everything is prepared. Therefore, you may have some false starts before this child actually arrives. The more prepared you are and the more prepared the baby's room is, the sooner your Libra will arrive.

Venus rules beauty and many of the most beautiful physical specimens (models of wonderful physical proportions, and so on) are born under this sign. That's why your baby is likely to be extremely attractive when it's born and have a special radiance and angelic expression. It will have a softness and a light quality that automatically attracts attention and makes people want to primp and pamper it.

Beware of becoming the infant Libran's willing servant because they act so much like the little prince or princess from day one that it's easy to fall under their regal spell. You'll need to maintain some of the control, otherwise you may spend all your time dancing to your Libran's tune. Set a routine that suits you or you'll be running around in circles all day.

It is best to set a rhythm and schedule for feeding, bathing and sleeping that you can stick to for this baby. Rhythm and routine are the two basic rules where tiny Librans are concerned. Letting the baby set the routine will turn the entire family's life into a circus because the Libran tends to have lots of whims, fancies and indecisive qualities. What it wants or enjoys today will be different tomorrow.

While this child may have frequent changes of mind, he or she will not like it one bit if you abruptly change your mind or your routine. If you do, this little one can become surprisingly petulant, sulky and possibly even a bit withdrawn. These babies know how to sulk up a storm to get their own way and they're masterful at flirting from the very beginning!

If you want to be a stage mother or father, you could have a great actor or performer on your hands. Natural performers, when Librans start walking and talking they're soon dancing around in a very appealing, funny, adorable and magnetic way. It's the kind of baby who will hold on to the side of the crib or playpen and be quite happy jigging away to music which it hears in its imagination.

Expect this to be a happy, wonderful individual to be around when it feels like being fun, and also for it to be a trifle moody when it suits it to be. This baby knows how to play the game of life to win and its idea of winning is to have its every wish and whim fulfilled.

Being stubborn and wilful, it will have a strong mind of its own and will delight in out-smarting you or getting its own way. You will find your world tends to revolve around your Libran but your chores will seem like labours of love because there's something so appealing and special about this baby and you'll know it. Little Librans like to sleep, even if it's at irregular times or odd patterns.

Librans have very clear food preferences and very specific 'people' or 'toy' preferences as well. This baby doesn't wait to develop its preferences, it seems to be born with lots of strong likes and dislikes. A Libran knows from day one what it wants and doesn't want. You will be talking to the trees if you attempt to get your baby Libra to do things your way all the time. There will probably be times when you'll enter into a battle of wills, but somehow this little bundle of joy can charm you eventually into seeing things his or her way. After all, didn't the Goddess Venus in Greek mythology always get what she wanted by fair means or foul. Well that's the underlying mythological energy you're dealing with here, Venus or Eros in baby form. Have fun!

The Libra toddler through teen

Librans are quite concerned about the impression they're making on others so they work very hard at being polite and acting grown up.

The Libran's development and youth is sure to be almost as challenging for you as it is for them. This little one loves to play and sing and dance around, but that's only half of the picture. Librans often have frustrations growing up because they have a very hard time deciding what they want. If you place your Libra toddler on the floor surrounded by five different toys, he or she will pick up the blue ball, give it a quick squeeze and then drop it and go after the red fire engine. Once they ring the bell and give the engine a shove, they're on to the teddy bear even before they fire engine stops rolling. They give the teddy bear an affectionate kiss, set it beside them and crawl towards the toy horn — get halfway there, then abruptly turn around and head back for the blue ball. It's not that the Libra has a short attention span, as some may believe, it is actually because Libra has a deep desire to choose the toy or activity that will be most fulfilling and they have a difficult time deciding which one that is!

You can make their life a little easier by limiting their choices. Give them one or two toys to choose from, or suggest they play with them both at the same time. Perhaps the teddy bear would like to ride on the red fire engine. If your little one is tired, cranky or hungry, don't overburden him or her with choices and decision-making. Simply hand your Libra one of their favourites and nonchalantly take all other options out of their sight.

Little Libras are delighted by shiny objects — the more expensive, the better. Given the choice between a sparkling bauble and a gold ring, the Libra will instinctively reach for the more valuable item. And while you may be proud to know your little one has such wonderful taste, you may be sorry if you leave your diamond earrings or silver cuff-links within his or her reach.

It is important to give your Libra guidelines about what he or she is permitted to play with and what is off-limits because by the time a Libra is three they already have a preference for 'real' things over 'play' things. I had the chance to see a great example of this one afternoon when I was visiting a friend who had a three-year-old Libra son. When I arrived, Josh proudly told me he helped his mum run the vacuum cleaner that morning. Cybil explained she had spilled powder on the bathroom rug and when Josh saw how the sweeper 'made the powder disappear' he was mesmerised. 'It really did make the powder disappear, Athena — just like magic!' Josh chimed in.

Later that day, as Cybil and I were talking, Josh came into the living room pushing his toy sweeper and frowning. He said, 'Let's throw this old thing away, Mum, it doesn't even work.' There's nothing like the real thing for a Libra!

Most Libra youngsters show signs of creative ability by the time they're four or five years old. Librans seek harmony so music and artwork often appeal to them. Many of these children love music and nearly all of them enjoy looking at beautiful artwork and creating their own masterpieces. This is generally the age when the Libra will begin to assert him or herself. They may have gone through a bit of rebellion around age two, but for the Libran age four or five is the time when they really begin to voice their preferences and they also expect to get what they want.

The more outlets they have for creative expression, the less frustrating this phase will be for everyone in the family — and the neighbours, too! While Librans can be very quiet, they can also raise the roof with their strong lungs and well-developed vocal cords. But don't worry, this stage is generally over by the time Libra goes off to Year One.

When Libra goes off to school he or she will look amusingly like a miniature adult going off to work. Librans are very concerned about the impression they make so they work at being polite and acting grown-up.

One of the greatest insults you can dish out to a Year-One or Year-Two Libran is to call them a baby. So be sure you treat your growing Libra with respect and don't tease him or her about acting younger then their age. They can grow up way too fast as it is, and they'll some day thank you for encouraging them to enjoy being a child while they could.

Librans take learning seriously and they tend to be good students. Of course there are exceptions, because some Librans are only interested in learning the things that appeal to them personally. You'll need to show this type of Libra all of the benefits to learning the things they don't like if you want them to keep an open mind. One of the benefits they will appreciate is the idea that if they learn about a bunch of different things, they will have a better life and can do more of what they want to do. Positive reinforcement and reasoning work much better with this child than black and white rules and ultimatums.

Librans understand the idea of fairness at an early age, but their own judgment is limited when they are young so there will be times when they upset one of their playmates by refusing to share toys or insist the other child do as they say. In an effort to get his or her own idea of their fair share, a young Libra can become very selfish and bossy at times.

In some ways this bossy character trait helps to balance Librans' deep concern with other people's opinions of them. The Librans who don't have this strong independent streak can become preoccupied with other people's feedback. Here's an important tip: If your Libra acts like they don't need your love and support or their friends' approval, don't believe it for a second! This is Librans' way of trying to shut themselves off and dodge their emotions rather than examine them. Be sure to consistently show your Libra that you love and believe in them, particularly as they reach and experience adolescence.

The years between ten and fourteen can be especially tumultuous for a Libra who desperately wants to be an adult, but isn't quite prepared to act like one. And it can be very confusing and frustrating for the people around Libra because at this age Librans are beginning to make many of their own important choices and decisions and they have a ton of anxiety about whether they're making the right ones.

To complicate matters, they try to suppress their own feelings of insecurity by acting as if they know-it-all and have their entire world in complete and total control. This Libran tendency is enough to make even the most patient and understanding parent want to rub it in when the Libra falls on his or her face.

While comments like, 'I told you so', may feel good to say, they do a lot of harm to the Libra and to your parent-child relationship in the long run. One of the most helpful things you can do at this stage of the Libran's life is to maintain the overall harmony of the household and give your Libra frequent praise and acknowledgment as well as appropriate — but not belittling — reprimands when he or she breaks the rules. This will help them to know you're there for them and, no matter how shaky the outside world or their inner emotions feel, they can count on their home and family as a stable and comfortable place.

I should warn you that when the Libra becomes a teen and begins dating, you may have a difficult time keeping up with all the different names and faces. One of my editors who has a Libran teenage daughter jokes that she is planning to install a revolving door to ease the traffic flow.

Librans have lots of friends and acquaintances and lots of dates. Don't encourage them to limit themselves at this age or they may revert to this pattern later in life. This is definitely the time to encourage them to have fun and avoid getting too serious too soon. But no matter what you say or do, your Libra will not be able to escape breaking a few hearts and having their own heart wounded a few times, too. Better that they begin to learn about emotional realities and broken illusions now instead of later.

The young Libran adult is clearly a thinker and is often the emergent leader among groups of friends. Librans also have an easy ability and lots of fun playing matchmaker, and your Libra may spend hours on the phone giving advice to his or her friends. The matchmaker, the peacemaker and the counsellor are all natural roles for Libra, and playing these roles helps to polish and refine some of the skills they will continue to benefit from throughout their adult life.

SCORPIO

[24 october — 22 november]

scorpio scorpio scorpio scorpio scorpio
scorpio scorpio scorpio scorpio scorpio
scorpio scorpio scorpio scorpio scorpio
scorpio scorpio scorpio scorpio scorpio

scorpio scorpio scorpio scorpio scorpio
scorpio scorpio scorpio scorpio scorpio
scorpio scorpio scorpio scorpio scorpio
scorpio scorpio scorpio scorpio scorpio
scorpio scorpio scorpio scorpio scorpio
scorpio scorpio scorpio scorpio scorpio
scorpio scorpio scorpio scorpio scorpio

element: water

planetary ruler: pluto

symbol: the scorpion

quality: fixed (= stability)

colours: deep reds and soft creams

gem: topaz and malachite

best companions: pisces and cancer

strongest virtues: tenacity, loyalty,

and self-honesty

traits to improve: intolerance, fear of change,

rushing to judgments of others

deepest desire: to live your truths, yet still do

whatever else you want (and not be caught for it)

Scorpio celebrities

Bill Gates, Indira Gandhi, Julia Roberts, Helen Reddy, Goldie Hawn,

Joan Sutherland, John Singleton, Whoopi Goldberg, Johnny Carson,

Pele, Hillary Rodham Clinton, Ted Turner, John Cleese, Winona Ryder,

Henry Winkler, Charles Bronson, Leonardo DiCaprio, Sally Field,

Calista Flockhart, David Schwimmer, Richard Dreyfuss, Jodie Foster,

Bo Derek, Lauren Holly, Demi Moore, Jane Pauley, Roseanne Barr,

Maria Shriver, Marla Maples Trump, Danny De Vito, Prince Charles,

Martin Scorcese, Calvin Klein, Meg Ryan, Pablo Picasso, Lyle Lovett,

Cary Elwes, Sean 'Puff Daddy' Combs, Dolph Lundgren, Jaclyn Smith,

Marie Antoinette, Carl Sagan, Yanni, Vivien Leigh, Nadia Comaneci,

Ike Turner, Billy Graham, Tonya Harding, Lisa Bonet, Ru Paul,

Linda Evans, Bryan Adams, Elke Sommer, Art Garfunkel and

Sam Shepherd.

[General outlook]

Good news! The new millennium brings to Scorpios fresh ways of looking at life. The themes of self-expression, love, creativity, confidence, inspiration and passion abound — in a nut-shell, the things you like best. The emotional dramas of the past decade are left behind and you stride ahead with brand new optimism.

However, you know that success now depends upon you. That is why, as we progress into the new millennium, so many Scorpios will have a growing sense of self-sufficiency and a stronger responsibility towards taking care of you and yours. The new millennium is an unbeatable time to make your dreams come true. It is time to write out your wish-list and send it to the stars. Be bold and brave and most of all have faith in yourself, destiny and others.

Romance

Getting who you want is often not the issue where relationships are concerned for Scorpios. However, finding the right person to support your long-term goals, love your everyday moods or shortcomings, understand your feelings and fit in with your dreams and desires is often much harder. As much as you love to dominate, you hate to be dominated and this is one of the new millennium issues you will be facing. Single Scorpios attract partners who challenge them with power struggles, while married Scorpios also learn to deal with the balance of power in their union. Be willing to yield, and you'll discover that your life continues to abound with love, romance and passion. Compromising and seeing the other person's point of view are extremely vital to ensure ongoing success in relationships now.

Health

Like a caterpillar transforming into a butterfly, Scorpios enter the new millennium with the opportunity to say goodbye to an old way of life and to say hello to a brand new one. Your transformation includes image, diet, exercise and relaxation. There has never been a better time to give yourself a complete physical, mental and spiritual makeover. Remember that your body is your temple, so take good care of it.

Finance

You Scorpios are some of the most brilliant money-makers in the world (think of Bill Gates, Jane Fonda, Ted Turner and even Australia's talented larrikin, John Singleton) but that doesn't mean that you don't work hard and long for your money either. Because Scorpios' 'resilience and perseverance' come naturally, if at first you don't become wealthy, you keep on trying. Your sheer doggedness is what often leads you to your own form of money tree! The testing times you faced during the last years of the twentieth century put many Scorpios into a financial quandary and encouraged them to explore new ways of earning income. The good news is now you have excellent opportunities to turn the tables around towards positive flow again and get ahead in the money stakes. You are more decisive and sure of what you want financially than ever before, and although you don't like to talk money, do make sure that you are receiving the financial rewards you deserve from investments or joint ventures.

Career

When it comes to ambition and stamina, you Scorpios are unbeatable. End-of-century problems, delays or bad decisions in your working life are forgotten as new millennium optimism grabs hold. Breaking barriers and setting yourself challenges is all-important. Keep in mind, too, that your talents and abilities are valid in many different career areas. Don't close old doors before new ones open. Keeping your options open is the key to your success. Also be prepared to explore new career areas, including those which are at this time so new conceptually that they are still unexplored and untested in terms of how they will unfold as business ventures.

[Millennium wildcards to watch for]

If there is anything you need to be careful about, it is new millennium power struggles, lavishness and restlessness. As the new millennium dawns, make sure you set yourself realistic plans for all areas of your life — work, money, love, health, personal development and so on. Focus your energies in specific directions, set yourself realistic boundaries. There are many distractions surrounding you, and it will be easy to get off track. Keep in mind that get-rich plans or risky schemes will bring you no good. Be steady, Scorpio, stay on target and you'll attract into your life whatever it is you want most.

> *You usually know exactly what you want,*
> *and what to do to get it. However, once it is*
> *yours, you sometimes feel trapped in anxiety,*
> *wondering if you have done the right thing*
> *after all.*

Combine desire, passion, uniqueness, intensity, genius, nerve, power and glory. Mix these characteristics up, then blend them with a serving of gentle, and not so gentle aggravation. Add a dash of the dictator plus a good pinch of generosity and tyranny, and you have created the cosmic cocktail known as 'the Scorpio'. You Scorpios are special. Even the name Scorpio stands out from the other zodiac names. Others seldom realise how powerful you are.

Rather than shouting about your conquests from the rooftops (like the more bold and audacious Fire signs, Aries, Leo and Sagittarius), you keep your most potent power contained within you and use it on special occasions. Small wonder you Scorpios are not only some of the most awesome and powerful people on the planet, you are also one of the cosmic world's best-kept secrets. You are seldom who you appear to be on the surface and your life is often not what it seems to be at all.

Since you are astrologically aligned with Pluto — the most awesome of all the planets and the God who ruled the underworld in Greek mythology — life for you is not meant to be a stroll down easy street. It is more than likely that you may need to go down to the very deepest and darkest realms of human experience to realise how nice it is to be on planet Earth surrounded with your mates, family and pets. You may even have to lose the things or people you value to know what all the things you have around you truly mean to you and to realise that your family and friends are your highest heartfelt priorities. Life is designed to teach you all kinds of lessons, and it does this with you the tough way — because tough is really the best way you learn things.

Just because you may have a tough side to your character doesn't mean that you aren't an emotional pushover or a highly sensitive being as well. The fact that you are both hard and soft is the wonderful contradiction about your personality. You can be as hard as nails or as soft as the most pliable putty, dependent upon the day, the time, the place, and the situation you are facing.

Certain people can wrap you around their little fingers; others will not get the time of day from you, even if they grovel. When you commit yourself to someone, or truly love somebody, your power often flies out the window and you become more of a victim of love or a follower of love than a leader of love. In fact, your loved ones often have more influence on you than you want to admit because you consciously or unconsciously keep them in mind when it comes to deciding what pathway to walk in life and making other major decisions. Sometimes you actually hold yourself back so that others can keep up with you.

Life has many distinctive phases and stages where you are concerned, Scorpio. You were born with the determination, energy and tenacity to manifest your greatest dreams or conversely to create your own worst nightmares. Such is the double-edged sword power of planet Pluto and your symbol — the Scorpion. Being born under the Scorpion tells you that you have sting, tenacity and strong survival instincts.

Usually you live life more intensely than most and your intensity and energy draw to you people, situations and experiences that are out of the ordinary. Your energy field also naturally attracts opportunities and therefore choices. The trouble is that many of the positive options that present themselves contain hidden challenges. That is why your life's course is more of a winding road than a straight journey most of the time.

Even if life does take you on strange journeys, both inwardly and outwardly, it is most fortunate and timely that your powerful ruling planet, Pluto, provides you with a wealth of strong characteristics and powerful qualities to help you to surmount challenges and overcome all sorts of obstacles in life. You come onto this planet well prepared survive any kind of test, challenge or dilemma.

You generally have an incredibly sharp and highly discerning form of intelligence, a wide variety of natural talents, style or flair that is quite different from those around you, and often a great sense of charm, too. This charm is the source of your secret power. It takes the sting that you have within you and in a moment turns it into a magic wand instead. When you decide to wave your magic wand, you can be quite a smoothie and a most entertaining companion (but only if you want to be).

You can also be very funny (think of Scorpios Goldie Hawn and Whoopi Goldberg), even a riot at times. However, even in fun, you do not like to be on the receiving end of other people's criticisms, jokes or put downs. You have your boundaries and you are extremely determined about keeping these boundaries in exactly the place that you want them to be.

Being a Cancer myself, I am naturally in awe of Scorpio's magnificent, powerful and intense desire nature. Scorpio is to me the most effective of all the signs (when they are in 'full forwards' mode). Look at the world's richest man, Scorpio Bill Gates of Microsoft (who coincidentally was born the same day as Julia Roberts — but in different years of course). Bill is one example of the positive influence of Scorpio.

There are many charismatic and delightful Scorpios, like John Cleese, Danny De Vito, Meg Ryan, Joan Sutherland and Leonardo Di Caprio. However, remember this sign does have its sting. On the bleaker side, cult leader Charles Manson is certainly the darker manifestation of this sign's innermost power.

Being powerful has its pain and its pleasure. Choosing between positive and negative behaviour (or good or evil) is often a decision that Scorpios need to face in their lives. Another choice many of your sign need to make is between your love for power and the power of love.

In life, having power is a huge responsibility — and you have plenty of power coiled up within you — often with enough left over to change or destroy the world all on your own, if you really got yourself going. Being a Scorpio is no simple matter because you are frequently in touch with the bright and dark sides of yourself simultaneously.

Wilful and headstrong, you can have a hard time taking no for an answer even when no is actually in your best interest. What you want and what is good for you often are poles apart. But amazingly, even when you take risks that backfire, like the cat, you seem to have your own form of nine lives. It is almost as though you enjoy playing risk-taking games with Lady Luck and the forces that control your existence, just to see how much control you can wield over destiny, others and yourself.

In many ways you are a control or power addict (even if this only applies in some areas of your life, or at certain times of your life). Because you love to be in control, the way you operate, the relationships you become involved in, and the dreams you set your sights upon sometimes are quite extraordinary. You are prepared to go off after higher prizes or bigger dreams than most people.

Naturally, the higher you aim, the greater the possibility of the fall you might experience. And when you do fall from grace or power or out of love, you can find yourself more beaten, bruised and battered emotionally, spiritually and psychologically than is bearable. But your endless quest to get what you want or whom you want is exactly the fuel that spurs you on from one weird and wonderful experience to another. You are prepared to rise and fall in the name of gaining love, experience, control, experimentation and — best of all — success!

Many Scorpios are hugely successful. 'Making it' means a great deal to you because you have a tremendous admiration and love for power and for those who hold it. In your most determined (or bloody-minded) frame of mind, you can be the epitome of someone who is willing to march into Hell for your own cause. At times, you can also have a kamikaze approach to situations, where you might feel that you would rather sacrifice yourself than surrender.

Just as the Scorpion can turn its sting on itself if it is cornered, you often become self-sabotaging or unreasonable when life does not go the way you planned, expected or designed it to go. One of the hardest things for you Scorpios to accept is that you are not master over all things. In fact, destiny, fate and fortune all play an enormous role in your existence. You cannot have power over your destiny and so while you may like these forces of fate when they work for you and you're on top of the world, you curse them when they get in the way of your well-laid plans. The hidden realms, the unconscious and the metaphysical and subliminal energy worlds all weave their magic web around you. This web is the web of karma and soul-power as much as it is fate and destiny doing its work upon you.

Truth be known, you wouldn't really want to escape from the magic world of destiny's decrees. The unseen powers or forces of fate are far more closely aligned to you than any other sign of the zodiac. Once you realise that fate and destiny are your metaphysical mother and father, you might begin to appreciate the domino effect fate and fortune play in your life. Therefore it is most important for you to hand over some of your power to destiny. Have faith in the hidden, more fateful forces that influence your existence.

Probably the hardest lesson in life of all for you to learn, Scorpio, is that in reality you don't know everything after all, but you sure enjoy pretending that you do. And what is best of all for you is that others believe you do know everything and that you have a trick or two up your sleeve, so who is really fooling who?

Others give you lots of support, encouragement and admiration, too. Your deep connections to the unseen metaphysical forces of the universe give you enormous sex appeal. You Scorpios often have more sex appeal in your little finger than most signs have in their entire bodies. What you have isn't a physical thing, it's a cosmic chemistry thing! And this sex appeal is both a help and a hindrance and can make and break you.

Sex can run your life (when your desire nature gets out of control) and it can align you with some extremely strange people — in sexual relationships as well as in other relationships. Your sex appeal is impossible to describe and on a superficial level it isn't necessarily apparent. For example, while you may appear reserved, distant and unyielding at times, there's a tension or a suggestion that lingers in the air around you (something like a sexual aura). Underneath your physical veneer there is an enormous amount of passion waiting to be unleashed. Because of the volatile nature of this unusual force, you are wise to use your irresistible charms carefully, Scorpio, because your red-hot passions — when unchecked — can burst into flames of destruction.

There are likely to be times when you will need to take charge of the passions and infatuations that are driving your life. If you don't master your sexual energy field, it will end up mastering you. Your intense inner desires can pave a smooth path or run you in circles, depending on whether you harness and use them or you let them use you. When you use your self-discipline, you can avoid your passions' wild goose chases and propel yourself to great success. When you let your passions control you, you often run into trouble which can create chaos in all kinds of areas of life — including and involving your relationships, health, finances, promises, matters of conscience and even the law.

Even though you love the chase of love, sex and romance, surprisingly many of you Scorpios gauge your real success by your material conquests and accomplishments more than your emotional or physical ones. You assess your success or status in life by your range of power, the amounts of money you have accrued and the height of the position you hold at work and in your family.

Being a somewhat driven sign, you also seek a more intangible type of success in the form of living up to your fullest and highest potential. Where you find yourself not progressing or getting what you want, you can become extremely despondent. A depressed Scorpio is like fate letting forth the furies. It can be both tragic and frightening. In fact, your negative and dark thoughts are your greatest enemies and most formidable opponents.

Nobody on this planet can ever beat you up half as much as you can beat yourself up. You can be your own toughest critic and your own worst enemy as well. It is vital for you to operate in the light and have bright thoughts so it is important be especially choosy about the company you keep because chances are you attract some unscrupulous or shady characters into your life. These people are reflections of your own dark side and for that reason they are sometimes difficult to resist.

You Scorpios are not the sign to trifle with because you also are capable of being quite vengeful. A beautiful, intelligent and street-wise Scorpio girlfriend of mine started dating the eldest and somewhat wild-at-heart son of one of New York's powerful political families. From the first day they met she influenced his life in a very positive fashion. She gave him a newfound sense of responsibility, goals and purpose and set his wayward lifestyle within new boundaries. And in certain areas of his existence he truly needed new boundaries, too. He (an Aries) had many established wild ways, and lived somewhat of a rather shallow eat-drink-be-merry, live-for-the-moment, forget-about-tomorrow existence. My friend's influence saw him moderate his drinking and stop smoking, and his rowdy late nights out on the town became less frequent. Soon he improved his health, put life back into his sagging career as a lawyer, started playing sport on a regular basis and generally got himself back into tip-top shape.

Throughout all this, he was crazy about her. He was also thrilled by the way she had influenced his life in such a positive fashion and could not wait to introduce her to his family, whom he assumed would praise and adore her as he did. However, because she was not from the same social background as he was, just as soon as his family met her they unjustly turned against her without considering the benefits she had created.

From that first meeting on, his parents criticised, disagreed with or put down everything she said, did, dressed in or commented upon. They went all out in their attempt to turn their son against her. However, they underestimated her Scorpio field of power and his deep love for her. When her boyfriend's family were ridiculously mean to her, my friend turned the tables and closed ranks on them. She decided that she wanted nothing to do with them at all, and as the son was so madly in love with her he ended up walking away from them, too, closing all connections with his family.

That was six years ago. After that, they married (in a beautiful private marriage ceremony without informing his parents) and now have two lovely children, a boy and a girl. The children have never seen their paternal grandparents — and probably never will if my Scorpio friend has her way. So her husband's family not only lost their son but also their grandchildren. If his parents had known more about astrology, they would have realised they took on the wrong person when they took on my Scorpio friend! No matter what battles are being waged around you, you Scorpios usually end up winning the war, even if you lose some of the battles along the way.

Waging battles is part of your world. Some of you may confront difficulties in forms such as alcohol, sex addiction or even drugs. Others may battle society's traditions, family members or business adversaries. This should not truly faze you. As a Scorpio, in many different ways you are meant to face numerous battles and tests of faith in your life. Mythology and the stars reveal that you are well equipped to take on and survive these challenges because your ruling planet, Pluto, rules the underworld, or the darker side of life.

Battling, or your tendency to take the hard road (or to adopt a hard line with others), even quite appeals to you. Compromise doesn't come easily to you and you usually have strong views and opinions. In fact you Scorpios can be one of the most black and white signs of all. In your mind, most situations and people you deal with can be all good or all bad. Finding moderation or half measures can be a tough call where you are concerned. You can be an extremist in the way you deal with situations, handle relationships, or judge, oppose or support other people or causes. You may even conduct your world, business or relationships with a 'do or die' approach. Tact is often not your finest quality and the ultimatum is something you are excellent at handing out and terrible at taking.

In fairness to you, however, if someone uses logic and tugs on your heartstrings a little, you can be very gracious. You have a particularly soft spot for the underdog and while you do attempt to keep this tenderheartedness hidden, people who know you well can often see it. However, few people can penetrate your public veneer and really get to know you. While you are often gregarious, friendly, honest, open, and peaceful on the outside, there is a lot happening on the inside that you do not reveal.

Your public personality is charming — often in a quiet sort of way — and you have a soft-spoken authority that makes people stop to listen when you speak. Of course, there are Scorpios who are loud, overwhelming and boisterous, and who love to be the centre of attention. However, unless they are in the entertainment business and profit from being centre-stage, the 'hey, look at me' type of Scorpios are in the minority. Secrecy means a lot to you, and keeping your affairs private can become a sore point.

When you have something to say, you do not mince words, and you generally only comment on topics you really know about. You rarely share your true inner thoughts with anyone but you will gladly question someone else about theirs. You believe any inquiry is fair game, and you do not think you are prying even if someone accuses you of it. People with thin skin cautiously refrain from asking for your opinion, but your honesty — stinging as it can be — is a rare and precious quality.

The ability to negotiate compromises is a great skill of yours and you make a terrific mediator, counsellor, negotiator or dealmaker for others. And when you offer praise, it is usually with complete sincerity. You praise others when they do a job well or they excel in some way, but you do not do so without merit. You know that it takes willpower, focus and energy to earn, win or claim your goals and dreams. So you do not waste resources or words.

You intuitively know that nothing and no one is unreachable, and you manage to come up with deals or arrangements that might be out of the question for everyone else. Winning is always important to you and you are a natural game-player. You know that everything and everyone has a price, and you have a quick talent for discovering what it is. You also know how to shrewdly read between the lines of conversations and faces, and you are not easily fooled.

However, when it comes to your life, you sometimes fool yourself. There are times when you think you know best and you dig in your heels and will not move forwards or change. Few Scorpios trust change, even when you are the ones making it happen. You like to keep everything (and everyone) in the place of your choosing. Since you are extremely independent, you can also be stubborn and strong-willed. You seldom listen to others' advice, even when they are offering you invaluable insights or opinions.

However, should you freely choose to change your mind about something or someone and switch mental channels, you switch completely. As a Scorpio, you are known for keeping your commitments, but when you do move on from something or someone, you rarely explain why or look back. This sometimes earns you the reputation of having the coldest heart of the zodiac.

When others do you wrong you seldom forgive or forget. And when you say goodbye to something or someone, that chapter of your life is often closed in a way that leaves the other person or the situation you left behind in some kind of chaos. However, you do not slam doors behind you easily or without a great deal of thought. As a rule, whatever it is that makes this happen builds up for a long time until you eventually reach your breaking point.

Fortunately, when the breaking point comes, you Scorpios can take care of yourselves very well. You have a keen and strong personal survival instinct. This serves you well in all areas of life because you can generally turn upsets or showdowns around to your advantage — eventually. When those rare occasions occur and someone does get the better of you in business, romance, or finance, you can become the embodiment of dark powers and forces.

There are many good reasons that many astrologers say, 'Never cross a Scorpio'. Being in the position where you have to take it, rather than hand it out, wounds you deeply. You can be over-reactive if or when others get the better of you. Try not to take defeat or rejection too seriously! Try to remember that everyone, sometime in their life has to take a loss, comeuppance or defeat — even you. You are human . . . after all!

Sometimes you feel as though you have been defeated when instead you are actually being presented with a winning hand of cards. Pluto, your ruling planet, is the planet of rebirth and transformation and the way it weaves its magic is often through destroying one situation that surrounds you to rebuild it anew. Consequently, some of the worst times of your life are merely the creation time that precedes the best period of your life. You frequently have to go through hell to reach heaven or lose something or someone to find something or someone better in the future.

Remember, Scorpio, your ego can be your biggest strength and motivation, but it can also be your greatest challenge and lead to your undoing. The more you feed your ego, the bigger it becomes, and the more difficult it is to control. Also, because you are born under the powerful sign of Scorpio, you are often automatically handed a great deal of respect and admiration from the world at large or from those around you.

You can lose touch with certain relationship sensitivities or delicate feelings simply because others succumb to your will so often. But even if you do get a trifle big for your boots at times, when all is said and done Scorpio, life usually smiles upon you, and you are the sign of the zodiac that usually ends up having the best times, the most incredible life, the greatest love affairs and the loudest last laugh of all.

Scorpio is a Water sign

To your advantage, you can be a terrific actor when you need to be because you usually have a deep emotional understanding of others and the polished ability to hide your own feelings. You truly do have a guardian angel, but yours is more like a Hell's Angel type of angel who hovers over you and picks you up and dusts you off when you need it most.

To your disadvantage, you can have a hard time trusting people. Not even your closest friends escape some of your suspicions, and you keep so much inside that there are times your anger boils over and rolls out like a tidal wave wiping out everyone and everything in your path.

[Insights into your sign]

The bright side: You have a great deal to offer, yourself, others and the world at large. One of your greatest strengths is your ability to tap into your intuition. When you utilise this gift, your inspired purpose of self-mastery gains clear focus.

The shadow: You can be your own worst enemy when you become obsessed with something or someone. At times like these, you end up creating your own nemesis.

Characteristics >	Benefits >	Drawbacks >
Ambitious	Self-starter	Power-hungry
Determined	Steel will	Bloody-minded
Emotional	Deep feelings	Paranoid
Energetic	High stamina	Explosive
Imaginative	Creative	Neurotic
Independent	Self-reliant	Selfish
Influential	Persuasive	Manipulative
Magnetic	Attract your desires	Attract trouble
Mystical	Mysterious	Raise suspicions
Passionate	Intense	Violent temper
Perceptive	Keen observer	Critical
Philosophical	Love wisdom	Judgmental
Powerful	Steel force	Bully
Quiet	Contained	Brooding
Secretive	Self-sufficient	Closed up
Selective	Observant	Fussy
Sensitive	Emotionally in touch	Alcoholism
Sexy	Master of seduction	Lack true intimacy
Subtle	Delicate	Crafty
Tenacious	Persevering	Stubborn
Unyielding	Firm	Unmovable

[Looking beneath the surface of your sign]

The underlying and sometimes very secret reasons behind your actions are often more revealing than the actions themselves. Even if you're one of the most divine Scorpios, you can still let all that power swell your head at times. The saying, 'All's fair in love and war' is part of the Scorpion creed. But beware, Scorpio, when you set out to satisfy your passions at any cost, you may end up over your head. And when you feel your life is out of control, you're tempted to use your stinging and deadly poison — and suffer the consequences.

Try to relax and let some things go. Your lust for control can be head-spinning, and besides, as much as you like to think you're running the show, deep inside you know there are plenty of forces that are running you! So take some time out to play. And remember that you always have a choice, and you're never really trapped, Scorpio, unless you believe there's no way out. There's a difference between committing to a goal or an idea and chaining yourself to a sinking ship when you could swim to shore instead.

[How to tune into your sign's powers]

> *Trust in destiny, yourself and others.*

> *Compromise when necessary.*

> *Accept change rather than fight it.*

The Scorpio woman

When she wants to, this lady can wrap a man around her little finger with one hand tied behind her back.

She is a deep thinker, an intense feeler and has a powerful inquiring mind. The Scorpio woman is one of the most magical, powerful, and yet surprisingly level-headed women on the planet. She is much stronger than her zodiac sisters, even though she may look as cute as a button and as gentle as a lamb. She is born with natural power and she probably started wielding it in the cradle when her daddy and mummy were kept running around in circles after her at a very early age (without even knowing she was running them around, too).

While the Scorpio gal often gives an appearance of being the great girl-next-door type — the type the boys in the neighbourhood all dream about at night (like Scorpio Julia Roberts) — or 'her daddy's little darling' type, don't mistake her for a 'little missy'. Ms Scorpio is also often perfectly capable when it comes to changing a tyre, playing football or generally wearing the pants and getting the job done on any level of existence when she needs to. The thing that is sometimes not too apparent from her external appearance is her self-sufficiency and her independence.

Real relationships can be something she aspires to but has difficulty adjusting into. Because she has so much inner strength, she often has unusual relationships with men, and sometimes she intimidates them. A part of her knows subliminally that she can (and may even consistently be able to) give any man a true run for his money. (Just look at powerful energy Scorpios Goldie Hawn, Julia Roberts, Hillary Rodham Clinton, and Maria Shriver.) So don't be fooled by Ms Scorpio's big laughing eyes, her cute giggle, her most appealing and sometimes seductive look, or her brave front. She is quite a complicated package and one you probably will never get a chance to unwrap sufficiently to discern exactly what exists underneath the top layers.

The big question that daunts many Scorpio women is, 'Am I really as nice and as perfect as I want to be?' Confidence is the rocket fuel of her life, and confidence is often something that takes some special drumming up for her. Frequently Ms Scorpio is quite a mystery to herself, too.

Although she knows her strengths and her limitations better than any other female of the zodiac, there is still an edge to her that says 'I'm extremely vulnerable underneath'. But she shouldn't believe this self-talk too much. The truth is that she is both inwardly vulnerable and powerful at the same time. However, she tends to be her own best critic and her own best adviser, too, and neither insult nor flattery from others does much to change the image or opinion she has of herself.

She's no stranger to emotions, and although she keeps them well concealed, they affect her deeply and can make her vulnerable in areas where she would normally keep up her guard. Consequently, she's had her fingers and her feelings burnt a few times, and might be slow to extend her hand in friendship. As much as she shines in her romantic and professional life, it is in the areas of home and family that Ms Scorpio generally finds her perfect niche. She can be one of the best mothers of the zodiac, but also one of the most obsessive and possessive.

[How Scorpio women operate]

Social

The Scorpio woman's public image is so well packaged that it's hard to believe she is experiencing the same ups and downs in life as the rest of us. She often has the brightest smile (just think of Scorpios Meg Ryan and Goldie Hawn) and you seldom see her looking depressed, at least in public. This lady is one of the world's best actresses and even if her heart is broken, she can still get up and put on a happy face — if she wants to.

Friendship is an area that Ms Scorpio treats as selectively as some people choose their heart surgeon. She likes to have the highest quality friends and usually they are hard for her to find. Often she becomes extremely disillusioned by the people who make up her inner circle. If someone really lets her down more than once, she usually prefers to be alone rather than put up with second best.

Just as she picks her friends, she is also choosy about which social invitations she accepts. She's even more discerning when she makes out the guest list for one of her own parties or get-togethers, especially if it's in her home. Her home — whether it's a cottage on the beach, or a townhouse in the city — is her sanctuary. Her bedroom is often her luxurious fortress and when she wants to hide away from the world, this is where you'll find her. Her home is where she gets to have everything exactly as she wants it.

She likes her privacy and she's not keen on people dropping in, so no matter how good your intentions are — telephone first. That is, if you have her number. There's a good chance it's unlisted. She prefers to be the one to initiate new relationships, and her criteria can be rather challenging. She's a natural born philosopher, and her best friends are candid and comfortable with her prying into their thoughts and beliefs.

The less interest someone shows in Scorpio's opinions and private life, the more she likes them. However, if she wants to talk to you about her secrets, love affairs or dreams, she is likely to be amazingly open and descriptive regarding the multitude of things both positive and negative that are happening in her life (but only when she wants to share).

Love and family

Ms Scorpio is the type who has her own unique kind of sexual chemistry or human feminine magnetism. She has a deeply seductive beauty that is both intriguing and distracting. (Picture Scorpios Marla Maple Trump, Lauren Hutton, Meg Ryan and Demi Moore.) Unless she's going through some sort of troubled times, her eyes flash with sparkling hypnotic charm and her coy smile suggests she knows your deepest secrets. And she might — a Scorpio woman is a psychic radar; she can pick up on who you are and what you're all about just from sitting across a table from you. She has refined intuition and is very adept at seeing right through other people's masks and motives.

She's also extraordinarily skilled in the art of romantic conquest. A Scorpio woman can walk into a room, smile seductively and walk away with the man she chooses, even if he already has a date for the evening. Few can compete with a Scorpio in the area of romance, and many women are incredibly jealous of her success. This lady can wrap a man around her little finger with one hand tied behind her back. She's frequently accused of playing by her own rules but she rarely agrees to play by anyone else's. All's fair to a Scorpio, and her coy tactics and smooth manoeuvres generally prove to be reliable when it comes to getting whomever, or whatever, she sets her sights on.

Ms Scorpio is not the love-'em and leave-'em type. She usually is looking for her lifelong partner. This can work both against and for her. If she meets the right man she often has the best marriage or partnership of anyone on the planet. However, unfortunately, meeting her Mr Right rarely seems to happen just like in the movies.

Frequently, when Ms Scorpio meets the man who she considers to be hot in the cot, she quickly and immediately assumes that he's marriage material, too. Using sex as her gauge or marriage-meter is one of the ways she can totally miss the mark. Because she is highly sexual, she can put sex up on a level of worship and then associate the man who came along with the sex with the same degree of worship. That is why, when it comes to living life on everyday levels, Ms Scorpio surprisingly often seems to settle for a man who isn't really fit to shine her high-heels.

She may race around telling everyone she has met her prince when before too long has passed her family and close friends quickly realise that she actually has gotten involved with a toad. Even when the realisation hits home that they have not met their prince after all, Ms Scorpio can misguidedly stick with her original assessment. Many times Scorpio women stay with their man just because they jumped into the relationship too quickly, got their lives complicated and now don't want to deal with the realisation that they created their own romantic nemesis. Moving on and cutting emotional or romantic ties often is the hardest thing for a Scorpio woman to do.

She will often drive a man to leave her by nagging him to death rather than just tell him goodbye, sorry — it just didn't work out. That is why many Scorpio women remain in relationships for years or a lifetime with men they do not respect. Where men are concerned, love and respect add up to the same thing for Ms Scorpio. And as respect is one of the greatest qualities that she assesses her life by, if deep down inside she doesn't respect her man she ends up loathing him.

Being such a capable and independent woman, when Ms Scorpio is single — although this leaves a huge gap in her life — she's actually sometimes more fulfilled than when she's in a relationship because she only has herself to please. But this doesn't last for long because the man-hunter in her can never be put to rest, só when she's not in a committed relationship she's conducting continuous interviews to fill the open position. She's critical of potential partners but once she gives in to her emotions, her heart can rule her head — at least temporarily.

A Scorpio woman likes a strong, virile man who is equal to, or superior to her, in intelligence, wealth, and power. However, finding a man who can live up to her desires and expectations is like looking for a needle in a haystack. Still, only a strong, loyal, and secure man can dance and dally with a Scorpio without being bitten and that's why so many men steer a course around her. Subliminally, many of them innately realise that they've met their match and they go out looking for easier pickings. Or if they are man enough, they will instead know that what they have found, although not necessarily an easy experience to handle, will turn out to be the love of their lifetime.

As a mother, a Scorpio woman has an iron fist and a pillow-soft heart. Her children play by the rules but also learn how to appeal to her softer side to sway her. And considering how objective a Scorpio can be about most things in life, she is far from objective when it comes to her own children. Some Scorpios totally refuse to look at their own creations with a critical eye.

Consequently, the Scorpio mother is great at supporting her kids' ambitions and desires, but not so great at helping them to recognise and strengthen their weak spots. She's also extremely protective and will take on anyone who even hints at giving one of her children a hard time. And that includes their father, who rarely has any chance of overriding her decisions.

Career

Where career is concerned, this woman can leave the competition far behind her. She usually has a business brain and she uses it well. She knows her potential is infinite, and she thrives on the opportunity to learn new skills and develop more resources. She can tackle almost any job. She uses her talents and abilities in such a remarkable way that she often ends up running the company. She has a lust for success and everything that comes with it, especially money and power. She might enjoy fame as well, but most of the time she prefers her privacy. Even if she makes a career out of acting or modelling or other areas that make her well known, she still manages to keep her distance from public scrutiny.

As much as she likes being praised and doted on, she also enjoys being a background player. Ms Scorpio loves pulling the strings and she often uses this talent well in her work. It's difficult to predict which profession a Scorpio will choose but she's often drawn to mystery and mayhem. She finds people fascinating and loves to observe them and theorise about their actions and motives. Her intuition often jumps in and fills in the gaps, and she can find her way through a problem, faster than most people can tie their shoes.

Scorpios make exceptional detectives, scientists, therapists, healers, investigative reporters, and journalists. She might work in a career that involves counselling others because she's often very good at getting to the root of issues that escape those less discerning than her.

Financial

Ms Scorpio has huge admiration and respect for the security, independence and comfort that money stacked away under the bed, in a foreign bank account, or in gold bars can bring. She loves money as much as she values love and sex — which is quite a lot. When she's really focused she can do well financially, but for a Scorpio, doing well is rarely good enough.

She wants to build her own empire and if she can't build her own, she'll try to marry someone who already has. However, if she doesn't marry money, it often serves her best financially because that encourages her to go out and make it herself. She does prefer to be financially independent and rarely trusts others enough to let them manage her finances.

Many millionaires and even some billionaires (look at Scorpio Bill Gates) are born under the sign of Scorpio, and some of them hit rock bottom before they begin to build their impressive financial portfolios. But then, rock bottom is a mere illusion for a Scorpio because their ruling planet Pluto's power of regeneration never fails to give new birth to the Scorpio, no matter how disastrous the financial crash.

Once Ms Scorpio has risen to the top of the financial sphere she generally has an easy time staying there and enjoying the rewards. She often generates some of her wealth through real estate. Her selective tastes pay off big time when it comes to buying property, and she has an uncanny knack for buying land just before its value skyrockets.

Physical

This is the dancing girl of the zodiac, the one who can do a flamingo, tap dance an Irish jig and a cha cha without missing a beat. Not only can she be an incredible athlete but she can also do something that not many others can do and that is look good while she is doing it! A Scorpio woman has such a powerful, often metaphysical, form of physical beauty that she can look glamorous in her high school physical edication uniform.

The word glamour is actually part of her magic. It describes a spell that the ancient women of wisdom used to wrap around themselves in order to make themselves attractive. Well, I firmly believe that a Scorpio woman innately has this same ability to make herself stand out, or appear unusually glamorous. Whether she is thin, a little plump, short or tall, she still has some kind of magical form of sex appeal or glamour. If she's wrapped in her black satin evening gown, she's bewitching enough to make you forget your name because she can truly bedazzle you. She has penetrating eyes and can hypnotise a crowd as she (without any apparent effort) flashes a glance across a room.

She generally has a strong constitution and is frequently very agile and light on her feet. Many Scorpio women are gymnasts and acrobats and they tend to be very coordinated and fearless at the same time. (Olympic ice skater Oksana Baiul is a Scorpio, and so is Olympic gymnast Nadia Comaneci.)

She feels her best when she stays physically active and exercise frees her mind and keeps her body running at optimum performance. But she sometimes takes her health for granted and pushes her body beyond its human limit. She can get away with this at times, but when a Scorpio really overdoes it, she ends up being forced to take a few days off to recover.

These are the times her friends will be expected to deliver piping hot soup, fresh tropical fruits, and chocolate-covered peanuts and raisins. Even with all of her friends waiting on her hand and foot, she can be a difficult patient because she's extra hard to please when she doesn't feel well.

As a Water sign, Scorpio is susceptible to stress-related health conditions and also environmental pollutants. She probably drinks clear mountain spring water and may have a top-rated filtration system in her home. But her emotions and her internal reactions to other people are usually her biggest health challenges. When a Scorpio woman feels defeated or down on her luck she can turn to some really excessive behaviours. She might eat a dozen cream-filled doughnuts or drink two bottles of wine, but whatever she does, you can bet she'll pay the price for it by the way she feels the next day.

Mental

The Scorpio woman is very intelligent even if she is more street-smart than highly educated. She always wants to know the ins and outs of everything and she knows how to ask the right question to get the right answer. She is intrigued by the unknown and looks forward to learning more about it with a sense of excitement. She probably believes (at least on an inner or subconscious level) that her mind is her true power and she probably receives some guidance from her sixth sense, but she may not consciously acknowledge this inner voice.

She's no doubt philosophical in some sort of way and she might even be a fan of Plato or Khalil Gibran or study with one of today's philosophers. She may be drawn to astrology or ancient mysteries and she's probably infatuated with the idea of magic. The Scorpio woman who practises mind control learns that her ability to create her dreams is extensive, and she's wise to be cautious about what she wishes for — since she very well may get it.

Many Scorpio women love practical jokes and she can pull off the most unusual and creative pranks. She also likes to learn new things, not from others, but by doing them herself. She's quick to accept an opportunity for hands-on training in any area of life she wants to learn about.

Spiritual

Ms Scorpio is very religious, spiritual and devout in the way that she structures her life. However, she often has little tolerance when it comes to dealing with, or being part of, organised religions. Because she operates so close to temptation, there are times she may choose to go to Confession, or do charitable deeds to make herself feel better about any past sins.

This occurs when she feels the urge to purge her soul and connect with the higher forces, usually for some specific reason — like she has lost her way, feels abandoned by life or needs to replenish her drained physical and emotional batteries. She will go out of her way to become as pure of spirit as possible, and this may include visiting places like ashrams in India or going to meditation or yoga classes.

She is often attracted to sitting in a church (sometimes of any denomination) not to attend a specific service but to humble herself to the higher forces that she knows hold the deciding votes when it comes to how her life evolves.

When she sits in quiet reflection she often talks to her own special god, goddess or creator and she has some of her most intensely meaningful conversations and can receive powerful messages and insights at these moments. That isn't to say, however, that whatever she is devout about today (or the god or goddess she feels closest with today) won't be different in a few years, or even next week.

It's not unusual to meet a Scorpio who has abandoned her childhood religion but still practises some of its dogma in an almost subconscious sort of way. Nevertheless, whatever she chooses to do, she'll do it with faith and love. A Scorpio woman innately knows that all paths will eventually lead her back to her origin, her creator or unconditional love.

The Scorpio man

Scorpio is a master of midnight romance, and he demonstrates his passion and virility with delicious delicacy and raw strength.

Want to fly to the moon, crash land on Mars or circle Saturn? If you want to really explore the unknown, without a parachute, then a Scorpio man (if he wants to) has the astrological power at his disposal to take you on the cosmic adventure of a lifetime. Now the big question is, will you survive the adventure? Well, that answer is for you to find out. Just be aware that you had better be daring and prepared for anything and everything when you involve yourself with a man born under the sign of Scorpio. He is not a man to take lightly (because he is certain to make a huge imprint upon your life).

He can also be confusing because he will be the perfect man and one of the more imperfect men, too, all rolled up into one. He is a mixed package — the Scorpio male is the super-hero one day and the court jester the next. He can swing like a pendulum in his emotional output, too. He may be fawning, attentive and seductive one moment then standoffish and self-absorbed straight after. However, he usually has a good reason for being one way or the other. He likes to play whichever role has the most power or influence to help him get his way. He also does not particularly like to put himself out for anybody else, although he probably thinks he does!

Now, the Scorpio man has the ability to get away with many things that other men would never be forgiven. That is because he has a unique brand of charisma, and he is often extremely appealing in his own way to look at, too. No matter how he appears outwardly, don't assume that he is not well equipped to get what he wants, especially if he wants it badly enough.

Mr Scorpio innately knows the magical spells of seduction. He was born under a dazzling sexual star and his physical looks are not necessarily his main drawcard. His personal appeal, sexually and otherwise, is of a subtle, 'read between the lines' type. When he is pursuing a gal, trying to win a bet or wheeling and dealing, he does it with his own brand and style. He has that 'hidden under the surface' type of mysterious appeal.

And what a talker. This man can truly charm the birds out of the trees, if he wants to. Mr Scorpio began polishing his communication skills when he was still in nappies. All babies cry when they're hungry, but a baby Scorpio can cry in such a way that you know if he wants peas or carrots. And so at an early age he begins a lifetime of issuing orders in the polite form of requests.

The amazing thing is that a Scorpio man is so magnetically powerful that he can usually get people to do exactly what he wants, whether he has any real authority or not. A prime example of a male Scorpio who most stands out as a high-achiever in our modern world is Bill Gates of Microsoft. Not far behind are American business moguls, Scorpios Calvin Klein and Ted Turner, who both so aptly exhibit top Scorpio power and strength. Mr Scorpio may be your best friend's brother, the guy next door or the man who drives you crazy at the health club when you see him flex his muscles.

Wherever he is and whatever he is, you are likely to notice him without even realising that you are noticing him. And whether your Scorpio is a media magnate or the guy next door, you'd be wise to make him a friend, not your foe. Never underestimate a Scorpio man. He is not a pushover; he is more of a bulldozer type of individual. However, he does his bulldozing in such a way that you seldom see it coming.

[How Scorpio men operate]

Social

The Scorpio man projects a feeling of cool certainty and confidence. He can appear quiet, innocent, serious, ambitious, energetic or imaginative, but rest assured, whatever image he's projecting, there's much more to him than meets the eye. And speaking of eyes, watch a Scorpio's eyes when he's talking about an issue he feels passionate about and you'll get a sneak preview of the intensity that's within his composed exterior.

But even with a thousand peeks into the core of a Scorpio, you'll be as uncertain about who he really is as you were the day you met him. And to make matters more complex, he's remarkably capable of mimicking the traits of the other zodiac signs.

Some Scorpion men are so skilful at going incognito they can pass as Sagittarians. But, sociable as he may be, his animated conversation with you doesn't necessarily mean he wants to be your friend. Take no offence, because a Scorpio can enjoy working side by side with someone for years before he even considers inviting them to a social outing. His suspicious nature makes him very wary of inviting newcomers into his life, and as much as he desires companions, he sometimes chooses to be alone.

Most Scorpio men have a handful of close friends and an address book filled with the names of casual friends, business prospects, and everyone important, prominent, or famous that he's ever met. And just about everyone in his book will gladly accept an invitation that he extends. He can be very entertaining because he's always thinking and feeling at the same time.

He might also be a prankster and surprise you with his original schemes. One of his favourite ways to have fun is to pretend he's the one in charge when he's not. I once watched a Scorpio tell more than thirty people waiting in line for a ticket outlet to open that the concert had already sold out. They all went home and when the ticket window opened he was first in line. He bought two tickets and laughed all the way to the front row of the theatre.

Love and family

A Scorpio man's blend of passion and intellect can at the very least place him in the running for the title of most magnetic heartbreaker on the planet. This isn't to say he sets out to do any deliberate damage; it's just that he knows exactly what he wants, and as soon as he detects something that isn't compatible with his idea of a mate, he steps out for a beer and doesn't return. If he does return after he decides you're not Ms Right, it's often because his search for the perfect mate has exhausted him, or he's tired of being alone. Be wary because he probably isn't planning to stay indefinitely.

Women worship at Scorpio's sexual altar and he seems to have the powerful ability to bewitch his partners. Even women who are dominant in other relationships rarely succeed in wielding any influence over a Scorpio whatsoever. Scorpio likes to rule over his own heart and head rather than permit either of them to dictate his actions.

There are times when his thoughts run away with themselves and his emotions run away with him. Generally, Scorpio is Mr Cool. Even when a red-hot relationship tempts him, he usually has the self-control to walk away without a backward glance if it doesn't fit into his lifetime master plan.

At this point you may be wondering if there are any benefits to a love affair with a Scorpio, so I will confidently tell you the answer is yes. He can be incredibly perceptive, creatively imaginative and profoundly sensitive. He is also likely to have a magic wand that he knows how to use at the right time in the right way.

His inner energy and power are infinite and he is just as interested in helping his mate to accomplish her goals and pleasures as he is in achieving his own. Did I mention that he's incredibly sexy? A Scorpio is a master of midnight romance and he demonstrates his passion and virility with delicious delicacy and raw strength. If you're his soulmate, you're in for the most exciting, though somewhat volatile, time of your life.

As a father a Scorpio commands obedience and respect and might be a little on the strict side. He loves his children with all of his heart but he doesn't tolerate defiance of any sort and he expects every member of the family to contribute to the common good. He especially enjoys his little ones when they're big enough to bring him the newspaper and help out with the chores. He's particularly protective of his family, too, and heaven help anything or anybody who encroaches or trespasses on the sanctuary of his home and family.

Career

Mr Scorpio loves to be captain of his own ship. And he doesn't like taking instructions from others unless they are teaching him something he wants to learn. However, although he is a natural loner and leader, if he has to work as part of a team, he is willing to patiently play the role of subordinate, even when he believes his qualifications are superior to those of his employer or administrator.

He does his job with energy, efficiency, and obvious ease. He's a valuable and productive employee in any profession and his loyalty goes to the individual signing his pay cheque. He doesn't let his personal opinions get in the way of his responsibilities and he's not one to stand around the cappuccino machine exchanging corporate gossip.

He considers himself completely responsible for his work and he won't make excuses or place blame on others when he's made an error. He's also a believer in the statement, 'Take no credit, take no blame'. And praise doesn't rate higher than financial reward. He's not necessarily just looking for recognition to feed his ego, he likes fair return for a job well done, too.

He knows what he can do, and other people's opinions of him can sometimes mean very little when it comes to his self-esteem. It is what he thinks about himself in terms of value that counts. He can be his own harshest critic and judge. Creatively employed, his independent spirit can take off with unique ideas, and if he's an artist or writer, his work is often condemned for breaking the rules of its genre — and then eventually praised for setting a new standard. Picasso is a perfect example of a Scorpio artist.

Scorpios can be found in every profession on Earth but his dominant traits combine to make him especially good at acting, advertising, writing, management, research, investigative work, and psychology. He is often drawn to one of the healing professions, and his strong energy and diagnostic intuition help him to rise to the top of his chosen field of practice.

Financial

Although a Scorpio has the power of the universe at his disposal, he won't rest until he makes enough money to maintain complete control over his present conditions and follow through with his future plans. Many Scorpio men are entrepreneurs and they generally make about fifty per cent of their income from privately owned businesses. If he doesn't own a company, he probably works for one that pays him well and provides valuable employee benefits.

As for the rest of his income, you may never know where that comes from, even if you're his wife. He always has some secrets and while his financial dealings may be completely legal and above board, he believes it's a good idea to keep his personal and professional business to himself. And his sealed lips help him to maintain his privacy while he makes his fortune and builds his empire.

Scorpio men enjoy all of the benefits that money provides and many of them are pleasantly familiar with the lifestyles of the rich and famous. It's not unusual for a Scorpio to achieve millionaire status well before he's forty years old. But the opportunity to make millions may present itself at any point in his life.

Physical

It doesn't matter how a Scorpio man looks, he's always a giant on the inside, and other places, where it really counts. Actually, he usually looks pretty good on the outside, too. He may not be what you'd call model material as he's likely to have more of a unique look than a stereotyped one. Scorpio men are known for their piercing eyes, well-toned physiques, unequalled endurance, and powerful energy fields. They're also known for their calm yet stoical expression that hides nearly all of their deep emotions. And perhaps that's where their health trouble begins.

Nearly all of Mr Scorpio's health problems are created by his own churning emotions, which he holds tightly inside. A Scorpio man has a hidden fear that if he lets go of or tames his passionate emotions, he'll lose his determination as well. Of course his intellect knows this isn't true but his subconscious fears can taint his outlook.

Most Scorpion men learn that one of the best ways to release stress is sex and other exercise, and they often find they're good at both. The main thing is for him to work up a sweat a few times a week. And it's very important for a Scorpio to make gentle stretching part of his daily routine to help balance some of his rigid thinking and flex his manly muscle(s).

All in all, the Scorpio man has a strong constitution and if he takes care of himself he will enjoy good health well into his later years. When he does get sick, he has an amazing ability to bounce back. Consequently, he's sometimes tempted to work too long and play too hard.

All Water signs have a penchant for overindulgence of some sort, and Scorpio's favourites include food, alcohol, and women. But he doesn't allow himself to binge too frequently. A Scorpio often experiences the pleasure and pain of numerous vices before he's even out of his teens. But for him that's a good time and a good way to learn some early lessons. And he nearly always has enough will power and determination to overcome any bad habits, except that sometimes alcohol can be his downfall.

Mental

The Scorpio man has been questioning everything ever since he took his first breath. His natural curiosity leads him to seek knowledge and wisdom everywhere he goes. He seems to know that the quality of his questions determines the quality of his life. That's why he burrows beneath the surface of life and situations and often is one of the best investigative minds around. He likes to get to the bottom of things and he certainly doesn't take what he's told or what he sees at face value. When it comes to sorting facts, figures and information, he's a four-star kind of guy.

Some of his best storytelling is birthed from his ongoing study of human behaviour and his sharp perceptions. He does embellish true accounts and adds a dash of fantasy to the situation, but these combine to produce a hilarious account of events and situations. He also writes some wonderful letters, e-mails and postcards, the type that are wrought with detail and wit. Writing is a healthy outlet for a Scorpio and some of those who you would never guess would keep a journal actually do. (But it will be absolutely off-limits to curious eyes, and you would be wise to respect his privacy.)

He likes to look to the past as well as the future when it comes to finding out information. He's intrigued by mystery and might even fantasise about finding the remains of an ancient civilisation. He probably loves to travel but doesn't travel as much as he'd like to because he gets accustomed to routine.

Often his work and his inquiries take him to foreign lands. At some time in his life he is likely to experiment with psychedelic drugs or consume vast quantities of alcohol to experience altered states of mind. Many Scorpios practise meditation or some form of mental exercises to focus and stretch their minds.

Spiritual

Because he travels the path of temptation throughout his life, Mr Scorpio often is looking for strength of will. Sometimes he'll find it through finding God. However, most Scorpios like to run their own show, and this means they can even turn their back on the creator and have such a strong connection to fate, fortune and free will that they more or less just coast their way through life believing that what will be will be.

Because he is a researcher by nature, the Scorpio man has the power to tap into some of the most enlightening spiritual information on — and off — the planet. His attraction to ancient mysteries reveals many truths and opens some hidden doors. A Scorpio may not understand how he does it, but if he's observant he'll notice that he attracts people into his life just by thinking about them or desiring their knowledge.

He may have a theory that life and death are merely gateways through realms of existence, and at least some of his friends consider him 'out there' in a big way. He also might reject the whole spirituality concept and choose to believe that we're born, we live, we die.

But no matter what his conscious mind says, his subconscious is always connected to the spiritual realms, and whether he knows it or not, he is probably far more attuned to his creator than most others on this planet.

The Scorpio baby

This is the high and holy roller baby of the zodiac. Whatever the Scorpio baby wants, the Scorpio baby gets.

Regarded as the passion and love baby of the zodiac, the arrival of this little Scorpio into your life will not only influence your future but this baby has what it takes to influence the future of the world!

There's a powerful subliminal force surrounding the Scorpio baby so prepare for a new dimension of experience in your life. Scorpios are destined for a life filled with acts of fate and fortune. This is the tiny babe who holds within its power the ability to change the set-up and make-up of your entire existence. No matter how smart you may be, this baby will keep you guessing.

Just when you think you've figured out a Scorpio infant he or she will turn around and do the exact opposite of what you had anticipated. Mystery is part of the Scorpio design and some mysteries are not meant to be solved. Something like the Egyptian Sphinx, Scorpios, even when they're still in nappies, evoke a sense of awe, and are surrounded by unanswered questions.

Prepare to go through many extremes of highs and lows because the little Scorpio has an innate desire to lead rather than follow. From the moment it's born, this baby definitely has a mind and destiny of its own. Scorpio babies don't arrive into your life by accident. The Scorpio comes as a gift.

Astrologically, the Scorpio is meant to be a great teacher of life to his or her parents. Scorpios also tend to have destinies interwoven with their parents and other family members.

Sooner or later you'll discover what an important role this tiny, innocent, vulnerable baby is going to play in your future — and it's likely to make an enormous impact on you, in more ways than one.

Ruled by Pluto, the planet of subliminal hidden power, Scorpios can sometimes make others feel a bit uneasy. Even as an infant a Scorpio has eyes that are both compelling and mysterious. Unlike many babies, who are looking for stability, Scorpios often thrive on change. That's understandable since Pluto is the planet of transformation, regeneration and change.

So by all means and fashions, this little bundle will guarantee that your life will go through a variety of changes, possibly in a very dramatic way. This baby is very much a child of destiny. There may be unusual conditions surrounding its conception or birth (the Scorpio baby doesn't do things by the book). During the actual birth, Scorpio also likes to have his or her own game plan, so expect the unexpected.

Being a child of destiny, the Scorpio baby is strongly linked and connected to the soul world. It's subliminally attuned to the metaphysical realms — so its arrival in the earth realm is quite a shock and a transition. And because of its unique psychological soul connection, this baby is not overly thrilled about its abrupt arrival on planet Earth, and it sometimes takes a few months before it settles into its physical routine.

Scorpio newborns are likely to have iridescent or radiant glows surrounding them. (It's their remnant energy field from the soul world.) There will be times when they have a distant dreamy look and a sweet smile, and they will be enchanting to watch and cuddle. But at other times, they can be a bit sad, and may cry easily. This stage will pass most smoothly if you are patient and loving because Scorpios have a tougher time than most adjusting to terrestrial life.

That's why so many Scorpio babies love to withdraw into themselves and appear to be pondering their own thoughts. This little mite may also love to sleep and will certainly enjoy dreaming. Be careful not to abruptly wake a Scorpio baby or it could be dawn before the startled infant settles down enough to fall back to sleep.

When the Scorpio baby is awake, he or she may enjoy following you around the room with their eyes. Scorpios can say volumes with their eyes and are known for being able to fix a very intense focus or gaze on you, almost as if you're a guilty party in something. This is one of the ways Scorpios tell you they want something, and they won't withdraw this gaze until you attend to it. These are persistent, powerful babies who tend to get their own way, whether you know it at the time, or not.

Because Scorpios are so strongly linked to other unseen and metaphysical realms of existence, they can experience intense emotions, which may cause some rather dramatic mood swings. Scorpios also have a certain wise knowingness, and can often see right into the depths of your soul. These wee people express themselves in mysterious ways. They are likely to have strong powers of auto-suggestion, sometimes so strong that they can silently wake you up at night so you'll check on them and change their nappy or bring them their bottle.

Scorpios also have some drastic taste changes, and this trait is sometimes exaggerated when they're babies. One day your little Scorpio will love to eat his peas and carrots, and the next day he may fling them across the room. Anticipate having an extremely interesting, love-filled, and joyous life with this one.

Although there may be times when your Scorpio appears to be taking his or her time in certain areas of development or expression, he or she will excel in other areas. And before long it all evens out and your offspring takes on the role of the true triumphant trooper that they are. Scorpio babies innately know when to hold their cards, and when to play them. Rarely will this wee one throw all his or her cards on the table at once.

The Scorpio baby is a power unto itself so you'll need to develop your patience because this little one isn't cut out to do things simply to please you. Scorpios have their own inner compasses and are set on their own path. This inner direction gives Scorpios high intellect, winning charm, and fascinating personalities. Before long your Scorpio baby will develop into a somewhat provocative talker and walker and . . . that's just the beginning. The Scorpio baby is going to fill your life and your heart with much more than you imagine. This is no ordinary child. The Scorpio soul is a very special one indeed.

The Scorpio toddler through teen

> *Scorpios build lots of dream castles, and their dreams should be encouraged because they have what it takes to make them come true.*

Scorpio toddlers have entrancing eyes and winning smiles, and it's a good thing because even at this young age they love to win. They love to win your attention, your praise, your laughs and smiles, but most of all, they love to win their own way! This is the path of the competitive and self-confident Scorpio throughout his or her life, and the early years determine whether they develop the habit of looking on the bright side or focusing on the shadows.

When the little Scorpio is between the ages of two and four, you can still catch a glimpse of how their mind works by watching their eyes. (Later in life most Scorpions master the poker face and don't give anything away by their expressions or their eyes.) But look closely at the eyes of a three-year-old Scorpio when they are told not to eat any more lollies or not to pull the dog's tail and you will see their eyes shift back and forth in an internal debate. You can almost see an angel on one of their shoulders and the guy with the pitchfork on the other — both of them trying to encourage your Scorpio in their direction.

But the truth is that Scorpio, even from a very young age, is following his or her own path. It may seem like the devil's winning on some days — like when your Scorpio tot writes his name in magic marker on your white kitchen walls or stuffs another cupcake in her mouth just as you say, 'no more cupcakes!' But on other days this little one will practically pulsate with sweetness and light. He or she will be a little angel at such times, picking up toys without being asked, sitting quietly while the adults talk, and taking their own dinner dishes to the kitchen sink.

Of course, most parents try to steer their Scorpios in the angelic direction, but you should be warned that applying excessive pressure to a Scorpio often leads them to do exactly the opposite of what you want them to do! This can be particularly dreadful during the dating years, but for now your little one will stand his or her ground in a less dramatic fashion by doing things like refusing to get under the bed covers when bedtime comes or refusing to come back inside the house until you tell her she can have a kitten.

Scorpios must be guided with logic, sound reasoning, and compassionate understanding. This is the best way for them to learn how to manage their own desires and emotions, which will help them to function much more smoothly throughout their lives.

Most parents of Scorpios need to worry less than parents of children born under other signs about their offspring being easily led. Scorpios tend to be leaders rather than followers. Not always, but more often than not, Scorpio children will make their own choices as to whether they want to go along with the crowds. The Scorpio doesn't mind playing alone, so even if all the other kids are heading for the swing he'll keep building his sand castle if that's what he wants to do.

Scorpios build lots of dream castles when they're young. And while their ideas may sound like castles in the air, their dreams and aspirations should be encouraged because they have what it takes to build the foundations beneath them and make them come true. The seven-year-old Scorpio who declares that she's planning to be a millionaire probably is seriously planning it, and she has every chance of achieving that dream if she studies, applies her wisdom, and holds fast to her vision. Scorpios who lead fulfilling lives tend to have visions for the future that are bigger than most, and this innate tendency is obvious from the time they are seven or eight years old.

If you ever meet a seven or eight-year-old Scorpio who has a piggy bank, I guarantee you they can tell you what they're saving for! This is a great way to catch a glimpse of a Scorpio's vision for the future. I saw this demonstrated again recently when I heard a seven-year-old Scorpio's father reading his son's savings account statement to him. He had already saved $700. I asked David what he was saving for, and he explained that he was planning to build 'something sort of like Disney World' when he got older, and he knew for such a big project, he needed to begin saving now!

Be warned that Scorpios are very competitive at times, and while it's tempting, as a parent or teacher to use this to motivate Scorpio to move in the direction you want him or her to go, be careful not to over-develop this mentality. By the age of nine or ten, Scorpio may be twice as competitive as his or her friends, so this is a trait that you probably won't want to encourage too much. Scorpios have the spirit of competition flowing through their veins, and helping them learn how to balance that drive to come out on top is very valuable. Consider involving them in some projects that require teamwork so they can experience the value of cooperating. These projects, particularly if they are done with friends and incorporate fun, surprise, or reward, will help to instil a positive connection with the idea of working together. Take your Scorpio youngster out to dinner at their favourite restaurant or make a contribution to their savings account to reward them for their good deeds, but don't go overboard.

There will be times, especially as your Scorpio goes through adolescence and the early teen years, when you will wonder if some alien force has taken control of your formerly sweet child. Up until about ten or eleven years old, your Scorpio will swing back and forth between winning your praise and getting your reprimand. But once they hit twelve or thirteen, these kids can turn into hell on wheels. It's not so much what they do or what they say, it's more of an attitude and a posturing. Basically, all they're really doing is trying to learn how to be adults and so they tend to mimic their mentors or favourite TV characters.

Needless to say this is a great time to gently steer your Scorpio offspring in the direction of a strong role model or two. These years can be difficult for Scorpios because they have an inborn tendency towards being eternally loyal to their family members and those they accept into their small circle of friends. The first few times Scorpio finds out that their best friend has repeated one of his or her secrets, or that one of their first loves is moving on to greener pastures, it can really throw them for a loop. During these turbulent years the Scorpio does more brooding than they will for the rest of their life. But don't despair, because this stage only lasts for about five or six years.

One of the most helpful things you can do for a young Scorpio is to reinforce his or her desire to succeed in life by encouraging them to learn, study, and ask questions. The more the Scorpio learns, the more likely it is that he or she will make the choices that will lead to the fulfilment of their highest dreams and most inspired vision or purpose for life.

SAGITTARIUS

[23 november — 21 december]

sagittarius sagittarius sagittarius sagittarius
sagittarius sagittarius sagittarius sagittarius
sagittarius sagittarius sagittarius sagittarius
sagittarius sagittarius sagittarius sagittarius
sagittarius sagittarius sagittarius sagittarius
sagittarius sagittarius sagittarius sagittarius
sagittarius sagittarius sagittarius sagittarius
sagittarius sagittarius sagittarius sagittarius
sagittarius sagittarius sagittarius sagittarius
sagittarius sagittarius sagittarius sagittarius
sagittarius sagittarius sagittarius sagittarius
sagittarius sagittarius sagittarius sagittarius
sagittarius sagittarius sagittarius sagittarius
sagittarius sagittarius sagittarius sagittarius
sagittarius sagittarius sagittarius sagittarius
sagittarius sagittarius sagittarius sagittarius
sagittarius sagittarius sagittarius sagittarius
sagittarius sagittarius sagittarius sagittarius
sagittarius sagittarius sagittarius sagittarius
sagittarius sagittarius sagittarius sagittarius
sagittarius sagittarius sagittarius sagittarius
sagittarius sagittarius sagittarius sagittarius
sagittarius sagittarius sagittarius sagittarius
sagittarius sagittarius sagittarius sagittarius

element: fire

planetary ruler: jupiter

symbol: the archer

quality: mutable (= flexibility)

colours: light blues and yellow

gem: turquoise and diamonds

best companions: aries and leo

strongest virtues: adventurous, fearless

approach to love and life and a wonderfully

positive attitude to life

traits to improve: stubbornness, wilfulness,

thinking that you know everything

deepest desire: to do what you love

Sagittarius celebrities

Kerry Packer, John F. Kennedy Jnr, Kim Basinger, Frank Sinatra,

Mariel Hemingway, Don Johnson, Caroline Kennedy Schlossberg,

Gary Hart, Kirk Douglas, Tina Turner, Anna Nicole Smith, Boris Becker,

Bette Midler, Katarina Witt, Jeff Bridges, Billy Idol, Maggie Tabberer,

Daryl Hannah, Christina Applegate, Brad Pitt, Bruce Lee, Judd Nelson,

Ben Stiller, Woody Allen, Britney Spears, Jane Fonda, Monica Seles,

Gianni Versace, Ray Martin, Teri Hatcher, Noel Coward, Jane Austen,

Katie Holmes, Sinead O'Connor, Steven Spielberg, Alyssa Milano,

Chris Evert, Walt Disney, Nostradamus, Ozzy Osborne, Lou Rawls,

Amy Grant, Jimi Hendrix, Brendan Fraser, Tyra Banks, Marisa Tomei,

Jim Morrison, Winston Churchill, Dionne Warwick, Don Johnson,

Christina Aguilera, Lee Remick, Beau Bridges, Kenneth Branagh,

Robin Givens, Susan Dey, Dick Clark and Diane Ladd.

Sagittarius in the new millennium

[General outlook]

Continuously coming up with your best, keeping other people happy, and learning new skills and talents took up a great deal of time, energy and focus throughout the latter years of the old millennium. For a variety of unusual reasons, many Sagittarians have breathed a sigh of relief that the new millennium has arrived. Fresh astro-energy is just what you need. A major upheaval in your romantic, financial or professional world gave you more end-of-century excitement, drama and challenge than you anticipated. The good news is that the new millennium brings you the cake — and the icing, too!

Positive planetary energy is on your side. This is a brilliant time for turning things in your favour, and making headway where love, money and work are concerned. Use your creativity and be kind to yourself. Remember that sometimes it's necessary to take one step back in order to take two forwards.

Romance

Dealing with some very unpredictable and unusual people has kept you on your toes for quite some time as far as relationships go. Therefore, many Sagittarians have not had real inner peace with their relationships. Instead, they have had to wonder what tomorrow will bring for them. Now new and exciting twists affect your love life as we enter the new millennium. The good news is you are more in tune with your love partner or spouse than ever before. Your union is solid and you grow together. For single Sagittarians a change in image or attitude attracts into your sphere a compatible and loving partner. Although your relationship might suffer teething problems, keep in mind that all good things take time. Patience will work wonders in relationship issues now, so do not feel you need to reach cloud nine overnight with that someone special. Allow the relationship time to grow at its own healthy pace.

Health

While you need a fairly considered approach to maintaining good health, and cannot afford to run yourself into the ground, new millennium magic is kind to physically robust Sagittarians. Most of you actually begin the new era sparkling with good health, and those who don't start it in tip-top condition find that their ability to heal and recuperate from ill health suddenly improves.

Many of you are inspired by your partner or family members to lose weight, start a new sport or give up a past bad habit. Put in a little effort and your health and wellbeing will glow. Remember, too, that a good night's sleep, or a holiday away from your usual routine, is worth its weight in gold for your sign!

Finance

Forward-thinking Sagittarius is always on the cutting edge of investment and financial planning. Just as well. You come into a small windfall as the new millennium gets underway. But whether your booty is self-made or heaven-sent, get ready to make it work well for you. Wise investment is absolutely necessary, or lavish spending will whittle it away. Remember, think abundance and you'll create abundance. It is time for you to watch your pennies (or your smaller investments or savings) in the new millennium; these pennies (if saved and collected) can make you richer than you imagine.

Career

Exciting new opportunities arise for Sagittarians in their work and professional spheres. Your talents, skills and experience are in higher demand now and never before have you felt so much faith in your own abilities. This is also a highly creative phase for Archers. Don't be satisfied with toeing the line. It's time to use your ingenuity and really make a difference in your work world. Be prepared to expand your work and career horizons. Many amazing opportunities are opening in new areas. Foreign people and locations are also likely to suddenly play a key role in the directions your career takes in the future.

[Millennium wildcards to watch for]

Life is meant to be a winding road for your sign as it is through the unexpected detours or changing conditions that you confront that you learn your greatest lessons and eventually find out what makes you tick. You are the sign that subliminally longs for adventure and a-thousand-and-one new experiences yet the thought that the grass is greener elsewhere can sometimes stop you from reaching your highest achievement. Variety makes you tick and is an important ingredient of your lifestyle, but your personal challenge now is to streamline your life. It's far too easy for Sagittarians to pack their bags on a whim to pursue a new relationship, job, hobby or lifestyle. But freedom and stability can go hand-in-hand. Be cautious. Value what you already have before looking for something new.

Understanding Sagittarius

You have friends all over the place and you probably have at least a few who walk on the wild side. But you have a super hero ability to escape danger and triumph over difficulty in the twenty-fourth hour.

Feel lucky? Well if you are a Sagittarius, you should. After all, you have won the cosmic lottery by being born under this magnificent sign. However, this celestial advantage still is no guarantee that you can't make a mess of things. In fact, you were born lucky, because you need to be lucky, and you do test your luck all the time. When it comes to having the good things in life you usually have more success than most. But that doesn't also mean you always have money to burn. It could be that you are rich in many ways, but not always when it comes to having money in the bank! You may be rich in spirit, true friendships or opportunity.

In many forms, luck is all around you. Yet many of you never truly appreciate just how lucky you are. This luck takes so many wide and diverse forms it can be hard to recognise. Also, for a lucky sign, it is quite amazing how much upheaval, drama and chaos you attract. But no matter what presents itself in your path — whether it turns out to be a real dragon you need to face, or merely a paper tiger — like a cat with its nine lives, you manage to land on your feet.

The zodiac's most prolific and creative trailblazers are Sagittarians. You often leave a legacy behind you, like Sagittarians Nostradamus, Beethoven and Walt Disney. Many Sagittarians do end up in the spotlight because of their incredible talent, determination and competitive nature. You can be super-stars like Sagittarians, Brad Pitt, Tina Turner, Kim Basinger, Britney Spears and sadly missed stars like John F Kennedy Jnr. You make great athletes like Bruce Lee, Boris Becker, Monica Seles and Chris Evert and you are found journeying everywhere and anywhere because you are this planet's most prolific adventurers and free spirits.

Because you love to take chances, you frequently go to extremes. Moreover, your free spirit can shock others who are less free than you are. You can say and do things that others would seldom imagine saying and doing. You sometimes like to test authority. As a child, you were likely to be the one who touched the wet paint or walked on the grass just because there was a sign that said don't.

In later years, you climb your own form of Everest, then do it all over again to prove the first time wasn't just a fluke! You love to test your luck and break through boundaries, especially boundaries that other people set before you. Putting yourself into fate and fortune's hands appeals to you, whether this takes the form of travelling around the globe, punting on the horses, exploring cyberspace or simply running as close to the edge of life as possible.

When it comes to your zodiac ruler, you Sagittarians are aligned with the highest of the high and mighty. Your ruling planet, Jupiter, is the most important Roman God, ruler of the heavens. Jupiter in Greek mythology was king of all the gods, the party thrower and the gift giver. Lots of Jupiter's 'let's party' influence rubs off on you, and you tend to be either the life of the party, or a party-giver yourself. Because your ruler rules the heavens, your head and thoughts are often up in the sky — and many pilots are born under your sign. Your connection to Jupiter is another reason why you intuitively know the sky is definitely not the limit.

Your zodiac symbol is the Archer. This Archer connection encourages you to aim high, but it also is an indication that you need to have a target or goal in mind, otherwise you are a most ineffective Archer who shoots the arrows all over the place. When you are inspired and loving what you do, that is when you are most on target. When you love what you do, you can be quite dazzling.

When you are at your highest energy peaks, you also can make others around you feel more energised or conversely, they instead may suddenly feel more exhausted than they really are. There are definitely times when you are wonderful to know, and other times when it can be tough just being in the same room with you. When you get out of the flow, you can be one of the more unsettled (emotionally, physically and spiritually) of the zodiac signs.

Your symbol, the Archer, also represents your direct, straightforward manner, your high aims and your love of nature. Your symbol also represents you as half man, half horse. It is interesting to make mention here that many of your sign love horses — if not riding them, betting on them. The Archer symbol is also an indication that unless you are accurate your arrows can fall short of their true mark.

Because you are frequently surrounded by opportunities, making choices can also confuse and baffle you. When faced with making a decision, it can sometimes be tough for you to settle on just one thing, one person or one desire. Your ruler Jupiter's motto is — the more the merrier. This motto can lead you into all kinds of peculiar situations. You may eat, drink and be merry to an extreme or take on more debts or responsibilities than you can comfortably handle. Throughout your life, you often discover (sometimes the hard way) how important it is to practise moderation.

However, wanting to have it all serves you as well. Your high spirits make you positive thinkers (most of you anyway). Naturally, you do not think positive thoughts all the time. And just because you have high spirits (or are lucky) does not mean that bad things don't happen to you, too. When bad things occur you can lose faith in your own good luck — but only temporarily. Like most of us, you have your ho-hum, doldrums days, yet you do seem to have the real blues less than the majority.

Life frequently takes a fortunate turn for you and that is when bad news suddenly, or eventually, transforms into good news. As an example, one of my Sagittarian girlfriends is a great skier (several years ago she was close to being an Olympic contender). She was a downhill speed daredevil. One day my friend lost control skiing, and ended up in hospital with multiple fractures. Now, the happy part to this story is that the physician who put her leg back together again was not just a brilliant doctor but also a dreamboat. Because my friend had to spend a long time in hospital, she naturally got to know her doctor well. She returned home well healed, and sporting a huge diamond engagement ring on her finger, courtesy of the gorgeous medico. From her disastrous accident she found true love. Thus is many a tale of woe later transformed into a tale of triumph when it relates to a Sagittarian.

Time both doesn't matter to you, yet still manages to means everything as well. Even if you avoid watching the clock (and I know several Sagittarians who refuse to wear a watch), no matter what you are doing, you are usually in a hurry. You like things to happen quickly, and most Sagittarians are not patient people. However, as you grow older and learn through experiences (especially once you have your own children) life generally teaches you the value of patience.

While you don't like fiddling with gadgets to find out how to work them (especially technical things like video machines or computers), when you truly want or need to learn something, you can be a super-quick learner. Once your inner curiosity is aroused, your mind keeps thinking about things — even while you're sleeping. Many of you Sagittarians actually talk in your sleep, rehearse conversations or work out problems while sleeping. This extra sleepy-time activity can involve big arm and leg movements, which often makes getting a good night's sleep not so easy for your sleeping companions.

Encyclopedias are often a great investment for you because you Sagittarians wonder about lots of things and ask tons of questions that seem — on the surface — mainly to be unanswerable. You think about the great mysteries of life. You may even be quite a philosopher and ponder over the possibilities of god, the goddess, religion, reincarnation and eternity. You may not know the answers, but you certainly have your ideas and are willing to share them.

You are often anxious to hear about other people's points of view on just about any subject under the sun, moon and stars. And what some might consider to be a mission impossible can be a piece of cake to you. You generally believe it's realistic to aim for miracles and you inspire others to do the same. You have a certainty and a confidence that makes others go along with your ideas and plans.

You're an ambitious goal setter and you usually try to exceed your goals — just to make sure you achieve them. You love to know everything and that means you often want to discover, experience and understand everything and everyone — and particularly understand things about yourself. Other people often fascinate you and you can enjoy talking to old, young, attractive and not so attractive, if you are curious to learn about them. You are apt to strike up a conversation with just about anyone who crosses your path.

As long as you feel you're making progress in your life and your explorations, you operate in a state of harmony and you feel content with your lot. However, because you usually expect life to fall into place for you, you can take disappointment to heart when things don't turn out according to your best-laid plans. And you can be a hard judge of yourself, often sad and sorry about the things you should have or could have done better.

When you get down in the doldrums, you probably like to take a break from work and maybe from your relationship and friends. At times like this you can go surfing, rock climbing, shopping, sailing, riding, gambling — exploring whatever it is that gives you a chance to escape from the world, even if temporarily. Sometimes a little solitude is very rejuvenating, but you don't desire to have solitude all that often, just when you know you need to catch up with your inner self again.

When something isn't working well for Sagittarius, putting on a happy face is something many of you are great at doing. This means that when you are at your lowest ebb those around you often have no idea that you feel downhearted. You like to keep your image up, even when you are worried or going through difficult times. You may be in a marriage that is wearing you down, a job that is boring you stir crazy, or be worried about finances or health matters.

No matter how overwhelmed you feel, you will continue to push these issues aside. You can hide your problems with a smile or your famous dry wit and sarcasm, and people rarely suspect you're anything but right on track, when you are not on track at all. And keeping your doubts, fears, or unhappiness to yourself, that's the way you like it best. You don't like to talk about the bad news, just the good news, and are much more sensitive and reflective than others around you usually ever guess.

While this is admirable on some levels, this side to your character often represents your childish tendency to ignore or run away from problems. You do not like dealing with upsetting things or people. You often wish that unhappy conditions would just sort themselves out without any active participation from you.

You Sagittarius have your breaking point, though. When you have really had enough, and the pretence is broken, then you take immediate action. That is when you will walk out the door or make a decision, from which there is no turning back. This turnabout side of you often surprises people who thought they knew you well. At these times, you can be unmovable. No amount of persuasion or cajoling from others can then stop you from doing what you do want to do. However, it often takes an extreme situation for you to reach this turning point.

You often give out mixed messages to others, and in all kinds of ways you can be foolhardy and brave at the same time. Some of you may even like to live dangerously and race around on a Harley-Davidson motorbike, fly stunt planes or otherwise live life in the fast lane. In fact, the role of a modern-day Indiana Jones (or Ms Indiana Jones) fits you well (small wonder that the originator of the Indiana Jones movies, Steven Spielberg, is a Sagittarian).

You have a great sense of self, too, and you often also like to come across as a charmer. You are friendly and like to be the centre of attention. It comes quite naturally to you to surround yourself with lots of activity and a variety of interesting companions. This social side to your character usually helps you to get through any rare moments or days of doom and gloom. And Sagittarians, it's really not that good for you to play the hermit role for long.

Ruled by Jupiter, you are cosmically designed to be out in the world surrounded by interesting and unusual people. When you're in your true flow you like to hang out with your friends and have fun. However, when you are not in your true flow, you may just surround yourself with even more friends and have even more fun. When you are down you often try harder and put more work into socialising. When you are hitting your true Sagittarian stride you can be one of the most likable and most personable signs of the zodiac.

When you need to be, you're generally fearless and you're probably more daring and willing to take risks than most of the people you know — not just physical risks either. You tend to trust strangers and acquaintances more than your friends think you should. And you will trust your instincts. Socially you are very open-minded. Basically, you'll go just about anywhere with anyone just to see what will happen.

You love going into other people's worlds to see how they live and to glean an insight into the way they think. That is why travel is often a source of inspiration and revelation to you, and many of your sign are to be found working in the travel industries. You mix well with others and you can bring out the best in people. You can be the kind of person that others trust — they will take off their superficial masks to reveal their deepest darkest secrets or true nature when they are with you.

Fleeting romances frequently occur with Sagittarius. Plus it is likely that some of the most memorable moments of your life involve the crazy times you have shared with your good friends and also with intriguing strangers.

Though you are often casual about relationships, friendships, comradeship, love and passion all mean a great deal to you, and these are the foundation stones of your existence. You could do most things on your own very well, but you choose to share your journey and your experiences with others, because you know that sharing makes the experience richer and more rewarding.

Your ability to mix, match and merge into the thick of things helps you move through circles of society and beyond in all types of ways. You're just as comfortable at a formal dinner party as you are at a beach barbecue. You are likely to have friends of every race, occupation and income level and you probably have at least a few who walk on the wild side. But even your most far-out friends look at you with wide eyes when they hear about some of your antics and adventures. By the way Sagittarians, you can also tell some amazingly tall stories that others believe.

Probably the thing a Sagittarius hates the most is living a boring life. You don't like spaces or gaps in your life so you fill these in as quickly as possible with dramas, activities, plans, projects or other distractions. However, you're not one to bask in your own achievements, prosperity, even success or failures for long because you're anxious to get on with the next thrilling chapter of your life. But you do like other people to know about your accomplishments and conquests and you're not too bashful to broadcast (sometimes loudly) your own great talents, triumphs or even plans for future successes.

What is so wonderful about you is that you can even laugh at your own failures, (although possibly there are some you are careful not to share, except to those you really trust). You're sometimes accused of being too pushy or too driven but when it comes right down to it, you really don't give undue attention to what other people think about you. You believe in yourself, and that is one of the most wonderful gifts of all about being a Sagittarian. Then again, if you didn't believe in you, it wouldn't be realistic to expect others to believe in you, would it?

You love to eat, drink and be merry (and as some have said of Sagittarians — they, eat, drink and re-marry). By the way, there are many Sagittarians with weight problems, because they love food so much, they become obsessive about it. But whether you are overweight, overworked or over-stressed, nothing can keep you down for long. Sagittarians know even the darkest times lead back to the light and you drive onwards with humour as your companion and intuition as your guide. You are the sign that usually ends up having the last laugh — sometimes even if having that laugh means laughing mostly at yourself.

Sagittarius is a Fire sign

To your advantage, you love and appreciate life and you really make the most of every opportunity to live your dreams. You have a very contagious, childlike enthusiasm at times and when you're excited about something, you're like the Energiser bunny — you can keep going and going! You like to lead the pack and the thrill you get out of blazing your own trail keeps you motivated and excited about your life.

When you take the time to slow down a bit you usually enjoy going out into the woods and communing with nature. You have a special bond with plants and trees and all the furry and feathered creatures. And you love to be outside in the sun, breathing in the fresh air — two things that help you to stay healthy. You also have a casual kind of optimism which refuses to accept defeat and you have a genuine interest in helping others.

To your disadvantage, you sometimes rely on your charm, good looks and good fortune to carry you through. While you're anxious to work on projects you think are interesting or fun, you're at your worst when you are forced to complete boring jobs or ones you don't like. These are the times you're not above taking advantage of someone who admires you by allowing them to do your dirty or dull work.

You can be outspoken and there's a good chance that your associates, and even some of your friends, are a little bit intimidated by you.

[Insights into your sign]

The bright side: You are naturally optimistic and have the power to land on your feet after any sort of upset or challenge.

The shadow: It's hard for you to walk your talk. You can be unreliable and tend to exaggerate. Sometimes you misrepresent the facts to an extent that you get into legal or other types of trouble.

Characteristics >	Benefits >	Drawbacks >
Adaptable	Free-spirited	Unreliable
Ambitious	Big thinker	Over the top extremist
Athletic	Healthy	Take good health for granted
Candid	Honest	Hurtful
Confident	Self-assured	Annoyingly arrogant
Curious	Strong desire to learn	Nosy
Egocentric	Individualistic	Showy
Energetic	Lots of vitality	Hyperactive
Enthusiastic	Inspired	Fanatical
Generous	Gracious	Extravagant
Impatient	Eager	Attract danger
Impulsive	Spontaneous	Irrational
Intelligent	Independent thinker	Scattered thoughts
Logical	Good learner	Think too much
Optimistic	Positive thinker	Unrealistic
Overindulgent	Have fun	Weak will
Persuasive	Influential	Forceful
Philosophical	Open-minded	Too easily influenced
Reckless	Daring	Operate close to the edge
Restless	Energy to burn	Can't relax
Talkative	Friendly	Exhausting

[Looking beneath the surface of your sign]

Sagittarius's hidden traits are merely the darker side of your most glowing characteristics. For example, your risk-taking can turn into recklessness and your confidence can swell up into a big head. That's when you unplug your cosmic connection and go about satisfying all of your most hedonistic whims and desires. These sensory experiences can feel so wonderful that you throw moderation to the wind and welcome overindulgence with open arms. Many Sagittarians face serious health, weight and financial crises because of over-indulgence.

But sometimes you just want to have fun! And that's one of the reasons you're so wonderful. Nevertheless, when you let your temptations and passions lead the way, you find yourself way off course. There is great insight and wisdom in the saying, 'Things of the material realm will never truly satisfy the soul', and some Sagittarians find it helpful to remind themselves of this now and again.

[How to tune into your sign's powers]

> *Instead of attempting to do everything at once — do one thing well.*

> *Learn the incredible value of patience.*

> *Set your sights on a specific target before you commence any action.*

The Sagittarius woman

She's outspoken, smart and powerfully seductive. She can weave her wildest fantasies into your dreams and wrap herself around your heart — but only when it suits her.

'I am woman, hear me roar' kind of sums up this firebrand woman of the zodiac. While she's very feminine, her brand of feminine has an unusual potent edge to it. Most Sagittarian women are powerful in a somewhat radical way (look at Jane Fonda, Sinead O'Connor, Kim Basinger and Bette Midler).

She has a mind of her own and has strong ideas about what she wants, what she believes in and what is right and wrong with the world in general. She can fight for peace or the underdog or spend her time fighting her own inner demons. However, Ms Sagittarius is likely to wage more battles than one would expect during her lifetime. Her ability to be something of a crusader can come of a surprise because she can be very, very funny and can even play the cutesy pie role to the nth degree. She can probably tap dance, juggle, windsurf, ski and even rollerblade backwards beautifully.

Underneath all the fun and games and (sometimes) ingenuous behaviour, she wants to be taken seriously. Although she can come across as an easygoing, fun-loving kind of gal, the Sagittarian woman is an ambitious idealist who believes she has a responsibility to make a difference in the world.

She sees herself as a woman on a mission, so she's often supporting some type of cause or movement. A Sagittarian may be trying to save the planet, the whales, or the rainforests, or working for some other humanitarian cause that has caught her impassioned nature. Or she might simply be trying to save herself or her variety of lost animals, friends or wayward boyfriends that come into her life. And even if she isn't trying to save the world or alter the record books, whatever she's doing, she's a go-getter.

She takes action and she's confident, impatient and generous, and she's outspoken, philosophical and powerfully seductive. She can weave her wildest (and mildest) fantasies into your dreams and wrap herself around your heart. But only when it suits her. If she isn't in the right frame of mind to impress you or pursue her ideals, she won't bother. There are definitely times she says one thing and then goes out and does the opposite. She can be quite tough to follow at times.

However, she does place a high value on truth, loyalty, trust and sincere affection. And the tougher she acts on the outside, the more vulnerable she often is on the inside. She's goal-oriented and she sets her sights high. She can flounder without a clear purpose and if she's not inspired about her life she can suffer from melancholy and depression and even become a heavy drinker or pill popper.

She can be one of her own toughest critics and expects to be able to perform at her best 24 hours a day. She expects so much from herself because, astrologically, Sagittarian women have a great goddess heritage. The original zodiac symbol for Sagittarius was the image of the goddess Artemis. In the original symbol for Sagittarius (before it became the Archer who is half man, half horse) Artemis was depicted as a warrior-huntress on horseback. She was armed with bow and arrows and carried a double-bladed lunar axe in her bejewelled girdle. This symbol was used until the male influence of astrology overwhelmed it about 2000 years ago.

Artemis was an excellent horsewoman and ferocious fighter who swept into battle astride her horse, brandishing her bow high. She was worshipped by the Amazons, who have now disappeared in the mists of myth, together with many others like the Atlanteans. She was also both the great huntress and protector of animals. She was worshipped as the triple-person goddess — daughter, mother and grandmother. In communities such as Sparta, her worship continued up into the fifth century BC. Artemis has incredible grace and athletic ability, and many Sagittarian women have these same qualities today. No wonder Sagittarians, with this cosmic birthright, feel so driven to excel and prove themselves over and over.

[How Sagittarian women operate]

Social

She can have the appearance of a tomboy, but don't let that fool you — a Sagittarian woman's feminine side is alive and blooming. She might often hang out in jeans and a T-shirt without make-up or adornment. The next time you see her, she is strutting her stuff in a red spandex dress with the little-nothing-top and super-high heels to match. A quick look through a Sagittarian's wardrobe will reveal the diversity of her lifestyle. Business suits, casuals, sports equipment and tracksuit pants, jeans and more jeans, a few hats and her favourite dressing gown. All my Sagittarian girlfriends have a 'favourite dressing gown'. Whether it's of tattered terrytowelling, or pure silk, it's the one she'll be wearing if you drop in and catch her by surprise.

If you want to find her at home, you'd better call first because she gives the term social butterfly a new meaning. She has at least a dozen good friends and her evenings and weekends are booked a month in advance. Just check out the invitations stuck on her fridge if you're curious about her upcoming plans.

Sagittarians' fridges have a personality of their own. The outside is plastered with overlapping party invitations, pictures of her kids (if she has any) and her friends' kids, pizza coupons, a couple of comic strips or funny sayings and an inspirational message or two. On the inside, either there's so much food you can serve lunch to the entire street or no matter how you combine the ingredients you can't make a single meal.

For fun she likes to go out to dinner with her friends and she loves movies — complete with lollies and ice cream for her sweet tooth. She probably likes dancing and might be into watching or playing a few sports. Most Sagittarian women are nature-lovers so she probably likes camping, hiking, horseback riding or maybe even white water rafting or rock climbing. Chances are she has a soft spot for animals and either has a pet, or wants one.

She's a caring and loyal friend and she listens with her head and speaks from her heart. She's wonderfully generous and enjoys spoiling her friends with her impressive hospitality and backyard barbecues.

Love and family

Men are sometimes in awe of the Sagittarian woman. They can see her free spirit and independence but they also notice her childlike qualities — she can be petulant and quite contrary. She's perfectly capable of taking care of herself but she doesn't like to be alone unless it's by her own choice. She can be the most friendly woman you've ever met but she also sets strong boundaries, and her outspoken nature can even intimidate some of the most confident men. It is hard to know with a come-on whether she is giving someone special treatment or flirting because she's so friendly and open with everyone.

She's intelligent and logical in all areas of her life — except romance. When it comes to love, a Sagittarian woman can be too smart for her own good, meaning that instead of trusting her heart, she plays head games with herself. This makes her one of the most confusing zodiac signs for a man to understand.

She can be straightforward to the core. Her honesty is sometimes confusing to men who are accustomed to coy women who rarely say what's on their minds. But she does have the potential to scheme, especially if she knows that to win her man is not going to be as easy as she thought. She vacillates between being self-assured and feeling vulnerable, which sends mixed messages and adds to the confusion. But underneath her generally confident exterior, she's every bit as sensitive to rejection as the next person.

Her fear of rejection doesn't stop her from going all out when she wants something or someone. I have a Sagittarian girlfriend who is usually pretty reserved, but when she gets going she can dance (not quite naked, but almost) on the tabletops. We were together at a social gathering at a friend's apartment in New York and there was a totally gorgeous hunk quietly smouldering with sex appeal (and totally aware of his magnetism) standing alone in the corner. He was so stunning that everyone avoided him except my friend, who cheekily sauntered up to him and said, 'I'm sure I know you, you look familiar'. He smiled, and she added, 'I know what it is. You look exactly like my third husband'. The guy was so taken aback, all he could say was 'Really. How many times have you been married?' to which my Sagittarian friend replied, 'Twice!'

But not all Sagittarians are that sassy. A Sagittarian woman who's experienced a broken heart may not act much like her risk-taking sisters. She's probably wearing a full suit of emotional armour for protection. This woman will literally bite her tongue before she speaks from her heart again. In spite of her optimism in the other areas of her life, she takes a long time to recover when her feelings have been trampled. This type of Sagittarian sometimes treats the ones she loves the most with her worst behaviour. It doesn't seem to make much sense, but it's her way of weeding out the faint-hearted.

When it comes to marriage, you may be surprised to see how widely Sagittarian women can vary in their choices. Some want marriage and a family more than anything else in the world. Others can take it or leave it. And some see matrimony as a prison sentence and have no interest whatsoever. I've yet to meet a Sagittarian woman who likes to take orders, so if she does marry, the union will be based on equality. She's more than willing to do her mate a favour every now and again but he needs to ask her politely and show his appreciation.

She also won't stand for any type of jealousy or insecurity. She may find it flattering or reassuring on a small scale but she expects her partner to respect and trust her. And anyone who questions her loyalty had better do so from a distance because her Archer arrows can fly fast and hit their mark with outstanding accuracy. A Sagittarian's sharp, piercing look or curt remark is enough to set most people back for a day or more. She's also been known to stomp her feet and throw an occasional plate, but these little tantrums are usually caused by frustration more than anger. Either way, she's likely to dismiss the entire episode within hours because she's not the type to hold a grudge.

When it comes to things maternal, the Sagittarian woman is an A-plus mum and her children (and her children's friends) adore her. She truly enjoys each phase of her children's growth and development, including the 'terrible twos', which she actually finds somewhat entertaining. Her children are encouraged to use their minds and generally begin thinking for themselves at an early age. A Sagittarian can relate well with children her entire life because she never loses the magic of seeing the world through the eyes of a child. And if you see her sitting on the floor finger-painting with her kids, she'll be having more fun than the lot of them.

Career

She's ambitious, enterprising and also hard-working. No wonder Ms Sagittarius is often one of the zodiac's best entrepreneurs and is sought after in the workplace. No matter what she does for a living (and she makes a good performer, lawyer, personal stylist, and teacher), she puts her full force of energy into her job. Many Sagittarians have fulfilling careers in the media, hospitality and beauty industries, literature, journalism and travel-related areas.

Communication skills are usually high for this sign and novelist Louisa May Alcott, who wrote *Little Women* and other books with females in primary roles, was a Sagittarian. Also because of the vitality that comes naturally to this sign, there are many Sagittarian women who excel in sports, such as tennis stars Monica Seles and Chris Evert and in track events there is still nobody to replace the incredible record-setting Jackie Florence Joyner (whose spirit lives on to inspire others).

Sagittarian women make good students so they often go into higher education. They can make excellent researchers, archaeologists or scientists. The fields that seem to appeal to them most are working with children and animals, advertising and public relations, foreign affairs, education, the performing arts and the tourism industry.

Whatever career she selects, a Sagittarian is likely to change her occupation or the emphasis of her career many times over the course of her lifetime. She's most satisfied with her professional role if she can see that it's making an impact on the lives of others. She also needs a good bit of flexibility in a job and doesn't like to be forced into conforming to a standard routine. But regardless of what type of work she's doing, she will probably do it very well — when she wants to.

Financial

Sagittarian women are considered some of the zodiac's most fortunate when it comes to money. It's not because there are scores of Sagittarian millionaires, although there are many. It's more that opportunities for financial reward present themselves frequently and money practically falls from the sky when a Ms Sagittarian really needs it.

But wealth has two faces and so does luck, and both wealth and luck can create advantages and disadvantages for a Sagittarian. On one hand, a Sagittarian who's making a lot of money usually enjoys the pleasures, conveniences and freedom that it brings. But on the other hand, she may become bored or disenchanted if she stays in a job only for the income and her heart's no longer in it. She also does not necessarily feel fulfilled if she gets her money easily. She has a strong work ethic and likes to make her own money if possible, rather than have access to someone else's.

She can be a tough businesswoman if she sets her sights on success. Most of the time a Sagittarian woman will use her logic and her intuition to make the best financial decisions and choices. In addition, because of that, she usually has enough cash-flow for her luxuries or other indulgences and manages to keep her spending habits within her budget. But, every now and again (often as some sort of 'I can afford it, so I'll buy it' type of statement to herself or someone else), she goes off on a wild shopping spree or splurges on something she doesn't really need, like her dream car or an exotic holiday.

Physical

A Sagittarian woman has a cool look, a warm smile and bright, lively eyes that don't miss a thing. (Sagittarians Kim Basinger, Maggie Tabberer, Jamie Lee Curtis and Bette Midler all have dancing eyes.) Some Sagittarians are petite and fairy-like and others are taller and more commanding in stature. But either way, she's strong, healthy and probably athletic. Warning: Sagittarian women often have weight issues. Regular exercise is vital. The heavier she is, the more weighed down she feels and the more depressed she often becomes. And there are few people more miserable than a sluggish and depressed Sagittarian.

When Ms Sagittarius looks good, she feels her best and most confident. She's also dramatic at times and she uses sweeping gestures that are expressive but not always graceful. Her movements are most fluid when she's playing one of her favourite sports or when she's dancing. Yet for all her coordination and athletic abilities, the Sagittarian woman can be unbelievably clumsy at times.

If she's in a big hurry, she can walk (or run) straight into a wall without even seeing it until she hits it head-on! I once watched a Sagittarian knock over three wine glasses and spill the cheese fondue on the rug — all in an effort to catch the biscuits she dropped first. When her mind is elsewhere, her body's automatic pilot shuts down and she might be described as hell on wheels at times like these.

Her potential for good health is excellent and she can exercise and play for a long time before she tires out. When she does get sick, it's usually her body's way of telling her to slow down and take a break. Her healing and recuperative powers are well-developed so she rarely suffers from long, lingering illness. And that's a good thing because she's too impatient to lie in bed for more than a few days at a time. Some Sagittarians have sensitive livers and should avoid drinking alcohol and caffeine. Others may experience problems with their hips and thighs.

A Sagittarian's public optimism can help to keep her immune system strong, but her private bouts of depression wreak havoc on her nervous system and use up a ton of energy. When she's really feeling low, she may not bother to get out of bed. But these are the times it's more important than ever for her to get up, go outside and take a brisk walk.

Mental

A Sagittarian woman is driven by her curious, restless mind. She's a mental explorer and she is curious about everything and everybody. Her intelligence and logic help her to work through problems and her impatient and impulsive nature make it easy for her to make decisions quickly.

She's a quick thinker and doesn't have much patience for people who are not as smart as she is. She has a definite idea of what's right and what's wrong. She can be quite stubborn and it can take a lot of time, energy and smooth talking to convince her to change her mind. She likes to come to her own conclusions and when she decides to change her mind, she changes it in an instant.

She always interested in learning something new, but she doesn't want to be brain-washed either. Fate plays an enormous role in her mental evolution. She's destined to meet some very unusual and enlightened people on her journey through life and their ideas will greatly affect her concepts and attitudes, for both better and worse.

There are many teachers on a Sagittarian's pathway and they're all prepared to take her to the next phase of her terrestrial experience. She will adore some of them and despise others, but she'll learn a valuable lesson from each one. The men who she becomes involved with probably exert the greatest influence on her thinking and attitudes.

Spiritual

The sign of Sagittarius is also the sign of the sage or wise counsellor. A Sagittarian woman knows she has friends in heavenly places but she might not spend much time thinking about them. She can get incredibly caught up in the material world and completely forget that planet Earth is merely her educational space station. She may be involved with some form of religion, but chances are she disagrees with at least a few of its teachings.

Sagittarian women can be sceptical about some religious teachings because they like to have proof. Many of them are atheists, which relates back to the influence of their goddess Artemis (their original zodiac symbol). Artemis refused to accept the male energy as the dominating one, so intrinsically, many Sagittarian women have difficulty embracing a solitary male figure as the only creator.

She listens to other people's viewpoints about spirituality, but at the same time, she believes that the morals and ethics she finds in her heart are true, and she uses these heartfelt insights as her spiritual compass. When she focuses on her spirituality or gets involved in ritual (such as prayer, meditation or church services) she sometimes catches a glimpse of infinity.

Ms Sagittarius is completely capable of developing inner peace and outer tranquillity if she's willing to apply herself to the task. If she does yoga, takes long walks or simply stops to contemplate the beauty of nature, her experiences in life tend to reveal more of their meanings to her. And she really thrives in all areas of her existence when she connects mind, body and spirit.

The Sagittarius man

His zest for life and persuasive charm make him nearly impossible to resist. And when he does what he's inspired to do, he twinkles and shines like a star!

Mr Sagittarius is the cosmic cowboy of the zodiac. He loves to get out and ride the world range in his own form and fashion and he can be quite a firebrand in his own way. As booze, mateship, football, barbecues, surfing and a free spirit all come under the rulership of the sign of Sagittarius, living in Australia is often like finding heaven on earth for a true Sagittarian man. Not that he has to be interested in football, booze or surfing, but the Sagittarian man enjoys the good life and living in the Lucky Country often suits him down to a tee.

When he is in true form, he is the zodiac's most at ease charmer. On an exaggerated level, the charismatic character Paul Hogan portrayed in *Crocodile Dundee*, with the twinkle in his eye, his free-spirited independent nature and his magical way of dealing with nature and the ladies (also in an exaggerated fashion) captured the heart and soul qualities of a Sagittarian man's free-spirited personality.

He is often a people-person (and if he's heterosexual, he is very much a man who loves women). He has a genuine interest in other people and loves to be in the thick of whatever is happening around him. He can be adventurous, foolhardy and extremely rebellious. If he decides to take the more wayward course in life, he can be quite the rascal. When he gets caught up in the high life or wilder sides of life, his answer to everything can be, 'Party-on'. Then he will live for the day and forget about tomorrow; his way of life may revolve more around sex, drugs and rock 'n' roll than on building a solid life foundation.

He often thinks that tomorrow will automatically take care of itself because he has a highly optimistic outlook. However, his party-on phase often runs a fast course, due to the fact that in this mode he is highly accident-prone, he runs his health into the ground (often to the point where he has to straighten up or he will end up with severe health problems) or can run foul of the law.

Once he completes the 'live for the moment and to hell with tomorrow' phase — or another way of saying that is — if he survives this wayward stage (and be aware that some Sagittarian men stay in this phase throughout their entire lives), then he gets on with higher priorities. That is when he becomes the great bloke, a brilliant businessman, a model citizen or even quite a brilliant teacher and philosopher. When he continues in the party-on mode, however, he often ends up sad, sore and sorry for himself in later life.

Once he gets his rebellious streak out of the way, the Sagittarian man is usually highly ambitious in all areas of his life. He's curious about all sorts of things and all kinds of people and he doesn't see the same limits and boundaries other people see. His energy and enthusiasm stem from an infinite source and he's often a few steps ahead of everyone else. Having a highly competitive nature, he is a natural gambler. He loves winning and gets a big charge out of being the first one past the chequered flag. But unlike Leo, who gets satisfaction from competing with and defeating others, the Sagittarian man is almost always in a race with himself.

He's confident and sometimes a bit (or even greatly) egocentric. He finds himself extremely interesting and has probably been studying every aspect of himself from the day in his crib when he first discovered his toes. Yet while he can be engrossed in himself at times, he's also completely fascinated with other people! He's a philosopher (like legendary Sagittarian Nostradamus) of sorts and he also might be the most outspoken man you know. He isn't malicious and has no desire to hurt anyone (usually) but he does speak his mind. And while he steps on a few toes now and then, his opinion is often respected and his advice is often sought after and highly regarded.

And even if he acts as if he doesn't want to be thanked or praised — he really does love it. As Sagittarian Mark Twain so brilliantly said, 'I can live for two months on a good compliment!' Sagittarians need those compliments to stack up more than most. He has a tremendous will of his own that often attracts criticism rather than praise. He can be extremely stubborn and won't be over-shadowed or brow-beaten even in early childhood.

Friends of mine have a seven-year-old Sagittarian son who can be a big handful because he's so active. He hardly stops for a minute. One rainy day when I was visiting his parents he was stuck indoors and everything seemed to go wrong for him. He was under everyone's feet. Finally his parents, overwhelmed and frustrated with his non-stop boisterous behaviour, insisted he sit quietly at his desk and read a book. He sat head down, fuming, then with defiance glared up and said, 'Mummy, I may look like I'm reading my book on the outside, but inside I'm still noisy and running around'.

You'll find out in all manner of ways, a Sagittarian can't be suppressed, controlled or outsmarted. He won't be instructed or contained (even if he occasionally gives an appearance of going along with your demands or desires when they don't coincide with his own). But in so many ways his spirit is his charm and he makes music in the way he stirs up such an unusual field of energy around himself (Beethoven was a Sagittarian). He is the genius, the fool and the trickster all rolled up into one. He is what he is . . . a free spirit — and he will never let you or the world forget it.

[How Sagittarian men operate]

Social

Sagittarian men are often regarded as heart-throbs. Just look at Brad Pitt and the now legendary John F. Kennedy Jr as examples. The Sagittarian man nearly always has a circle of people around him and he's likely to be at its centre. He's a social magnet and his frank disposition and bright, flashing eyes attract attention wherever he goes.

He has a lot of friends, a ton of acquaintances and a growing list of people he wants to meet. Ask one of your Sagittarian friends who he'd like to meet and he'll probably name some celebrities, a couple of professional athletes, a handful of international experts and a world leader or two. He might already know some of the questions he'd ask if he meets them, and he just might have a few idealistic causes to pitch.

Another Sagittarian strength is that he has practically mastered the art of suspending judgment when it comes to people's appearance. The old adage 'Don't judge a book by its cover' has profound meaning to a Sagittarian and he can give you countless examples in his own life when this advice has proven to be wise. He takes a sincere interest in the lives of his friends and willingly helps them when they need it. He also enthusiastically supports education and all forms of learning and he may even contribute to a scholarship fund in his community or be involved with youth groups or other community projects.

He's adventurous, too. If he has the chance to do it (especially when he is younger) his favourite activity is travelling and there are few places on Earth or beyond that he isn't curious to see. All sorts of physical activities arouse his interest and a lot of his social time is spent either watching or playing sport outdoors. Nature has a healing effect on him, so he often goes out of his way to position himself in the great outdoors. But indoors holds lots of fun times for him, too. Being a man of many social parts, he also likes parties, funny or thought-provoking movies and all types of music and books.

Love and family

Mr Sagittarian can make a wonderful boyfriend, husband, father and son. However, he can also be one of the most exciting yet exasperating men in the zodiac. His passion for living and his persuasive charm make him nearly impossible to resist. He has a talent for enjoying whatever he does and he can turn taking out the garbage into an action-packed adventure. He doesn't beat around the bush and his straightforward comments can be hard to swallow at times but his compliments are treasures of sincerity.

When it comes to love and romance, he has earned a reputation as a heartbreaker. Not all of them, but many Sagittarian men look for their mates through the process of elimination. While this technique may not be the most expedient, it suits him well as he's rarely in a hurry to make a romantic commitment. He loves his freedom and anyone who attempts to curtail his activities or monitor his friendships is setting herself up for a fall. He won't put up with jealousy and if you treat him with suspicion you get to see him in his raging glory. If you love a Sagittarian, you must trust him. The two go hand in hand as far as he's concerned. And if you question him or check his coat pockets for other women's phone numbers, you're only torturing yourself. If he strays, he'll probably be the first one to tell you (or he will leave evidence to the effect that he is straying in strategic positions for you to find). If you are involved with a Sagittarian man and are concerned about the possibility of his infidelity, worrying about that possibility in advance does nothing to prevent it. You are better off facing facts and either bowing out or letting him have his head rather than making any attempts to curb him.

Mr Sagittarius will not be ruled by other people's whims, wishes or insecurities. Give him some rope and he usually won't want to wander anyway. Once he makes a real commitment he can be the most loyal of companions and he treats his mate with tender love and gentle understanding.

He's looking for a woman who is as enthusiastic about living as he is. He also wants someone who's intelligent, honest and independent. He's particularly interested in a woman who has an element of mystery about her and a well-designed life of her own. He's too much of a free spirit to enjoy having a woman cling to him so in many ways he's looking for a woman who is a lot like him — independent and a free spirit.

When he finds that special someone who truly loves, trusts and believes in him, together they have the power to fly to the moon without a rocket. While he may delay making an emotional commitment, once he finds his mate he is often one of the most committed men around.

As a father, a Sagittarian will probably take more interest in his children once they begin talking. He'll share the task of taking care of them from the start but it frustrates him not to know what's going on in their minds. However, when his children are old enough to communicate with him, his bond with them really deepens. He loves their observations of the world and he learns just as much from his kids as they learn from him. He thoroughly enjoys three-year-olds who are going through their 'why?' stage and has an awful lot in common with them. He's also on the tolerant side because he believes children need to learn from their own mistakes. He likes to take them on outdoor excursions and he's interested in their thoughts and opinions.

Career

Whether he's a surfer (surfing the ocean's waves or the Internet), a weather reporter, an advertising executive or promoter, the Sagittarian man feels most fulfilled in careers that rely on his pioneering spirit and his philosophical mind. His life-long devotion to learning makes him a very creative teacher in any area of life — and like Sagittarian Socrates — if others ask his opinions, he urges them to observe, question and think things out for themselves.

If he chooses teaching as a profession, it's likely to be in the form of adult education or seminars he develops himself. However, being such free spirits, Sagittarians usually avoid any job that makes them operate within set boundaries. He loves to be able to act spontaneously and to think on his feet. He firmly believes the way to fall behind is to follow the crowd. This belief makes him innovative and he can often be found trailblazing where others in his profession haven't dared to go.

His career (which is often connected with the mind) can lead him into exploring various new fields of technology, new concepts of spirituality, modern and ancient philosophies or other originality-based industries.

A Sagittarian male often starts his own business, but if he works for someone else he's sure to carve out a niche or cultivate a special skill that makes him difficult to replace. Many Sagittarians' athletic abilities pave the way for careers in professional sports and their desire to be in the spotlight may lead them into acting, professional speaking or some aspect of the performing arts (Sagittarians Jeff Bridges, Woody Allen, Steven Spielberg, and Kirk Douglas are some examples).

The Sagittarian's love of nature and animals often leads him to a career like veterinary care or even zoo-keeping. You'll also find Sagittarians in positions involving travel, sales or marketing. Many Sagittarians are entertaining tour guides, record-breaking salesmen and visionary marketing executives.

Financial

Sagittarian men often live by the seat of their pants when it comes to finances. Many of them have an 'easy come, easy go' attitude to money. Fortunately, a Sagittarian man is said to be among the luckiest in the zodiac when it comes to money and he needs to be because no one risks their financial security as often as he is likely to. He is the kind who can be tempted into get-rich-quick schemes and often needs someone else to manage his cash-flow.

He has a naturally generous nature, so he is capable of spending his money every week and ending up with nothing by the time next week rolls around. However, Lady Luck majestically appears to bail him out when he really needs it. When he's on track, he has a knack for seeing future trends and his profit-making hunches usually pay off for him. However, he can be an excessive gambler — one who loses his shirt one day and then wins it back the next. Gambling has sent scores of Sagittarians into bankruptcy as his history of luck entices him to believe the next big win is just around the bend. But bankruptcy isn't the worst thing that can happen to a Sagittarian man and he is soon back on his feet again hunting for a new opportunity.

Mr Sagittarius can be a super salesman, especially when it comes to selling himself. He's also a creative idea man and he has no problem going out and pitching his own ideas to get financial backing and support. He knows it's mainly a matter of contacting the industry or people who stand to profit most from his plans and he's great at determining who they are.

Physical

Most Sagittarian men are strong, agile and active. However, if he gets too involved in the high life, he quickly loses these qualities. He can be great-looking with eyes that sparkle with light and a warm genuine smile. He's often graceful in his movements and many Sagittarian men are great footballers, excellent runners and talented athletes. But that doesn't mean he won't knock a cup off the counter and cut his hand trying to pick up the pieces.

He has a reputation for episodes of clumsiness every now and again but he's generally very coordinated. The Sagittarian man excels in many sports and has especially skilled hand—eye coordination. It's no surprise that the Archer is fast and has good aim and he can usually play any sport well. Because his zodiac symbol is the Archer — half man, half horse — archery might appeal to him, as well as all forms of horse riding, including polo. If he isn't riding them, he can also enjoy punting on the horses as well.

He has loads of energy and he regularly exercises. He's at his best when he's following a consistent fitness program that includes aerobic exercise and strength training. However, when he stops exercising, he often experiences trouble keeping his weight down. Some Sagittarian men truly pack on the pounds and have many self-created health problems because they have allowed their weight to get out of control. Especially after the age of forty, he finds he can no longer live the high life he used to without paying a physical price for it.

His legs and particularly his thighs are the most sensitive area of his body, according to astrology. He needs to make sure he does some leg and back stretching to keep his body flexible and toned. If he doesn't exercise, chances are he's restless and possibly reckless as well. These traits coupled with his impulsive nature can result in accidents and injuries, but they're generally not too severe. Many Sagittarians learn that when their mind is buzzing with activity, a tough workout can do the trick and calm him down.

As a Fire sign, his potential for good health is excellent but he needs to make time in his schedule to relax. He has a tendency to schedule more than he can realistically accomplish and he frequently pushes himself into overdrive to get everything done. Just watching a Sagittarian can be tiring at times. In fact, he creates most of his own health problems by over-working his body and over-stressing his mind. The body parts most often affected by his over-exertion are his liver, his hips and his thighs, but his troubles are rarely chronic. If he does get sick, he can usually recuperate quickly, providing he's willing to spend a few days resting.

Mental

While he may go through times when he seems as if he is disorganised and unfocused, that's usually just an indication that he has other things on his mind, or he can see no real value to the matter he is meant to be focused upon. When he is in true flow, the Sagittarian can be a quick learner and a fast assimilator of information — but only when he is interested in the subject matter.

The Sagittarian male is a perpetual student of life. He has an unquenchable curiosity about the workings of the universe and a fascination with the mechanics of the human mind. Sagittarians tend to be highly intelligent and a number of them score as geniuses on IQ tests. He's most intrigued by questions that appear unanswerable and his entire life might be considered a journey of sorts. He seeks the knowledge of experts and respects the commonsense of people who live simple lives.

He's often philosophical in his thinking and he takes little for granted. He believes in questioning common knowledge and he knows many so-called facts are really just myths or legends that have been passed down through the ages. He's a bit intolerant of ignorance but he's willing to help anyone who has a true desire to learn. Some Sagittarians devote their lives to dispelling myths and setting records straight.

Spiritual

Whether it is through those magical moments that he experiences when he is surfing, flying planes or enjoying nature through the great outdoors, Mr Sagittarius is likely to be innately connected to his creator. After all, his sign is the sign of the sage and some Sagittarians spend a lot of time in their private thoughts — pondering the mysteries of life. Some Sagittarian men commence their lives, following the religious path of their parents. Some may continue on this path throughout their lives and at least a few will find their vocation in religion. But many Sagittarians begin to look critically at their inner beliefs by the time they're in their teens. After they explore religions, some Sagittarians delight in being free thinkers, putting down anything they feel is religious pomposity.

Other Sagittarians love to make fun through religious concepts. Sagittarian Woody Allen, for example, has made many insightful humorous quips and comments about God, spirituality and religion. My personal favourite quote of his is 'How to make God laugh? Tell him your future plans'. My next favourite is 'I'm not afraid of dying, I just don't want to be there when it happens!'

But even if they seem to be light-hearted about religion, the Sagittarian's life and drive are often more spiritually and religiously based than it may appear to those who think they know him well. There is often a lot going on inside him that's not apparent outside. The Sagittarian's mind is one of the most curious.

He's not one to swallow a lot of dogma and he will openly question what appear to be inconsistencies within belief systems. Still, he's rational enough to realise people need some sort of support structure and every belief system can be of service in some way. He also might believe that no theology structured by humans can accurately portray God.

The Sagittarian man who focuses his energy upon spiritual matters can learn some amazing truths about himself and all living creatures. He may develop a gift for intuition or prophecy, or have remarkable dreams and inspired visions. Because of his desire to explore all realms, he may even get into taking psychedelic drugs in his wild-child years, not just to be a rule-breaker but also to experience altered states of consciousness. Should he truly be touched or affected by a spiritual or religious experience, some Sagittarians feel such a strong pull that they will devote their lives to walking a spiritual path.

The Sagittarius baby

You've never seen a faster tummy wriggler than a Sagittarian baby on the move. Because this baby is such a mover and shaker, you need to keep an extra close watch over it.

The Sagittarius baby is born with the zodiac's lucky silver spoon in its mouth. Expect your tiny Archer to be extra-special. He or she is destined, according to the stars, to be given many opportunities to live the life a fortunate few can ever expect.

The Sagittarian infant is an extra-special bundle of joy. Born with Jupiter (Jove), the benevolent god in astrology, as its ruler, astrologers regard Sagittarians as born lucky. Everything about this baby and its birth is somehow more exciting and bigger than normal — including weight and length at birth. Women carrying future Sagittarians often crave odd combinations of food and can have fierce appetites. The cosmic imprint of the Sagittarius identity, even as a baby, can be summed up by the word big. This can be big in thoughts, actions and deeds or when they get old enough to spend money — big on spending!

Enthusiasm, optimism, courage and creativity are often very strongly imprinted upon this child's character and surround its entrance into the world. Your Sagittarian is likely to come into the world with a rush. Many Sagittarians are born when they're least expected or may be a bit premature. Some say the Sagittarian baby loves to arrive at an inconvenient time and place — like in the car on the way to the hospital.

This is the adventurous spirit from the first moment of life! And this curious, action-loving spirit will also let you know he or she has a unique time clock. The hours the Sagittarian babe sleeps or stays awake are likely to be extraordinary or different in some way from others. Sagittarians can be rebellious and fight for independence even when they're just a few months old. They're just letting you know that freedom is their first love and early rebellion gives you an idea and some preparation for the months and years to come.

The Sagittarian is born with a special brand of personality, so the birth of a little Archer means you're about to have an amazing companion. He or she has a fascinating personality that radiates and illuminates all around. A baby Sagittarian also tends to be easygoing and is usually quite adaptable.

This is the type of newborn who can handle a bit of schedule changing as far as eating and sleeping goes and will generally not be too disgruntled by change. These babies don't cry very often unless they're really upset, over-tired or under-fed. They have a natural capacity to find things that amuse them or entertain them, like watching mobiles or moving their little fingers and toes.

Usually the Sagittarian baby doesn't demand as much attention as others but they still love to have it. When you find this little one disgruntled or hostile, he or she might be feeling cramped or restricted. This sign is after all the freedom sign of the zodiac. Sagittarian babies like room to move and don't like to be restricted, especially physically. If you wrap these ones tightly in blankets or bundle them up too tightly, they'll probably feel claustrophobic and closed in. Even holding a Sagittarian baby too tightly can create a sense of discomfort for them and can make them very cranky. They need to be able to wriggle and kick, sometimes just as a way to express themselves. Freedom of movement, with your careful holding, or in their crib, can make a world of difference to this baby's feelings of inner and outer comfort.

Even though this child is happy to do its own thing, that doesn't mean you're safely off the nurturing hook and can get on with your own devices. Because this baby is such a mover and shaker, you need to keep an extra close watch over it. Sagittarians are adventurers and explorers. They're amazingly creative and are willing to take some rather big risks. These infants can't be left unattended even for a second unless they're in a truly safe place. Even then, these babies will often find a way out of their cribs or play areas, so check on them often, although you believe they are safe.

The little Archer (even when it's in the womb) can wriggle into strange positions or strange places. It will (when more advanced) be a great crawler, climber and even before you know it, a runner. You've never seen a faster tummy wriggler than a Sagittarian baby on the move. It can be faster than the roadrunner, heading for anything and everything (even out the door) before you realise what's happening.

Most Sagittarians love to get outdoors and see what's going on and babies are no different. They also love pets, toys, rattles, shakers, gizmos and gadgets and since they're the sign of excess — the more the merrier. Do be warned and remember that a Sagittarian baby doesn't know any limits!

Little Sagittarians generally walk, talk and do just about anything they possibly can earlier than most other babies. However, they probably won't be interested in expanding their vocabulary for some time. Lots of Sagittarian toddlers seem to have more fun making noise, than making small talk. But don't worry, the little Archer has no intention of getting too slow a start in life, so put on your runners and get ready for a journey in the fast lane — not just while they're a baby, but right through life!

The Sagittarius toddler through teen

Sagittarians of all ages are freedom-lovers and really dislike being confined or forced to do anything they don't want to do.

You'll need a pair of running shoes just to keep up with this little one's antics around the house, from pillar to post and back again. And long before he or she can talk, your little Archer is wondering about and questioning everything from 'How do the lights work?' to 'How long is it going to be before I can drive?'

Sagittarian toddlers already have an expansive capacity to think and process information and they have enough physical and mental energy to fuel their whole neighbourhood — if only it could be harnessed. Even in those rare moments when a Sagittarian child is sitting still, you can almost hear their minds racing a hundred miles a minute.

Little Archers are determined to learn how to walk as soon as possible and once they do there's no stopping them. They love to try new things and they often have a fearless quality. I can't overemphasise the importance of teaching Sagittarians about safety as soon as they can begin to understand. Telling a Sagittarian not to stick a fork in an electrical outlet will not be enough.

You need to tell the Archer the dangers — in some detail — about what will happen if they do. For example, 'Don't stick your fork into the wall socket, Johnny, because if you do, it will feel like someone dropped a car on your head and your heart could stop beating, which means you'll probably miss your birthday this year and I'll have to give your new toys to your brother'. Granted, this example is exaggerated and on the morbid side, but your Sagittarian really will need you to help them think through consequences — especially when they're young and very, very curious. Most parents of Sagittarians learn how to communicate like this eventually because it's often their best chance to help the Archer avoid all sorts of injuries.

One of the really great things about the Sagittarian child's curiosity and desire for new experiences is that you can introduce him or her to many different environments with lots of different people and they'll fit in and feel comfortable almost immediately. This tot isn't one to hide shyly behind you as you introduce him to new friends or relatives and they probably won't cry much when you first begin to leave them in other people's care for the day.

Sagittarians tend to be sociable from the start and even if your Archer has some other astrological influences that makes them a bit more of an introvert, they have a tendency to continue to open up more and more as they grow older. And by the way, while your Sagittarian will certainly grow older, he or she will never grow up. In fact, even the phrase 'Grow up!' can rub a Sagittarian the wrong way.

And get ready for some live entertainment because by the time the Archer is only four or five years old, they're natural performers. They love to show off by demonstrating their new skills for you and reciting their knowledge and they're looking for your applause, praise and approval. It's important at this age to take the time to watch and listen to your little Sagittarian because they're in the process of building their self-esteem and testing themselves against the world. On the other hand, most parents are not able to devote their entire day and night to following the line-up of Sagittarian commands — 'Watch me swing.' 'Look at me climb up the sliding board!' 'Listen to me sing my ABCs.' 'I can count to ten on my fingers — watch me!'

One of my girlfriends in Australia has a Sagittarian son and when he was four she had a little platform stage built for him. Then every night before dinner, for about fifteen minutes, the little Archer had his time in the spotlight to show off all of his new abilities and observations of the day. She ingeniously encouraged her son and he no longer demanded her total attention all day long.

As the Sagittarian reaches school-age, their ability to pull the wool over your eyes is already being developed. These kids just love to have secrets and they love to sneak about imagining themselves as private investigators, powerful magicians, smooth pick-pockets and top spies. As long as the Archer keeps these games of imagination in the fantasy realm, all is well, But some Sagittarians have an inborn thirst for going beyond imagining. You'll need to keep a close eye and an objective view of your Sagittarian while you attempt to educate them about the benefits of honesty and integrity.

Another way to channel Sagittarians' energy in a productive direction is to get involved in their learning process. When they're learning how to read, make a game of it. When they're learning about animals, take them to the zoo or to a farm so they experience what they're hearing about in school.

Most Archers have a life-long fascination with the stars so they will be mesmerised by the challenge of finding and learning the names of the constellations and charting the path of the moon with its waxing and waning. Sagittarian youngsters love to learn but sitting still in a classroom all day is sometimes more than they can take. They want to be out there in the world —

tasting, touching, feeling, hearing and smelling real-life people and events. The more you can combine action with learning, the more they will learn.

Sagittarians of all ages are freedom-lovers and really dislike being confined or forced to do things they don't want to do. They're also impulsive and sometimes reckless in their play, in attending to their responsibilities, and in their handling of money.

This independent nature will temper itself in some ways as the Sagittarian gets into his or her twenties but until then — and especially during the Archer's teen years — this independent streak can be maddening for parents and teachers. You'll need to guarantee them a slot of 'free time' each day if you want them to cooperate during other parts of the day.

Remember that your Sagittarian is a natural explorer so you're wise to have the talk about the birds and the bees much earlier than most parents. Make sure your Archer has accurate information about sex and the full picture of what doing it can lead to because nearly all Sagittarians are fascinated by this adult domain. But most of them are looking only at the aspects of pleasure and ignoring all of the potential headaches and dramas.

Be honest and direct with Sagittarian teenagers because this is the form of communication they respect the most and have the easiest time understanding. And be ready for them to be brutally honest and sometimes completely tactless in return. The ability to spontaneously share their honest opinions is both a blessing and a curse in a Sagittarian's life and in the lives of those around them. Over time they'll begin to learn more gentle ways of expressing their truths, but they will still feel compelled to add their frank opinions or arguments, whether you want to hear them or not.

The young adult Sagittarian needs your love much more than your advice or even your wisdom. Regardless of what you tell them, they probably won't be content until they've experienced life's lessons themselves.

Most Sagittarians want to make a statement to the world rather than go with the flow and quietly fit in. Treat them like you would treat a close friend — with honesty, loyalty, respect and an open mind — and they will continue to share with you and trust you throughout their life, whether they're surfing the big waves in Hawaii, exploring the secret mysteries of the Great Pyramid of Giza, hiking in the Himalayas or unveiling the hidden powers of the mind.

CAPRICORN

[22 december — 20 january]

element: earth

planetary ruler: saturn

symbol: the goat

quality: cardinal (= activity)

colours: greens and golds

gem: white onyx and moonstone

best companions: taurus and virgo

strongest virtues: your disciplined approach,

organisational skills, and consistency

traits to improve: clinging to the past, inability

to forgive others, taking life too seriously

deepest desire: not to miss

out on a moment of life's magic

Capricorn celebrities

Pat Rafter, Kevin Costner, Carolyn Bessette-Kennedy, Ricky Martin,

Annie Lennox, Sissy Spacek, Donna Summer, Denzel Washington,

Anthony Hopkins, Rowan Atkinson, Marilyn Manson, Nicholas Cage,

Ted Danson, Tiger Woods, Rudyard Kipling, David Bowie, Kirstie Alley,

Jack Jones, Jim Carrey, Kate Moss, Muhammad Ali, Al Capone,

Christy Turlington, Jude Law, Mel Gibson, Jim Bakker, Diane Keaton,

Rod Stewart, Marianne Faithfull, George Foreman, Julia Louis-Dreyfus,

Dolly Parton, Tippi Hedren, Paul Keating, Val Kilmer, Shirley Bassey,

Linda Kozlowski, Tracey Ullman, Cuba Gooding Jr, Victoria Principal,

Pat Benatar, Marquis de Sade, Michael Crawford, Faye Dunaway,

Lloyd Bridges, Aristotle Onassis, Mary Tyler Moore, Ava Gardner,

Diane Sawyer, Marlene Dietrich, John Denver, Cary Grant, Sade,

Eartha Kitt and David Lynch (born on the cusp of Aquarius).

[General outlook]

Get ready Capricorn! The new millennium symbolises fresh astrological energy for you. New people, projects and places will enter your life. There has never been a better time for challenges. If you have ever said to yourself, 'I could never do that', then think again — because anything is possible in the new millennium with so much powerful and positive astrological energy surrounding you. Like a magnificent butterfly leaving its cocoon, you are ready to make a transformation and spread your wings. Trust yourself and above all, be kind to yourself. This is a learning phase and one in which you will learn tremendously from your mistakes. Remember, too, that keeping a smile on your face and doing whatever it takes to maintain a positive outlook will work miracles.

Romance

Be ready to have a few unsettled times with relationships early into the new millennium. Your natural reserves of patience get a good working out as the new millennium dawns. Married Capricorns support their spouses emotionally through a tough time regarding family or professional matters. Many single Capricorns may even feel that they will never meet their soulmate. However, Capricorns, be patient and keep believing in your lucky stars. You are advised to hang in there. Just when you least expect it, love and romance take surprising turns, proving that Cupid is alive and well in the twenty-first century (and looking out for you). Be loving, be tender and you'll open your heart to new levels of intimacy.

Health

Your legs and back are the sensitive areas of your body as we enter the new millennium, Capricorn. As long as you do not put yourself under too much stress or strain, with a little effort, you can and will enjoy good health as the new millennium turns the corner. Use your famed Capricorn self-discipline to your advantage and give up any non-healthy vice (such as smoking, drinking too much alcohol or coffee, late nights and so on). You will see how leading a balanced lifestyle will have wonderful side-effects on your romantic life, too.

Finance

How you handle your finances can literally make the difference between your life turning out to be a 'happy' or 'sad'. Do not kid yourself that money doesn't make your world go round, or, conversely, that any lack of money can grind your world to a halt. For all kinds of reasons, it is most important for you to feel that you are on top financially because if you're not, you soon lose your sense of self-worth and vision for the future. As potentials and pitfalls abound for you in the moneymaking arena and your new millennium advice is 'play it safe'. It's easy to be influenced by your family and friends' bright (and not so bright) ideas on finance, but the truth is you are your best financial adviser now. When it comes to money matters, the best combination is to trust your own instincts and your ability for thorough research. With a little effort, you'll create a small pot of gold at the end of the rainbow during the first five years of the new millennium and continuing on after that as well.

Career

While it may not always be perfect, at least into the new millennium your working life is definitely not dull. Shifts and changes surrounding your work and certain competitive or bossy colleagues may put you on the alert, but don't let them throw you. The beauty of this phase is that you are learning that the only constant thing in your (working) life is change! Be open to constructive criticism. In fact, there is a career mentor out there — waiting to help you move up the ladder. It's time to show others just what you are made of. Keep focusing on career goals and refuse to allow others to stop you from reaching them.

[Millennium wildcards to watch for]

You self-doubting Capricorns are often your own worst enemies and as the new millennium dawns you will have a tendency to beat yourselves up, and worry overtime if things don't go according to your finely tuned plans. Keep in mind that it is sometimes necessary to take one step back before taking two steps forwards in life! That is how we learn our best lessons.

Be patient. Understand that any obstacles you find in your way are just stepping-stones to success. Any major obstacles may also indicate that destiny has another plan in store for you. Marvel at the way life unfolds before you. This new millennium is a blessed and an exciting time for Capricorns to be on planet Earth. Enjoy.

> *Whether you're in the boardroom making deals or in the bedroom making love, you do it in Capricorn style with a steady laser beam focus, a flair of originality and an abundance of ability.*

Whether you are on top of the ladder of success or in the process of climbing it, you Capricorns have a huge list of useful personality traits to help you make it to the top. Characteristics like patience, perseverance, determination, independence and tenacity all come naturally to you. Your strength lies in the fact that nothing (or no experience) is wasted with you. You learn quickly and have a capacity for being prepared to go the distance when you really want something (or someone).

Your astrological symbol is the Goat and its sturdy hooves represent your sure-footed approach to life while the Goat's horns show your ability to butt through tough obstacles. You have the vision, power and true grit to make it to the top and you can do it all alone if necessary. Surprisingly, some of you Capricorns do prefer to go it alone. When you are ambitious or have fixed goals in your mind, your motto is 'You're welcome to step in front of me, but if you can't keep up, please step aside'.

But to know one Capricorn is not to know them all. Astrologically, Capricorns fall distinctly into three groups. The first group (the majority of Capricorns) is the up and at 'em, aim-for-the-stars type. This group is aligned with the resilient and resourceful mountain goat. Charged with ambition, this mountain goat Capricorn is intent upon climbing higher in the world.

The second group of Capricorns is aligned with the more docile garden goat. These Capricorns are not so interested in climbing the ladder of success and seek out less challenging and more predictable routines. Content to stay on solid ground they will go to great lengths to side-step adventure. Sometimes this group of Capricorns live their entire lives in the same town (sometimes in the same house). These Capricorns feel their best when they let the world and time pass them by.

The third group of Capricorns are a combination of the mountain and garden goat in their drives and characteristics. If you are this type, you tend to run hot and cold when it comes to fulfilling your ambition, fame and fortune. These goats have a taste for both lifestyles and often feel tugged and pulled between the two.

These Capricorns alternate between moving in the fast lane of life (where everything happens at once) and coasting along in the slow lane. It can be quite amazing to see the difference in their attitudes, behaviour and focus in these two speeds and cycles.

All Capricorns tend to switch back and forth between fast and slow speed to varying degrees and that is why many of you are driven to work like fury all week, then withdraw to a country retreat, put on slippers and dressing-gown, disconnect the telephone, switch on the television and hibernate on weekends.

However, being in your slow cycle doesn't necessarily mean you have peace of mind on the inside. Your sign worries a great deal about security — especially, when it comes to ensuring you have emotional, financial and health security in the future. Sometimes your fear of being ill-prepared for the future is the driving force that makes you work harder than other people.

Many of you Capricorns are prepared to put in more effort than most to secure tomorrow and build the future of your dreams. In fact, you are one of the most organised, determined and strong-willed signs of all. When you are at your best, you can juggle and handle many tasks well. And because you can be multi-talented, many Capricorns are capable of climbing the ladder of success, and knowing how to build the ladder as well.

The trouble with all this working overtime, keeping up with your careers or other projects, is that you often find yourself with very little spare time. It's important for you to carve out time for your personal life because your family and friends as well as love and romance mean a great deal to you. Nearly every Capricorn has a powerful desire to share life with the 'right' person.

You have many and diverse dreams to share so you crave a close relationship with someone who is loving, warm and sensitive — particularly someone who is compassionate and understands you. Instead, however, many of you find yourselves in a relationship with someone who is more concerned with you understanding them (than with whether they understand you or not). Sometimes those who are needy attract you because you do tend to love to play caretaker. You are willing to play this role, but only if your mate is appreciative with both words and actions.

Nevertheless, true love isn't something that happens easily for you. You often keep people at arm's length with your 'I'm all right Jack' attitude. You also fear rejection and when you feel out of your emotional depth this can stop you from trusting others and expressing your true feelings. Opening your heart can be quite a task for you at times (that is why so many of you have pets — that way you can open your heart and know you won't get it kicked closed again).

Both in love and in business, karma plays a big role in your lives (and many say Capricorns are old souls come back to Earth to go through some kind of inner transformation and learn new insights). Whatever is going on around you at any time in your life, be prepared, because destiny will test you in many ways, Capricorns. When it does, remember that life's hardest lessons frequently deliver you the sweetest rewards. You are something like the Cinderella or the Cinder-fella of the zodiac. The saddest tragedy or hardship often turns out to have a fairytale ending for you, so be patient and never forget the story about the Prince and the glass slipper, because for you this fabled slipper really does exist.

In fact, many fables and legends come true for Capricorns. Stories of your success — as well as your trials and tribulations — have been written up in history books for aeons. Some of the greatest folk legends and historical tales exist about Capricorns — ranging from Jesus, Joan of Arc, Muhammad Ali and the legendary Elvis Presley as some awe-inspiring Capricorn examples.

Many of you Capricorns do make a contribution or difference to our world in a variety of fields of endeavour. Some contribute in ways where you become famous, while others make a difference by working behind the scenes. Many Capricorns work at careers that provide a helping hand for others. There is something in the Capricorn nature that makes you very protective of the underdog and you can be a fabulous 'saviour figure' in the lives of those who need your help (after all, you are born under the same sign as Jesus). You are unique and are also one of the most socially present of all the zodiac signs. You Capricorns are an excellent sign to have on any team (especially where you and others are united together — either in a cause or sharing similar goals).

While you may give an outer appearance of being capable and efficient, often you are quite insecure within yourself. Sometimes your emotional or romantic insecurities can be traced back almost to the cradle. It is quite amazing how many of you Capricorns go through unusual circumstances with your parents.

You may have been adopted or separated from one or both of your parents when you were a baby or a small child. In some cases, one of your parents may have suffered from illness, been emotionally remote in some way, appeared to be a tough judge of your behaviour or talents or simply seemed disinterested in you as you were growing up. Even if you have gone through some tough times in your younger years, usually you do manage to rise above these early fears or unhappy memories. Moreover, the saying, 'whatever doesn't kill you makes you stronger' often applies to you.

Throughout your life, you frequently feel as though you are carrying the weight of the world on your shoulders (possibly a reason why so many of you do seem to suffer from back problems). While sometimes this 'carrying a heavy load of responsibility' does apply to you because others put their responsibilities on your shoulders, the irony is that you Capricorns tend to bring on many of your problems yourselves. You do this by taking on too many projects and saying yes to too many people.

On top of that, although you are not a classic example of a perfectionist, you can be very hard to please at times. Even when things go right for you, you often wish they had gone even better. You also love to have everything turn out according to your best-laid plans. Detours, delays and obstacles throw you off your pace or get you out of step.

Unpleasant surprises, uncertainty and upheavals are conditions you really do not enjoy. That is why your sign likes to carefully plan for the future and doesn't like to take chances. In addition, you Capricorns are naturally cautious by nature. This encourages you to set up all kinds of boundaries in your life because in many ways, you know what you can or cannot handle and you want to work within certain perimeters.

To your advantage, you are a great leader and organiser and you understand your own inner strengths, weaknesses and resources better than most people. You are fair in most areas, but if anything or anyone threatens your emotional or financial security, you can become a tough opponent or competitor. However, conflict or showdowns can be hard on you and the anxiety you sometimes harbour over regrets and future fears can develop into nervous illness or chronic ailments.

While you enjoy some excitement, you do not handle chaos well at all. In fact, many of you will go to great lengths to keep life under control and avoid any disruption. Many of you Capricorns are control addicts. Because of this desire to keep everything contained, controlled and running to plan, you naturally attract chaos into your life. Chaos occurs because, like it or not, that's the way you grow and learn and the reason why fate occasionally steps in to deliberately bump you onto a new path.

Life sometimes brings you down a peg or two deliberately. Humility is often a hard lesson for you to learn as you can be one of the most stubborn signs of all. If you really have your heart and mind set on a particular goal, you will continue down dead-end streets, refusing to acknowledge you missed your turn a few miles back. However, this obstinate streak of independence serves you well in the long run. It also provides you with extraordinary inner power, takes you on some of the most amazing adventures, and sometimes takes others along for the ride of their lives, too.

In astrology, your ruling planet is Saturn, and what a mighty, magnificent and magnanimous planet it is. Saturn is a planet that is greatly under-rated in most astrology books. Saturn is the planet of karma, lessons and responsibility. It is also the planet of judgment and cause and effect. In mythology, Saturn is the Roman god who presided over the sowing and reaping of grain. It reveals how what you put into life, spiritually, emotionally, physically and energy-wise is exactly what you eventually get back (whether you like it or not)!

Because of Saturn life is a serious matter to you, and even small things can worry and distract you. However, like excellent wine, you age well and with time, you usually become more mellow and philosophical in your outlook and develop a light-hearted perspective. Although many astrology books represent you as workaholics, you are not just an 'all business and no fun' kind of gal or guy.

While you're down-to-earth, you can also be incredibly funny, whimsical and surprisingly psychic. Your instincts, intuitions and unusually visionary imagination are your hidden and sometimes unrecognised but extremely useful talents. What is so great about these talents is that you can apply them to practical use. Learning to blend your psychic ability, creativity and determination gives you the turbo power to achieve the loftiest goals and climb the highest mountains.

You are not only talented yourself, you also appreciate beauty and talent (and may even work in these areas). Many of your sign can paint wonderful art, play inspired music or arrange a garden, home or other environment magnificently. However, there are times when you are too preoccupied or busy to notice the beauty around you.

Toni, one of my Capricorn friends who edited this book for me, travelled across the world to climb Mount Sinai, and many Capricorns — like their astrological symbol the mountain goat — do love to climb mountains. Her aim was to watch the sunrise. On her upward journey, she said that she was so busy focusing on getting to its peak for sunrise that afterward she deeply regretted that she did not stop to really admire the dazzling stars that magnificently illuminated the dark desert sky. That 'reaching the top of the mountain' syndrome really gets to you Capricorns. It can be such a strong focus or even a distraction that you sometimes forget to smell the roses, or appreciate the night's loveliest stars along the way.

It's this same drive to get to the top that places many of your sign at the pinnacle of the corporate, social or domestic ladder and you frequently excel in all three domains at once. Whether you are in the boardroom making deals or in the bedroom making love, you do it in Capricorn style. When you want something to go well, you have the ability to do it with laser beam focus, a flair of originality and an abundance of ability.

Another Capricorn friend Jennifer (who is in the hospitality business) can plan a gourmet meal for 200 black-tie guests, play the stock exchange, get the children safely off to school and oversee the organisation of a multi-level company all in the same day. What makes me applaud and envy her most is the fact that she still has time to have a manicure (and a pedicure) and work out on her treadmill in between. Now not all Capricorns are so wonderfully efficient with their time. There are those Capricorns who prefer to sit around and wait for lightning or fortune to strike them before they get the ball of life rolling. These Capricorns use time differently. They bide their time where the other Capricorns use it up like clock-efficient dynamos.

Nevertheless, those Capricorns who are true blue organisers can run the world single-handedly (and I know this from my many experiences with them). Camilla, another Capricorn friend, organises an annual Christmas dinner in Australia for everyone who has nowhere to go or for those who want to escape from family affairs or other complicated Christmas responsibilities. Sometimes fifty to seventy people arrive at her small home. Camilla sets up wonderfully decorated outdoor trestle tables for a sit-down meal for all of us. We are all told to invite anyone we know who was going to be alone on Christmas night. Our contribution is to cook something and bring it with us.

Several years ago I cooked my first turkey for Camilla's Christmas celebration and it looked beautiful sitting on the buffet table with several other turkeys and a wide array of traditional side dishes. However, since I am not someone who spends much time in the kitchen, and this was my first attempt at turkey roasting, when Camilla stuck the carving fork into it the turkey collapsed with the equivalent of a puff of smoke and a theatrical and embarrassing 'poof'.

Being a classy Capricorn, Camilla just laughed and without meaning any put-down said, 'I'll bet Athena cooked this one!' (As an aside here, I will reveal that from when we were married many years ago my husband John, a Sagittarian, has requested that I never cook him a meal, and I have only cooked two, under emergency kind of conditions.) However, with or without the embarrassing non-contribution of my 'baked to a poof' turkey, the night was a wonderful, heart-warming, fun-filled success. It resonated with true Christmas goodwill and spirit.

Thanks to Camilla, who is a wonderful and generous event and life organiser, everybody's night was magical. Like many a true Capricorn, Camilla contributes her talents in organisation not just for her own benefit, but also to give all of us less organised beings a more meaningful and wonderful life than we would ever manage to create without her. As I mentioned earlier, Capricorns can indeed be a great sign to have on your team.

Another wonderful thing about most Capricorns is that you actually do what you set out to do, instead of just talking about it. When you have a task in hand, you are detail-oriented and follow through on dotting all the i's and crossing all the t's. You love to take care of loose ends before they trip you up. You make long-term plans and establish future objectives and you are disciplined enough to keep your attention on your next step.

Some Sun signs are the Jack or Jill of all trades and master of few. But a true blue Capricorn operating at the highest expression of your sign's potential manages to master many skills. That is why you're placed well ahead of others in terms of survival instinct and fulfilment. If I was going to be stuck on a desert island with someone, I would hope it is a well-organised, take care of what is essential, Capricorn.

Not only are you often superb organisers, but you've also been blessed with some great bonuses — a fabulous head for business and a body designed for love — just to name two. But of course, nobody, not even you, is perfect. Your downside is that you constantly challenge yourself and never think you have done as much as you could have/should have done. No one is tougher on you than you can be yourself.

Because you are so hard on yourself, you like to keep many of your shortcomings concealed and you also have a very private side. You can sometimes feel very much alone, wondering if anyone will ever truly understand you or love you. This line of thinking can lead to melancholy (sometimes even severe depression), and feeds the illusion that there is an ultimate star marked 'happiness' just out of your reach.

Your occasional blue moods creep in like a psychological fog. While you try to override these moods, these moments of melancholy slow you down long enough to catch your busy breath. It is important during any blue-moon times that you reflect on how much you have already accomplished and remember how far you have come!

One of the biggest challenges you confront in life is learning to appreciate what you have done before you start to worry about what has not been done. You can get lost in your too-many-things-to-do list and lose sight of your admirable string of abundant accomplishments. You tend to focus on the events and situations that are not going as planned and overlook your own victories.

You crave praise and acceptance from others because you withhold them from yourself. Learning to love yourself exactly as you are is the purpose of your Earth expedition. This purpose takes you through highs and lows of all sorts. However, when you begin to see your own shining light, Capricorn, you earn your golden wings and no longer need to push yourself to race up life's many mountains. Even when you earn your wings, though, hang on to your sturdy Capricorn Goat hooves because they are very useful in the Earth realm.

• • • • • • (Capricorn is an Earth sign

To your advantage, you have a strong sense of survival that keeps you going when you are in the midst of difficult situations and encourages you to persevere when others might give up. This keen survival instinct also helps you detect danger — almost like a built-in form of radar — and repeatedly saves you from accidents and injuries.

You have a talent for seeing the big picture, while keeping your focus on the next few steps. You know how to plan and make the right moves now to help you in the future. You also have the awareness necessary to wisely take advantage of all the opportunities that come your way.

To your disadvantage, you can lack self-discipline and be extremely weak-willed at times, which is a lot different from being stubborn. You know what's best for you, but sometimes you just cannot get up out of your easy chair to do it. You are sometimes inconsistent in the application of your knowledge and you can be the champion of not practising what you preach or taking your own good advice!

[Insights into your sign]

The bright side: One of your greatest strengths is your ability to stay focused on a goal until you achieve it — no matter how long it takes or how difficult the climb.

The shadow: You often miss the beauty and magnificence of the moment because your focus is nearly always on tomorrow.

[Looking beneath the surface of your sign]

Too often you entertain thoughts like, 'No one will ever love me enough', 'Life's not fair', 'I'm too fat', 'I'm too thin', 'I'm all alone', 'Nobody cares', and 'I do everything for others, but they don't do the same for me'. Yet, the more you desire affection or attention, the better you play the aloof and detached role. You desperately want to be needed, but you sometimes act as if you do not need anyone but yourself.

Secretly, you hope if you are very, very good the world will see you are worthy of praise or acknowledgment. Your need to prove something to others is an exaggeration of your desire to prove something to yourself. You struggle when there is no reason to struggle and you worry about possibilities that may never become problems.

When you face your dreaded fears you learn some of your most valuable lessons and awaken your most profound inner wisdom. You were born with a sense that you were destined for something important, and you are. Life's many challenges may delay your destiny, but you can overcome any barrier and rise to any height.

Characteristics >	Benefits >	Drawbacks >
Admired	Good role model	Fall from your pedestal
Ambitious	Set goals	Have trouble relaxing
Caring	Take care of friends	Overprotective
Classic	Realistic	Pretentious
Clever	Good reasoning	Sarcastic, act superior
Critical	Detail-oriented	Quick to notice faults
Cautious	Resilience	Stick-in-the-mud
Determined	Persevering	Won't quit even if you should
Goal-oriented	Focused	Always thinking about tomorrow
Honest	Trustworthy	Holier than thou
Hospitable	Generous	Others take advantage
Melancholy	Introspective	Downright depressed
Powerful	Strong leader	Bossy
Practical	Down to earth	Don't make wishes
Quiet	Good listeners	Switched off
Reliable	Respected	Boring
Responsible	Self-reliant	Know-it-all
Sensible	Good head for business	Old-fashioned
Serious	Mature outlook	Rarely laugh (about yourself)
Social climber	Good networker	Impressionable
Stubborn	Get your way	Stay aboard sinking ship

> *Lighten up and try not to take yourself so seriously.*
> *Let bygones be bygones.*
> *Use your confidence and certainty to pave your way to success.*

(The Capricorn woman

> *It's a rare occasion when the Capricorn woman doesn't get what — or who — she sets her sights on.*

You usually get a complete package with a Capricorn woman. She can be the total knockout to look at, too (think of Capricorns, Faye Dunaway and Ava Gardner as examples), with amazing bone structure, a magnificent smile and laughing type eyes. She's quick-thinking, talented and a compassionate, caring person as well. Moreover, whether she is a knockout beauty or not, she is still the gal you are proud to have as a mother, sister, friend, wife or companion.

In a powerful and confident way she is extremely feminine, and she usually has a great sense of style and a load of personality. She doesn't bow down to the dictates of fashion, but nevertheless she manages to be fashionable in her own unique way. Like Capricorn supermodels Kate Moss and Christy Turlington, Saturn-directed women are often just as comfortable in a sparkling ball gown as they are in faded blue jeans. While she may turn heads, she doesn't do this intentionally. Ms Capricorn usually does not try to stand out in a crowd — unless she wants to — and she definitely does not want to draw negative attention to herself by her appearance or behaviour.

She has an abundance of sincerity and class but she rarely appreciates the depth of her own qualities or beauty. The Capricorn woman can be found just about anywhere doing practically anything with almost anyone. But, rest assured she's always subconsciously or consciously moving in the direction of her goals.

She can be a huge social success and is sought after as a friend. Many admire her for her quick wit, her discriminating taste and her ability to say what she means (like Capricorn actress Julia Louis-Dreyfus when she was portraying the character Elaine in 'Seinfeld'). She is a 'doer' not just a talker. And she doesn't tolerate fools too well, although she does have a tendency to fight for the underdog!

She's generally a model of diplomacy and she's capable of smiling sweetly when she might rather take your head off. She sets goals and likes to have fixed plans in place so she knows exactly where she is heading next. She is usually quite happy putting in the time, energy and discipline to get to where she wants to go and she leaves no stone unturned. Ms Capricorn also understands she needs to climb the various rungs of the ladder of success before she can reach its top.

When she likes you, Ms Capricorn is truly a great friend and a tremendous support to those who are part of her cosmic team or crew. However, if she doesn't like you, she may not even give you the time of day. She can be self-righteous at times and can also have a difficult time understanding other people's incompetence. Tolerance is not one of her more developed virtues, but usually if she has children she does develop tolerance in abundance.

[How Capricorn women operate]

Social

For a person who is serious by nature, Ms Capricorn can be quite a social butterfly. She knows an 'all work and no play' attitude has a price. When she's in the mood for fun and the right invitations arrive, she transforms herself into a unique kind of party girl. However, dressing for a party can be tough for her. It's not uncommon for a Capricorn woman to try on six or seven of her most stunning outfits and then decide she has nothing to wear. She's usually not extravagant in her clothes buying, but she is self-conscious about her figure or form in some way. She will go to great lengths to look her best.

Parties are often more than just a party to her, too; they provide her with an opportunity to meet people. She's usually on a mission — looking either for Mr Right or her next business contact. She has an inborn sense that knows the value of networking and she does her best to surround herself with people who will be helpful to her or who are talented, innovative or entertaining.

Because she often has a lot happening in her life, sometimes it can be hard to keep up with her. As she tends to overbook herself, she's nearly always in a hurry. Whether for social reasons or other ones, taking care of business (her own or other people's) comes naturally to her. She is a natural organiser and often takes on more than her fair share of responsibility when something needs to be done.

She often works for charities or takes care of other people in some way. If she is playing hostess, the parties she plans are usually very successful. She will put a tremendous amount of thought, effort and creativity into them and, generally, if she does something, she likes to do it well. She's a staunch believer in time-honoured tradition, loves family values, and her parents probably drummed it into her that if something is worth doing, it is worth doing well. She sets extremely high standards and can be a tough critic of herself.

Yet even Ms Capricorn (as much as she would like to be) is not always sugar and spice and all things nice. She faces her own form of inner demons and temptations. Even with her traditional and reserved nature, Ms Capricorn still occasionally likes to rub elbows with some of the people on the seamier side of town. She finds this darker side of living fascinating and alluring. And on a rare occasion, usually when she's far away from home, a Capricorn woman will do the unthinkable — forget all about tomorrow, throw caution to the wind and let down her hair. That is when she can get herself into some very unusual (even scandalous type) situations, the kind that could be written up in the tabloids and sometimes are.

Love and family

A dynamic combination of earthy sex appeal and confidence create an aura around the Capricorn woman that both attracts men and intimidates the hell out of them! She has a natural ability to freeze, tease and then please, turning on the charm with the flash of a smile that says 'look but don't touch'. She can waltz away with the distinction of being the most alluring flirt at a party and then refuse all telephone calls the following day. A man with his eye on a woman of Saturn had better be clever, funny, very secure and have a pair of hiking boots next to his handmade leather shoes.

Ms Capricorn is very determined to find her Prince Charming and she will let little stand in her way. She's looking for a man who's secure enough to allow her to be whomever or whatever she wants to be. He needs to be tolerant and supportive to live in harmony with her insecurities and her determination — but usually he's more than adequately rewarded for his dedication to her. She's not always the best companion because she's busy thinking about other things, but when she does give her mate attention, she can take him to the heights of ecstasy. But be warned, she's almost never easygoing.

She's something of a perfectionist and that makes her a hard one to please, both in business and in love. She has very high expectations of others and herself and she wants a man who values security as much or more than she does. She's impressed with men who are go-getters like herself, but usually ends up with someone who will allow her to call most of the shots. Once she's selected her mate, she demurely allows him to believe that committing to each other is his idea.

Once she's in a committed relationship or married (Capricorns often choose not to tie the knot of matrimony, but still 'commit' to someone), she generally prefers to continue up her career path. She's more than capable of working full-time and sharing the responsibilities of the home. However, there are those Capricorns who choose to leave their jobs to devote their attention to homemaking and she can be very content doing this. She'll proudly support her husband and family in their endeavours and she'll expect them to do the same for her. And by the way, every man marrying a Capricorn is also marrying her family. Don't be fooled by the infrequency of her visits 'home'. I assure you she has every intention of dunking you unmercifully into the family bath of fire at the next reunion or holiday gathering.

You may pay the price with your in-laws, but you reap the rewards with your own family. A Capricorn mother is firm but joyful with her children. She takes them on nature walks and generally gets them to do things with her that are educational, rather than simply filling in time. She throws theme parties for their birthdays and will even help them to fill up water balloons or get into all kinds of shenanigans just for fun — as long as everyone helps to clean up the mess after the mayhem is over.

Career

This woman can run a corporation, manage an estate or wait on tables with equal ease and grace. But you'll most likely find her in a position that has an established routine. She likes to know what she's about to do and feels more relaxed when she knows she can do it well. She takes pride in everything she does and she likes to be the best in her field or the best tipped on her shift.

Many Capricorns are multi-talented and it's not uncommon for them to have more than one career going at the same time. They often express their talent as writers, journalists, professional speakers, artists and musicians (Joan Baez, Naomi Judd and Dolly Parton are all Capricorns). Many Capricorn women excel as professional athletes, golfers, skaters and gymnasts. Capricorns are natural negotiators and are perfect for positions in public relations and human affairs. They also do well as consultants, herbalists and healers.

Regardless of her chosen career, a Capricorn woman's ideal is reaching the top and she's prepared to do whatever it takes and work as hard as necessary to get there. If she finds out that a top-level position won't be available soon enough to suit her, she may lose interest in her current employer and find another place where she can aspire to the pinnacle. She's not pushy or showy about her climb. In fact, she can be rather quiet and coy about it and before you know it she's moving into her new penthouse office with President or Manager engraved on the door.

Financial

Once a Capricorn woman learns to trust her own financial instincts, she practically floats to the top of the financial sphere. But you probably don't see the hours she devotes to researching the real estate market, reading about investments and percentage rates or poring over statistics and stock exchange forecasts.

Many Capricorn women do end up wealthy, but sometimes you would not know it from the way they live or how they dress. Ms Capricorn is not one to flaunt her possessions and when it comes to money, she's the most modest of all. Even if she marries a billionaire who she knows will love her forever, she will have her own bank accounts and continue to work if she can manage it. She does not totally like to hand her future financial security over to anyone. That is why she often becomes irritable, fretful or rundown if she stops making her own money and begins to live on her husband's income (even if he is more than happy with this arrangement).

Especially financially, a Capricorn woman's biggest obstacle is that she often lacks faith in her own self-worth. She readily recognises other people's value and how they are good at what they do and that they deserve big salaries and so on, but she tends to underestimate her own. Until she can clearly see what she is worth, she may practically give away her skills and talents. She even feels uncomfortable discussing money and she often has anxieties about her expenses even when she has plenty of money to pay the bills.

Physical

Capricorn women possess a classic beauty that is often quite striking. Supermodels Christy Turlington, Kate Moss and legendary entertainer Gypsy Rose Lee are all Capricorns. Ms Capricorn may have a soothing voice and can have a calming influence on others, even when she is in turmoil herself. She can disarm man, woman or child by smiling with her eyes, which radiate charisma and strength simultaneously. This woman is truly a light unto herself.

In spite of this, she may want nearly constant reassurance that she is attractive and desirable. Especially in her younger years, she wants to be pretty more than anything else. A young Capricorn female often places beauty over brains. Even as this child blooms into a woman and appreciates the value of her intelligence, she yearns to be considered beautiful. A man involved with a Capricorn woman needs to think before he speaks — especially when she asks him how she looks as they head out the door. 'You look fine', is not an acceptable response and will send her pouting back to her wardrobe. If you want to please her, tell her she looks stunning, radiant and beautiful.

One of Ms Capricorn's greatest beauty assets is her clear, smooth skin. Many Capricorns are blessed with this physical trait but they also need to devote some time to keep it healthy. Her skin is sometimes on the dry side, but if she drinks lots of pure water and uses moisturisers consistently, she can keep her youthful glow well into her later years. Many Capricorns become more attractive and more physically fit in the second half of their lives and Capricorn grandmothers are known for their bright, dancing eyes and firm features.

The Capricorn woman has strong, sometimes larger than average hands and feet (or her hands and feet may have a peculiar shape to them). When this is true of her, she may be self-conscious about them and wish they were smaller or prettier. However, she knows her hands and feet serve her well. Whether she's giving a relaxing back massage, kneading homemade bread dough or climbing life's mountains, she has great power to call upon. She also has a natural resistance to disease and often lives well into her nineties.

When she does get sick, chances are she has worried herself into that condition. She suffers from skin rashes or hives, which are triggered by overexertion or stress, and a nervous stomach that is further irritated by improper food combining and poor food choices. This woman can eat a bag of potato chips and a box of chocolates and try to make up for the splurge with a diet soft drink.

Capricorn women need to take special care of their bones and joints, as these tend to be vulnerable areas. Making a habit of eating a healthy amount of calcium and getting lots of outdoor exercise helps this woman more than she wants to admit. If you want to support her efforts, invite her to go on a walk with you. But don't tell her she should exercise or she'll spend the day sulking because you think she's fat.

Mental

Mentally, she's quick, clever and rational and has a polished ability to weigh both sides of a situation before making a decision. She usually treats her mind better than her body and spends more time reading self-improvement books than romance novels. Her top interests are learning, advancing and furthering her ambitions.

She does not have a need or even a desire to tell everyone what she knows and there are times when she remains silent for diplomatic reasons. Consequently, she is sometimes greatly underestimated. But a Capricorn knows how to make this work in her favour and before long she politely passes her competitors on the road to success. She is wise enough to adapt to changes and look for the hidden benefit in every apparent obstacle. She does not dwell on failures, but stays diligently focused on the light ahead.

She may not be able to spout off factual data and trivia at a moment's notice, but her mind works in such a highly organised manner that her research and reports are unparalleled. She is also imaginative and resourceful, so she can solve problems that leave others scratching their heads in confusion. As a Capricorn is a woman born under the influence of the planet Saturn, she has an innate ability to process and synthesise information rapidly, mentally relating it with all other 'mind files', and putting what seems useful to her project or personal journey into action immediately.

Spiritual

Whether she lives in the city, the country or the outback she is likely to have a home that somehow feels a little like a church, a sanctuary or a retreat in some way. She may even have religious crosses on the walls, little shrines of some kind (even if the shrine simply is represented by family photos), perfumed candles and glorious flowers positioned in the right places around the room.

Because she loves tradition and structure, many Capricorn women practise some type of organised and traditional form of religion. However, those who were brought up Catholics often end up straying from this particular doctrine because in their adult years they cannot find themselves accepting a religion that is still not open-minded enough to accept women at the top of its hierarchy.

Whether a churchgoer or not, Ms Capricorn has her own unique link with her creator. She probably has her own special guardian angel, too (and subliminally she is aware of this guardian angel connection). She knows in her heart that her faith (or lack of faith) contributes to and affects her entire existence.

Should she occasionally project an image of disinterest when it comes to heavenly matters this is because she is so busy taking care of earthly matters. Sometimes it may take a life crisis or family drama to remind her of the comfort and sustenance that prayer, religion, meditation and faith provide.

If she can find enough time to explore her innermost world, she is likely to be delighted with what she finds. She often possesses heightened psychic abilities and is probably good at seeing or hearing other people's silent thoughts and innately knowing when to take action or hold back. Being out among nature not only heals her, but also is where she feels closest to her special god or goddess. When she views the sun setting, watches the ocean waves crashing upon the shoreline or sees the moon rising, often a tear of gratitude and love appears in her eyes. While she may believe that luck is something you create for yourself and that superstitions are foolish pastimes for the weak-minded, she does believe in faith, magic and miracles.

The Capricorn man

To find him in a crowded room, look for guy with the serious expression who's gazing out the window, and rowing up the river of dreams.

Like Capricorn Mel Gibson, the twinkle in Mr Capricorn's eyes hints that there's often more to him than his steely, sometimes serious, disposition suggests. Nevertheless, don't be fooled by the twinkle in his eyes, either. This guy has a mission to make it to the top and anything not on the path is generally considered a damned intrusion.

Mr Capricorn likes to travel a straight path and if you want to take him off on a detour, it had better be for a good reason. There are exceptions that happily delay his determined approach towards his goals, and falling in love is one of them. But a Capricorn man is just as cautious in romantic matters as he is in business and he won't easily permit his heart to lead him astray.

He is determined, dedicated and independent. Yet, while this strong and driven man gives the impression of needing no one — he silently yearns for people to welcome him, adore him and respect him. He also wants people to like him and appreciate his abilities. But, whether you do or don't like him, the Capricorn man stays on track.

Capricorns Louis Pasteur and Isaac Newton were so 'on track' they were ahead of their time. Newton's law of gravitation, which is now accepted as obvious, was at first scoffed at and ridiculed. And when Pasteur first introduced his method of killing unsafe bacteria in food many people thought he was foolish, but pasteurisation is a common practice today. Like diehard Capricorns, neither Newton nor Pasteur allowed public opinion to stand in the way of their pursuit of truth and possibility.

Mr Capricorn is aware of his inner power, so his primary rule is to 'go for it' — with patience. He's a planner and an organiser and he generally knows exactly where he's going and how to proceed. He expects hurdles along the way and he's great at jumping them, slipping under them or discreetly going around them. His combination of dominant character traits nearly always adds up to a successful venture and often results in a big round of applause (just look at the success that Capricorns like Kevin Costner, Ricky Martin and Rod Stewart have achieved, capitalising upon their Capricorn talent and sex appeal).

[How Capricorn men operate]

Social

The Capricorn man loves being invited to parties but he doesn't always enjoy them once he gets there. Unless he's interested in making business or romantic contacts by going, he'd sometimes rather work late at the office or retire early so he can be fresh for tomorrow's business meeting or his football game. When he does accept a party invitation, he often graciously arrives with a tasteful gift for the host and then seems almost self-conscious when he offers it. To find him in a crowded room, look for the guy with the serious expression who's gazing out the window, rowing up the river of dreams. Never mind that he's at the hottest social event of the season with people laughing and dancing all around him, his serious stance is his self-made fort designed to discourage all but those who have a true desire to get to know him.

Of course, there are Capricorn men with strong planetary influence from the Sun or from Jupiter who can be the legendary life of the party (look at Capricorn actor–comedian Jim Carrey). But in general, a Capricorn man is polite and friendly in a reserved manner and he's sometimes accused of being snobbish when in fact he's just being quiet and observant. Even at the most exciting parties and social outings, he can be a stuffed shirt because he feels compelled to conduct himself with the utmost social grace.

He's far from a saint and every once in a while (sometimes more frequently — Al Capone was a Capricorn) he loosens his tie and takes a walk on the wild side of life. When he lets his hair down, he often does it in such as full-on way that the desire to let his hair down doesn't erupt again for quite some time. But most of the time his monthly meetings with his accountant or lawyer, followed by a friendly game of poker are about as much social stimulation as he wants or needs. He usually values comfort and relaxation over excitement and loves to spend time with his friends and family because that's when he can really be himself.

His hobbies are often centred in the outdoors because the Capricorn has a close bond with nature. He probably likes to walk through the bush and many Capricorns love going fishing. His favourite movies have exhilarating action heroes who save the day. He likes to experience excitement through the movies where there's no real risk or inconvenience. He enjoys both a friendly round of golf and a competitive one (like Capricorn golf champion Tiger Woods), but his social life will nearly always take a back seat to his hobbies, career and his family.

Love and family

The Capricorn man has one of the warmest hearts in the zodiac but don't expect him to wear it on his sleeve. He's uncomfortable with public displays of affection and, frankly, even private displays of affection are reserved for those truly special occasions — like his wedding day. He loves to be adored by women but his refined poker face won't show it and while he understands the rules in courtship, he doesn't always want to play the game.

He sometimes fantasises about being a romantic, but this guy will propose marriage in the second page of a letter after telling you the mundane details of his day on the first page. But where he falls short on romance, he rises tall on lovemaking, loyalty, appreciation and support. He's a warm, sexy and affectionate lover, and he gives wonderful bear hugs and back rubs, too (he may even be a physiotherapist or chiropractor). His heart knows the depths of passion (sometimes in a very kinky fashion) but you may need to know him intimately before you see his more steamy side.

As well as being sexy, believe it or not, Mr Serious Capricorn can be funny, too (and Jim Carrey again is a great example of this)! It's often not the sort of slapstick humour that has people rolling on the floor, but rather a dry sarcastic remark that lingers in your mind and finds you smiling again a week later. Capricorns Steve Allen and Andy Rooney both are great at this kind of humour. One of Capricorn's favourite topics to joke about is his family, but he won't think it's funny if you chime in. He's the only one permitted to make fun of his own clan. And by the way, his clan rules. That marriage proposal was written only after Mother decided that you were acceptable for her son.

The Capricorn man is looking for a mate who understands and supports his goals. Chances are he'll select a woman who's reserved in her behaviour and conservative in all sorts of ways — including the way she dresses. She'll have a deep love for children, be a good cook and probably be a 'neat-nik'. A woman with her hopes set on a Capricorn man can increase her chance of winning his heart by showering his mother and family members with attention. Bake cakes for his mother, take soup to his sick brother and go shopping with his sister.

He is definitely worth winning, as a Capricorn man is the epitome of a faithful husband and a devoted breadwinner. He may not spend many relaxing evenings at home, but he usually makes it home for dinner and a quick kiss before he heads back to the office or to his moonlight job. And when he does take a night off, he can make up for lost time with his gentle touch and skilful lovemaking manoeuvres.

As a father, a Capricorn attempts to be firm but the truth is his children can often charm him into a more lenient state of mind. He believes his responsibility is to provide them with a solid foundation for the future and help them discover their own strengths and talents. He attends his daughter's piano recitals with pride and reads his son's book reports with genuine interest. If his children are interested in sports, they have an advantage over their friends because most Capricorn dads are natural coaches, encouraging practice and instilling confidence as he teaches the basics of the game.

Career

The Capricorn man can diligently climb to the peak of any career path but he leans towards positions that have structure and routine built in. He likes schedules, time slots and organisational meetings because efficiency is his middle name. He's creative in his ideas and solutions but practical in their application. He takes his work seriously and he works just as diligently as an employee as he does when he owns the company.

Capricorns excel in teaching, banking, engineering and architecture. They're also quite content to work in humdrum type jobs if the security and money make it worth his while. Many Goats enjoy careers in public service or community relations, real estate and marketing. Some of the best writers are Capricorns — Rudyard Kipling, Edgar Allan Poe and J. D. Salinger are just a few examples.

As well, some of the most talented actors of our time are Capricorns — like Lloyd Bridges, Kevin Costner, Ted Danson, Robert Duval, Mel Gibson and James Earl Jones. But no matter what profession a Capricorn chooses, he's typically successful and respected. And if he's in charge, better yet. He's not into glitz but a nice office with a well-made leather chair sounds like a good place to operate command central.

Somewhat surprisingly, Capricorns also are extremely creative. Their conservative traits tend to repress these talents in favour of more traditional careers but the Capricorns who follow their inspirations can gain prominence in literature, art, music, sports and entertainment. (Capricorn Elvis Presley shifted the music scene and Tiger Woods re-wrote the history of golf.)

To the up and running Capricorn, walking on water (and sometimes being nailed to the cross) is part of the daily routine. They don't think it's a spectacular ability; they see it as merely doing whatever is needed to achieve their goals. And if they need a miracle to get to their next destination, they can usually think of a way to organise one.

Financial

Remember that there are three different types of Capricorn (the ambitious, the passive and those who swing between these two extremes), so when it comes to finances some of the richest and poorest men in this world are born under this sign. Some Capricorns may even find that living off social security works for them, but most Capricorns aspire to make as much money as Greek shipping magnate Aristotle Onassis made during his lifetime — and he was a Capricorn.

The Capricorn man who is focused on building a fortune is the type who keeps the first dollar he ever earned and saves it as a lucky charm. This sort of Capricorn begins saving for his retirement before he's old enough to hold a job. Since his main focus is on tomorrow and the days after, he's careful to plan for the future in a realistic and wise way.

He makes his fortune one step at a time, taking only the most calculated risks and following all the rules of sound financial planning. A Capricorn man likes to own a house, rather than rent, and buy his car, rather than lease. He doesn't like to owe anyone money and he sleeps easier when he has no debts. Sometimes Capricorns have a reputation for being stingy. They can actually be very generous but they refuse to pay more for something than what it's reasonably worth. If there's someone in your office who brings their lunch every day, chances are he's a Capricorn or there's a Capricorn at home influencing this habit.

Physical

The Capricorn man comes in many manly shapes and sizes (look at Val Kilmer, Mel Gibson, Kevin Costner, Ricky Martin, Humphrey Bogart, Cary Grant, Anthony Hopkins and Rod Stewart as prime examples), but he usually has both feet – clad in sensible shoes or the very latest and trendiest sneakers – planted on the ground. He might stand so steady he appears to be growing out of the very piece of earth or floor on which he's standing. There's often a calm gentleness in his strong demeanour and his voice is both authoritative and soothing. He displays an air of certainty that, with practice, becomes as much a part of his physical appearance as his straight nose and chiselled jaw line.

Capricorn men generally enjoy exercise and they often make good long-distance and cross-country runners. They also make talented ball players with their steady feet and capable hands. Capricorn's balanced, busy lifestyle and rational thinking prevent him from wasting too much energy. He has great endurance and the capacity for a long, healthy life. It's not uncommon for a Capricorn man to outlive most of his friends and even some of his children. But he can be his own worst enemy in the physical arena. No amount of moderate living and exercise can completely override his doomsday attitude; he can be the world's worst hypochondriac. A Capricorn man is wise to make healthy choices in his nutrition, to avoid smoking, limit caffeine and alcohol and get a moderate amount of exercise every day.

His hands and feet, symbolically the most important body parts for his life-long climb, are sometimes afflicted with conditions like arthritis, tinea and psoriasis. And when a Capricorn is on the verge of a summit that he's a bit afraid of, don't be surprised if he sprains an ankle, twists his knee or even breaks a leg. (His bones are the part of his body in astrology that are most crucial.)

This is sometimes his way of forcing himself to stop and reconsider his plans before he commits to his next critical step. His stomach is also an area that expresses anxiety and he should remember that he's not a goat in actuality when it comes to eating. But he loves good food and in martyr-like fashion the Goat offers to finish the food on his kids' plates, so it won't go to waste. He usually has a sweet tooth and probably has a steady supply of ice cream in his freezer.

Mental

He has the ability of a skilled chess player to calculate moves and plan well into the future. His certainty and serious nature support his methodical thinking and make him a worthy contender in any arena. He's grateful for his intellectual ability but never quite satisfied. He always wants to learn more, understand more and improve more.

He loves to solve mysteries and unravel mental puzzles. He finds new information stimulating, especially if a 'mind stretch' is required to grasp it. Because of his ability to think and reason even under pressure, he's a valuable member of any company or organisation. Regardless of his career choice, his attention to fine details takes his work to a higher level. If he's an architect, his buildings come to life; if he's a teacher, his students lean forwards in anticipation of his next word. If he says something, he wants it to be well worth saying and possibly repeating.

He's able to link information from all areas of life to form an ever-expanding cross-referenced file of knowledge. And he can jump to remarkably accurate conclusions. Never underestimate the mental prowess of a Capricorn. Even if he appears to be the least qualified or too young and inexperienced for the competition, he can win (look at Capricorn Tiger Woods as an example).

He's probably still a member of the church or religion he grew up in but that doesn't mean his mind is closed to other ideas and perspectives. He presents a very conservative front and may scoff at the idea of anything supernatural, but he definitely knows his zodiac sign is Capricorn and no doubt recognises himself in the description.

He's intrigued by the thought of living many lifetimes and in some ways he hopes it's true. But his down-to-earth nature often persuades him that the only real things are those he can perceive with his five basic senses.

He generally admits he's had some pretty odd coincidences though. On some level he may believe we all have a sixth sense lying dormant within us. But he's often too focused on the material plane to test his theory and cultivate his own psychic abilities.

He is often interested in interpreting his dreams. He looks for insights, information and advantages in all areas of his life and if his dreams can help him to understand something better and support his mission he's all for it. Many inspired thoughts and ideas find their way to him through his dream states, whether he realises it or not. And his quiet and contemplative mind finds many moments to ponder the questions of his existence and his purpose.

He seems to know that the quality of his questions determines the quality of his life. And he has a secret theory that there's a hierarchy of worlds beyond this one and if the truth is known, he probably spends more time in these realms than he dares to admit even to himself!

The Capricorn baby

[*The Capricorn baby is the wise, serious, distant and delicate baby of the zodiac.*

See the baby with the wrinkled, crinkled facial expression, possibly with the naturally spiked-up hairstyle? If you look closer, it probably has its tiny little hand rolled up into a tight fist and seems to have an innate desire to keep moving its legs like an athlete, scissoring its way from side to side. The Capricorn baby begins to prepare itself early for climbing to the top of life's mountains. Its first attempts at accomplishing this feat, however, are destined to take place in a horizontal position. That's often why an infant Capricorn cries when it is tucked in too tightly and can't move its legs around freely. It's ready to climb, even when it can't yet crawl.

This Capricorn baby usually says hello to the world by yelling at the top of its tiny lungs! The tiny 'Goat' is likely to spend much of its time asserting itself through wailing (and to make their point they perpetrate this wailing at a high-pitched level). When truly letting it rip, this child's wail can sound more like a mountain-top form of Swiss yodelling. It has a ring to it that seems to permeate any sound/pitch barrier and some Capricorns' parents claim it's the kind of wail that can break glass.

If anything traumatic happens to the newborn Goat during its very early days or months on the planet, the shock to its lungs and self-expression can create all kinds of side-effects, from asthma and other bronchial problems to allergies, and it can even develop a stutter in later life.

Also I have observed that many Capricorn babies seem to have the appearance of the Buddha as they develop. By the Buddha, I mean that rotund, plump tummy look, and many Capricorn littlies go through a phase where they are quite plump and bald, too. For some reason, many baby Capricorns seem to have a talent for being contortionists and can move their faces and foreheads around in quite a novel and entertaining-to-watch fashion.

Whether this facial contortion is created by a need to express some secret inner thought or emotion, the pain of gas or some other physical reactions, Capricorn babies appear to be more facially active than most other babies. So don't be surprised if your Capricorn offspring is the centre of attention in the nursery.

Capricorns are born under the influence of the planet Saturn — the planet ruling parenthood, family structure, the foundations of life, the later years of life, the gleaning of wisdom through experiencing delays and the value of learning patience. As an offshoot or side-effect from this planetary influence, often from the day the Capricorn baby is conceived there seem to be delays or something requiring patience and perseverance surrounding this one's birth.

It may be that its parents have waited some time for this baby to come along or that they have some unusual age difference, like the man is considerably older than his wife, or vice versa. Also with this delay factor in force, when the birth is approaching there may be several false starts or uncertainties surrounding the birth itself. However once the Capricorn baby is born, its path to the top of whatever mountains in life he or she chooses has begun. As the baby Goat grows up, its parents often wonder and marvel at how it manages to hook up with the people and contacts it needs to make it to the top.

There is usually an intangible other-world quality about Capricorn babies. Without being able to put your finger on it exactly, there is something different about them. Some seem to be born with almost an illuminated aura surrounding them; an aura which becomes invisible within a few days of the birth.

Many astrologers believe these little ones are great old souls coming back to earth again and many a parent of a Capricorn child has agreed with them. There's a feeling of wisdom surrounding this baby that is so obvious people will comment on it. This child will look more developed or mature during its childhood, too. As the baby 'Goat' develops and goes through its baby growth process, it is likely to do some things that are quite extraordinary and at times appear to be miraculous or mysterious.

In attitude and behaviour, small Capricorns take themselves, other people and even toys very seriously. They love to have a routine as far as eating and sleeping are concerned. Baby Goats really seem to taste their food and feel and sense objects or toys when they touch them. They are very focused and anxious to learn and develop. They're also wary of life and won't jump quickly into anything. The Capricorn baby may seem to be a slow developer at times but this is just its way of easing into things, rather than jumping into them.

This wee mite has an innate sense of what is right and wrong and is likely, very early in life, to realise what it can and can't do. Most Capricorn babes learn their boundaries very quickly and seem to understand the words 'yes' and 'no' much sooner than other babies. If you're the parent of this baby it's important to keep a vibration of love surrounding you because Capricorn babies are the most connected subliminally to their parents.

They have a strong instinct for whether they're being accepted or rejected and will remember this feeling or sense of connection or disconnection subliminally for all their lives. Babyhood and childhood play enormous roles in the Capricorn's emotional and psychological development. The connection to the mother in particular can be significant. In later life you can tell a lot about a Capricorn (the dark or light emotional baggage they are carrying) by the way they talk about or don't discuss their childhood and their connection or disconnection with their parents (or one parent in particular).

Due to its Saturn rulership (the planet of delay and restriction) it could take time for this baby to walk and talk and it may appear to be a slow developer because of this. When it does walk or talk, you should really applaud and show your approval. It loves recognition of its achievements and records in the deepest realms of its innate being exactly what effect it has upon you when it performs certain actions or reactions.

Even if your baby is a slow developer, remember this child has a natural tendency for taking its own wise and good time to do things because of its inner caution and a strong sense for self-preservation given to it by the planet Saturn. Remember also, this little soul isn't in a hurry to prove anything. It realises life is a journey made up of many steps. It knows it has plenty of time and this baby prefers to get things right, rather than do things haphazardly just to impress others. Therefore it may be extremely fearful if pressed to perform beyond and above its sense of safety.

The physical, material realms of experience mean a lot to this wee person. The Capricorn baby is a sensualist, will love to be caressed and will adore all the pleasures life offers including tasty food and good milk — particularly mother's milk. However, it is extremely sensitive so the mother will need to be careful what she eats as her diet could easily upset the Capricorn's delicate stomach.

The love the Capricorn baby has for nurturing itself through good eating will be reflected later on in its life as a taste for good living. And from birth the Capricorn usually likes routine, organisation and scheduling. It likes patterns and rhythms. It doesn't like change or surprises. It also likes gentleness, soft sounds and plenty of things to look at and focus attention on. These infants often pay particular attention to their own booties — as Capricorn babies often have a great fascination for observing and playing with their own hands and feet!

The Capricorn toddler through teen

The way to help the Capricorn child succeed is to focus very much on what they're doing right and very little on what they're doing wrong.

The next time you see a photograph of a toddler dressed up in mummy's make-up and pearls or daddy's tie and hat, take a good look at their face. If they have a grown-up expression and a serious-looking nature, you can almost bet he or she's a Capricorn. These children tend to be serious in their thinking and they often relate better to grown-ups or older kids than they do to children their own age. This little one doesn't want to play school, unless they get to be the teacher or better yet the principal. These kids want to play office.

Little Capricorns — from the time they're born and right on through their lives — are creatures of routine, schedule and habit. They do much better and feel more secure when they know what's expected of them and they thrive when they're praised and acknowledged for doing well. This is particularly important in the early years as the Capricorn begins learning to walk and talk.

If the Goat can see that failing is part of the learning process, then he or she will be more willing to try new and different things as they grow older. If, however, Capricorns are severely criticised or made fun of when they make mistakes, they will often grow up and be afraid to try anything new. This type of stagnation is deadly to a Capricorn youngster whose inner nature is to climb higher and higher to reach their goals.

In fact, the way to help Capricorns succeed is to focus very much on what they're doing right and very little on what they're doing wrong. They're their own worst and most severe critics so when they make a mistake they are really hard on themselves. In fact, these little people can get so upset about making a mistake that they end up making a whole string of mistakes because they were so shook up about the first one. Help them to put it all in perspective so they're willing to keep trying, even when they seem to be failing more often than succeeding.

Capricorn children sometimes need help to loosen up and be willing to play and have fun without following a particular plan. You might hear your four- or five-year-old Capricorn say to a friend, 'Okay, first we'll play ball and then we'll play video games and then after that, if we have time, we'll play with our dolls'. Capricorns often have an air of authority about them and lots of times their friends will go along with them without even thinking about it.

Encourage some spontaneity in your Capricorn to help balance all that serious planning and worrying. They'll have plenty of time during their adult life for that. For now, you might explain to them that their job is to learn about life and have fun! And be sure not to add to your little Goat's worries by discussing adult types of problems in front of him or her.

Little Goats are more drawn to toys and games which have a purpose than to abstract types of playing and rough-housing. Baby boomer Capricorns are still reminiscing about the board game called 'Life' which allowed them to spin the wheel and move a token around the board to simulate things that happen in real life. First get a job and buy a car, then get married, buy insurance, pay taxes, have kids, and then upon retirement choose between the poor house and the millionaire mansion. Most Goats will make it to the millionaire mansion because, even in a game, they dread the thought of the poor house.

Capricorns, by nature, have a fear or insecurity about not measuring up or not being good enough. This inner fear is partially responsible for their success but it is also what stops them from taking a chance or trying something new that could lead to even greater success and more opportunities. These anxieties often come to the surface when it is time for Capricorn to go off to school.

Some of these children will begin having nightmares or stomach disorders because of their anxiety about the unknown future. Tell them as much as you can about what is coming. Give them an idea about what school is like and what is expected of them. You might even take them to their new school and show them their classroom before their first day so they feel prepared. Capricorns are very good at acting confident even when they are scared so it will be up to you to anticipate and recognise their anxieties and help them to prepare — rather than worry.

During their pre-adolescent years of about age eight through to ten, the Capricorn really enjoys adult company and conversation. They're careful listeners and are attuned to the adult nuances hidden between the lines.

They're trying to figure it all out and they look forward to the day when they're in charge of their own lives. I remember a Capricorn who lived on my block when I was still at high school. She was only about nine years old and she loved to visit the adults in the neighbourhood, particularly the ones who were retired. I would see her sitting on my neighbours' back porches chatting with them for hours. Young Capricorns respect and appreciate people who have experienced life and have some wisdom to share.

Just keep in mind that the 'kid' wants to be a grown-up Goat more than anything else. When Capricorns are entering their teen years, they begin to be pre-occupied with questions and plans for their adult life. The question, 'What am I going to be when I grow up?' suddenly takes on new urgency — usually around Year Eight or Nine.

While the other kids will just be wondering if they should take Spanish or French for their language option, Capricorns are sending away for information from prospective universities or institutes. But regardless of how focused they are about their future Capricorns also begin to stand up and take serious notice of the opposite sex at about this age. Because of their intensity, a Capricorn can break a heart and have his or her own broken all in a matter of hours.

Young Capricorns tend to get attached to people quickly and have a hard time with break-ups, even if they initiate them. Help them to remember that they have a lot they want to accomplish before they settle into a long-term relationship and resist the urge to remind them that they're still kids. Capricorns are very serious about their emotions and helping them to cultivate a sense of humour will serve them well throughout their lives.

Capricorns are natural leaders and they often serve as the captain of their class or football team. They usually get good marks, especially in the subjects they like. But in spite of all these strengths the Capricorn teen is extremely self-conscious and self-critical, and criticism from parents, teachers and friends only exaggerates their low sense of self-worth.

Make it a habit to notice and openly recognise and appreciate their good traits. Tell them you appreciate the fact that they're responsible and good at taking care of themselves. Praise them for their achievements and affirm your belief in them and your support for their dreams. Assure them that even the worst times in life sometimes lead to the best times, and encourage them to look on the bright side of life.

AQUARIUS

[21 january — 19 february]

aquarius aquarius aquarius aquarius
aquarius aquarius aquarius aquarius
aquarius aquarius aquarius aquarius
aquarius aquarius aquarius aquarius

aquarius aquarius aquarius aquarius
aquarius aquarius aquarius aquarius
aquarius aquarius aquarius aquarius
aquarius aquarius aquarius aquarius
aquarius aquarius aquarius aquarius
aquarius aquarius aquarius aquarius
aquarius aquarius aquarius aquarius

element: air

planetary ruler: uranus

symbol: the water-bearer

quality: fixed (= stability)

colours: electric blues and violet

gem: sapphires and opals

best companions: gemini and libra

strongest virtues: reliability, artistic talents,

and bright vision of the future

traits to improve: emotional detachment, fear

of rejection, lack of appreciation for themselves

deepest desire: sharing their

lives with the right people

Aquarius celebrities

Andrew Peacock, Molly Meldrum, Matt Dillon, Michael Hutchence,

John Travolta, Ellen DeGeneres, Neil Diamond, Paul Newman,

Cybill Shepherd, Bridget Fonda, Mozart, Alan Alda, Rene Russo,

Heather Graham, Oprah Winfrey, Christie Brinkley, Tom Selleck,

Phil Collins, Minnie Driver, Sherilyn Flynn, Boris Yeltsin, Farrah Fawcett,

Oscar De La Hoya, Mia Farrow, Barbara Hershey, Zsa Zsa Gabor,

Charles Dickens, Greg Norman, Placido Domingo, Geena Davis,

Princess Stefanie and Princess Caroline of Monaco, Prince Andrew,

Natassia Kinski, Athina Onassis, John McEnroe, Gene Hackman,

Boris Spassky, Lisa Marie Presley, Claire Bloom, Jane Seymour,

Jennifer Aniston, Jennifer Jason Lee, Benny Hill, Ronald Regan,

Emma Lee Bunton (Baby Spice), Vanessa Redgrave, Morgan Fairchild,

Sheryl Crow, Stockard Channing, John Belushi and Linda Blair.

[General outlook]

The new millennium signifies big changes for Aquarians. The final years of the last century challenged you in many ways. This phase continues and the lens through which you see the world is changing little by little. However, even where you have confronted some tough challenges in recent years, better times are ahead of you. There are extremely positive vibrations surrounding you where romance, work, money matters, new friendships and family affairs are concerned.

Above all, the new millennium is a creative and constructive time for Water-bearers. You realise now (because of wisdom earned in the past) that you cannot approach new problems with old solutions. Treat every experience, however negative it may seem, as a way to learn, love and grow. This is a wonderful time to make your dreams come true.

Romance

Single Aquarians find a partner more in tune with their internal rhythms while married Aquarians move towards making their relationship based more on honesty, equality and mutual co-operation. Although your partner may push your buttons, your love relationship is forcing you to grow much more than you realise. 'Love really does make the world go around', and this statement is your new millennium motto. Be bold, be brave and let love and romance light up your life. Also, remember that love takes many forms, and do not exclude loving your life, your gifts and your talents, too.

Health

Being a fixed sign (a sign that doesn't like change), some of you Aquarians had the worst health you ever had as the old millennium ended, especially those Aquarians who held deep apprehension about the future. However, Aquarians who could adapt to change and had the faith and free spirit to embrace it greet the new millennium in good health. Many, in fact, eagerly begin a new health or fitness program (possibly inspired by the fact that you have been through upsets because of other people's health problem or even your own). This is a great time to make all kinds of healthy changes and begin the new millennium with a fresh and vital outlook on life. Above all, learning to meditate or studying and perfecting other relaxation techniques will help you achieve true 'mind, body and spirit' fitness. Sometimes it's necessary to 'clear out' old and jumbled thoughts in your mind to let new inspiration enter.

Finance

Many Aquarians have learned their financial lessons the hard way over the past few years. Some of you have taken financial or investment risks and lost, while others have merely ignored cash-flow problems in the hope they would go away.

Luckily, you are now moving towards a new financial era of enormous potential for abundance and prosperity. Money matters look positive for Water-bearers as the new millennium dawns, and sharing your luck with family and friends (or even a charity) will give you great satisfaction. Enlisting the help of a reputable financial adviser will also help you make more money to put away for a rainy day.

Career

Whatever work role you have selected or whether you are a homemaker, it is still important for you to be up-to-the-minute with the cutting-edge world of technology — because your sign rules technology. For many reasons, you should be prepared to move forwards careerwise, armed with sufficient information, knowledge and understanding about technological advances and products. Fortunately, your Aquarius creative career flair, combined with the experience you have gained over the past few years, give you a winning combination where work and career matters are concerned. The new millennium signifies new career directions are opening around you and many Aquarians start their own business or move into a different field of work. Whatever occurs, be aware that your greatest successes are found when you work as part of a team. Don't go it alone. Teamwork will help create miracles.

[Millennium wildcards to watch for]

Our relationships with others provide us with a mirror of ourselves, which helps us to grow and evolve. However, as the new millennium dawns you may wonder what it is exactly that you have done to deserve so many dramas in your relationships. Don't be surprised if feelings of jealousy, frustration or anger arise where a close love relationship is concerned. Use a close friend as a sounding board or let out pent-up emotions by playing competitive sport. Expressing yourself verbally or physically will help you find an inner equilibrium.

Understanding Aquarius

> *Getting you Aquarians to move out of your minds and into your hearts is sometimes like trying to get an elephant to climb through the eye of a needle.*

If you were the misfit at school, or seemed different from others in various situations or stages of your life, don't worry too much about it because this misfit factor is often part of the Aquarian experience. In fact, I remember the first astrology books I used to read years ago usually wrote up Aquarians as the Lone Rangers of the zodiac. There are probably several occasions when you have pondered how different or unusual your thoughts are compared with others.

Some people might even have hinted that you were going to great lengths to try to be different from others (especially like the time you dyed your hair bright green or blue when you were in your teens, changed your name to Sunrise Rainbow or joined the flower power group back in the '60s). However, dyed hair or not, for an Aquarian, just being yourself is being different. When you try to fit in and conform to the ways of the world, that is when you usually lose your way in life. Attempting to fit in and please others can often cause you stress and frustration.

Being different (or an original) is what you are all about! You are who you are because that is exactly who you're supposed to be. The Forces of the Universe have gone to enormous lengths to make every one of you Aquarians a total original. That is why, if you really look around, you will discover that no two of you Aquarians seem anything alike.

You are sometimes outstanding in your uniqueness and extremely creative, too, like Aquarians Yoko Ono, Mozart, Zsa Zsa Gabor, Axl Rose, Greg Norman and Lisa Marie Presley. When you were made, the universe was intent upon creating a special one-off individual, so, if you are an Aquarian who feels misunderstood, or alone even when surrounded by others, this is probably because you truly are operating in a league all of your own.

Life suddenly becomes a whole lot easier once you understand that you're functioning on a different (and sometimes higher) vibration than those around you simply because you are an Aquarian. Once you come to grips with your individuality, you learn to rely more on your own unique perceptions and keep many of your thoughts to yourself. Nevertheless, there will be many occasions when your somewhat different attitude towards life startles others (sometimes even you), and no matter how carefully you guard your silent pearls of wisdom and try to be like everyone else, your behaviour is sometimes confusing, even to your closest friends.

You yearn to fly high and take everyone with you, but sometimes the heights are too dizzying for others' down-to-earth tastes and views. That is why you will go through phases of your life where you need to be willing to leave people behind. Although you don't like change for the sake of change itself, there will be times when you need to move on, put the past behind you and find new friends or partners. These are the times when you need to link up with those who are prepared to fly at the same crazy heights that you relish.

While your special uniqueness may sometimes make you feel that you need to work harder than others to fit in to the world, or sometimes makes you feel alone, nevertheless there are abundant benefits to being born an Aquarian. It means that you march to the beat of your own special magic drum. And you are likely to lead an exceptional life, too. Princesses Stephanie and Caroline of Monaco, Oprah Winfrey, John Travolta and John McEnroe are great examples of modern-day Aquarians who have their own unique way of living their lives and who have broken some establishment rules in their desire to do their own thing!

When you do your own thing, even when others judge you harshly or friends betray you, it is not in your nature to seek vengeance. You truly believe in the philosophy of live and let live and you do what you can to remain free of society's restrictions. This attitude makes you a wonderful friend, too.

In your outlook and behaviour, you are possibly at least a little eccentric. You thrive on doing things in your own way and in your own time. You generally don't like to keep schedules or make plans too far in advance because it's hard for you to predict what might be happening two or three weeks down the road.

This doesn't mean that you do not appreciate the value of routine. However, when you're in a position with a rigid schedule and predictable routine, you can sometimes become physically unwell, restless and depressed. As much as you love structure and routine, a repetitious lifestyle can be a double-edged sword for you. Because your sign needs more activity than most, both mentally and physically, you sometimes do need to break away from structure and routine. These are the times it is imperative that you take a day off and seek an adventure that promises novelty and excitement.

You need to shake a leg in more ways than one because the circulation system of your body is your weakest physical point. That is why physical exercise is crucial for your wellbeing. You need regular exercise for your body and mind to remain in balance, and self-relaxation techniques and gentle stretching can work wonders for your mind and nervous system.

The expression, 'necessity is the mother of invention' applies to you, too. To your great advantage, because you have an inventive mind (and often a lateral way of thinking) you rarely encounter a problem you cannot find at least five different ways to solve. When your fellow Aquarian Thomas Edison wanted to improve upon the safety and effectiveness of the old gaslights, he invented the light bulb. Not that inventing the light bulb was enough for him, either. After he invented the light bulb and patented another 1093 inventions, humble Thomas Edison was quoted as saying, 'We don't know one-tenth of one per cent about anything'. Only you Aquarians with your open mind usually realise how little we humans actually do know.

It is no accident that an Aquarian invented electricity because your sign is astrologically aligned with electricity. Your ruling planet (or one of your rulers), Uranus, rules electricity and in terms of your quick mind, your creative spark (or bright ideas), like electricity, can sometimes light up a room without the help of a light bulb. Interestingly, your innovative mind and creativity can sometimes be a hindrance. Often you Aquarians lead extremely fortunate, sometimes even exceptional lives, where you're surrounded with great gifts and blessed with unique talents and abilities. However, because you can be so caught up in your internal dialogue and mentally distracted from the real world, it often takes a crisis for you to discover just how blessed and lucky you truly are.

Sometimes the world at large doesn't even exist for you (and in this way you can be a little similar to the cartoon character from some years back, Mr Magoo, when he used to go on his 'separate reality' journeys through life). You can be weighing up so many different thoughts that you lose track of the original destination, question or plan. You can wear odd socks, lock your keys in the car and forget what day it is but, amazingly, still work out the mechanisms of the universe. Distraction comes easily to you, yet your cyclical type of thinking allows you to see the most amazing connections and subplots between events and people — even if you do occasionally forget the main theme. Learning to increase your power of concentration can help you put your bright ideas into action. Your solutions can have a big impact on the people around you and sometimes on the entire world.

Your symbol in astrology is the Water-bearer. Because of this, you are sometimes mistaken as a Water sign when you are an Air sign. In the Aquarian symbol, the water being poured by the maiden represents water from the ocean of knowledge. The jug the maiden holds depicts the higher forces from above showering you with the gift of wisdom. Consequently, you have access to incredible insights, but as an Air sign, you can also think far too much for your own benefit. Too many thoughts sometimes make you lose your connection to your natural (almost psychic) open-minded intuition and inspiration.

You can out-think and go against your own intuition or better judgment and your mind sometimes stops you from opening your heart and connecting with others to the degree that you would love to do. Always remember, Aquarius, that too much thinking can both make you and break you. You need to learn to open up your heart because it isn't healthy to be all mind and not enough heart. You can neglect your body and spirit because you are busy thinking.

Getting you Aquarians to move out of your minds and into your hearts is sometimes like trying to get an elephant to climb through the eye of a needle. Too many thoughts can even make you neurotic, paranoid and fearful and many Aquarians don't take the best care of their health. However, it is true that those of you who get into healthy living often set tremendous examples for the rest of us — as you Aquarians can be extremely self-disciplined when you choose to be.

You sometimes prefer to live life through your thoughts, rather than in reality. You may spend a great deal of time thinking about your options, choices or possibilities. However, getting you to take action on these options can require some kind of showdown to occur. You can prefer to think, rather than act! This applies to romance, too. Falling in love isn't something that you find comfortable. In fact, it can really shake your world and interfere with your inner musing.

Your continuous analysing process often interferes with experiencing the deeper heartfelt connection of true love. Feelings or emotions often make you vulnerable, so many of you actually attempt to avoid really getting close to others, simply because when you get too close or care too much, these feelings can make you feel like an endangered species. This desire to keep your mental space (and at times your heart) at a distance from others can create all kinds of strange character traits within you — some of which you recognise for what they are, others that are not too apparent on the surface. Many a hermit, an eccentric and a radical have been born under your sign.

In your efforts to find romance in a distanced way, many Aquarian women read romance novels or watch romantic movies rather than allowing themselves to become involved with the real thing. Also, Aquarian men may (for example) read *Playboy* — for the articles and interviews of course (or so they claim) — in an attempt to make that romantic human connection without having to truly face their own emotions or emotional needs on a real-life level.

Your ruling planet, Uranus, is the ancient Greek sky god and was the first ruler of the universe. This planet does not manifest its influence emotionally, however, it affects you through a higher-minded, inspiration-based energy flow. Therefore, Uranus generally makes its imprint upon you in mind-connected ways. Uranus is also the planet that rules lightning and electricity so it has incredible and indomitable power. Uranus brings change into play — change of mind, change of circumstance or condition, and change of heart, too (the kind that zaps you like a bolt from the blue).

Uranus also rules the unexpected. Now if you are attuned to Uranus, you've probably had more change in your life than some slot machines! Under Uranus, unexpected happenings and occurrences make up a big part of your everyday life, and while this influence may sometimes feel a little crazy, the intensity of electric energy that surrounds you really teaches you to appreciate and enjoy the present moment. You also appreciate the value of checking out everything that is going on around you, and of keeping your back covered, too. The Boy Scout motto, 'Be prepared' was probably written with an Aquarian in mind because operating under Uranus means that anything and everything can happen in an instant.

Given the unique combination of intense and unusual flows of energy that influences Aquarians, it is no real surprise that so many Aquarians live their lives on the border between creative genius and crazy chaos. It is interesting to note that there are more Aquarians than any other sign in the American Hall of Fame and there are more Aquarians than any other sign in psychiatric hospitals.

Where you do not experience dramatic changes in your daily life, or if certain areas of your life are constant and very stable, it is likely that you are not operating completely under Uranus's influence. The conservative planet Saturn was your primary ruler until Uranus moved into that position. Many Aquarians (especially the older ones) still feel more pulled towards Saturn's slower-moving energy fields, and if this is true for you, your nature and disposition are probably more serious than your Aquarian starmates, who are guided more strongly by Uranus.

These days, most Aquarians operate mainly under Uranus-type energy, with a nice balanced (anchoring) touch of Saturn's calmer influence. This most diversified planetary combination provides all Aquarians with a very special blend of energy highs and lows, mental dexterity and character traits. It can sometimes make you feel torn in two different directions as Uranus dares you to be different at the same time as Saturn is whispering in your ear, 'stick to tried and tested methods'. If you ever feel like you are going crazy, this combination of Uranus and Saturn energy pulling you in opposite directions is likely to be the source of many of your unsettled feelings.

Finding the balance between order and chaos is often a great test for you Aquarians. You can be extremely wise and smart, and then sometimes go out and do something very foolish. But since an Aquarian's life is about learning through experience, it is through taking chances, especially the ones that backfire on you, that you often acquire your greatest gifts of wisdom.

Knowing Uranus's capacity to create chaos, and Saturn's talent for creating order, you might wish, 'if only I was operating under the more stabilising influence of Saturn' — but don't be too hasty. There are many amazing benefits to be gained from being attuned to both Saturn and Uranus. Saturn represents the past, and Uranus represents the future. Saturn on its downside can make your life pedestrian, predictable and wearisome. Saturn can also block some of your creative vision and make you stubbornly cling to conventional ways.

Uranus, on the other hand, is your futuristic planet, and does the opposite of Saturn. Uranus prods you into action by reminding you that you never know what tomorrow will hold. This Aquarian reality means less stability, but it also means more excitement, surprise and electrifying moments. When Uranus is not tempered, however, it makes you feel highly-strung and sometimes even nervous and neurotic. Whereas under Saturn you may be a builder, under Uranus you become a creator.

Uranus rules genius thinking, technology and scientific breakthroughs. It makes you a student of life. It also rules inspiration and the higher cosmic connections (like inspired writing, painting and insights). Saturn makes you a teacher of life but also encourages you to set boundaries and leads to your feelings of being overwhelmed when you are pushed beyond your comfort zone. When you are attached to the power that emanates from Uranus, it provides you with high-octave, cosmic forceful energy. If you follow these Uranus-inspired thoughts, whether you recognise it or not, you have the potential to be a creative genius. (Mozart, Boris Spassky, Norman Rockwell and Charles Dickens are all Aquarians.)

Uranus, because its influence can be so sizzling and buzzy, can make you a dazzling type of person who impacts the world in an unusual and charismatic way. Uranus puts your head up in the realm of distant stars. That is why many of you often find that although you are living in the world, there is a private part of you that is not really connected to the world at all. Many Aquarians have enough going on within them, on the inner levels of operation, that your own inner world keeps you company. You truly have the capacity to be your own 'best friend' or companion.

Your unusual personality magnetically attracts all sorts of adventures, offbeat characters and mysterious opportunities into your life. It is likely that you're attracted to people who are unusual in some way (usually creative people) and you often find yourself surrounded by a group of associates or friends who look like they have nothing in common with you or with each other! But you have the innate capacity to see far beyond the appearances of things in general because (operating under Uranus) you are one of the least judgmental of all the zodiac signs. (Conversely, those Aquarians who operate more under Saturn can be extremely judgmental.)

You usually feel comfortable with even the oddest outsiders and your inquisitive mind, in its quest for truth, accepts all sorts of differences of appearance, outlook and beliefs in others. Because of these character traits, there are times in your life when you hook up with crowds who are into questionable, and possibly even sometimes illegal, activities. While you are more susceptible to being influenced by your friends when you're younger, you can end up in some serious trouble at any age if you're not careful regarding the company you keep.

Fortunately, you have powerful resilience (and stubbornness) within you, too. Often you Aquarians have an unparalleled talent to reinvent your circumstances and come out a winner, but your ability to rise above adversity and triumph makes others very jealous. Sometimes people misinterpret your free-flowing type of energy as apathy and think you don't care about them, others or the things that are happening around you, when in fact you are just handling things in your own independent-minded fashion. In reality, you're very introspectively sensitive and occasionally need to detach from the outer world to give yourself a break.

When you are mentally overloaded you flip off one of your mental switches and go out to lunch in your own cosmic cafe! When you are in this frame of mind, nothing others say or do is likely to really get through to you. When you need to take time out, you take it. Moreover, you take it in some strange ways. Because of your uniqueness, most Aquarians know what it's like to be misunderstood and you occasionally feel a deep isolation that comes from being ahead of your time in your thinking.

You can suffer from your unconscious and often unrecognised ability to look into the future, or for being too smart in your ideas or concepts. As an example, when Aquarian Galileo openly embraced the idea that the earth revolves around the sun, he was harassed, ridiculed and put under house arrest! Even after his belief was proven accurate, he still was not pardoned by the Catholic Church until more than 340 years after his death.

I heard a great story about an Aquarian professional athlete who showed the true colours of his zodiac sign by his big-hearted actions. This athlete was leaving the stadium after winning a championship game and a man who seemed totally heartbroken came up to him to congratulate him and ask him for help. The heartbroken man said his son loved to play football but he had been seriously hurt in a car accident and would never walk again without having expensive surgery. The man had no insurance and did not know how he could tell his son that he could never play football again. The Aquarian athlete's heart went out to this man and he wrote him a cheque for $10 000.

'Tell your son he will play football again', he said as he handed it to the man.

Several months later when the athlete returned to the same town he learned from local sources (who had heard of his generosity) that the man he gave the money to had lied about the boy's plight.

When the Aquarian heard this he smiled ear to ear and asked, 'You mean his son can still walk and play football without having surgery?'

'Yes', said the local source. 'The man's son was never in a car accident.'

'Thank God', said the athlete, 'I couldn't stop thinking about that little boy'.

Some people thought the athlete should have been angry or sued the man to get his money back, but that's not the way you Aquarians generally think. When something tugs on your heartstrings, you care in a deep, significant fashion. You want to help people, take care of lost dogs, and attend to the needy wherever they are. However, you are often taken advantage of, and people sometimes let you down badly. Nevertheless, you keep bouncing back. In fact, you have an amazing belief in people, even though you have been stabbed in the back many times and know from past experience that bending over backwards for people often lands you on your bottom, instead of at the top of their thank you list!

Sometimes people can be so tiresome or unsettling to be around that you sometimes prefer the company of animals, trees and your own fantasies. You tend to swing back and forth between total immersion in the world and complete withdrawal. Aquarians can be hermits, celebrities and everything in between.

Since your home is often a reflection of your unique mind, unusual colour combinations and patterns abound in your furnishings and decorations. Whether you live alone or with a roommate or partner, you strongly influence the space around you. And everything you touch is affected by your Aquarian style and energy. Your gift to the world is your originality and you clear a path to the future almost as easily as you ride the waves of life.

Aquarius is an Air sign

To your advantage, you can make your dreams come true, especially when you have a purpose bigger than yourself. You're a seeker of truth and you know the deepest wisdom is within you. You study everything and everyone, including yourself, and you diligently attempt to find the missing pieces of life's puzzle. You find tradition interesting but that doesn't mean you follow it.

To your disadvantage, you can be strongly influenced by chaotic environments and other outside distractions. You can be easily side-tracked and have so many projects going at the same time that it seems to take forever to finish even one of them.

You may have days when you feel like you're watching your life, instead of participating in it. You can be very self-critical and when you are reflective you often see your weaknesses instead of focusing on your strengths.

[Insights into your sign]

The bright side: One of your greatest strengths is your unique and inventive mind. There are many imitations, but you are a true original.

The shadow: Being original creates some of your most difficult tests in life and sometimes turns you into an outsider or misfit.

[Looking beneath the surface of your sign]

Your hidden traits are so skilfully kept under wraps that even your closest friends rarely see your darker side. But you can dip a blue mood and change it into black despair in the blink of an eye. Your creativity is great for lots of things, but it can also exaggerate the problems in your life and make something bad appear even worse than it is. When you're doing what you love to do, you overflow with energy and your inspired energy spreads out and lifts the spirits of people all around.

When you're floundering, you may exhaust yourself. Your mind is like Grand Central Station, with trains of thought coming and going around the clock and the hum of a thousand conversations in the background. Part of this lifetime for you, Aquarius, is learning how to focus your mind. That means you attract situations that teach you how to concentrate. The situations you attract to learn these lessons aren't always pretty, but once you master this mind game, you rise to new heights. You yearn to be understood but not very many people are ready to

Characteristics >	Benefits >	Drawbacks >
Amiable	Good-natured	Easily distracted
Analytical	Good mind	Pre-occupied with self
Assertive	Responsible	One-eyed
Detached	Free-thinker	Prone to accidents
Eccentric	Unique character	Out of step
Genius	Bright ideas	Misunderstood
Honest	Sincere	Startling
Humane	Kind	Exploited
Independent	Self-sufficient	Refuse good advice
Innovative	New approaches	Constant change
Inventive	Creative ideas	Ahead of your time
Original	Pioneering	Ridiculed
Outspoken	Candid	Unrestrained
Patient	Composed	Repress frustration
Popular	Well liked	Put on pedestal
Probing	Thorough	Prying
Progressive	Clear inner vision	Easily bored
Serene	Peaceful	Drifter
Tolerant	Understanding	Taken advantage of
Tranquil	Soothing	Subdued passions
Unbiased	Objective	Self-righteous

see the world through your crystalline eyes. So, you sometimes feel more isolated when you're with others than when you're alone. This can lead to days of solitude, sulking about your uniqueness. The truth is you would hate to be like everyone else, but you still think other people's lives are somehow easier than yours.

[How to tune into your sign's powers]

> *Remember that all boundaries are actually just illusions.*

> *Celebrate your individuality.*

> *Dare to be different!*

> *She's a natural flirt and just a flash of her smile can melt most road blocks. She loves trying new things and she'll do almost anything at least once.*

If one woman of the zodiac has her head in the stars, it is Ms Aquarius. Her subliminal connection to the cosmos is much more pronounced than the other signs, and this sometimes gives her an appearance of being rather dizzy, zany or unpredictable. She needs more time to herself than most and sometimes actually enjoys her own company much more than being in a social setting. She probably doesn't smile as much as other signs of the zodiac, laugh as frequently, chase after romance or let down her hair in gay abandonment, but when she does turn on the charm, Ms Aquarius has a unique form of feminine magic within her that can be dazzling to behold.

She's the woman the guys wonder about and the women feel somewhat threatened by, because the Aquarian woman is a question within a question. She is not an easy individual to get to know, and in many ways, it is not just others who wonder what she is all about — Ms Aquarius is constantly trying to get to know herself. She has a wide range of interests, values freedom above most things, and is generally comfortable with all levels of society.

While most other signs measure their worth through the way others view them or through their connections with others, Ms Aquarius is like a spring breeze, touching everyone but belonging to no one. She's sweet and charming but sometimes a bit stand-offish, or even distant. Moreover, she's so unpredictable she can easily surprise or even shock you. She has a habit of turning up in the most unusual places, doing the last thing you expect of her. She may act friendly or even be seductive, appealing and flirtatious one moment, then the next moment she may give off a feeling that she doesn't even know that others exist. She is the woman of the zodiac who can run hot and cold more than most, but she has this tendency because she usually has so many important matters or considerations constantly through her mind.

Ms Aquarius does not normally structure her life within the usual boundaries that other women of the zodiac acknowledge or work within. She will get involved in situations or relationships that others would think extreme, unfeminine, unusual or unappealing. She dares to be different and her unconventional attitudes, beliefs and approach can make her many friends and some enemies, too. She can be quite a go-getter and high achiever if she sets her sights on success, and success doesn't usually mean the same thing to her as it means to others.

Ms Aquarius loves a good cause. Whether her cause is to save the whales, build an orphanage or work for the school tuck-shop, she generally wants to serve the world at large, rather than serve her own satisfaction. The big picture or the larger concept often appeal to her much more than trivia or pettiness. She is often a fighter for the underdog and generally is a lot stronger in will than her external countenance may suggest. She especially hates to give in and can be quite a control person if she feels she needs to be.

Males often influence her life in an unexpected way and she has many times had some kind of important revelation, character building or other exchange — or lack of exchange — through the circumstances surrounding her and her father (for both positive and negative effect). Her childhood relationships often shape her independent nature and make an ongoing impact upon the way she handles and structures her relationships.

At school, she probably did things that broke the rules or upset authority in some form because, from an early age, Ms Aquarius has an inborn tendency to do things in new and different ways. Experimentation means a great deal to her. She knows more than ten different routes to the supermarket, rearranges her furniture once every few months and changes her hair style or colour at least once a year. She may wear her dress backwards, join Volunteers Abroad, start an acting career or find a cure for a terminal disease.

There is really no telling where an Aquarian woman is heading and she's the first to admit it. Even if she stays in one spot and seems impervious to change, her thoughts travel vast distances. She has a flexible plan of action but there are so many unexpected occurrences in her life she doesn't rule anything out.

Although extremely independent, she is very interested in others and what makes them tick! She has a special kind of magic that stems from her acceptance of others and her certainty that everyone has something special to offer. She's quite possibly the most popular woman you know but she may also be the loneliest, as well as the most misunderstood. Often Ms Aquarius settles on independence rather than joining a team. However, she loves to work in teams, too — but can find dealing with other people is hard to handle for extended periods (unless she is in a leadership position in the group — and she often is). Whatever Ms Aquarius does, she does it her way. She's a rare gem, a woman of the future, and her originality influences every area of her life.

[How Aquarian women operate]

Social

An Aquarian woman has a reputation for being invited to more parties, special events and weddings than she can possibly attend. When she's in one of her sociable moods she goes to as many as she can. And when she doesn't feel like going out, she stays home and works on her hobbies, writes in her diary or gets lost in a movie. She usually doesn't spend a lot of time with one person and she's often with a small group of friends. She makes friends easily and everywhere she goes. She's knows the names of her dentist's children, sends the guy at the ticket outlet a birthday card each year and is on a first name basis with the tellers at her bank.

She's a graceful 'fairy godmother' type, who loves to circulate her kindness, humanity and generosity among friends and strangers alike. She may not think that she has many enemies or adversaries, but people are often jealous of her and create obstacles behind the scenes and behind her back. But Ms Aquarius has enough power to dissolve most road blocks and when that doesn't work she slips into her magic wings and flies over them. She loves trying new things and will do almost anything at least once. She's curious and her personal research projects take her on all sorts of adventures.

She savours her freedom and her independence and while she's often spontaneous, she can be deliberate in her decisions, too. And by the way, if she asks for your opinion, it's more out of an interest to learn how you think and less because she's seeking your advice. An Aquarian woman doesn't have a typical day, but one of her days off work might look something like this: She has a hot steaming shower and drinks a glass of fresh orange juice; jumps into a pair of jeans that are so outdated, they're stylish; pulls a sweater on — inside out — runs a brush through her hair, puts on her pearl necklace, her hiking boots and a touch of make-up, and heads for the neighbourhood coffee shop to meet two of her friends.

Her afternoon could include a long walk, a matinee, an audition or an art show. She may have to choose between a party, a concert and a play, or she might go to all three. She can change clothes and accessories several times in a day, and each time she creates a look so uncommon that — for better or for worse — she's guaranteed to turn heads.

Love and family

An Aquarian woman can be incredibly confusing in all spheres of life but she's most confusing to those who are trying to develop a romance with her. Most of her dating relationships grow out of friendships and this is one of the reasons it's hard to figure out if her interest is growing or if she's just being extra friendly. She's a natural flirt and when she flashes her smile she's bewitching.

This woman has everything she needs to be a loving and faithful partner but she treasures her freedom and maintains her independence even if she marries her soulmate. She's looking for a lover and a friend. She wants someone who's willing to share some of her interests and she's anxious to try some of his. Any man who's considering taking his friendship with an Aquarian to a more intimate level had better have an abundance of personal security.

No matter how much she loves her partner, she holds on to her other friends — male and female — and thinks nothing of making plans with her friends that don't include her mate. She believes space in a relationship is needed for love to grow. As a rule, an Aquarian woman hopes to find a partner who's as much of an individual as she is or who at least questions things most people take for granted.

Appearances don't matter to her as much as spirit, mind and personality, and she often has her most fulfilling relationships with men who are quite a bit younger or older than her. She's tolerant of all sorts of habits and indiscretions but she won't stay with anyone who is untrue to himself.

In most cases an Aquarian woman eventually gets married, and sometimes more than once. A woman with the influence of Uranus is trusting and understanding, patient and caring. She values honesty and once the commitment is firm, she's faithful and loyal. She treats her husband with the same amount of trust she expects from him. She won't call his office to see if he's really working late and she won't check his pockets for phone numbers, even if he comes home smelling like perfume.

She's not naive, it's just that when she forms a partnership she treats her other half with complete confidence until he gives her a clear reason not to. But, be warned, if a situation becomes intolerable, Ms Aquarius's heart cools quickly and before long she's off on her own again. If you treat her with respect and honesty and don't demand too much attention from her, she's one of the greatest gifts the universe can send into your life.

When an Aquarian decides to embark on the adventure of motherhood she has a number of transitions to make. The idea of having a new life depend on her can be a bit frightening but she adjusts with a little time. She shows her children the same amount of tolerance and respect as she gives to her adult friends and she helps them learn the value of honesty and the importance of questioning what they see and hear — even when she's the one talking.

She rarely punishes her children for mistakes that they admit and she cultivates an open relationship within the family that stands firm, even through adolescence. She's one of the favourite mothers among her kids' friends because she's fun, she listens with genuine interest and she has enough magic dust up her sleeve to turn a frown into a smile. She often has pets, too, that bound all over the place, creating some additional excitement in the household.

Career

An Aquarian can easily spend the first half of her life exploring different jobs, career paths and fields of study. She usually has a deep yearning to earn an income doing something she loves to do. She also likes to do things her own way. So her originality keeps her from seeking a position that demands conformity and her spontaneous nature resists routines.

Many Aquarian women work as freelance artists, writers or photographers and others hire out their services as consultants, run quaint shops or art galleries or work for a florist or in a bakery. (Lots of Aquarian women have extra sensitive noses so they really appreciate the fragrance of flowers and the soothing aroma of fresh baked bread.)

There's a chance she has her own business and it's not unusual for an Aquarian to work at several different jobs to earn a living. Uranus accents her inventiveness and creativity and keeps her on the path of truth. She may be an inventor, a researcher or a scientist or she could pursue something like social work or counselling. There's no shortage of Aquarians in the entertainment business (Ellen DeGeneres, Geena Davis, Bridget Fonda, Heather Graham, Molly Ringwald, Jane Seymour and Cybill Shepherd are all Aquarians) and acting, singing and comedy all appeal to her.

Most Aquarians aren't driven primarily by a desire for money so their career choices tend to reflect their beliefs and interests. Unless she's at a low point in her life, you can almost bet an Aquarian woman is doing a job she likes, or a job she believes makes a difference. She sometimes seems disorganised and there are peaks and valleys in her productivity. But when she's hot, she can set the world on fire with her accomplishments!

Financial

Just when you think an Aquarian woman can't possibly throw you for another mental loop, the topic of money comes up and her reasoning sends you reeling. She's every bit as innovative with how she manages her finances as she is with her clothing and furnishings. Her accountant rarely endorses her methods but grudgingly admits whatever she's doing is working.

Many Aquarians are content to live simple lives with few possessions and little or no debt. Others enjoy life's pleasures and comforts a bit more but they usually won't take out a big loan to buy them. They like having a limited amount of monthly expenses so they have more options for how to spend and save the money that's left over. Occasionally an Aquarian woman will worry about cash-flow, but unless she is going through a divorce settlement or some other kind of financial dilemma, her financial position isn't likely to be the highest on the list of her life's priorities.

She loves to have money in abundance, but if she doesn't have this opportunity to have money to do whatever she wants, she is extremely skilled at living a great life on whatever resources she does have. After all she is one of the more inventive signs of the zodiac so she can transform situations around so that they work well for her, with money or without it. She knows things have a way of working out, and as long as she's focused on her objectives the universe supports her.

Ms Aquarius is often quite lucky with money matters too. She practically falls into investment opportunities that pay high dividends and she's probably won money more than a few times in her life. Some Aquarians become quite wealthy through extraordinary circumstances. An Aquarian woman who's inspired and following her heart moves steadily in the direction of success, accumulating the accolades and profits as she goes.

However, money alone is not enough to make her heart sing. She needs more than money to complete her world — and she will seldom compromise her principles to get money, or if she does, she won't compromise them for longer than she needs to.

Physical

'Now you see her, now you don't' applies to the Aquarian woman. She operates in two ways physically. She will put herself together in a way that puts her physical appearance under wraps and do whatever she can not to be noticed. Or, if there is a need for it, she can turn heads in a way that snaps people wide awake in an instant. Much of her physical charm stems from her innermost light. She has dreamy eyes that sparkle with light and flash with questions and her vitality gives her a fresh and glowing beauty.

Even a quiet Aquarian radiates a high vibration and can shift the atmosphere in a room simply by walking in. She often has smooth, silky skin and soft hair that blows in the wind, or looks as though it has been. Her clothes can often be composed of the widest assortment of bits and pieces and mismatched colours under the sun, moon and stars. She can be incredibly stylish one day and the next day look like she picked her clothes out of a laundry basket in the dark.

Her appearance changes with her moods and she may have more fun mixing than she does matching. She doesn't always care what she wears; she is quite happy feeling more comfortable than stylish. However, when she wants to dress for success or to make an impact, she mostly manages to do this, in a style that is all of her own. Many Aquarian women become fashion trendsetters simply because of their unique, different approach to fashion (with Aquarian Farrah Fawcett being a prime example).

Ms Aquarius comes in many different sizes, shapes and personalities (because she is the most unique individual sign of the zodiac and usually no two Aquarian women are anything alike). However, she probably has a gentle voice and a winning smile. Her movements are flowing and graceful and she's usually agile and strong. Her general disposition is easygoing and she manages to keep her cool under most circumstances. Her outlook on life helps keep her healthy, but she can always benefit by getting more exercise. The majority of her life takes place in her mind, so her body is often ignored. She needs to remember good nutrition, exercise, sunshine and fresh air all increase her mind's capacity to function. Plus, they do wonders for her physical and mental health. But an Aquarian woman is somewhat resistant to advice so rather than encourage her to exercise, invite her to go swimming or hiking with you.

As an Air sign, an Aquarian woman's circulation is vital to her wellbeing. She can keep her system working smoothly by walking each day or going on a leisurely bike ride. Yoga is also a great choice for an Aquarian because it stimulates the spinal column and redistributes the body's vital energies. An Aquarian woman is wise to learn at least two methods of self-relaxation to help her nervous system carry away her stress. Sleepless nights, allergy attacks or stomach disorders are sometimes signs she has tension that needs to be released. Singing, taking photographs, dancing, lying in the sun, writing, deep breathing and meditation can all help to keep an Aquarian in healthy balance.

When she does get sick an Aquarian often seeks the assistance of alternative medicine or naturopathic remedies. She might use acupuncture, massage techniques or other therapies which work with the meridians that carry energy through the body and release pent up tension and emotional blocks. She often benefits by taking vitamins, and herbal supplements, organic fruit, and vegetable juices give her system a big boost.

As a Water-bearer, she's naturally drawn to the seashore but if it's too far to go, soaking in a hot bath and drinking crystal clear water can help her to relax.

An Aquarian woman sometimes has problems with her knees, shins and ankles and she could be susceptible to varicose veins. She's also somewhat accident-prone, especially while she's functioning on automatic pilot. But overall she has the potential to be a picture of health if she takes care of herself.

Mental

The mental planes are the centre of Ms Aquarian's world — that is why it is so important that she keeps her mind entertained — thinking healthy positive thoughts — and avoids any pastimes or relationships that cause her mental unrest or dilemma. Alcohol and drugs have a negative effect upon her mental outlook and she needs to take care of her mind (through the thoughts she thinks and the pastimes she involves her mind in) as if it were the most delicate orchid.

She is gifted intellectually, although she may not be rational in her thinking. She's broad-minded, analytical and very inventive. She often views the world from a higher vantage point and she can frequently see the hidden order in what appears to be chaos. This perspective gives her a great sense of freedom in her thinking and influences the way she lives. She's comfortably independent and nearly everything about her is just slightly off-centre.

She's a riddle to others and a mystery to herself. She probably knows her thoughts have the power to create and transform her world, but she frequently seeks diversions to avoid hearing her mind speak. An Aquarian woman is unbiased, not judgmental and highly tolerant of everyone she knows and meets. Her friendly manner and honest approach help her conduct her informal surveys on human behaviour and her progressive nature pushes ahead through any problem she confronts.

Unfortunately, the Aquarian woman can be a tough critic of herself, and she can suffer from high anxieties, panic attacks and insomnia if she loses faith in herself, destiny or others. Sometimes she has to remind herself to be grateful for what she does have (or has accomplished), rather than focus on the things that may not be going to plan. She is often a lot better off than she gives herself credit for. The moment she remembers to count her blessings, her life changes because she starts to put her mind-magic to work in a positive way. However, if she focuses on dark clouds, she usually attracts more of the same.

Spiritual

Being of an inquisitive turn of mind, the topic of religion is often a matter that the Aquarian woman puts a great deal of thought into. After her initial exposure to established religions, Ms Aquarius can become quite alternative in outlook and may even join up with others in forming a new kind of spiritual group or religion herself. She likes to be different, and she appreciates and recognises the value of having an individual viewpoint of life, so where any religion tends to put rules, regulations and routines around connecting to the higher powers, she often finds it difficult to conform to doctrine or authority.

When she has had the time to think about all the various options and possibilities, often the Aquarian woman decides to keep her mind open when it comes to religion. Sometimes she may, however, adopt the viewpoint of the agnostic, and if so, she holds firm to this belief until she finds evidence for adopting another stance.

However, if she develops her spiritual insight and intuition, her own mystical or magical life experiences could change her mind. It is her personal connection with the holy areas of life which hit her religious or spiritual heart. While she may learn from personal spiritual experience or insights, she looks for her individual experience or truth in religion and she's sceptical of all forms of blind faith.

She knows the finite human mind can't understand the infinite universe and she might even get angry about the way theologians pass off their theories as great truths. Her investigations expose many of the lies society has passed down through the ages, but the closer she gets to the truth, the more she realises most people prefer the illusion.

She is wise enough to know the truth is always in the hands of the few, not the many, so she quietly tucks her discoveries into her spiritual scrapbook. If she's diligent and attracts the teachers she desires along her path, an Aquarian woman can find the answers to her deepest questions and shine light upon her darkest fears.

The Aquarius man

Getting to know an Aquarian man is a little like finding your way through an intricate maze the size of Australia. He has so many highways and byways running through his mind you'll need a good map and a fast car, just to keep up with him.

The Aquarian man is not going to be a person who you can figure out in a moment, a day, a week, a year or even a lifetime. More of an enigma than an open book, this man usually keeps a tremendous amount bottled up inside. Generally, he has a great deal on his mind, and he likes it that way! His varied and abundant thoughts provide him with a magical means for creating a private domain or world, all of his own.

Moreover, his musing, concepts and mental daydreams are not idle thinking or wasted energy. These constant mental churnings afford him his most brilliant realisations, insights and breakthroughs. He also enjoys having inner dialogue-type conversations with himself, and in the course of these conversations, he can come up with theories, decisions and breakthroughs which revolutionise his existence — and sometimes even change the world.

He may have many mates, good friends, associates and close contacts in his life, and he often enjoys these relationships immensely, but they can exist, for him, more on a social superficial level rather than on a close intensely personal one. While there may be many times he wishes he could share his real thoughts and the private aspects of his world with others, it is unlikely that many can ever enter or share his private space. On the rare occasion that he does meet a like-minded person, he often truly has found his best mate or friend, his soulmate or his greatest teacher or student.

When Mr Aquarius truly connects with someone on a deeply personal level, from that moment his life alters quite dramatically. However, the instances of this magical mind connection, or mind-body-and-spirit connection, taking place, are few and far between. When he is really out of beat or out of tune with those around him, he can spend a lot of time feeling a little like a stranger in a strange world.

He is the introverted extrovert, meaning that he gives out lots of mixed messages on all kinds of levels. However, in his general outlook, the Aquarian man is usually one of a kind! He can appear in any profession, but is likely to have an 'I'll do it my way' approach to whatever he does. He can appear a traditionalist in some ways, but then he will do something that breaks all the rules. He is broad-minded, unpredictable and controversial.

His patience, tolerance and amiability give the impression he's tranquil to the core, but his behaviour rarely reflects what's really going on beneath the surface. He is no ordinary, everyday kind of guy. He is the kind whose still waters run extremely deep. He is driven by his search for truth (or at least truth in the terms that mean something to him), and he won't hesitate to challenge an expert or an authority if he thinks they're in error. His questioning mind rarely rests and he believes each person is responsible for finding his or her own way in life.

He lives by standards and ethics he has devised for himself and, chances are, his personal guidelines have little to do with society's rules and expectations. People may see his approach to some situations as selfish, but because he isn't one to attempt to change his course to suit others, even if he is being selfish, it isn't a mean-spirited characteristic on his part. The truth is that he doesn't know how to live any other way. It is easy for him to upset or offend others.

He's ahead of his time and his ideas and behaviour can trigger a wide array of emotions and opinions from those who value conformity and follow the ways of tradition.

Although he loves his private space and time alone, he can, nevertheless, be quite fascinated by others. He has a gift for discovering something special about each person he meets and he treats most of the people he meets as if they were already his friends. He finds great satisfaction in offering his assistance, and he goes out of his way to do favours and make thoughtful gestures for others. He is often a group organiser or a team leader, as he deals well with groups and team spirit activities. However, he often prefers to deal with society as a whole, rather than as individuals, because when he has dealt with individuals in the past, they have frequently disappointed him.

[How Aquarian men operate]

Social

Getting to know an Aquarian man is a little like finding your way through an intricate maze the size of Australia. He has so many highways and byways running through his mind you'll need a good map and a fast car just to keep up with him. And while the Aquarian is sometimes accused of trying to be confusing or mysterious, he is often most perplexing to himself. He's a social party hopper one day and dreads the thought of budging from the solitude of his home the next.

He's the holder of life's secrets and people are drawn to him for as many different reasons as there are stars in the heavens. He treats everyone with the same amount of respect, curiosity and ease, and people who normally feel uncomfortable with strangers respond to him like a long lost friend. If you have a hard time finding people who understand you, you will probably feel an immediate bond with an Aquarian man.

Even people who are in the public eye can relax, let down their hair and put up their feet when they're with him. He's not particularly impressed with celebrity, fame or fortune and he usually accepts life's gifts and lessons with some degree of objectivity. He knows most things are not what they appear to be, so he doesn't get as worked up about the past or the future as most people do.

You're just as likely to see him at a black-tie dinner as you are to see him sitting on a park bench, sharing a sandwich and discussing the meaning of life with a bag lady. He's an interested listener and is great at helping people arrive at their own conclusions by asking them the right questions. He finds the human mind fascinating and can listen to someone else's thoughts and theories for hours on end. The more he learns about other people, the more he understands himself. He often asks his friends for their opinions, but he's usually not looking for their advice. He wants to be sure he has thought of as many options as he can and hearing other people's ideas can sometimes inspire his own.

He enjoys all sorts of activities, parties and games. Variety is a staple, rather than a spice, for an Aquarian. So he follows the trail of novelty making his own innovations along the way. He probably spends more of his time in mental pursuits than in physical exercise, but if he has an interest in sports he can be a very talented sportsperson. An Aquarian wants to learn every position on the team and play them all well. His composure makes him a powerful contender and his wide outlook keeps him from dropping the ball or letting down his team when under pressure.

Love and family

An Aquarian man can take you to the furthest reaches of the galaxy but he'll probably sometimes leave you feeling as though you are tagging along for the ride, rather than sharing the experience with him. If you complain that he isn't giving you quite enough attention, he understands and sympathises with your feelings — but that usually doesn't change a thing. If you have fallen under the enchanting spell of an Aquarian man you will need to widen your view and realise that being with an Aquarian man is not going to always be a time of 'moonlight and roses'. You will have times when you will need to entertain yourself, as he is likely to have many things on his mind.

Just because he is preoccupied doesn't mean that he doesn't commit himself to you, either. When an Aquarian man falls for you, he let's you know his feelings, but he just doesn't feel that once he has shared his heart and soul with you, he has to do this on a regular basis.

If you are the kind of woman who needs heaps of affection, reassurance and attention, he may not be able to satisfy this emotional need. You may even have times when you think he is a bit too distant to be able to keep you happy, and maybe you need to go out and continue your quest for true love. But once you look into the deep, soulful eyes of an Aquarian the criteria for your ideal man may melt into a distant memory and you will realise that he is going to be an unusual romantic experience, but one that you cannot simply resist anyway.

He is totally different from other men, so he operates with a different set of criteria in every department of his life. Romantically (if and when he wants to be), he can be quite irresistible. An Aquarian man has quiet charisma and charming mystique. Even a woman who has sworn off relationships can get pulled into his aura like a magnet. I remember the day I came home and found two messages on my answering machine from one of my Capricorn girlfriends. The first message said she was taking a break from the dating game for a while to focus on her career. The second message — that came in only two hours after the first — said she met this amazing man who was an Aquarian and she was already crazy about him.

This man can be the most irresistible of all and it is often his independence that surrounds him like an invisible cloak, or his detached kind of sex appeal, that makes him so attractive. There's nothing like a mystery (or a sense that a man isn't really that available to you) to keep a zodiac girl on her cosmic toes — and Mr Aquarian does just that.

He's very popular, too. The Aquarian knows people all over town and has more friends and acquaintances than he can count. However, he also has his quiet side, and often has a retreat or some place he disappears to, when he needs his space. He has lots of associates, acquaintances and friends (but possibly very few friends that he would truly call 'close' ones).

Women number among some of his greatest friendships, too, and in fact, some of Mr Aquarius's greatest love affairs are begun as friendships. And be forewarned, as spontaneous as he is, he hesitates to make any sort of commitment no matter how casual. He may spend every Saturday night with the same woman, but that leaves six days open for just about anything else. He won't lie to a direct question, but he also won't offer you details or explanations about what he does when he isn't with you, unless he wants you to know.

An Aquarian man takes his time where marriage is concerned and if a woman is too impatient to wait for him, so be it. He'll wish her well with no hard feelings because he knows that before long someone else will be bidding for his heart. Sometimes an Aquarian holds out longer than he intended, though, and may be a bachelor well into his fifties. But he has no regrets and if he truly decides he wants a mate, he can easily find one, regardless of his age or condition. Most Aquarian men do marry eventually, but they usually resist the first few urges to propose.

Once this man says, 'I do', he means it. He's honest and loyal and he accepts all sorts of differences in opinions, beliefs, education and upbringing. He's the faithful type and he trusts his wife beyond a shadow of a doubt. He's most content with a woman who's independent, alert and open-minded. She needs to have a life of her own, complete with her own friends and pastimes.

He loves spending time with his lover but there are still a few million people he hasn't had the pleasure of meeting yet so he can't possibly stay home every night. But he's a warm and loving husband and on those occasions when his wife complains she's married to a ghost, he can make his presence felt in so many delightful ways, she's certain he is alive and very well.

As a father, an Aquarian is a rare find. He treats his children with love and open affection and he's proud to be their friend and provider. He sees himself as a fortunate man entrusted with the care of nurturing young minds and he's careful not to force his own values and ethics upon them. He believes his role is to help them find their own way in the world and he does the best he can. He has just as much pride in their victories as he has compassion for their losses and when they have something to say, he really listens.

Career

He is extremely creative and can work in just about any area or field that takes his fancy. He also is the kind who can work at a career that doesn't really interest him because he can have his mind elsewhere while he goes about his work anyway. His interest in people often leads him into social service types of professions. He may find his niche in a non-profit organisation or in some aspect of social work or counselling. He frequently works for human or animal rights and he probably puts in a lot more time than he gets paid for but money is rarely his highest priority.

If he is making a big income it's often just a side benefit to doing what he really loves and wants to do. His ability to tune into the genius energy provided by his ruling planet Uranus heightens his creativity and inventiveness, and Aquarians have made some of the most amazing inventions and discoveries (remember, Charles Darwin and Thomas Edison were Aquarians). His wide-ranging but organised thoughts can lead to a successful writing career, as it did for Aquarians Lewis Carroll, Charles Dickens and Jules Verne.

In addition, many Aquarians are philosophers, sociologists, psychologists and anthropologists. If he doesn't pursue one of the sciences he may be drawn to the arts. He has talents he has yet to discover and there's a chance he has a good hand and eye for photography, sketching or painting (Norman Rockwell was an Aquarian).

Some Aquarians have an innate desire to become actors (like Aquarians John Travolta, Tom Selleck, Gene Hackman and Paul Newman), and he may have staged performances for his family when he was still in primary school. The idea of getting to play different characters and try on different personalities is very appealing to him and more than a few Aquarians are hot box-office attractions.

He is often quite a brilliant businessman, too (but not always), and can turn his career into a really big money-spinner if he has that business knack. But whatever he does, you can be sure he's doing it the way he thinks it should be done, regardless of the rest of the world's opinion.

Financial

Money plays an interesting part in the life of an Aquarian but it might be more interesting to you than it is to him. Chances are, he can take it or leave it and this outlook meets with disapproval and raised eyebrows from his accountants. He wants to earn enough to pay his bills and buy what he needs but he usually isn't overly interested in material pleasures. If he seeks money it's often for some philanthropic purpose or to fund his travels and expeditions. He likes to take on jobs that cover most of his expenses and he prefers to have others look after all the financial details of his everyday existence.

However, if this doesn't work for him, he may become an incredibly efficient and effective money manager. Usually after someone else has either cheated him or dropped the financial ball on him, he suddenly becomes inspired enough to learn to master his own financial possibilities and options.

While Mr Aquarius can be extremely generous, he does not like wastefulness. He does his best to avoid frivolous expenses and he finds extravagance ghastly. In fact, it may be one of the few things he has a difficult time putting up with. He tries to avoid spending up big on his credit cards and borrowing money because he feels claustrophobic or overwhelmed when he's in debt. The Aquarian man can have a knack for attracting money from the oddest places when he needs it.

Fate often favours him when it comes to money matters. He may be about to head to the bank to take out the dreaded loan, and a few moments before he leaves he will receive a cheque in the mail from someone he helped five years earlier, or someone slips an anonymous money order under his door that says 'Thanks'. The expression 'somebody up there, likes him' often applies to Mr Aquarius in the realm of finances.

As an Aquarian gets older he begins to see more value in making investments and if he can afford it, he hires a financial consultant to help him sort through his options. In his younger days, however, he usually just wings his way through his finances — and these eventually do turn out well for him, but more by luck than good management.

Physical

The Aquarian man's appearance is as unpredictable as his actions. He wears what he feels like wearing, whether it's socially acceptable, appropriate or stylish. On some days he looks absolutely in vogue, but unless he has a real interest in fashion those days will be few and far between. He's usually the one at a casual party wearing a tailored suit with tennis shoes; and he's the one at the awards banquet wearing a wrinkled shirt and slacks that don't match. And there's no guarantee his socks will match, either, or that his hair will be combed.

However, the surprise is that he still manages to look terrific. His off-the-cuff attitude to clothes and appearance often makes him a trendsetter or leader in style (because others try to copy his flair for looking different or unusual). He doesn't pay much attention to what others think about his looks anyway. Most Aquarian men have too many other things on their mind to give much thought to their wardrobes or appearance.

He's physically stronger than he looks, light on his feet and sometimes as graceful as a cat — when he's paying attention. But when his mind takes off for the cosmos he can forget about his body and stumble over his own feet. Even when his mind is with his body he may overlook his physical needs. It's not uncommon for an Aquarian to realise at midnight that he forgot to eat all day. He can also build up nervous energy until he suddenly feels so restless that he can barely sit still. He needs to get moderate exercise every day and make it a point to eat light, nutritious meals even if they're at odd hours of the day and night.

Aquarians are Air signs, so a strong circulatory system is vital for their good health. A sluggish circulation can create all sorts of nagging problems so it's important for the Aquarian man to fit aerobic exercise into his busy day. But when it comes to physical exertion, moderation is an Aquarian's key to staying in shape. Too much exercise or overexertion can have a negative affect and result in hives, allergies or other nervous disorders. His calm appearance makes him look stress-free but he can be high-strung internally.

Even so, an Aquarian man usually has good stamina, a healthy heart and excellent recuperation powers as a gift from nature — in fact, everything he needs to live a long and healthy life if he's willing to put just a bit of effort into it. Many Aquarians develop an interest in team sports and often the sports he likes most are associated with water. He might enjoy canoeing, being part of a rowing crew, swimming, diving or playing water polo. He's wise to protect his knees, shins and ankles in any sport or activity where they can be hurt because Aquarians have an inclination towards sprains and breaks of those body parts.

Mental

This is the zodiac male man with a mind of his own, and very few external conditions or influences can sway him once he has his mind made up. His mind is his true home and universe and he loves orbiting around inside his solar system of thoughts, as much as possible. A natural lateral thinker, an Aquarian man can step outside of a problem and see it from all sides, rather than seeing it only from his own point of view. This is a special gift and it serves him very well. But it also has drawbacks because he sees so many choices he doesn't know which one to pick. Consequently, he can be the stalemate champion when it comes to making decisions that don't need immediate attention.

Once he has put his thoughts together, he usually doesn't like to unscramble them and start off in a new direction again. He can be quite a stickler when it comes to having a fixed point of view. Changing his mind can be the toughest challenge for him. Amazingly, for such a widely diverse thinker, he can become quite stuck in his thinking at times and it can take some kind of major drama or turning point in his life to arise before he will alter his decisions or way of thinking.

Surprisingly though, an Aquarian's habits of reserving judgment, being patient and showing tolerance, don't stand in the way of his spontaneity. There's nothing like the fresh winds of change to an Aquarian, and change often does him the world of good, too.

His ruling planet, Uranus, connects him with the potential to be a creative genius and he has every possibility of imagining and inventing an object or method that can change people's lives. But sometimes an Aquarian is so ahead of his time his ideas are scoffed at and ridiculed. That won't stop him, though. He follows his own intuitions and no one's opinion has much power over him.

Spiritual

An Aquarian's views on spirituality can be as unconventional as the rest of his lifestyle and he has a natural ability to upset people who follow a particular religious doctrine. He doesn't criticise their beliefs but he won't politely nod and agree with them, either. He's a spiritual scientist and explorer in many ways and he examines and compares different faiths and religious writings in an objective manner. He rarely accepts the traditional teachings of religion in totality but he might pick bits and pieces from many religions and merge them together to form his own unique belief system.

The less conventional, quite individualised religions or spiritual beliefs often appeal to him, more than the mass-consciousness-designed ones. He may become involved in a spiritual quest himself. However, his quest is likely to be one that he keeps to himself. He may be a spiritual or religious student for a long time before others know of his involvement.

The typical Aquarian rarely wants to convert anyone else to his way of thinking because he knows everyone has their own light to follow. It's ironic that a number of religious sects have been founded on the belief systems of Aquarians after their deaths. The Church of New Jerusalem, for example, was founded by the followers of Aquarian, Emanuel Swedenborg after he died. Swedenborg himself had no interest in forming a new religious sect based on his beliefs. He was just living the way he felt inspired to live. But there's something in the glint of an Aquarian man's eyes that makes people believe he knows the way.

He sees the great questions of life as engaging puzzles and might put some time into researching them. He loves unravelling a mystery and his search for universal truths leads him on to many different planes of thought. Born under the sign that rules astrology, many evolved Aquarians know the secrets of the stars and that the stars are the original version of the greatest story ever told — a story that was later personified and translated into human terms.

The Aquarius baby

> Throw away those 'How to bring up baby' books — an Aquarian baby doesn't do anything 'by the book'.

An Aquarian baby is a truly unique individual, and no book has ever been written that will be able to tell you how to understand or care for your Aquarian offspring. When all is said and done, the onus is on you to closely observe and get to know this little person for yourself.

You will need to learn to do things spontaneously and to handle the most unusual and unexpected of conditions. The Aquarian baby is no ordinary child. He or she is a special individual who requires you to learn a new way of dealing with responsibilities and parenthood. No matter what you're expecting, there is wisdom in maintaining an open expectation about parenting and exactly how to fulfil the needs of your beautiful but unpredictable bundle of joy.

Chances are, you'll experience a lot of change in your everyday life, routine and everything else because your Aquarian baby is going to turn out to be (in some form or another) your truest and possibly toughest teacher in life. Its way of doing this teaching may be subtle or not so subtle, but new realms of feeling and understanding, and possibly intensified compassion and even tolerance, are about to become a big part of your reality. This little one is designed and ordained to teach you some new beliefs, philosophies and life-patterns even before it's walking and talking.

You'll learn these things whether you want to or not and your lessons will come in a variety of forms involving dimensions of both pain and pleasure! Born under the planet Uranus (the astrological link to the individual expression of genius), the Aquarian baby will operate in a league of its own and in many ways it can perform miracles and change the world, simply because this child has its own unique way of expressing itself and will always do things its own way.

While this infant doesn't follow the standard rules, it's not necessarily a rebel, either. Its rule-breaking is more lateral than literal. Its spirit makes it more a free-thinker, attuned by fate to its own brand of unique individuality. This is the baby who is likely to be the most misunderstood or most misinterpreted in its needs and desires because it operates on a special wavelength — one that is true to itself, rather than designed to fit into the world at large.

If the little one begins its individual approach to living on planet Earth in true Aquarian style, then from its conception through to its actual birth, the events and circumstances that surround its origins and beginnings are likely to be different from what is most generally expected about this time period of a baby's formation and coming into being. This occurs because this soul has its own way of doing things, even if doing things the proven way appears to be the best way. This is the baby of the unexpected and the unusual, and a strong sense of self generally surrounds this individual from birth through to old age.

The Aquarian is, after all, the most original thinker of the zodiac. Consequently throughout gestation, its birth and its first few months, its growth and evolvement may be somewhat of a mystery or puzzle. The lesson this tiny person is destined to teach you (and the doctors or whomsoever else comes into contact with it) is that you need to come up with new ways to understand, guide and most of all, deal with your own emotions as you learn.

That's why, from the moment you find out this baby is on the way, you can't really set plans, patterns and routines and stick to them. When the baby is earthbound and has arrived, the same rule (that there are no rules where this tot is concerned) continues as far as feeding or sleeping go. Sometimes this infant will eat and drink like it's a giant, other times it won't have any interest at all in food. This baby will be a sound sleeper one week, then want to stay up bright and alert — no sleep needed at all — for the next week. The best thing you can do with an Aquarian baby is learn to compromise from the start.

Once it moves into the phase of growth that involves walking and talking, this little one's talent for setting its own speed and pace will be very obvious! He or she will either do everything at a particularly early age or be extremely slow about getting its walking and talking in full motion. Whatever path it chooses, for this baby both timings are perfect. Remember, your offspring has an internal inner-destiny clock that runs at exactly the right speed for the baby's complete and happy development.

Time has different rules and meanings where the Aquarian baby is concerned and it has a tendency to respond to its own unique inner clock, rather than be run by any outside influence (an attitude and behaviour trait that is likely to continue on throughout the rest of its life).

Therefore, if you want your Aquarian infant to be the same as everyone else's baby, you're going to be waging an unwinnable battle against certain powerful astrological forces. These forces decree that your child is a world unto itself and the earthlyworld has to fit in with it, rather than the other way around.

If you try to make your little Aquarian fit in, you will also make life a more difficult experience unnecessarily. Remember you're the student with this baby, whether you choose to be or not. With the Aquarian babe in your home, there will be an adventure a day and a lesson to learn as well, but also more than one or two miracles or mysteries to marvel at.

Being born under the sign of Aquarius (which means that unusual or unexpected influences are powerful foundations in this small individual's destiny), this baby's birth is likely to be a lot different than expected. Aquarians of every age are notorious for being early or late and so you can be fairly certain that your baby will not show up at the predicted time for its birth. Before this infant is born it loves to create an element of surprise around everything it does and to make those around it begin to second-guess its next move.

Be warned, surprise is a constant companion when you're dealing with this little babe. Just when you think you have it all organised or figured out the most incredible twist or turn of events will arise to see things moving in a different direction. You need to loosen up and let go of expectations to make this baby really feel at home and stop yourself from over-reacting to minor dramas.

As mentioned earlier, this child will turn into Rip Van Winkle one week then not want to sleep for days on end. To flow in harmony with this newly landed earth angel, simply live each day a step, a minute, an hour at a time — and put away your own assumptions for now. You can't expect anything to go as planned and you have to be prepared to go with what is, not what you assume or predict. Sooner or later you'll begin to appreciate that almost everything you think you should do, or need to do, has to be reconsidered on a moment-to-moment basis.

From the very beginning, even without it being noticeable, this baby will have a definite mind and development program uniquely its own. It has a rhythm and inner dance beat that only it can hear and it lives by it. To try to alter this and make your bundle of joy similar to others is to try to turn the tides in the ocean. You will just make life tough and unhappy for everyone, particularly your little one. Allow your infant to be the 'individual' it is destined to be. Left to develop at its own pace, this is a well-adjusted and happy baby. It just wants to do things its own way, and that's exactly what will happen — eventually.

The Aquarius toddler through teen

Aquarians are magical and charming children. The world is their classroom and they love to be surrounded by variety and diversity of all types.

Aquarius toddlers, by the time they're two, are already asserting themselves and taking control over as much as they can. This is the little one who will want to try to do everything independantly. Of course, doing things for themselves at the age of two or three usually means more work for their parents or care-givers.

Spills and accidents are par for the course in these early years until your little Water-bearer becomes a bit bigger and has more strength and dexterity. Most small Aquarians want to hold their own cups, wash their own faces and decide which clothes to wear. They aren't trying to be difficult; they just have a clear sense of what they want and what they don't want. And they definitely want things to be done their way!

It's usually a bit unsettling to the mother or father of a three-year-old Aquarian to hear how certain and absolute this child sometimes sounds, but you'd better get used to it because this isn't a phase — it's a way of life. There may be times when you find it frustrating but try to remember that for an Aquarian, the 'I want to do things my way' attitude leads to plenty of original creations and lots of personal success. Try to supply your little one with lots of safe, fun and healthy options. Little Water-bearers love playing in the water, for instance, so plan some extra time for their bath so they can play with all of their bath toys. These kids often are interested in learning to swim at an early age and it's a great idea to teach them because they're drawn like magnets to swimming pools, ponds and creeks.

Other favourite activities for Aquarians around the ages of three or four are playing with modelling clay, colouring and painting, drawing and playing musical instruments. The xylophone, harmonica, and tin flute are sure be around as long as there are Aquarians.

Aquarians are magical and charming children. They're sometimes a bit precocious but that's part of their mystery and obvious uniqueness. These children stand out from the crowd by virtue of some intangible essence you can't quite put your finger on. They're just a bit different and they have a special sort of creative energy around them all the time.

There are any number of things an adult can learn and discover through the eyes of an Aquarius child and there will be moments when you feel as if your child has the wisdom of the ages. Help your Aquarian to grow up as slowly as he or she can.

By the age of four or five, your Aquarian is ready and usually willing to go off to pre-school. They enjoy the variety of toys and activities and they like meeting other children and experiencing a new world.

They might rebel against the rules a bit but many Aquarians are more willing to follow the rules at school than they are at home. It's not too soon to have a frank talk with your Aquarian about the choices they make. Help them understand that each of their choices has consequences and that it's a good idea to find out about the consequences before they make a choice.

Aquarians understand this type of logic, but you'll need to follow through with these children or they'll soon disregard your parental authority altogether. For example, if you say they must put away their building blocks before they can go outside to play with their friends — stand your ground. The best you can give your Aquarian is a firm foundation of guidelines and rules and a flexible array of possibilities within those guidelines.

Water-bearers tend to be highly intelligent so even when they're in Year One or Year Two they're old enough to understand some complex ideas. In fact, Aquarians often do better with abstract thinking than they do with concrete concepts that are carved in stone. It's their nature to question things many people automatically accept as true. And as annoying or embarrassing as that can be at times, it also why so many Aquarians leave an immortal impact on the world.

Don't be surprised if your Aquarian has a vivid or graphic imagination that shows up in school artwork and written reports or essays. This creative streak can really start blossoming when they're seven or eight and begin to creatively share their ideas and concepts in words and pictures. I should mention that Aquarians think it's more fun to be creative than to be accurate, so their writing, and even their verbal accounts of events, will tend to be exaggerated in some ways. The best thing to do is keep them supplied with lots of paper, computer disk space or art materials so they have a ready outlet for their creative expression.

As Aquarians enter adolescence they usually begin diverting some of their creative energy into their social lives. Aquarians love to have lots of friends who are all very different from each other. The world is their classroom and they enjoy being surrounded by variety and diversity of all types. Lots of Aquarians become particularly chatty at this age in their attempt to communicate their thoughts and questions to the world and get a response. In fact, this yearning to communicate — to understand others and to be understood — is a running theme in an Aquarian's life.

While other adolescents and teens are struggling to fit in, the Aquarian is wearing different-coloured socks, trying out an outrageous new hair style and modelling the styles that will be all the rage in about five years! But most Aquarians' parents have less trouble with their children's appearance than they have with their opinions. Young Aquarians love to challenge traditions and belief systems — particularly yours. Just hang on because this ride gets a bit bumpier before it smooths out again.

The teen years tend to be the most difficult for you and your Aquarian to endure and grow through. This is his or her last chance to assert their own authority before going to uni or moving out of the house. They spread their wings and flap around a lot during these years, mostly in preparation for being on their own for real. It may be tempting at these times to humble your Aquarian with a smart remark or reminder that they're still living under your roof, but these kinds of comments will just widen the gap between you.

There are plenty of other people standing in line to challenge and humble an Aquarian. You're better off focusing on being his or her friend because the same Aquarians who have been saying they can't wait to be on their own tend to get worried as the time approaches. So no matter how cocky a young adult Aquarian may act, you can be sure there's a bit of vulnerability and uncertainty lurking underneath that mask.

One of the best ways to help prepare your Aquarian for the world is to help him or her to value education and learning. The more they learn about their opportunities and choices in life, the better they will be at making choices and decisions that are in their best interests. The more an Aquarian learns about life and the laws of the universe the more fulfilling their life can be.

The Aquarians who are the most fulfilled tend to be focused on some great question or research or on bringing to fruition some dream or goal that's bigger than they are. Help them to realise they're stars in the making, and they'll radiate with energy, creativity and a special something that is all their own.

PISCES

[20 february — 20 march]

pisces pisces pisces pisces pisces pisces
pisces pisces pisces pisces pisces pisces
pisces pisces pisces pisces pisces pisces
pisces pisces pisces pisces pisces pisces

pisces pisces pisces pisces pisces pisces
pisces pisces pisces pisces pisces pisces
pisces pisces pisces pisces pisces pisces
pisces pisces pisces pisces pisces pisces
pisces pisces pisces pisces pisces pisces
pisces pisces pisces pisces pisces pisces

element: water

planetary ruler: neptune

symbol: the fish

quality: mutable (= flexibility)

colours: greens and deep blues

gem: chrysolite and moonstone

best companions: cancer and scorpio

strongest virtues: intuition, adaptability and

creative approach to life

traits to improve: self-indulgence,

over-sensitive responses, lack of faith

in the future

deepest desire: to meet your true soulmate

Pisces celebrities

Albert Einstein, Elizabeth Taylor, Robert Altman, Drew Barrymore,

Ivana Trump, Peter Fonda, Joanne Woodward, Mikhail Gorbachev,

Prince Edward of England, Rupert Murdoch, Billy Zane, Michael Caine,

Vanessa Williams, Prince Albert of Monaco, Edward (Ted) Kennedy,

Antonio Sabato Jr, Bruce Willis, Sharon Stone, Cindy Crawford,

Sidney Poitier, Jennifer Love Hewitt, Quincy Jones, Chelsea Clinton,

Niki Taylor, Jon Bon Jovi, Ivan Lendl, Kurt Cobain, Liza Minnelli,

Billy Crystal, Rob Lowe, Kurt Russell, Glenn Close, Holly Hunter,

Shaquille O'Neal, Willam Hurt, George Harrison, Michael Chang,

Michael Bolton, Patsy Kensit, Spike Lee, Jerry Lewis, Nina Simone,

Joanne Woodward, Lynn Redgrave, Barbara Feldon, Dana Delaney,

Nat 'King' Cole, Aidan Quinn, Andrew Shue, Queen Latifah, Téa Leoni,

Chuck Norris, Ron Howard, Tom Arnold and Tony Robbins.

[General outlook]

Pisces enter the new millennium excitedly juggling an abundance of ideas, jobs, relationships, hobbies and emotions. You have never had so many opportunities knocking at your door. But before you say yes to all of them, make it a priority to streamline your life. Concentrate on quality, not quantity. It is most important to keep your eye firmly fixed on specific goals, targets or outcomes throughout the introductory years of the new millennium, otherwise it will be far too easy to be sidetracked by situations that are not of true or real value to you.

In particular, you need to make a closure where an old romance, job or living situation is concerned. Putting an old ghost to rest will allow you to move forwards towards new experiences. There are many wonderful things occurring in your astro-sphere. Make a wish list for every area of your life for the next five years. Reach for the stars now; don't be shy to ask for even your most secret or previously seemingly impossible type of desires to be fulfilled. We are entering a new millennium on planet Earth and it's time to make your dreams come true.

Romance

Pisces float sweetly on cloud nine as new millennium love fever hits. Married Pisces discover that a mutual goal or project (possibly raising children, planning a holiday, or buying a house together) brings them closer to their partner in love and companionship.

Single Pisces exude an attractive gentleness that others find hard to ignore. Whatever your relationship status, you Pisces are among the lucky ones who know that love really does make the world go round. If love doesn't initially come to you as the new millennium starts to progress, be patient. Given time you will discover that Cupid does have you positioned high up on his hit list of 'must do's' where firing his love arrows is concerned in the new millennium.

Health

Being so sensitive, Pisces are a little like a human sponge. When other people upset you or make you angry, you tend to absorb their bad and most negative vibrations. Your health and wellbeing are finely attached to your emotions and when you are emotionally out of balance, health-related problems are likely to arise. Know that when you calm your mind, you heal your body as well. This entrance time to the new millennium is a wonderful time to learn more about the mind-body-emotion connection. Positive affirmations, meditation, yoga and other relaxation techniques will work wonderfully for you now and help you to turn any health problem into a positive energy flow again.

Finance

Although the new millennium begins with some cash-flow ups-and-downs, don't lose hope or feel financially defeated! There are wonderful monetary opportunities soon about to arise around you, Pisces, and with a little effort you can make leaps and bounds in your financial world. Do, however, examine your attitudes to money and wealth. If you don't believe you deserve abundance, then you won't receive it. For your sign, attitude is everything. Be positive and you'll attract whatever it is you desire. And, if you think you are lucky, you will be lucky with money (and other areas of your life), too.

Career

As the new millennium begins, making a positive impression at your workplace is more important than you realise. And although you most likely have the goods or talent already in terms of professional experience, convincing your employer or co-workers that you are a star performer is going to be all-important. Don't be shy about promoting yourself. This is one of those phases where blowing your own horn is absolutely necessary. Also be aware that your new millennium horoscope indicates that many of you Pisces will find your focus and attention is drawn away from career and directed more towards developing home, family and personal areas. This may encourage you to work from home, or commence a business with family or friends.

[Millennium wildcards to watch for]

The new millennium brings with it the feeling that anything is possible for Pisces. While it's wonderful to be open to new experiences be aware that many fleeting castle-in-the-air ideas are competing for your attention. Before jumping blindly into a new romance, job or living situation, listen to your inner feelings. Your heart never lies, so tune into your intuition. Armed with inner certainty that you are truly following your own star of destiny (rather than following society or other people's rules or dictates), you can't go wrong.

You're oceans away from others in your attitudes, beliefs and desires, and it's not uncommon for you to feel like a fish out of water.

Your sign, Pisces, rules sixth sense, rainbows, mists, clouds, fantasies, dreams, and illusion. Therefore, the surreal and hidden realms affect you more than any other sign of the zodiac — except for maybe Scorpios. Fantasy means a great deal to you, and may even hold more value to you than what is called 'reality'. Why is the invisible and intangible world so powerfully connected to your sign? Because your ruling planet is Neptune. Neptune is the God in Greek Mythology who rules the hidden, unseen depths of the oceans.

As we all know, there is so much more to any ocean than what is apparent upon its surface. It is a world within worlds. Also our earthly existence is not just a physical one. It too offers us worlds within worlds, too (our inner and outer lives being two of these worlds). You Pisces are more closely connected to these inner and outer otherworlds, and especially the non-physical realms, than the rest of us. That is why there is usually much more to you than meets the physical eye.

Because of your connection to Neptune even when you live on planet Earth with the rest of us, part of you is usually off somewhere else in your thoughts, dreams or consciousness. No wonder you sometimes complain that you feel like a fish out of water! Many of you spend most of your sleep and awake time living in your own innermost, private, creative world. Your inner life or world is often composed of many ongoing fantasies, schemes and dreams.

Sometimes we outsiders manage to catch a glimpse of your inner world. However, as your sign also rules the magic and phenomena that surround mirrors, reflections, images, holographs and mirages, really seeing what is inside you is not easy. You express your hidden sides often through the unique way you dress, wear your hair, your lifestyle or the career you create, the words you write, the things you say, the love you share with us, the music you make, or your unusual viewpoint.

We may also glimpse the secret side of yourself (or the private side) through the widely diverse range of emotions you seem to go through — unusual emotions; emotions that often seem to erupt within you from out of nowhere. Just as the ocean can suddenly become stormy, there is no one as accomplished at pulling so many surprise emotional punches as you.

Because of your connection to other worlds, many of you Pisces can love your sleep time more than most. A soft inviting bed can be the earthly cloud you withdraw to when you are world weary, sad or tired. Some Pisces' bedrooms can even be artistic or creative masterpieces of a kind and style quite exceptional to behold. Often you choose to live in unusual or even peculiar places (in beach huts, log cabins, converted railway carriages, on boats, or even in gypsy-type trailers). For recreation, you may enjoy skiing, swimming, surfing, having baths or simply walking along the seashore.

Because of your connection to the watery realms and other worlds, drinking alcohol can often be a big thing for your sign, too. Usually this eventually turns out to be a most unhealthy and unwise pursuit. Because of your inherent love for the ocean, some of you are even collectors of seashells, or have pictures or artwork representative of the ocean on your walls. Many beachgoers, boat-owners, fishermen, surfers, avid sunbathers and beach lifeguards are Pisces.

Neptune is also the planet of illusion, glamour, mystery, spirituality and deception. These unusual qualities are often what make other people feel drawn to you. When you're in your true energy flow (when you are not overly worried about something), it's easy for you to make new friends because people want to get to know you. There truly is something different about you.

As you are tapped into worlds that are often inaccessible to others, you can be prone to feel lonely. This complicates your existence because you are usually a true romantic. You seek out love and will often go to great lengths to find your true love. Being so receptive and emotional, romance and matters of the heart mean a great deal to you.

You are also adept at donning rose-coloured glasses when it comes to romantic attractions. Because you want to have romance in your life, you will sometimes create it, or pretend it is there, when it is not. It is at such times that you put others up on a pedestal and then suffer the consequences of seeing them fall from favour in your eyes.

The disillusionment you experience in your relationships often brings you crashing back to reality. You want your true love relationship to exist on cloud nine, but keeping it there, at least in this so-called 'real world' can be a mission impossible. Nothing else dashes your fantasies and your dreams as quickly as much as a romance that has gone wrong. When your Pisces heart is broken (particularly the hearts of the feminine Pisces) your heart doesn't just break. It fractures into many little pieces.

In some ways, you Pisces truly do have hearts of glass. However, amazingly (even though the damage you sustain sometimes appears irreparable), you recover and your broken heart magically mends. Usually full recovery only occurs, however, when a new romance comes along. Indeed, there is nothing like new romance to return a Pisces back to cloud nine. It will not matter how old you may be or what stage of life you are in (whether you are at kindergarten or in the retirement village), you Pisces do operate best when you have a special valentine to place upon the romantic pedestal which exists within your heart of hearts.

Relationships are your mirror of who you are in the outside world so whether you are relating to those around you emotionally or your dealings with others are business-related, other people affect your sense of self profoundly. This is because you are incredibly open and accessible to others (their needs, thoughts, attitudes and desires).

More than any other sign, those around you affect you both consciously and unconsciously. The cosmic or psychic connection you have with others colours your world and sets your wheels of destiny spinning. This thread that links you physhically to others can obviously work for and against you, depending upon your choice of companions. Often you discover that certain of your associates provide you with a great deal of faith, encouragement and support, while others drain you dry or lead you astray.

Throughout your years on this planet, you get a first-hand experience of how significantly your associations, relationships and exchanges with others affect your health, wealth, dreams, visions and destiny. Your life changes dramatically when you eventually learn the insightful meaning behind the expression, 'you can judge a person by the company they keep' and begin to use more discretion in your choice of confidants, business partners, lovers and companions in general.

As Neptune rules mystery, you are quite a mystery to the world at large, too. Lots of people may think they know you, but you will constantly do something that makes them realise that they don't know you after all. In addition, your physical appearance is often quite misleading. You can be a total contradiction in the way you dress, behave and act. Often your choice of career provides no real insight into what makes you tick, either.

Your personality is more multi-levelled than consistent, so the way you feel or act today can differ in the light of a new day. There are times when you are quite logical and other times when you are very irrational. You can be the genius, the introvert, the extrovert and the comedian all rolled up into one. You are not particularly constant in your moods, behaviour or attitudes, either. But, after all, is the ocean stable? Hardly! Because of your strong link to the hidden dimensions of existence, swings of mood, neurosis, paranoia and strung-out nerves are frequently things you may need to conquer.

Your link to the unseen areas of earthly existence, however, means that you have incredible vision, talent and creativity at your disposal. This psychic attunement, or realm of senses, that you automatically tap into can be a source of inspiration and creativity to you. However, tapping into this information or these insights usually only benefits you in the external world when you have some kind of anchor back to reality. You need to have one foot on the earth so that you can bring your other-worldly dreams and schemes into manifestation. Finding your particular anchor is often your life's quest; and your 'anchor' can take many forms. It may be the right partner, your family or home base, your career, having money in the bank. Or it may be something more intangible, like going surfing, having a spiritual belief, or even a philosophical understanding. However, if you are lucky enough to discover your anchor, it is wise for you to stick with it. Otherwise, you can sometimes become a drifter, a misfit and a lost soul. Without your anchor to the outer world, you can have trouble operating in the real world.

You can be so wrapped up in your own thoughts most of the time, that it is not uncommon for you to be extremely forgetful or appear to be eccentric. However, when the cosmic pieces fall into place for you, and you bridge the gap between fantasy, creativity and reality, you can become a true genius (like Pisces Albert Einstein) or a dazzling business success (like Pisces Rupert Murdoch and motivational speaker Tony Robbins).

Finding the fine-line passage or pathway that leads to success isn't easy for you. When you find it, however, you really do fly over the rainbow. That is when you can tap into an entire range of creativity that others cannot even begin to fathom. You can be the most truly amazing person. The skills or insights you catch a glimpse of through your innermost vision or senses (when you look through the cosmic mirror of your vivid imagination or fantasies) are often what provide you with your highest talents and livelihood.

When you tap into these celestial magic moments, when time, space and creativity connect for you, you can be inspired; you have the best of both worlds — the inner and the outer worlds. Those of you who reach this connection now and again become the Pisces artist, poet, sculptor, photographer, inventor, musician, advertising executive, designer, movie star, fashion designer and innovator.

You are also capable of being quite an accomplished fortune-teller (although you probably wouldn't think this). You generally have a clear vision of things to come; you often have an abundance of untapped psychic ability, and if you work on this inner talent, it can be exceptional. You Pisces often have dreams or hunches that prove true. For example, you sometimes know who is calling you (by instinct) before you answer the phone.

Many brilliant business people are born under your sign. Pisces people, like businessman Rupert Murdoch, have an ability to tune into business matters or pick up business trends or other insights from out of thin air, with remarkable accuracy. This talent, which you business Pisces possibly term business savvy, 'hunches' or 'calculated guesses', helps you tremendously when it comes to making the right moves at the right time.

Just as your symbol pictures two fish, with one fish swimming up and the other going in the opposite direction, life is not a simple process for you. You have times when you head up to the top of the ladder of life, and other times when you plunge down to the bottom rung again. As the ocean tides rise, fall, and go through changes, so does your life. Some of you end up living your everyday existence more in a state of chaos than in order. Chaos occurs when you somehow find yourself out of step with the world at large. Not all Pisces are independent and enterprising people. Many of you Pisces occasionally have a hard time motivating yourselves. The easy way out often tempts you.

Those people who you see sitting on their favourite bench at the beach every day, basking in the sun, picking up social security, or hanging out regularly at the TAB are often Pisces. Many of you Pisces prefer to avoid the fuss and bother of keeping up with the Joneses — and in fact, your desire to avoid dealing with the real world can become something of a personal and professional crusade. Staying away from responsibility or even commitment can be the way many of you decide to spend your lives. This escapism from the real world can also include escapism through alcohol and drugs. You can get into debt, run foul of the law or even end up incarcerated. Usually you pay a high price for taking what you think is the easy way out.

Life keeps you on your toes when you try to master your inner and outer worlds and merge them together. You try your best to be objective but your feelings can run roughshod over commonsense.

Particularly when things go wrong for you, your excessive emotions can take command. At times like this, you can sometimes blame your woes on destiny, or on other people. However, the instant you assume responsibility and look straight into your own heart and soul for the reason something may have gone awry, you make real progress.

You can also become extremely co-dependent or dependent upon others. The Pisces who stops looking towards others for support, and who manages to be their own support, often ends up a powerhouse of energy, creativity and inspiration.

Especially in your younger years, you are incredibly impressionable and vulnerable. Many of your sign are kind, gentle and extraordinarily sensitive. At school, your teachers, and their approach to you, can make you or break you.

Among a group of people, especially if placed in a competitive position, your emotional rivers flow deep, and you can be easily hurt. Your emotions run your life more than you like to admit and your talent for covering up how you really feel often disguises some deep wounds that run within you.

You can be quite melancholy at times and while you're quick to throw a lifeline to a friend in need, you're slow to grab one for yourself. You're sometimes tempted to resign yourself to your circumstances instead of putting the effort into changing your course. You can also crumble faster than you can fight back. Too often you give up on something, yourself or someone before the situation has been truly resolved.

Sticking it out is often what makes you learn about your own strengths and the abundant array of multi-dimensioned opportunities that exist behind a problem or a difficulty. However, although you often are distracted by your inner felt experiences, looking at the impressive list of Pisces celebrities page (at the start of this chapter) it becomes obvious that you Pisces certainly do have the zodiac power to make your brightest dreams come true.

One of the healthiest ways for you to calm your nerves and lift your spirits is to go out and listen to some great music. You probably like rock 'n' roll as much as jazz or classical. Your foot taps (almost automatically) to all sorts of rhythms and beats and you can get lost in a great song. Dancing is a great choice for Pisces, too. Moving to music heals your body and frees your mind and you never know who you might bump into on the dance floor. But if you feel too gloomy to sing or dance, at least treat yourself to a funny movie or go to a comedy club. Laughing unlocks your emotional flood gates and floats your stress — gently down the stream.

When stress is high, withdrawing to your own form of an ivory tower often works wonders for you. Most Pisceans need some solitude. It's a good idea to plan at least one night alone every week and at least an hour for yourself every day. You need to do something physical to release your inner tensions, too. When you don't get enough exercise and relaxation you can build up tension and feel like you might explode.

There's not a Pisces alive who hasn't been tempted to jump in the car and drive as far away as you can or take the first flight out of town, no matter where it's going, to escape from pressure, responsibility or challenges. However, spur of the moment decision-making and over-reaction is often more disruptive than helpful to you. Therefore, it's sometimes more sensible to plan your breaks from stress or your holidays well ahead of time. The funny thing is, even with all of your intuitive input, you don't seem to notice when it's time for you to take a break!

Here's a hint. The next time you walk three blocks down the street before you realise it's raining, go home and pack your bags for a weekend get-away. Pisces who don't take care of their mental and physical health are tempted to spend more time daydreaming and less time making their dreams come true.

Pisces is a Water sign

To your advantage, you have deep emotional understanding and a broad outlook about life. It's because of the way you see the big picture that your life can (at times) flow almost effortlessly and things seem to take care of themselves. As a Water sign you know life has its ebb and flow and you accept that as part of the plan.

You also have the magical capacity to share your love on a physical, mental and spiritual level. You feel very deep connections with people you love and you sometimes have a psychic sort of bond with your partner, your parents and your kids. And it's not unusual for your intuitions about your family members' lives to come true.

To your disadvantage, you tend to ignore what you need in favour of focusing your attention on others. This is very thoughtful of you but you have to admit it's sometimes (not always) a way to avoid whatever you think you should be doing for yourself. You Pisces have a hidden talent for somehow playing the co-star in your own life stories.

[Insights into your sign]

The bright side: Pisces is the Sun sign that represents eternity. One of your greatest strengths is your inner knowing that no matter how confusing things seem, everything that happens within and around you has a value, a meaning and a reason.

The shadow: Your easygoing attitude can sometimes lull you into a false sense of contentment and make it easy for you to rest on your laurels and find that you have missed the boat of life.

[Looking beneath the surface of your sign]

Your hidden traits also can come to the surface when you're emotionally distressed or physically exhausted. These are the times you can be

Characteristics >	Benefits >	Drawbacks >
Adaptable	Accept change	Unsteady
Charming	Have many friends	Lead people on
Compassionate	Genuine concern	Feel others' pain
Creative	Heightened imagination	Exaggerate
Emotional	Deep feelings	Melodramatic
Esoteric	Spiritually awakened	Misunderstood
Gentle	Soothing presence	Vulnerable
Graceful	Coordinated	Delicate
Humorous	Laughter is healing	Hide pain
Impressionable	Open-minded	Others take advantage of you
Intuitive	Strong cosmic link	Paranoid
Kind	Generous	Easy mark
Lovable	Warm relationships	Incite jealousy
Melancholy	Deep feelings	Depression
Psychic	Highly receptive	Highly strung
Resigned	Willing to yield	Give up too soon
Scattered	Broad interests	Absent-minded
Sensitive	Keen perception	Anxious
Talented	Array of special gifts	Not practical
Temperamental	Let off steam	Waste energy
Understanding	Compassionate	Easily hurt

temperamental (occasionally even rude), and possibly feel like you're going to yell, cry or scream at the drop of a hat. But your temper has the power to motivate you in a way that few of your other characteristics can do. And your occasional rudeness warns others there's more to you than meets the eye.

While there might be more gentle ways to let people know what you're thinking, a smart remark or sarcastic line usually gets the point across, too. But sometimes you blame someone else when you know you're the one in the driver's seat. Remember, Pisces, roadblocks are messages. You can bash your head up against them or you can sit down and have a picnic while you think of a way around them.

You have an easy time accepting others but you have a hard time accepting yourself. You dwell more on your weaknesses than you do on your strengths. This gives you a warped perception and tends to lower your feeling of self-worth. Try to celebrate your personal and professional victories and look for the silver lining in your own dark clouds.

[How to tune into your sign's powers]

> *Cultivate your self-discipline.*

> *Follow your inspirations.*

> *Act with integrity.*

The Pisces woman

She's an angel with gossamer wings, upon which disappointment is a heavy burden.

This Pisces dream girl of the zodiac is usually easy to recognise. She's often the girl or woman with the amazing-shaped enormous eyes (and possibly in extreme cases, with the heart or rose tattoo on her wrist). She's the zodiac dream girl because she sometimes seems to have stepped out of a dream herself — or she is living out her life through her dreams!

On those invisible chemistry levels of life, whatever the mythological 'It' of sensuality is, Ms Pisces has 'It'. While she may not be the best-looking of her group of girlfriends, she is probably far and away the most unique and unusual. Having 'It' is metaphysical as much as physical chemistry.

Whether consciously or not, Ms Pisces knows how to use this magical, invisible energy to her advantage. Even when she is wearing her old trackie pants and T-shirt, somehow Ms Pisces still looks appealing. She knows that she can be the enchantress when she wants or needs to be and when Ms Pisces chooses, she can be quite hypnotic in the way she applies her powers of autosuggestion. When she wants to send out a 'message' to others, she usually sends it psychically, on a mind level, as much as in actuality.

Because she is tapped into the cosmic phone system, whether Ms Pisces uses this internal 'message sending' power in business, home or family, she is usually successful in making her point and getting her message delivered. This power of autosuggestion especially applies in the dating and mating realms of operation. Aware of her own powers when she chooses, Ms Pisces can unabashedly flutter her eyelashes, wear the lowest necklines, come up with the cutest smile or have such a pretty laugh that she can turn grown men (and sometimes also women) into immediate suitors. She often also complements her already delicious fragrance of natural lacy femininity with soft-spoken charm.

When she has love, romance, sex or marriage in mind, she's sweet enough to lure bees away from flowers and she's alluring enough to attract the attention of men and the jealousy of women. Ms Pisces can be quite an audacious schemer, too, and has been known to find other people's boyfriends and husbands more attractive than she maybe should. However, 'All's fair in love and war' is often her motto, and if she sets her sights on a job, a man, a goal or a specific target, she usually is successful.

Not much stops her really, except herself! Her lack of confidence is often her greatest undoing, and no matter how many great successes she chalks up on life's scoreboard, her achievements seldom satisfy her. She can be exceptional in terms of success or accomplishment, yet still feel unworthy. Underneath her exterior, Ms Pisces is a complex package of positive and negative feedback. No wonder she laughs and cries more than most. But when it is all said and done, underneath her vulnerability, she's usually multi-talented, a wistful dreamer, thoughtful friend and incomparable lover.

And as much as you think you know her, you probably don't. Since she started dressing up as a small child in her mother's clothes, Ms Pisces has remained a great pretender, entertainer and performance-giver! Projecting an appearance of wide-eyed innocence and filled with vulnerable childlike wonder, she can seem as wholesome as a crunchy ripe apple (but do remember Eve offered Adam the apple, too).

When she wants to project a more raunchy impression (and Ms Pisces can be extremely raunchy) she flips a quick mental switch and rapidly moves away from playing her 'Ms vulnerable' role into something steamier. Then she will become as sensually decadent and as tempting as a hot fudge sundae with extra whipped cream and two cherries on top is to someone on a diet. One thing is certain — she is always much more than her veneer reveals.

Whether she is a housewife, a businesswoman or a student, generally she has her own style. The image she creates is usually unique to her, too. She may be into designer clothes or dress as if she is off to Woodstock (or somewhere, anywhere, between these two styles). She may wear a seashell handmade necklace one day, then diamonds the next. She loves bracelets, particularly charm bracelets that jingle when she moves. She often has a closet filled with a wild array of clothes.

She likes to be her own original production, and often she is a trendsetter (as Pisces Sharon Stone so aptly proves with her terrific and unique sense of style). When it comes to her beliefs, desires, thoughts, schemes and dreams, she's more eccentric, intuitive, imaginative and mystical than practical. She isn't likely to follow the popular vote. But just when you think you know what she'll come up with next, she will surprise you. She can be extremely contrary.

Caring about others comes naturally to her and although she loves time alone, nevertheless she is often quite a people person. She can be the touchy-feely kind who wants loads of cuddles, reassurance and affection. She is also someone who goes out of her way to 'feel good'. She may have candles and incense burning, love to meditate, do yoga or have some esoteric spiritual practices or other unusual superstitious traits.

Whatever she does, it seems to work well. When she isn't having one of her more stormy emotional days, she has a calming and soothing presence, and everyone from her friends through to the bankteller or her plumber loves her to phone or come into their presence when they feel frazzled or frustrated.

She can easily run the gamut of feminine expression and energy, and can be terrific at playing starring roles in her own life or on the stage. She can be an accomplished (but also inconsistent) actor and, indeed, can become an Academy Award winning actress (like Pisces Elizabeth Taylor).

However, remember that her ruling planet Neptune is the planet of illusion, the planet that rules the changing depths and rhythms of the stormy oceans. A Pisces woman may give off many impressions, or have the outer tranquillity of a cool stream, but internally her emotions can rise and fall and toss and turn like waves. Sometimes she feels overwhelmed if she plans too far ahead. It is enough for her to get through today.

Even when she is trying to be an open book, she nevertheless often remains an enigma to others, and to herself! She probably cannot explain how she can run out to buy a loaf of bread at the corner shop and come home two hours later with a new pair of earrings, the phone number of a gallery that might exhibit her paintings and a stray dog (or even a new man) in tow.

She travels a zigzagging road in life, with lots of intriguing side streets to explore (not to mention a run-in with several romantic pot-holes or detours as well). If you chart her life's course, it looks more like a tangled pile of colourful yarn than a designated path of any sort. But Ms Pisces is a woman who believes the process and wonder of getting somewhere or experiencing the journey is much more valuable and important than taking the direct route — or arriving on time. And in this belief, in her case, she is often right.

[How Pisces women operate]

Social

A Piscean woman has a spell-binding quality that delights her female friends and enchants just about every man who has the pleasure of meeting her. She radiates a warm glow and can heat up a room like a cosy fire. Young and old, rich and poor find solace at her hearth. And her heart is pure enough to see the hidden beauty in the ugliest of ducklings. She has a gentle grace, a compassionate nature and a kind spirit. She also has a special talent for helping her friends see themselves in ways that boost their self-esteem and their courage.

She has soft, flowing style and her life often has more in common with a fairytale than a soap opera. (Of course there are some dreadful fairytales, too.) Ms Piscean has the quiet certainty that everything is going to turn out just right. She is, without a doubt, the fairy godmother of the zodiac. She also has a sprinkling of magic operating in her life and good fortune has a way of arriving on her doorstep when she really needs it. Nevertheless, life is far from being a bowl of candy kisses for Ms Pisces.

Her strong emotions can override her logic and send her sailing into hot water. When her anger is aroused, she can be as temperamental as a Taurus and as sarcastic as a Leo. Her best friends know she's just letting off steam but her unreasonable and sometimes bewildering behaviour can be vexing none the less. When things aren't right within her, she can tend to take her bad mood out on others.

Most of the time, however, she's a warm, dry cove in a raging storm and a cool breeze on a hot summer day. She adapts well to any circumstance or situation and she often does it with a sense of humour. She relaxes on quiet evenings with close friends, good food and great conversation. And she parties at crowded dance clubs, music festivals and all sorts of concerts.

She loves the element of the unexpected in live performances and she might have a streak of entertainer or actress in her. It's been said again and again that Pisces people, more than other signs, truly see the world as their stage. And whether they head for Hollywood or star in their own home movies, they can portray themselves in a wide variety of roles.

Love and family

A Piscean woman truly improves with age. Her inner beauty blossoms throughout her life and it can't help but show up in her warm eyes and her brilliant smile. Just look at Elizabeth Taylor if you have any doubt that Piscean women become more appealing as they gather life's experience. She can swim circles around other women when it comes to awakening a man's virility and she can play Snow White or Cinderella with equal ease. But whether she's waiting for her prince to come or wishing her way to the ball, her life is always touched by drama and fantasy.

Wherever there's a Piscean woman, you'll see three or four men in her midst trying to capture her attention. What they probably don't realise is capturing her attention and winning her heart are two very different games with very different rules. She'll gladly give you her attention and even her laughter and a warm embrace or two but you'll need to be more than entertaining to make it through the gateway to her heart.

She's looking for a real man — the kind who can offer her his strong shoulder to lean on, and provide her with passionate times filled with romance and loving, too. He should have inner strength, stability and power. She usually knows what she wants in her man, and she needs her perfect match more than most. However, for one who needs a man, she can be amazingly independent. And while she can create a very comfortable lifestyle on her own, she prefers to have someone take care of her, to spoil her and fulfil her every whim and wish. Life is so much more pleasant that way for a Pisces woman.

It's not that she's lazy, it's just that she sometimes has a hard time getting enthused about earning a living and managing her finances when there are so many other more fascinating things to do. Anyway, underneath the surface of her liberated exterior, Ms Pisces is often quite an old-fashioned girl who wants an old-fashioned guy, just like dear old daddy!

When it comes to relationships, she is sensitive, sentimental and easily wounded. Some Piscean women (particularly those who experienced emotional traumas in their childhood), won't leave home without slipping into their emotional coat of armour. But the typical Piscean wears her vulnerability as gracefully as she wears jasmine and ribbons in her hair. She surrounds herself with dreams and fantasies and protects her heart with a bit of Neptune magic.

She's proficient in lovemaking and her gentle caresses and velvet soft kisses can bring the strongest man down to his knees — with a proposal on his lips and a diamond ring in his pocket. Only a man who's strong enough to be gentle can give a Piscean what she really wants in a relationship. He needs to treat her with abundant kindness at all times and happily accept her distant daydreaming, and even her complaining, although maybe he can't understand it. After all, she is an angel with gossamer wings upon which disappointment is a heavy burden.

Once she finds the man she's looking for, she treats him like her personal hero. She openly adores him, believes in him and depends on him. And she's genuinely grateful he rescued her from the real world. A Piscean woman won't try to upstage her mate and she doesn't expect him to account for his actions and decisions.

She trusts her partner entirely until he gives her a concrete reason to doubt him. If she ever doubts him, beware — hell hath no fury like a Pisces woman when she feels betrayed. However, if he behaves himself, he is very well treated. She stays out of his business, doesn't blame him for her problems and has no interest in changing him. It's no wonder other women hesitate to compete with a Pisces opponent. It's a rare occasion when she doesn't get her man.

In all fairness, I should mention that once the marriage is official, she may exert a bit more influence on her mate, but she's not a nagging or domineering wife. If anything, her husband's biggest complaint might be she's moody, too fragile physically and sometimes distant. She does have a tendency to spend a lot of time in her private world of thoughts, or worrying about her health, but this is her way of sorting through all of her emotions.

Some Piscean women are masterful cooks, and nearly all female Fish make loving mothers. She frequently assuages her little ones' biggest fears and she can often hear their silent hopes. She wants to give them everything they desire. She knows it's not in their best interests, but she has a difficult time restraining herself. She understands the frustrations of growing up and she remembers how much disappointment can hurt. She kisses away bruises and bakes away tears and she always makes time for her kids.

Career

A Piscean woman is extremely versatile when it comes to her career. She can turn her hand to almost anything and many Pisces women pursue a variety of occupations. But whatever she chooses should offer an outlet for her creativity and her imaginative mind. She thrives in atmospheres that support her sensitivity and permit flexibility in her work schedule. She is very affected by her work environment, too. Where her workplace is less than bright, she will become quite dull and lacklustre herself. For example, put a colourful Piscean cartoonist in a square office with four white walls and no windows and she'll begin to draw characters who give her readers nightmares instead of a good laugh.

She's often drawn to a career in the arts, but that doesn't mean she seeks centre stage. She can be happy designing costumes for the school play, running magazines, penning a novel, painting puppets for a children's TV special, or writing the jingle for a radio commercial. She can be an innovative fashion designer, a dreamy watercolour artist or a vibrant illustrator. Many Pisceans make striking models (Cindy Crawford and Niki Taylor), strong singers, and star actresses (Glenn Close, Elizabeth Taylor, Drew Barrymore, Bernadette Peters, and Joanne Woodward are Pisceans). They also make talented writers and skilful musicians and can be great teachers.

A Piscean woman relates to people of every age with complete comfort and understanding. Whether she's on the floor playing marbles with her Year Two pupils or playing gin rummy with a group of senior citizens, she blends right in. Many Pisces find fulfilling careers in social service organisations, mental health clinics and the medical fields. She can be a caring social worker, a perceptive counsellor and a powerful healer. She is also likely to love working with the under-privileged or needy, as she has a strong desire to do good deeds and cares greatly about those less fortunate than herself.

She also enjoys careers that involve travel, beauty and fantasy or illusion. But regardless of her choice, a Piscean woman is very disciplined about leaving her daydreams at home with her problems and arriving at the office like a breath of fresh air.

She does have the potential to be a little snippy (or even a lot snippy) at times, however, and there may be days she's obviously uninterested in any sort of small talk. She's a bit like a chameleon and tends to take on the attitudes of her co-workers and the tone of the office environment. So she's at her best when she works with people she really likes in surroundings that are bright and appealing.

Financial

If there's one sign who wishes money grew on trees (more than all other signs), it would have to be Ms Pisces. But once she comes to grips with the reality that it doesn't, it's amazing how innovative she can be in organising money-making projects on her own. She's generally a wise investor and has some very profitable hunches when it comes to buying and selling just about anything. She's not driven by the desire for money itself, but she's very interested in the options it provides and the freedom it gives her. However, she can be very extravagant and this can sometimes be her financial undoing. If she starts to spend too much, her shopping excesses can be hard to stop. Many a man has thrown in the towel with a Pisces woman, simply because of her over-extravagance.

A Piscean woman can be tempted into get-rich-quick schemes and she occasionally gets burned on a deal that turns out to be too hot to handle. But she has an amazing ability to recover from financial mishaps and when she's in over her head, she's charming enough to find people to bail her out. She's most fortunate when she's married to a partner who's skilled in managing money, and if he listens to her hunches and intuition, they stand to make a fortune together.

She's generous and altruistic and she makes substantial gifts to children's hospitals, community arts programs, social service organisations and research foundations. A Piscean woman is the queen of true charity. She often makes her donations anonymously and has genuine concern for other people and their positions in life. She can't stand the thought of a child going hungry or a mother being forced to give up her baby because of poverty and she often devotes a large portion of her income to philanthropic causes.

Physical

She can be a quite a spectacular knockout physically — although she possibly does not see herself that way. She has soft, compelling eyes that sparkle with the light of mystery and a warm, understanding smile that makes you wonder what she's thinking. Her skin is smooth and supple and her features are generally refined and striking. She nearly always has soft, silky hair and some say when the prince called, 'Rapunzel, Rapunzel, let down your hair', he was calling to a Pisces.

She's usually well endowed physically and as far as her body tone is concerned, she is usually more soft than lean. If she works out she often overcomes this tendency to be well padded, but her weight-watching can require quite a strict discipline and routine. She has wonderful light around her (her connection to the metaphysical realms) and often looks as if she is radiant or sparkling — especially when she is happy or contented. Some say the Pisces woman actually glows when she is pregnant, too.

A Piscean woman can have the most beautiful feet, with dainty polished toe nails at the ends of perfectly shaped toes. Unfortunately, they are also quite sensitive and she's prone to aches, bunions and corns. Her hands are frequently small and dainty, but some Pisceans have hands that are big enough to hold all the world's problems at once. Not many Pisces women are tall but their posture and poise makes them look taller and thinner than they are and their graceful movements can present the illusion they are walking on air.

Her potential for good health is excellent but being a Water sign, she's very sensitive to her environment and is prone to stress-related health conditions. When she confronts circumstances beyond her control, her health can instantly be affected. This is particularly true when she has emotional difficulties and inner turmoil. And because the core of her problems is frequently obscured, her illness can be difficult to diagnose. Consequently, it's not uncommon for a Piscean to receive incorrect medical advice or treatment. A Piscean should make it a habit to seek a second and third opinion when she faces a serious health decision.

When she's unhappy about something or someone, that is when she tends to over-eat (although some Pisces women actually lose their appetites — but not too many). A turtle moves faster than most Pisces women's metabolism so regular exercise is imperative for her.

She can exhaust herself with emotional stress and worrying and it takes her longer than most people to rebuild her immune system after it's crashed. Sleep is one of Ms Pisces best friends. It improves her mental outlook and boosts her stamina. If she develops an interest in yoga, meditation, swimming or walking, it works wonders to keep her calm and centred. It's not uncommon for a Piscean to learn some type of relaxation therapy.

A Piscean woman may have a talent for singing or dancing and many Piscean women are coordinated enough to be strong gymnasts and spectacular figure skaters.

Proper nutrition, moderate exercise, warm baths and soothing massages make a perfect combination for releasing tension and giving her body the gentle care it needs. She's greatly affected by the people she lives with and works with and family members can shift her mood from oceans away. Unhappy thoughts turn into physical problems very quickly for her.

Mental

A Piscean woman perplexes people her entire life when it comes to the way she thinks. From the time she's a child, she has her own way of seeing the world and her own way of participating in the action around her. She believes in magic because she experiences it. She believes in the mystery of the unknown because she senses it. Her thoughts are rarely like those of anyone she knows and her dreams and fantasies are in a league all their own. Her views on life are so different that if it weren't for her human form, people would be sure she was from another planet. And on top of all that individuality, she has a personality that sparkles with charm.

She's able to solve some of life's most challenging puzzles but she can't decide which pair of slippers to put on when she gets up in the morning. Her adaptability can be a great strength but also a considerable weakness. She is sometimes tempted to conform to a bad situation or to go along with the crowd when she knows it's not the best thing for her to do. But her emotions can veto her logic.

She has a bright sense of humour and her speech is nearly always articulate and descriptive. When she's worried or upset, she can turn her wit into biting sarcasm and let some harsh realities roll off her tongue. But her anger is fleeting and she soon returns to her kind, compassionate self. She has many mental pursuits and interests in life, but she isn't inspired by strictly intellectual endeavours. There has to be some sort of mystery to unravel or treasure to find for her to push her mind to its fullest potential.

Spiritual

A Piscean woman is fascinated and challenged by questions that can't be easily answered. She sees the universe as a question within a question and she's probably curious about her existence and intrigued about the afterlife. She believes all forms of religion serve a purpose and encourages people to follow their hearts and choose the spiritual path that serves them the best. It's not uncommon for a Piscean woman to spend her early adulthood learning about several faiths and belief systems and attending a variety of spiritual services. She often finds the vibrations and music more moving than the sermons but she's deeply touched by any ceremony that opens and lifts hearts.

The truth is most Piscean women are just as likely to be at a seance as in a church, synagogue or temple. She tends to be esoteric in her beliefs and ideas that sound outrageous to some people sound appealing and plausible to her. Her heightened gift of intuition helps her sort truth from marketing, especially when it comes to religions. She generally believes God is all-powerful and loves each person exactly as they are. She almost never buys into the threats of fire and brimstone and she suspects everyone will eventually find their way to some form of heaven.

When a Piscean woman has an inkling something is about to happen, it often does. In fact, it's frequently a series of accurate hunches that open her mind to psychic phenomena and encourage her to explore the sixth sense. She's in awe of the mind, body and soul connection and she realises humans know very little about their own true essence, let alone the universe. But she does know that when she opens her heart to her inner wisdom she gets some powerful results.

The Pisces man

A Piscean man blends naughty with nice and comes up with nirvana. He can make Lance Romance look like an amateur when it comes to winning and keeping a woman's heart.

One of the more complicated men of the zodiac, the Pisces man is the kind who keeps those around him constantly guessing what his next move is likely to be. Often when he makes his move, others are hugely surprised because his actions or choices are the last thing they expected. However, his associates are not alone in being astonished by the way he tackles or handles situations. Mr Pisces himself, is often the most stunned of all by his own thoughts, deeds and schemes.

The Pisces man can pursue his greatest ambitions and follow his most inspiring dreams. But that doesn't mean he does. Although Mr Pisces has the ability to achieve his goals, he's susceptible to every imaginable distraction and temptation along the way. He has countless opportunities to choose his own direction but he can quickly forget his plans and go along with the crowd instead. He has an easy way of fitting in, no matter where he is or whom he is with. And he has friends in high places as well as low. He seems to know that each individual is a vital part of the workings of the world and he lives his life accordingly.

However, there are definitely times when his choice of friends, confidants or advisers is questionable. Often he finds himself surrounded by people who are not helping him to get where he wants to go at all. He will hang in there, nevertheless, and sometimes learn the hard way that the company he keeps can make him as well as break him.

He has an open mind, a closed mouth and patient curiosity, which make him a perfect listener. Old men at the bus stop and lovers standing in line at the movie theatre tell him their problems and ask his advice. His dry cleaner complains to him about her mother-in-law, the pharmacist asks if he should buy his girlfriend red or yellow roses, and the man at the newsstand asks him the meaning of life.

As well as being a good listener he can be a fantastic storyteller (occasionally spinning tales that are too incredible to be true). Although he has a special story-telling talent, if he is trying to get his point across, or wants something special,

Mr Pisces will share his opinion, ideas or thoughts in a simple, concise and straightforward manner. He saves his poetry for sharing his emotions.

He's a natural romantic and Piscean men have long been praised as breathtaking lovers. He values truth (but often wanders away from it) and appreciates beauty (but often is fascinated by ugliness, too). He has a gentle spirit, but his gentle side may be hidden beneath a tough exterior. A Piscean man is far more sensitive and impressionable than he wants people to know. He is also capable of much more than most people imagine.

[How Pisces men operate]

Social

A Piscean man's social life can be as glittering as an episode of *Lifestyles of the Rich and Famous* or as simple as a regular trip to the local pub or RSL club. But whether a Piscean man is having a calm, relaxing evening or he's rocking and rolling with the music, you can bet he's with his friends (although there are some Pisces who are quite happy being loners, too).

In general, however, everyone is a Pisces' friend. He has few prejudices, so nearly everyone he meets is a potential buddy. Whether the people surrounding Mr Pisces are children, teenagers, are going through their mid-life crisis, or reminiscing about their earlier years in their old age, he is likely to be interested in what they have to say. He does tend to find his fellow earth-dwellers quite fascinating subjects.

He can be quite a 'gadabout'. Perhaps it's because fish don't have feet to help them stand still, but whatever the cause a Piscean man rarely stays in the same place for long. He likes to keep moving.

He may drive around a lot, run around, or constantly be doing something with his hands. He may even be professional traveller, truck driver or pilot. He often needs to break his routine, or catch up on the goings-on that are happening around him. Being stuck in one place makes him feel claustrophobic. Like the ocean that he is astrologically connected to, he needs to find his own form of feeling the rhythm of the waves and the rush of the current to feel fresh and alive.

He likes variety in people, too. He enjoys being around those who are different from him. He's most attracted to people who are emotional and creative and he's wise enough to choose his companions carefully, since he can be such a chameleon.

He does a fair job of avoiding real trouble but he occasionally gets pulled into someone else's pity party, and for a Pisces that's trouble enough. He relates deeply with other people's feelings and when he spends time with someone who's depressed, he may sink into his own melancholy mood. When he gets depressed, he can be a walking dark cloud. Often he just needs a break from pressure and he's right back on his feet again.

However, sometimes his lapses into a maudlin state of mind linger. When this occurs, it can take a huge effort to pull him out of the doldrums. Music, dancing, taking a hot or cold shower, going for surf, a swim or visiting friends often help. However, alcohol can be the worst form of pick-me-up for him. It usually does the reverse and puts-him-down further into the pits instead. The Pisces man with a drinking habit can have a big problem. Not only does alcohol often bring out the worst side to his character, drinking can become a habit that he finds almost impossible to beat.

He loves to be both a spectator and a participant of life as he knows it is just as much fun to be in the audience as it is to be up on the stage at times. He enjoys going to an art show, a reggae festival or talking to his goldfish, cat or dog. Don't laugh! He actually might even understand what his pooch is saying to him.

He can have an incredible psychic connection to children, pets and certain people. He can also be found strolling around in a bookshop, weeding his vegetable garden or playing footy. His interests are as varied as his opinions and his friends and he's open to all kinds of new experiences. He probably heads for water whenever he can and many Pisceans enjoy swimming, fishing, snorkelling, sailing, white-water rafting, surfing, skiing and lying on a warm beach with a cool breeze.

You can spot him at a beach by looking for the guy who's staring wistfully out to sea lost in his own private dreams. He has an elusive quality you can't quite put a finger on — he's as easy to pin down as a wave on the beach. He has lots of little secrets — some more innocent than others — and he likes to keep the details of his life to himself, even when there's nothing to hide (but there probably is something to hide anyway).

Love and family

There are few men more romantic than Pisces and none who know the *Book of Love* (or the *Kama Sutra*) cover-to-cover like he does. But then he should know it because he wrote it. No one has to remind a Piscean man to buy his girlfriend flowers for her birthday or send roses to his wife to say I love you. He makes Lance Romance look like an amateur when it comes to winning and keeping a woman's heart. He writes colourful love letters, sweet poetry and an occasional naughty rhyme or limerick.

He'll leave presents on your doorstep and sexy notes under your pillow. (And if the tooth fairy ever reads one she'll have a hard time keeping her mind on her job for the rest of the night.) A Piscean man blends naughty with nice and comes up with nirvana. He can sense your most private desires and bring your most erotic fantasies to life. He can also understand your emotions, empathise with your difficulties and offer a helping hand or shoulder to cry on. But don't expect his shoulder to be a dry one. It's most likely on the damp side from the string of visitors who sought his shoulder before you did. So go easy on him.

It's a rare Piscean man who can tell you exactly what he's looking for in a woman but he says he'll know her when he sees her. And while this approach may work for some, it's often a Piscean man's biggest pitfall. A Piscean man can be led by emotions and passions more than logic and a beautiful woman is difficult for him to resist. He can easily fall in love with the way a woman looks and fill in what's missing with his imagination.

He also has the capacity to fall in love with several women at once and keep them all dangling on his bachelor's heart-string. He can be a cad when it suits him and has the capacity to love and leave, too. He often gets into romantic trouble because he finds the grass greener elsewhere, or finds someone else's wife far more attractive than he should.

He can be a hopeless romantic at times and instead of seeing someone for who they really are, tends to put them on an unrealistic pedestal.

I can't say I've met many Pisces who are in a hurry to get married, so if wedding bells are a high priority you might do better to shower your attention on a Capricorn or a Taurus. That isn't to say a Pisces will never settle down. He will. But only in his own good time. If it's already too late for warnings and your heart is set on landing yourself a Pisces male fish, this is the perfect opportunity to cultivate your patience and test your sense of trust.

Every woman in a relationship with a Pisces realises, sooner or later, that she's the one in his heart — even if the rest of the world is on his doorstep. It's not uncommon for him to receive a call for help at 2 a.m. and head out the door to give his assistance. It's also not unusual for that call to come from one of his attractive female friends. (A woman needs to be pretty darned secure to deal with that!) But most Pisces men get their fill of philandering before they settle into a commitment (or at least we hope so). However, if he is a philanderer, he can be the slippery fish type of Pisces who will never really settle with one woman — so you'll need to be ready to weather some emotional storms.

As a father, a Pisces is his children's most heroic action figure, most creative storyteller and most musical toy. To say that his children adore him would be an understatement. He is without a doubt their all-round best buddy. He patiently listens to their dreams and ambitions, gives serious thought to their ideas and suggestions and praises them for using their imagination. He's an honoured guest at tea parties and he's frequently invited to feast and to fight side by side with the knights of the round table. He's not much for discipline but when he's successful in teaching his children to listen to their hearts and use their own minds, they grow up to be loving and thoughtful adults.

Career

There are a wide variety of occupational pools and professions in which Mr Pisces enjoys swimming. He's not much for a typical 9 to 5 lifestyle, although he can put up with one if his evenings are free for dreaming. He thrives in positions with flexible hours and he's happiest when he can put his creativity into his work.

Whether a Pisces' dream is to become an astronaut, a professional athlete, a Nobel Prize winning scientist or a renowned artist or musician, he has everything it takes to turn his wishes into reality. Piscean men have so many talents they often pursue more than one profession at a time, or they periodically change careers. One thing is certain. The Piscean male is as impressionable as the warm wet sand at the ocean's edge. Surround him with beauty and he paints a masterpiece on the ceiling of the Sistine Chapel. Immerse him in cold, hard reality and he writes *The Grapes of Wrath*.

A Piscean can truly excel in almost any field that's not restrictive. He can be a warm and wonderful school teacher, a thought-provoking philosopher, an understanding social worker and an astute healer. He can also make an award winning photographer, a talented craftsman and a cutting-edge designer or illustrator. He may even find himself becoming a movie star, a professional athlete or a super-model. But whatever he does it's guaranteed to have his mark of originality and his creative style.

Financial

A Piscean's favourite way to earn his riches is to inherit them. His next choice is to win them. His third choice is to marry them and his final choice is to work for them. He's not lazy in the stereotypical sense, although he can create a pretty convincing illusion that he is. I don't mean to gossip, but we all know a Piscean who swings in his hammock while his wife works two jobs. What we don't know is what he's accomplishing in his mind! After all, some of Piscean Albert Einstein's greatest ideas came to him through his imagination, his intuition and his dreams.

Most Pisces are quite a bit more mobile than the hammock man. The typical Piscean cares little for fame or fortune, yet for some reason he attracts lots of opportunities for both. And if he listens to his intuition and has a good investment counsellor he can make more money than most people know what to do with. But he never has any trouble whatsoever knowing what to do with his wealth because a Piscean can always find something to spend money on. And he's far from selfish. In addition to purchasing a collection of original artwork for himself, a Piscean millionaire is apt to buy a house for a homeless family or construct a new wing on the city library.

Physical

Picture Antonio Sabato Jnr's smile, Bruce Willis's eyes, Kurt Russell's dimples and Sidney Poitier's charm and you're on your way to creating an astrology textbook Piscean. But actually, the composite image is less appealing than each of these Piscean men individually. It's a Pisces' uniqueness that makes him so incredibly handsome. He often has soft hair, symmetrical features and graceful movements. If you've ever seen Tony Lockett weave his way down a football field, you know how agile and smooth the Piscean can be.

Watch the way a Piscean walks. He can convince you he's not quite touching the ground. But his feet will remind him he is. A Piscean man can have perfectly shaped feet but they're often afflicted with sprains, corns, ingrown toenails and bunions. A Piscean's hands have a story to tell, too. He might have the steady hands of a photographer, the nimble fingers of a pianist or the paint specks or charcoal smudges of an artist. Many Pisces men are self-conscious about their hands and feet. They tend to think they're either too big or too small. But chances are — they're just right.

He has the potential for an excellent bill of health but he has to do his part to take care of himself. He's often tempted to let his passions and indulgences sweep him away, and he's wise to make moderation one of his physical ten commandments. Pisceans should avoid taking drugs; even prescription pain killers and sleeping pills can become addictive for a Piscean and alcohol can be the most tempting bait of all.

If you overhear someone saying, 'He drinks like a fish', there's a good chance the person being talked about is a Pisces. But that doesn't mean all Pisces have drinking problems. There are plenty of fish who are disciplined enough to drink occasionally and many others who are content to stay away from the pubs altogether.

As a Water sign, a Piscean is exceptionally sensitive and vulnerable to his environment. He feels best when he lives in an area that has pure water and clean air, but he does okay in big cities with his household air purifiers and water filtration system. His physical appearance can portray a fairly accurate picture of his state of health but a Pisces can still fool you.

He tends to be sporadic in his exercise routine, overexerting himself one day and trading in his workout for a bag of potato chips the next. He has the best chance to maintain his health by doing some type of moderate aerobic exercise every day. A relaxing swim, a brisk walk or even a round of golf (if he doesn't use a cart), can be very energising and invigorating for a Pisces. It's also a good idea for him to work on his stretching and flexibility.

Mental

A Piscean male is a natural born researcher from day one and he often begins examining his world by conducting an in-depth analysis of his baby crib. He treats scientific explanations as theories because the way he sees it, humans have little real chance of discovering the laws of the universe in a laboratory. In fact it was Einstein, a Piscean, who asserted, 'There's no logical way to the discovery of the elementary laws of nature; there is only the way of intuition'. And most Pisceans are at no loss for intuition, or even an occasional premonition, for that matter.

The Piscean man develops his mind but he doesn't follow traditional methods or think common thoughts. He lets his imagination ask the questions and he tries to answer them with his reasoning and intuition. And sometimes he just forgets about what he has been taught and follows his emotions instead. He can be unpredictable at times and every now and again he'll even have a temper tantrum. But Neptune soon cools his head and before long he's restored to perfect composure.

A Piscean has some of his brightest ideas when he lets his mind wander off on its own. He needs to ponder a situation, look at all sides and then release it by going to a movie, taking a walk, playing a video game or whatever works to keep his mind off the question. Frequently an answer or idea will pop into his head from out of the blue and many Pisceans sleep with note pads by their beds to record interesting dreams. A Piscean man's mind is completely off on its own tangent. And while those who are more down to earth may not understand him, they benefit from his contributions to society, his unusual approach to life and his ability to come up with a different and original point of view.

Spiritual

Many Piscean men have a deep inner belief that the essence of God permeates everything in existence. Some Pisces feel this so strongly that their lives become a spiritual journey. (Mystic Edgar Cayce was a Pisces.) A Piscean man's convictions are usually based on his own spiritual experiences and his theories stem from the whisperings of his soul.

The sea speaks to him and so do the stars, the moon and the sun. He's tapped into a different wavelength and he occasionally has flashes of inspiration that lead him closer to his life's purpose. A Piscean man is often intrigued by astrology and may dabble in palmistry or read tarot cards or runes. He doesn't rule anything out.

Even the rare Piscean man who doesn't feel a strong spiritual stirring has a hunch there's a lot more going on than meets the eye. And every time he sees a magic trick or an optical illusion, it reminds him that life is more than what's on the surface, and human senses are easily fooled.

The Piscean man's world of imagination can be just as real to him as the physical world and this gives reality a very different twist. Many Pisces men truly believe there's some sort of a hidden order in the universe and perhaps that's why they're often intrigued by spiritual quests.

The Pisces baby

This is the magical baby who is surrounded by the super-celestial lights that shine from heaven above.

Have you ever thought about reaching up and touching the clouds? Well reaching up to touch the clouds is something similar to attempting to fully experience your Pisces baby. Your little Pisces is the celestial baby that comes to earth from the highest of the metaphysical astrological realms. Because it is from the higher channels of existence, it is certain to have something incredibly special about it. Rest assured your little angel has come to earth to have some extremely important learning experiences.

As this infant comes from the higher sources of existence, naturally it doesn't adapt quickly or easily to the demands of this planet. Indeed it is not usually at all well prepared for the full-on confrontation involved with operating under the various earth senses. Therefore, there's a possibility this baby will experience some physical health problems.

Allergies and other forms of stomach upsets or nervous type ailments often affect this newborn. It may have trouble with digestion or with areas connected to taking in earthly elements (food, air, water and so on) and assimilating these within its physical system. These health problems often occur (I believe) — as a direct result of its spirit or will becoming adjusted to operating in a human body and within earth's very dense and demanding environment.

Something like an earth angel (and you may even notice a lot of light surrounds this baby when it's born and remain around it for several hours or even a day or two after its birth), this baby is extremely psychic. Because it is so attuned to higher senses, this tot often operates on many different emotional and sensitive response levels than other babies. It's a delicate soul and it's likely to need a lot of your most special time and attention.

Because it is so highly attuned and so lacking in physical attachments, this tiny one may not like it too much when it comes to being born. Your Pisces baby has probably been most content and happy living in the shelter of its mother's comfortable, warm womb. It can be so safe, cosy and comfortable in there surrounded by its watery bubble. That's why many Piscean babies are so reluctant to be born and put up quite a struggle.

Naturally the delivery room isn't too welcoming a sight either for this brand new little soul. With all the hustle, bustle, bright lights and coldness its senses run rampant. Of all the star babies, this is the celestial one who needs more than anything else to enter into the earth's domain in a gentle fashion. The traumas it may experience at birth can be around it for a long time to come.

The birth itself can sometimes be quite an ordeal for this delicate soul. It innately longs for warmth and tenderness and a sense of belonging. When this baby is born it is wise for its mother to put a lot of loving energy into it and give it reassurance. In this case it is unwise to delay mother-child contact. This little mite needs love more than anything else.

In its quest for heartfelt love and attention, your Pisces baby will be a real cuddler and affection seeker. It will become upset and sometimes overly distraught about things that seem to be extremely ordinary. A shadow can startle it. A loud noise can terrify it. It will be very attached to its mother or father, or both. It could become upset even at a particularly early stage should its mother go out (or go away) leaving her baby with someone else. Or this child might become upset even if it only senses its mother has left the vicinity. This baby has an extremely sensitive nature and operates best surrounded by soft lights, muted colours (not bright) and harmonious gentle music. Just as it can be unsettled by harsh exterior conditions, conversely positive, gentle external conditions and its surrounding environment soothe it.

As he or she develops you will discover your Pisces baby is no natural daredevil. In fact, it is likely to be a trifle scared about just about everything and anything. This is not the baby you give the monster toy or hand around for all the relatives or siblings to nurse. It can be quite alarmed at being exposed to new people and to nature. Instead of big bold coloured toys, offer it soft delicate toys. It needs memories or stirrings of the celestial realms (the cloud forces) to surround it.

This baby adapts better in a smaller, non-threatening atmosphere. The wide open spaces are not something it probably attunes to well. In fact, it is likely not to enjoy journeying too far from familiar surroundings at first and will prefer to play in one location rather than roam around. Even when it becomes more mobile, this isn't the little person who goes exploring, unless of course it gets curious enough or distracted by the various shadows and lights around it to forget its natural anxieties.

In fact, chances are that this will be a dependent type of baby and child. It's more likely to want to cling to its mother than go looking for adventure. When it comes to letting its older siblings play with it or having family pets around it, be watchful and careful. This baby is not one who naturally adapts well to others and can find it unsettling to be exposed too quickly to too many different individuals or earthly elements.

The little Pisces loves to be sung a lullaby and will love it when you read stories, too. It has music and rhythm in its own soul and is likely to sing, jiggle and eventually dance at an early age.

But its initial time on this planet can be testing both for the baby and for its parents. Having spent the last nine months in its private ivory tower of the womb and enjoyed its seclusion, the Piscean newborn probably won't be too easy to please or understand. In fact, it is likely to enter this world quite cranky and crying loudly about being unhappily evicted from its private womb-dreamworld.

You will have to put a lot of time and energy into this baby because it will require some mollycoddling and will be very dependent upon its mother for quite some time. In fact, it could become upset if you move away from wherever the baby is located as it will sense whether your protective presence is close or removed. This baby has a very delicate nervous system so you need to cater to it, rather than expect it to quickly adapt.

The Pisces toddler through teen

Pisces want more than anything else to hold on to their dreams; so they sometimes believe what sounds good, instead of what's true.

Pisces toddlers are highly sensitive to their environment. They flinch at loud noises, squeeze their eyes shut in bright lights and put their hands over their ears when they hear music played poorly or a singing voice that's flat or out of tune. They seek smooth harmonious living in a quiet, predictable environment and most young Fish can be soothed with melodious music, soft lights and their favourite toy.

I should warn you that Pisces' sensitivity goes beyond their physical surroundings; these children are very tuned in to your moods and emotions and if there's conflict in the home, they will be strongly affected by it.

Treat your little Pisces with plenty of warm affection, honest praise and gentle guidance. These children generally respond better to quiet encouragement than loud commands. Also, they may not always readily volunteer information about what they like or what they want, so you may need to encourage them to share these things with you.

Since Pisces is a Water sign, you can usually bet they like to play with water. Pisces children — especially as they reach the age of four or five years old — love to splash in water fountains and jump in rain puddles. These little ones can learn to love swimming lessons at an early age if their parents participate with them and assure their safety. They love to blow bubbles and watch them float through the air. They look forward to wishing on the first star of the night and they don't mind going to bed quite as much as most children because Pisces love to dream.

Don't expect your Pisces child to anxiously look forward to going off to day care or pre-school. They may end up enjoying it very much and if they're enrolled with a good teacher or care-giver they'll definitely benefit from the experience. But they don't really like to do new things or meet new people, especially when they're this young. They may cry when you leave them with a baby-sitter or when you drop them off at pre-school, but once you're out of sight they will usually gather themselves together and turn their attention to their group.

You might want to keep in mind that your Pisces child will be strongly influenced by you, your opinions and your reactions. If you turn up your nose at eating broccoli, he or she probably will, too. Try to encourage your little one to make his or her own decisions or you will find they rely on you more than is desirable as they grow older and enter school.

Conversations with Pisces — especially around the ages of four to five — often go like this. Mum or Dad: 'Kathy, would you like to wear your pink sweater or your blue sweater?' Kathy: 'Which one do you want me to wear?' It can be a little exhausting at times but the more you help these kids gain confidence in making their own choices the better off they are. Naturally on some days and in some situations it will be easier or more appropriate to make their choices for them, but try not to make this a habit.

Once your Pisces is spending several hours a day with people outside your family, you will notice a variety of personality traits coming out that you hadn't seen before. Some say Pisces absorbs everything around them but I believe it is much more than this. Pisces is like a living mirror — reflecting whoever is in their presence. So if your Fish begins to exhibit some behaviours you're not fond of, it's a good idea to take an honest look at yourself and at the other friends and role models in your Pisces' life — including the ones on television.

It's not unusual for Pisces to play with and talk to friends and pets you can't see. These imaginary people and animals are often outer reflections of some of the personality traits the child is 'trying on' before exhibiting them in their own behaviour. But for a Pisces these fantasy friends can seem as real as the kid who lives next door and it's pointless to deny their existence — particularly since you can't prove you're right. Besides, if you ever see a Pisces talking to an invisible friend it will be enough to make you wonder if there is someone there you can't see. Nevertheless, either way, once Pisces goes off to primary school you will usually hear more about their classmates and less about their invisible pals.

Pisces tend to do well in school, providing they don't have an excess of fears or anxieties associated with their teachers or the other kids in their classes. They're usually bright learners and creative artists and many Pisces love to read. Surround them with lots of well-written and beautifully illustrated books, especially those classics in which children triumph.

Stay away from some of the more morbid fairytales because these will just invoke frightening and disturbing images for a Pisces. It's also a good idea to monitor the movies and television shows your Fish is watching. Many other children are less influenced by images as they grow older, but Pisceans tend to be influenced by pictures, sounds and vibrations throughout their lives.

Pisces, more so than many signs, have a heightened intuition and psychic sense. You may not even realise this about them because they often keep their hunches and thoughts to themselves. I remember the mother of a Pisces phoning me a few years ago because she found her daughter's intuition to be a little spooky and was trying to understand it. She said her nine-year-old daughter Sarah was reading a book in the family room while she was writing a shopping list in the kitchen. One of the items she wrote on the list was a crock-pot for an upcoming dinner party she was hosting. She said a few minutes later Sarah walked into to kitchen and asked, 'What's a crock-pot?' Conversations like this can become almost commonplace in a Pisces household.

But as psychic and intuitive as Pisces tend to be, they're also quite vulnerable. They can see the big picture, but they don't always see what's right in front of their eyes. Pisces, especially around adolescence, want more than ever to hold on to their dreams and they're often willing to believe what sounds good, over what's true. They generally need to experience a broken loyalty or a few disappointments before they begin to accept that wearing their rose-coloured glasses is not always in their best interest.

Be prepared for your teenage Pisces to experience all the dramas of dating and heartbreak because they yearn to be accepted and loved and rejection of any sort is very hard for them to stomach. There may be many tears during these years but there will also be some warm heart-to-heart talks if you're able to keep the lines of communication open and keep your own critical comments to yourself.

Help your Pisces to diversify his or her interests so not all of their energy and focus ends up on the opposite sex. There will be times when nothing you do will succeed in pulling Pisces out of themselves. When they're emotionally wounded and choose to withdraw, give them some time alone before you invite them to participate in one of their favourite activities like going to the movies, shopping, or visiting the new exhibit at the museum of art or science.

One of the most important roles a parent can play in the life of a young adult Pisces is to help them to balance their intake of ideas, impressions and information with the expression of their feelings, their creativity and their original thoughts. These people are destined for a very rich life and while they may experience some melancholy lows, they enjoy some truly exuberant highs in life.

·······(CONCLUSION

I believe our true purpose in each lifetime is to follow our hearts and intuition and have the courage to live our most inspired dreams. And we have everything we need to do this — inside of us — all the time.

Zodiac: Your astrology guide for the new millennium was written to help you discover your own magical qualities and awaken your most inspired dreams and visions for your life. It is no coincidence that the constellations that form the zodiac can be seen clearly from both the Northern and the Southern hemispheres of Earth. The zodiac is our path back to our origin — and forwards to our dreams. The truth is in the sky — and it is more enduring and more profound than most people can even imagine.

······●(ABOUT ATHENA STARWOMAN

Athena Starwoman began learning to read the stars before she could sing the ABCs. Her wise grandmother, also known as 'Starwoman', taught her the names of the constellations in the zodiac and by the time she was in Year One, she was already an adept astrologer.

Athena's life is devoted to mastering the science and artistry of astrology and sharing her ancient wisdom with others. She has travelled the world and studied with the most brilliant philosophical and metaphysical minds. She knows the secrets of the sun and the mystery of the moon and she follows her heart's desire.

Athena is today's leading international astrologer. Her last book (also published by HarperCollins), *How to Turn Your Ex-Boyfriend into a Toad*, can be purchased around the world.

You can read her words of wisdom exclusively in *Woman's Day* in Australia. You can also connect with Athena at www.Starwoman.com to get the latest and most up-to-date information about her and the astrological outlook.

You can hear Athena Starwoman's recorded weekly astrological updates for your sign by calling 1–900–957–014 for a cost of $0.95 per minute (mobiles and payphones extra).

You can also call Athena's Psychics and have a personal one-on-one consultation with one of Athena's highly qualified psychics by phoning 1–902–220–265. Cost of these calls to a live psychic is $4.95 per minute (mobiles and payphones extra).

If you would like to have your personal horoscope done by Athena, send A$85, your date, time and place of birth to Athena Starwoman, PO Box 235, Double Bay, NSW 2028, Australia.

www.starwoman.com

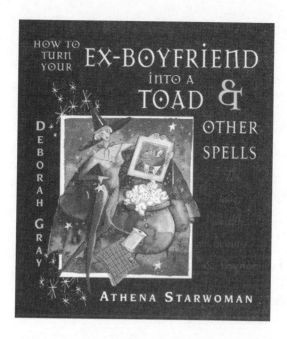

HOW TO TURN YOUR EX-BOYFRIEND INTO A TOAD & OTHER SPELLS

With this collection of ancient spells for modern times, Athena Starwoman and Deborah Gray share with you their Magic. The powerful spells encompass:

- Love and sex spells—a love goddess must have the right bedroom
- Naughty spells for naughty girls—don't get mad, get even
- Money and success spells—money will come when you're ready to receive it
- Me, me and I spells—what you think, you become
- Home and family spells—love comes in many forms
- The rest of your life spells—you create your own destiny

As the authors say, believe in yourself and in the absolute power of love. And remember, the best witches always look fabulous!

0–7322–5701–8
available from all good bookstores

HarperCollins*Publishers*